THE RATIONALITY OF BELIEF
AND THE PLURALITY OF FAITH

WILLIAM P. ALSTON
Visual Reproductions, Syracuse, N.Y.

The Rationality of Belief
&
the Plurality of Faith

ESSAYS IN HONOR OF

WILLIAM P. ALSTON

EDITED BY

THOMAS D. SENOR

CORNELL UNIVERSITY PRESS

ITHACA AND LONDON

1995

Chapter 8 appears with the permission of the author and copyright holder, Alvin Plantinga.

First published 1995 by Cornell University Press.

Printed in the United States of America

⊗ The paper in this book meets the minimum requirements of the American National Standard for Information Sciences— Permanence of Paper for Printed Library Materials, ANSI Z39.48-1984.

Library of Congress Cataloging-in-Publication Data

The rationality of belief and the plurality of faith : essays in honor of William P. Alston / edited by Thomas D. Senor.
  p. cm.
Includes bibliographical references and index.
ISBN 0-8014-3127-1 (alk. paper)
  1. Knowledge, Theory of (Religion) 2. Religious pluralism.
3. Religion—Philosophy. I. Alston, William P. II. Senor, Thomas D. (Thomas David), 1960– .
BL51.R294 1995
210—dc20   95-24730

For Bill Alston
with gratitude, respect, and love

Yet so much bounty is in God, such grace,
That who advance his glory, not thir own,
Them he himself to glory will advance.
    —Milton, *Paradise Regained,* 3.142–44

Contents

Contents

Acknowledgments

This book is the result of the hard work and good wishes of many people. First, thanks go to Al Goldman, who was the first to have the idea to do the book (i.e., for *me* to do it). Without his suggestion (and later encouragement) it is unlikely that the ball would have ever begun rolling. Next, thanks are due John Ackerman of Cornell University Press for having the wisdom to see what a fine idea this collection was, for advising me never to use the 'f-word' (festschrift) around a publisher, and for not holding it against me when I did. Others to whom appreciation is owed as early consultants are Peter van Inwagen, Jonathan Bennett, Al Plantinga, and Stewart Thau. I thank Jan Cover for offering good advice at various stages, having done this sort of thing himself a few years back. Eleonore Stump gets the credit for the quotation from Milton on the dedication page. Sue McDougal and Lisa Mowins have my gratitude for planning and throwing a terrific shindig at which this collection was announced. Thanks also to Krista Schimelpfenig for fielding calls from anxious contributors and for photocopying.

Of course, there would be no collection without the contributors. Not only have they written a fine book, they've been models of saintly patience through what has turned out to be a rather long process. And while all kept this project in confidence, some had to work very hard and show remarkable creativity to honor both the Ninth Commandment's injunction against lying and my editorial imperative: Thou shalt not tell Bill. To them, thanks for all the above and for putting up with an editor who didn't know what he was doing.

Acknowledgments

Final and most heartfelt thanks go to my family: to Dad for, well everything; and to my wife, Georgia, and children, Elisa, Kate, and Graham, for being tangible manifestations of the grace and unconditional love of God.

T. D. S.

THE RATIONALITY OF BELIEF
AND THE PLURALITY OF FAITH

Introduction

Thomas D. Senor

This is a collection of essays that centers on the theme of the epistemology of religious belief. As such it is not unique. The philosophy of religion has been flourishing of late, and epistemological issues have received more than their share of attention. It might seem that the distinctive feature of this book is that its authors all acknowledge a debt (professional and otherwise) to William P. Alston. But again, this is by no means a characteristic unique to this volume. Alston's influence has been pervasive in many recent books in the philosophy of religion and epistemology. What does make this volume unique is that each of the essays was written in Alston's honor.

It would be insulting to attempt to condense all Professor Alston has accomplished into a few short pages, so I will not even try. What I will do is highlight some the areas in which his work has been particularly influential and some of the features of that work. I shall then try to explain briefly why he is so admired and respected by his students and colleagues.

To say that Alston has had a productive career, especially in the past decade or so, is a gross understatement. His philosophical writing has culminated in the publication of five books: *Epistemic Justification* (1989), *Divine Nature and Human Language* (1989), *Perceiving God* (1991), *The Reliability of Sense Perception* (1993), and *A Realist Conception of Truth* (1995) (all from Cornell University Press).

In his writings in epistemology, Alston has focused on three themes: foundationalism, concepts of justification, and the internalism/externalism debate. Generally, he has been willing to defend unpopular

positions and resist trends. Since about mid-century, foundationalism
has had few defenders. Yet against coherentism, Alston defends the
possibility of immediate justification, that is, justification that is not
mediated by the epistemic warrant of other beliefs. The post-Gettier
literature has emphasized finding conditions that are necessary and
sufficient for a subject's being justified in believing a proposition. Those
who offered such analyses, however, rarely attempted to say anything
enlightening about the nature of justification, as if all philosophical
analysis required is a set of necessary and sufficient conditions impervi-
ous to counterexamples. In the midst of this came Alston's paper "Concepts of Epistemic Justification," in which he emphasizes the nature of
the concepts rather than their conditions of application.[1] Finally, in
the 1980s epistemologists were lining up behind the flags of either
internalism or externalism, although precisely what these theses were
and what distinctions were possible within each camp was not a matter
of public record. Alston first set his sights on clarifying the conceptual
terrain and proceeded to offer a sensible middle view that incorporated
contributions from each of the warring factions.

Alston's book *The Reliability of Sense Perception* is widely considered the
most thorough discussion of our confidence that the senses generally
provide us with true beliefs about the empirical world. In this work,
Alston argues that there is no epistemically noncircular way to show
that the senses are reliable. Yet he refuses to be led into skepticism,
holding instead that it is practically rational to regard the senses as
reliable even in the absence of a noncircular justification.

In the philosophy of religion, Alston has done important work on
theological language and philosophical theology. Yet despite the quality
of his papers in those areas, his most significant contribution here has
been at the point where philosophy of religion intersects with epistemology. In *Perceiving God*, Alston has given the philosophical community one of the century's most important works in the epistemology of
religious belief. Religious experience that a believer takes to be a direct
experience of God can, Alston argues, afford her prima facie justification for theistic belief as long as the belief is formed in accordance
with a socially established theistic doxastic practice. What makes Alston's book so significant is that it is written by a leading figure in
contemporary epistemology who is also well versed in contemporary
and classical theology and in mysticism. Thus, the discussion is of a
consistently high caliber whether it centers on epistemology, theology,
or the writings of the mystics. Once again, Alston courageously argues

[1] *Epistemic Justification*, pp. 81–114.

for a position that only a few years ago was not taken seriously in academic philosophy; in large part because of his writing, that has changed.

Although this introduction cannot begin to do justice to the depth and breadth of Alston's written work, neither should it ignore the other two important contributions of his career: editing and teaching. Although Alston has worked as an editorial consultant for many journals for many years and is the editor of the Cornell Studies in the Philosophy of Religion, his position as the first editor of *Faith and Philosophy* (the journal of the Society of Christian Philosophers) has been the most editorially influential. His tenure at *Faith and Philosophy* was marked by three features: the ascendance of a new journal in just a few years to be, arguably, the best journal of its kind; the speed with which a decision was reached on a paper; and the number of drafts that the typical paper had to go through before finally being accepted. The first two features have been universally applauded, but it is the third that is particularly vivid in some of our memories. It was this aspect of Alston's editorship that prompted Bruce Russell to say in a footnote to an article that appeared in *Faith and Philosophy:* "I have cursed Bill Alston in private and would like to thank him here in public for forcing me to work harder to improve this paper than I wanted to work. I hold him responsible for any errors that might remain."[2]

Nearly everyone I have spoken with about papers submitted to *Faith and Philosophy* during Alston's tenure has reported that his or her work was taken seriously and responded to respectfully. Of course, that doesn't mean that the arguments and analyses didn't take a beating; they almost certainly did. But the beatings were generally regarded as fair and given in order to make the paper a better piece of philosophy.

The final aspect of Alston's career that must be noted is his teaching. Today one frequently hears the claim that universities emphasize research at the expense of teaching. Bill Alston is living proof that the two can fit hand in glove. His publication record and international reputation speak to his research; those he has mentored testify to his influence as a teacher, particularly of graduate students.

For twenty-two years, Alston was a faculty member in the Philosophy Department at the University of Michigan. Among those who worked with him there were Robert Audi, George Mavrodes, Nelson Pike, Alvin Plantinga, William Rowe, Joseph Runzo, and William Wainwright, all people whose work contemporary philosophy of religion would be

[2] Bruce Russell, "The Persistent Problem of Evil," *Faith and Philosophy* 6, no. 2 (1989), 139.

considerably worse off without. Many others who were never his students owe a professional debt to him as well. Marilyn McCord Adams and Robert Adams overlapped with him on the Michigan faculty, and both have publicly acknowledged the influence of Alston on their careers.

While I was at Syracuse in the mid-1980s, neither I nor anyone else could understand how Alston was able to do all that he did and still give so generously of his time to students. Although his teaching load was light (usually one graduate seminar per semester), he put a great deal of time into the courses he taught. Each week he would arrive at the seminar with a file folder stuffed with pages of handwritten notes. Undoubtedly, some of these were written in earlier years, but he seemed to have an encyclopedic knowledge of the current literature before it was published and would often lecture on it from detailed notes. He also required short weekly papers that he would collect and grade before the next seminar. What I find striking is that, contrary to the way seminars are commonly taught, in Alston's graduate seminars students are the primary beneficiaries. Because he was doing research in the areas in which he taught, Alston naturally assigned students to read some of his work (he even told us to sleep with the prepublication typescript of his article "Concepts of Epistemic Justification" under our pillows). Yet the point of his seminar was never for him to use graduate students as a testing ground for his material. His concern was to make his students better scholars and philosophers.

Alston also voluntarily ran a philosophy of religion discussion group at Syracuse. He formed the group because an increasing number of graduate students were arriving with an interest in philosophy of religion, but only one graduate course a year was taught in this area. That Alston did this for the sake of his students was clear. All too often only two or three students (and no faculty) would join him in the Philosophy Department seminar room for a lunchtime session, and frequently he had to spend much of the time explaining what we would have seen for ourselves had we read the material carefully. I was always amazed that he was willing to take the time. Yet as long as two or more were gathered, he was happy to accommodate us.

In the summer of 1985, four or five of us wanted to learn something about Thomas Reid. We decided that we would form a reading/discussion group, and we asked Alston if he would be willing to grade the papers we wrote so that we could get credit for independent study. He agreed on the condition that we meet with him once a week and read according to a schedule he would produce. We happily complied (although we figured that this would mean less time for summer frolic than we had planned), and Alston taught a seminar on Reid to us during the summer, when he officially had no teaching responsibilities at all.

The list of courtesies Alston extended to his graduate students would not be complete without mentioning the Bible study group that met at his home. Not only were many graduate students interested in philosophy of religion, but several were practicing Christians who had come to work with Alston on issues of faith and reason. Alston's concern for his students has never stopped with their academic well-being. Every Thursday evening, Bill and his wife, Valerie, would have ten or so graduate students and close friends in their home for study and fellowship. The opportunity we had then is rare indeed. In matters of faith and spirit, publications and prestigious awards mean nothing; Alston allowed us to see him in a perspective in which the playing field was level and he was a fellow pilgrim.

Those who read Alston's writings are fortunate to have him as a fellow philosopher, those who have studied with him are lucky to have him as a mentor, and those who know him are blessed to have him as a friend.

This collection consists of eleven essays, divided into three parts, all of which in one way or another discuss issues important to the epistemology of religious belief.

Part I, "Natural Theology and the Knowledge of God," is composed of four essays. The first, Marilyn Adams's "Praying the *Proslogion:* Anselm's Theological Method," is a fascinating interpretation of Anselm's theological methodology as found in the *Proslogion.* Whereas this famous ontological argument is often understood and treated as a piece of natural theology that Anselm takes to be useful for apologetics, Adams argues that Anselm never intends for the argument to be compelling to the unbeliever. This is so, in large part, because the act of doing natural theology is, on Anselm's view, an interactive process with God as both the medium and the message. According to Adams, Anselm "treats all creative problem solving as essentially collaborative: the creature seeks, the Creator discloses, the creature articulates what it has seen." Despite the negative repercussions of the Fall on human cognition, God is able and willing to aid reason by revealing himself to us as a response to prayer. Adams concludes by suggesting that contemporary Christian philosophers heed Anselm's epistemology of philosophical theology.

Brian Leftow's "Can Philosophy Argue God's Existence?" concerns a topic that is important but generally neglected by analytic philosophers of religion. Arguments for God's existence are, naturally, liable to come under fire from philosophical atheists and agnostics. Frequently, religious philosophers themselves find problems with particular theistic arguments. There is a tradition within religion itself, however, that sees arguments that seek to prove God's existence as inherently misguided and perhaps even blasphemous and idolatrous. Leftow here considers an objection of this type, found in the writings of Karl Barth, that is specifically directed at cosmological arguments. In the end, Leftow finds the Barthian line worthy of serious attention but unconvincing.

The problem of evil has long been an intellectual (as well as spiritual) stumbling block for theists. And though the so-called logical problem of evil isn't discussed much these days, its empirical or probabilistic cohort is. No one in this century has done more to press this objection to theism than William Rowe. Rowe's contribution to this book is a rebuttal to a recent paper of Alston's on the empirical problem of evil. Rowe argues that it is more reasonable to think that, for a given instance of horrid evil, there is no overriding reason for it than to think that there is some reason, but that human cognizers aren't in a position to know it.

Essay 4 is a collaborative effort by Eleonore Stump and Norman Kretzmann. Once again epistemological issues are the focus, but this time the questions concern the nature of divine knowledge. Though theists commonly claim that God is omniscient, they are rather silent as to *how* God knows. Stump and Kretzmann look to the writings of Thomas Aquinas for help with this question. Initially, it appears that no help will be forthcoming. For though he does have a view about how God knows what He knows, Aquinas seems committed to other positions regarding the divine nature and human free will that are apparently inconsistent with what he says about God's knowledge. Stump and Kretzmann argue, however, that contrary to earlier interpretations of Aquinas, his view regarding divine knowledge is fully consistent with the rest of his philosophical theology as well as with human freedom. Thus, in addition to questions of the epistemology of human belief about the divine, this volume contains a consideration of divine belief about humans (and the rest of creation).

The book's second part, "The Epistemology of Religious Experience," begins with Robert Audi's "Religious Experience and the Practice Conception of Justification." Audi compares a conception of epistemic justification that plays an important role in Alston's *Perceiving God*, the 'practice' notion of justification, with two others: the Jamesian and the intuitionist. Having distinguished these notions, Audi turns his attention to a consideration of the epistemic value of religious experience according to each of these concepts. He then suggests that the practice conception is more plausible as an account of rationality, as opposed to justification. Audi concludes that a nondoxastic variety of faith deserves serious consideration and that a practice account of the rationality of faith, as opposed to the justification of belief, is quite attractive.

William Hasker's "The Epistemic Value of Religious Experience: Perceptual and Explanatory Models" is a comparison of two options for accounting for the epistemic importance of religious experience. Alston's perceptual model is contrasted with an explanatory model recently proposed by William Abraham. The perceptual model sees religious experience as similar in important ways to sensory experience. Under the right conditions, both modes of experience can produce prima facie justification directly, that is, without the aid of other beliefs. On the other hand, the explanatory model is essentially an inference to the best explanation account constructed to emphasize the similarity of religious belief systems to scientific theories. Hasker discusses in some detail Abraham's criticisms of the perceptual model and finds them lacking. Furthermore, Hasker argues that the prospects for experience to play an important role in justifying religious belief are best on the perceptual model.

William Wainwright's "Religious Language, Religious Experience, and Religious Pluralism," nicely segues from the section on religious experience to that of pluralism. Like many of the other essays in this volume, Wainwright's is largely concerned with Alston's work. While generally agreeing with Alston's approach to religious epistemology, Wainwright thinks that the problem of religious pluralism poses a serious problem, not only for epistemological claims of theists but for semantic claims as well. According to Wainwright, in order to show that certain terms can be predicated literally of God (as Alston has attempted), one must show that the theistic ways of conceptualizing God are superior to nontheistic ways. This leads Wainwright into a sophisticated discussion of Alston's religious epistemology in general and of his treatment of the plurality of faiths in particular. Wainwright attempts to show that a satisfactory solution of the problem of pluralism requires an argument of the superiority of one world-view over the others.

Wainwright leads us into the dominant issue of the book, and the subject of the volume's final part, "Religious Pluralism." Given that the world contains a variety of religions that make claims that are apparently inconsistent with one another, what should be the attitude of the Christian toward Islam, or of the Jew to Hinduism? The problem is particularly acute, it seems, if one's religious belief is grounded in religious experience. For the belief of those of other faiths might well be grounded in experience too. Many, John Hick being the most notable, argue that the fact of the plurality of faiths requires us to eschew a parochial view of our own religion; we should not think of our dogma as embodying *the* Truth and suppose the creeds of other religions are riddled with error. Alvin Plantinga disagrees. In "Pluralism: A Defense of Religious Exclusivism," Plantinga argues that the Christian is violating neither moral nor epistemic duty in believing the claims of Christianity to embody the truth, even if this means that, on her view, any religious claim inconsistent with the Christian creed is false. Furthermore, Plantinga argues, even the believer who is aware of the diversity of faith might *know* the claims of her religion if they are true.

It is hard to know how to summarize Peter van Inwagen's interesting essay. Van Inwagen describes what he terms the 'picture' of the religious pluralist. This is not a picture he likes. To accept it and then argue against the pluralist is to play a game van Inwagen thinks can't be won. Therefore, he presents his own picture, a model or theory of 'religion' from which an orthodox Christian can make sense of pluralism and other related topics. The result is a discussion that is bound to be as controversial as it is fascinating.

In "Perceiving God, World-Views, and Faith: Meeting the Problem of Religious Pluralism," Joseph Runzo adopts a more conciliatory attitude toward pluralism. Although he agrees with the essence of Alston's view, Runzo thinks Alston has not dealt adequately with the pluralist. An important part of Alston's argument for the justification of religious experience concerns the effect that taking part in the religion has on the life of the believer. Runzo argues that this test cannot confirm what Alston calls the 'Christian mystical practice', since, as John Hick has held, a fundamental claim of all the major religions is that following their teachings will lead one from self-centeredness to 'Reality-centeredness'. So, according to Runzo, this test will fail to support the Christian practice any more than the other practices. He concludes by suggesting that Alston's approach to the epistemology of religious experience could be aided by a larger role for the notion of 'faith'.

George Mavrodes's "Polytheism" concludes the volume. The title of this essay and its relation to the topic of pluralism need a bit of explaining. There are several reactions one can have to the plurality of faiths. One might say that one religion is 'right' and the others 'wrong'. Or one can say that although all religions are directed toward the same Reality, what they say about the Reality is generally false. Or one might take things more or less at face value and think that the different religions are simply describing different gods. Now it still might be that not all the claims of each religion could be true, but the reason would have to do not with ascribing inconsistent properties to the same Being but rather with ascribing to more than one being a property that could be had by at most one (i.e., being Creator of all contingent existents). One who adopts this last perspective is a polytheist in a straightforward sense of that term. Mavrodes believes that on one reading of the recent work of John Hick, Hick is a polytheist. After discussing Hick's *An Interpretation of Religion* and its Kantian approach to religious experience, Mavrodes concludes by considering the plausibility of poly—as opposed to mono—theism.

NATURAL THEOLOGY AND
THE KNOWLEDGE OF GOD

[1]

Praying the Proslogion:
Anselm's Theological Method

MARILYN MCCORD ADAMS

In 1978, the founding of the Society of Christian Philosophers and the adoption of its motto, *"Fides quaerens intellectum"* (faith in search of understanding), challenged its members to reassess the relationship between faith and philosophy. The thoroughly secular atmosphere of mid-twentieth-century British-American analytic philosophy had fostered compartmentalization. It was natural for some of us to leapfrog back to the middle ages for alternative models. Many take their inspiration from Aquinas, who pressed philosophical methods and results—conceptual frameworks, techniques of analysis and distinction-drawing, of arguments pro and contra—into the service of theology, distinguishing natural from revealed theology primarily on the basis of whether the premises could be known by unaided natural reason. For a different approach, I reach back to Anselm of Canterbury, the author of our slogan, and to the *Proslogion*, alternatively entitled thereby. Here Anselm offers his most intimate depiction of the Christian philosopher at work. Anselm invites his reader in, not only as a spectator to observe but as an apprentice-imitator to follow and do likewise.

Anselm's Audience

Anselm wrote the *Monologion* at the request of his monastic brothers.[1] In it he adapts the monastic method of meditation to new material,[2]

---

[1] References to the Latin text of Anselm are to F. S. Schmitt's critical edition, *S. Anselmi opera omnia,* (Edinburgh: Thomas Nelson Sons, 1946–61). The title of the work is followed by a comma; 'c.' stands for chapter; 'S I.93.3–4' abbreviates 'Schmitt edition, volume I, page 93, lines 3–4.'

[2] Cf. Benedicta Ward, "Introduction," *The Prayers and Meditations of St. Anselm with the Proslogion,* (Harmondsworth, England: Penguin, 1973), pp. 44–46. Ward sees the form

speaking "in the role of someone who by arguing silently with himself investigates what he does not know,"[3] thereby broadening his audience to include real or hypothetical[4] *"ignorantes"* who for one reason or another do not believe at the beginning. By contrast, the *Proslogion* was the product of Anselm's initiative,[5] the record of his project of simplification, a shorter route to *Monologion* conclusions regarding the being and well-being of God and creatures.[6] The *Proslogion*, too, is a spiritual exercise, whose genre alternates between meditation addressed to the soul that undertakes it, and prayer spoken directly to God.[7] Whereas the *Monologion*, inquiring as it does "concerning the rational basis of faith *(de ratione fidei)*,"[8] can be meditated as much by unbelievers as by those who have living faith, the *Proslogion* is written for believers, "in the role of one who tries to raise his mind to the contemplation of God and who seeks to understand *what he believes*."[9] Thus, Anselm entitles the work *Fides quaerens intellectum*[10] and orients the soul, in c. i, to the project of seeking God's face in prayer.[11]

The Dialectics of Inquiry

Dual Goals

Corresponding to Anselm's bipartite description of his project are two distinguishable but interrelated goals: (i) to "contemplate God," "see God's face"; and (ii) to understand what he or she believes. In the Prooemium, Anselm leads with the latter, describing his desire to find *unum argumentum* by which to establish what he had proved by the concatenation of many arguments in the *Monologion*.[12] By contrast, in

---

and method of both the *Monologion* and *Proslogion* as continuations of the tradition of *lectio divina*.

[3] *Proslogion*, Prooemium; S I.93.3–4: "in persona alicuius tacite secum ratiocinando quae nesciat investigantis, . . ."

[4] F. S. Schmitt conjectures that they are hypothetical in "Die wissenschaftliche Method in Anselms 'Cur Deus Homo,'" *Spicilegium Beccense* (Paris, 1959), p. 367.

[5] "Aestimans igitur quod me gaudebam invenisse, si scriptum esset, alicui legenti placiturum . . ." *Proslogion*, Prooemium; S I.93.20–21.

[6] Cf. *Proslogion*, Prooemium; S I.93.6–10. Cf. c. xxii; S I.117.1–2.

[7] Cf. Yves Cattin, "La prière de S. Anselme dans le *Proslogion*," *Revue des Sciences Philosophiques et Théologiques* 72 (1988), 373–96.

[8] *Proslogion*, Prooemium; S I.93.1–2; I.94.6–7.

[9] Ibid., Prooemium; S I.93.21–I.94.2: "sub persona conantis erigere mentem suam ad contemplandum deum et quaerentis intelligere *quod credit*."

[10] Ibid., Prooemium; S I.94.7.

[11] Ibid., c. i; S I.97.4–10.

[12] Ibid., Prooemium; S.I.93.4–21.

c. i of the work proper, Anselm begins with (i) the stirring of the mind to contemplate God.[13] Of the two, it is (i) the aim of seeing God's face that dominates and frames (ii) the project of understanding, while the latter (ii) is both subordinate to and partially constitutive of the former (i). If the topos of the *Monologion* is more generic—"the soul in search of goodness"—that of the *Proslogion* is a more particular version of the same—"the soul in search of God, the good that satisfies."[14]

This scheme of priorities is understandable, because, for Anselm, enjoying a vision of God is the telos of rational creatures, the that-for-which they were made.[15] Already in the *Monologion,* he had argued that "every rational being exists for this [purpose]: to love or refuse things to the extent that, by rational discernment, it judges them to be more or less good or not good"[16]—and concluded more particularly that "a rational creature is made for this [purpose]: to love the Supreme Being above all [other] goods, inasmuch as It is the Highest Good."[17] Since love seeks its object with all its powers,[18] "a rational creature ought to devote all its powers and will to remembering and understanding and loving the Highest Good—the [end] for which it knows itself to exist."[19] Moreover, this effort makes the soul into the best image of God and hence the best instrument for knowing God it can be.[20]

Similarly, the *Proslogion* emphasizes that God is to be sought with the whole self. This is explicit in the resolve of the work's concluding sentences:

> Meanwhile, then, let *my mind* meditate on it, *my tongue* speak of it. Let *my heart* love it, *my mouth* proclaim it. Let *my soul* hunger for it, *my flesh* thirst for it, *my whole substance* desire it, until I enter 'into the joy of my Lord', 'Who is' the triune and one God, 'Blessed forever. Amen.'[21]

[13] Ibid., c. i; S. I.97.3–10.

[14] Cf. Cattin, who identifes the topos of the *Proslogion* as "the soul in search of God" ("La prière de S. Anselme," p. 379).

[15] *Proslogion,* c. i; S I.98.14–15: "Denique ad te videndum factus sum . . ." Likewise, Anselm speaks of Adam's losing the "beatitudinem ad quam factus est" (S I.98.18).

[16] *Monologion,* c. lxviii; S I.78.25–I.79.1: "omne rationale ad hoc existere, ut sicut ratione discretionis aliquid magis vel minus bonum sive non bonum iudicat, ita magis vel minus id amet aut respuat."

[17] Ibid., c. lxviii; S I.79.2–3: "rationalem creaturam ad hoc esse factum, ut summam essentiam amet super omnia bona, sicut ipsa est summum bonum."

[18] Cf. ibid., c. lxxvi; S I.83.18–20.

[19] Ibid., c. lxviii; S I.79.2–5: "rationalem creaturam totum suum posse et velle ad memorandum et intelligendum et amandum summum bonum impendere debere, ad quod ipsum esse suum se cognoscit habere."

[20] Ibid., c. lxvi; S I.77.7–24; c. lxvii; S I.77.27–I.78.11.

[21] *Proslogion,* c. xxvi; S I.121.22–I.122.2: "Meditetur interim inde *mens mea,* loquatur *lingua mea.* Amet illud *cor meum,* sermocinetur *os meum.* Esuriat illud *anima mea,* sitiat

Moreover, like other prayers, the *Proslogion* works "to stir the reader's mind to love or fear of God, or to discussion of Him."[22] Following a tradition that reaches back through Benedict to Cassian to Origen, Anselm's prayers aim to stir the mind out of its inertia to thorough self-knowledge, which produces a wound in the heart *(compunctio cordis)*— sorrow for sin, dread of its consequences, anxiety over distance from God—which in turn leads to humble prayers for help, and resolves into a compunction of desire that energizes the soul's renewed search for God.[23] The text of the *Proslogion* proper is bracketed and punctuated by such prayer exercises, designed to stir *the emotions and will* (in cc. i, xiv–xviii, and xxiv–xxv),[24] so that the soul may seek by desiring and desire by seeking, with the hope of finding by loving and loving by finding.[25] Likewise, since intellect is counted among the soul's powers, the *intellectual* inquiry of the intervening chapters (cc. ii–xiii and xviii–xxiii) constitutes another avenue of approach to God.

In human beings, cognitive and affective powers interact. Just as the soul cannot will what it in no way thinks, so its ability to see is affected by its loves and choices. If both the *Monologion* and *Proslogion* trace human difficulties in knowing God to the ontological incommensuration between their natures,[26] the *Proslogion* emphasizes a different explanation, numbering the cognitive distance between God and humans among the consequences of Adam's fall—"from the Fatherland into exile, from the vision of God into our blindness"[27]—in the first instance, a failure of will! On the positive side, the prayerful stirring of will and emotions Godward (as in cc. i, xiv–xviii, and xxiv–xxvi) contributes to

---

caro mea, desideret *tota substantia mea,* donec intrem 'in gaudium domini' mei, 'qui est' trinus et unus deus 'benedictus in saecula. Amen.'"

[22] *Orationes sive meditationes,* Prologus; S III.3.2–4: "ad excitandam legentis mentem ad dei *amorem* vel *timorem,* seu ad suimet discussionem." Cf. *Proslogion,* c. i; S I.97.3.

[23] Ward, "Introduction," *Prayers and Meditations of Saint Anselm,* pp. 48–51. Cf. Cattin, "La prière de S. Anselme," p. 378; *Proslogion,* c. i; S I.100.10–11.

[24] Yves Cattin describes these three sections as "three broad shores of meditation and prayer" (La prière de S. Anselme," p. 377), but in fact the prayer and meditation never stop. The intellectual work continues in the second person addressed to God in cc. ii–xiii, xviii–xxiii, and xxvi. What distinguishes these three "shores" from the other passages is that they are focused and stirring the will and emotions, whereas the other prayers are part of the intellectual striving into God.

[25] *Proslogion,* c. i; S I.100.10–11: "Quaeram te desiderando, desiderem quaerendo. Inveniam amando, amem inveniendo."

[26] *Monologion,* c. xv; S I.28.5–7; c. xxviii; S I.45.25–26; I.46.2–29; c. xxxvi; S I.54.15–18; c. xxxvii; S I.55.12–14; c. xxxviii; S I.56.3–17; c. xliii; S I.60.5–7; c. xlviii; S I.59.15–16; c. lxiii; S I.5; c. lxiv; S I.74.30–1.75.16. *Proslogion,* c. ix; S I.107.4–I.108.9; c. xiv; S I.112.2–11; c. xv; S I.112.14–17; c. xvi; S I. 112.20–27. Cf. xxv; S I.120.17–20.

[27] *Proslogion,* c. i; S I.98, 16–99, 7; esp. S I.99, 4–5: "A patria in exsilium, a visione dei in caecitatem nostram." Cf. c. xviii; S I.114, 3–8.

the soul's focus and produces the motivational resolve necessary for sustained intellectual inquiry.

The insertion of the two *Proslogion* goals into the dynamics of prayer clarifies their interrelation.[28] In chapter i, the soul begins—at Divine invitation—with the lofty aim of (i) seeking God's face,[29] but its fall into the recognition of its own cognitive incapacities and their root in Adam's sin leads to humility, which expresses itself in a lowering of its sights to (ii) the second goal: "I do not try, Lord, [i] to penetrate your altitude, because my intellect does not compare with it at all; but I desire [ii] to understand a little bit *(aliquatenus intelligere)* your truth, which my heart believes and loves."[30] This project of "understanding a little bit" apparently occupies chapters ii–xiii. But when Anselm pauses to take stock (in cc. xiv–xviii), the first and higher goal of (i) seeing God's face becomes the standard against which the results are evaluated, and Anselm puzzles about how he could have reached the second goal of (ii) "understanding your truth a little bit" without attaining (i) the first:

> Well, my soul, have you found what you sought? You sought [i] God, and you have found [ii] that He is something highest of all, than which nothing better can be thought; and that He is Life itself, Light Itself, Wisdom Itself, Goodness Itself, Eternal Blessedness and Blessed Eternity; and that He is everywhere and always. Now if you have not found [i] your God, how is He this which you have found and which with certain truth and true certainty you *have understood* Him to be? But if you have found [Him], then why do you not experience *(sentis)* what you have found? Why does my soul not experience you, Lord God, if it has found you?[31]

Switching to visual imagery, Anselm restates the difficulty—if the Light and Truth that God is, are both the object and the medium of under-

---

[28] For a detailed mapping of the prayers in cc. i, xiv–xviii, see Cattin, "La prière de S. Anselme," pp. 375–87.

[29] *Proslogion*, c. i; S I.97.9–10.

[30] Ibid., c. i; S I.100.15–17: "Non tento, domine, [i] penetrare altitudinem tuam, quia nullatenus comparo illi intellectum meum; sed desidero [ii] aliquatenus intelligere veritatem tuam, quam credit et amat cor meum."

[31] Ibid., c. xiv; S I.111.8–15: "An invenisti, anima mea, quod quaerebas? Quaerebas [i] deum, et invenisti [ii] eum esse quiddam summum omnium, quo nihil melius cogitari potest; et hoc esse ipsam vitam, lucem, sapientiam, bonitatem, aeternam beatitudinem et beatam aeternitatem; et hoc esse ubique et semper. Nam si non invenisti [i] deum tuum: quomodo est ille hoc quod invenisti, et quod illum tam certa veritate et vera certitudine *intellexisti*? Si vero invenisti: quid est, quod *non sentis* quod invenisti? Cur non te sentit, domine deus, anima mea, si invenit te?"

standing, how can the soul [ii] understand anything *about* God, without [i] seeing God?[32]—and offers the resolution that understanding and vision come in degrees: "Or did it see truth and light but not yet see You, because [ii] it saw You to some extent *(aliquatenus)* but did not [i] see You *as You are?*"[33] Further reflection reveals that the cognitive inaccessibility of God to the soul is partly a function of the incommensuration of their natures—because "not only are You a greater than which cannot be thought, but you are something greater than could be thought"[34]—and hence to that degree permanent. Yet sin-produced blindness[35] can be repaired by God, and for this Anselm prays.[36] He then resumes the search for clearer understanding through cc. xviii–xxiii, when he finally stops to summarize the results by extolling the Goodness of God discovered thereby (cc. xxiv–xxv) and estimating its power to satisfy the soul (cc. xxv–xxvi).

The Genre of Alloquium

In the *Proslogion*, the exercise of understanding itself takes the form of a prayer: not a meditation (as in the *Monologion*) addressed by the soul to itself; not a dialogue (as in *De grammatico, De veritate, De libertate arbitrii, De casu diaboli,* and *Cur Deus homo*) in which the reader hears thoughts uttered by two different speakers; but *alloquium,* in which the soul *speaks to* God.[37] The soul begins by asking questions of,[38] addressing puzzles to,[39] and/or begging help from God.[40] Then God "illu-

---

[32] Ibid., c. xiv; S I.111.16–20: "An non invenit, quem invenit esse lucem et veritatem? Quomodo namque intellexit [ii] hoc, nisi [i] *videndo lucem et veritatem?* Aut potuit omnino [ii] aliquid intelligere de te, nisi .per 'lucem tuam et veritatem tuam'?"

[33] Ibid., c. xiv; S I.111.20–21: "An et veritas et lux est quod vidit, et tamen nondum te vidit, quia [ii] vidit te *aliquatenus,* sed non [i] vidit te *sicuti es?*"

[34] Ibid., cc. xiv–xv; S I.111.22–I.112.17, esp. S I.112.14–15: "non solum es quo maius cogitari nequit, sed es quiddam maius quam cogitari possit."

[35] Ibid., c. xvii; S I.113.8–15.

[36] Ibid., c. xviii; S I.113.18–I.114.13.

[37] Yves Cattin distinguishes the genre of *alloquium* from dialogue (where two voices are heard) but lumps it together with meditation, on the ground that Anselm speaks and no one replies ("La prière de S. Anselme," pp. 375–76). I think it is misleading to say that no one replies, however. God speaks within by disclosing, but Anselm has to put what is shown into words. Cf. *Proslogion,* c. xxvi; S I.121.4–6.

[38] *Proslogion,* c. ii; S I.101.4–7; c. vi; S I.104.20–25; c. vii; S I.105.9–11; c. viii; S I.106.5–8; c. ix; S I.106.18–I.107.3; c. x; S I.108.23–25; c. xi; S I.109.10–24; c. xviii; S I.114.14–18; c. xix; S I.115.7–9; c. xx; S I.115.18–20.

[39] Ibid., c. xiii; S I.110.12–19.

[40] Ibid., c. ii; S I.101.1–2; c. ix; S I.108.8–10; c. xiv; S I.111.23–I.112.11; c. xviii; S I.114.8–13.

mines" the soul so that it may "see,"[41] "teaches"[42] it that it may understand; Anselm begs, "tell your servant within, in his heart"[43] that he may know. It then belongs to the soul to articulate what God has revealed, usually couching the reasoning[44] and statement of results[45] in the form of second-person address to God, at intervals combining this with exclamations of thanks and praise.[46] In the few cases where explicit address is lacking, the context of continuing prayer is clear from what precedes and follows.[47]

Anselm puts the soul that prays the *Proslogion* in a position analogous to that of a philosophy student who seeks the teacher's help in refuting arguments for solipsism or proving the existence of other minds. (The difference, just mentioned, is that in the latter case, the teacher verbalizes his or her own thoughts, whereas in the *Proslogion*, the soul articulates what God shows.) Thus, Anselm takes for granted that human understanding is a work of collaboration, involving reciprocal initiative and response: the soul strives and seeks, thereby bringing the image of God that it *is* into clearer focus, tuning its instrument of knowledge as best it can; then God presses in and discloses; and the soul works to put into words what it has seen. Such a dynamic is already implicit in Anselm's Prooemium description of "his" discovery of the *unum argumentum*. He began (as in the *Monologion*) with meditation on an issue of philosophical theology:

> considering that [work = the *Monologion*] to be composed of a chain of many arguments, I began to ask myself whether perhaps *unum argumentum* could be found, which would need nothing other than itself for proving itself and which alone would be sufficient by itself to demonstrate [i] that God truly exists, [ii] that He is the highest

---

[41] Ibid., c. iv; S I.104.5–7; c. xiv; S I.111.22–23; I.112.5–6, 9–11; I.112.27–I.113,1.

[42] Ibid., c. ix; S I.108.11.

[43] Ibid., c. xxvi; S I.121.4–6; cf. S I.120.23–26; and c. xiv; S I.111.22–23.

[44] C. iii; S I.102.3–9; c. v; S I.104.11–17; c. ix; S I.107.4–I.108.20; c. x; S I.108.26–I.109.6; c. xi; S I.109.10–24; c. xiii; S I.110.20–I.111.3; c. xv; S I.112.14–17; c.xix; S I.115.10–15; c. xx; S I.115.21–I.116.3.

[45] Conclusions addressed to God: c. iii; S I.102.3–9; c. vi; S I.105.4–6; c. vii; S I.105.27–I.106.2; c. viii; S I.106.9–14; c. xi; S I.110.1–3; c. xii; S I.110.6–8; c. xvii; S I.113.8–15; c. xxii; S I.116.15–I.117.2; c. xxiii; S I.117.6–16.

[46] C. iv; S I.103.5–7; cf. the "shores" of prayer and praise in cc. i, xiv–xviii, and xxiv–xxvi.

[47] Twice the question is raised and/or reasoning begun in the second person, but then it continues without further address (c. ii; S I.101.7–I.102.3; c. iii; S I.102.6–I.103.2); once the question is raised without address but answered in the second person (c. xxi; S I.116.6–12); and twice the conclusion is stated without further address (c. iii; S I.102.9–11; c. xxiii; S I.117.16–22).

good, that needs no other, that [iii] all things need Him for their being and their well-being and [iv] whatever [else] we believe about the Divine Substance.[48]

He engaged the problem with persistence, but without success, until he decided to give up and turn his mind to other things—

> Often and eagerly, I would direct my thought to this goal. Sometimes what I sought seemed within reach; other times, it would flee from the mind's eye altogether. At last, despairing, I wanted to cease from the search of something impossible to find.[49]

—whereupon the solution began forcing itself upon him, contrary to his own initiative:

> But just when I wanted to exclude that thought from myself, lest it prevent my mind from occupying itself with other things on which I could make more progress, then it began more and more to force itself insistently upon me, unwilling and resistant as I was. Then one day when I was worn out from resisting its entreaties, what I had despaired of finding came to my conflicted mind, so that I eagerly embraced the line of thinking that I had anxiously warded off.[50]

Anselm then gave words to the insight by writing the *Proslogion*,[51] which is in any event dotted with *explicit* acknowledgments of Divine collaboration in the form of prayers for help, second-person address of reasoning to God, and exclamations of thanksgiving.

---

[48] *Proslogion*, Prooemium; S I.93.4–10: "considerans illud esse multorum concatenatione contextum argumentorum, coepi mecum quaerere, si forte posset inveniri unum argumentum, quod nullo alio ad se probandum quam se solo indigeret, et solum ad astruendum quia deus vere est, et quia est summum bonum nullo alio indigens, et quo omnia indigent ut sint et ut bene sint, et quaecumque de divina credimus substantia, sufficeret."

[49] Ibid., Prooemium; S I.93.10–13: "Ad quod cum saepe studioseque cogitationem converterem, atque aliquando mihi videretur iam posse capi quod quaerebam, aliquando mentis aciem omnino fugeret; tandem desperans volui cessare velut ab inquisitione rei quam inveniri esset impossibile."

[50] Ibid., Prooemium; S I.93.13–19: "Sed cum illam cogitationem, ne mentem meam frustra occupando ab aliis in quibus proficere possem impediret, penitus a me vellem excludere: tunc magis ac magic nolenti et defendenti se coepit cum importunitate quadem ingerere. Cum igitur quadam die vehementer eius importunitati resistendo fatigarer, in ipso cogitationem conflictu sic se obtulit quod desperaveram, ut studiose cogitationem amplecterer, quam sollicitus repellebam."

[51] Ibid., Prooemium; S I.93.20–21: "Aestimans igitur quod me gaudebam invenisse, si scriptum esset alicui legenti placiturum . . ."

Frequent commentary to the contrary, there is nothing paradoxical[52] or question-begging about the soul's asking God's help in finding arguments for Christian beliefs about the being and well-being of God, any more than in a student's asking the teacher for help in disproving solipsism or establishing the existence of other minds. But the method of *alloquium* does call on the soul undertaking the exercise, as on the commentator interpreting it, to observe a distinction between beliefs that are presupposed by the soul's (student's) requests for help, second-person address, and expressions of thanks, on the one hand, and those that figure as premises in arguments on the other. Some, but not all, of the former are theses to be proved by the latter: for example, the existence, power, wisdom, and goodness of God are the subject of Anselm's *Proslogion* arguments, but the doctrine of Adam's fall is not (the existence of the teacher's mind, but not his or her obligation to help the student as teacher of the class).

The *Unum Argumentum*—Scope and Strength

Anselm was confident that he had already given a reason for the faith that was in him in his *Monologion*. To his mind, its arguments lacked not cogency but unity and simplicity. For him, the methodological bias in favor of simplicity and unity in theories has its epistemological basis in the ancient maxim that "like is known by like"; its ontological foundation in the fact that God the Truth is self-sufficient, paradigm unity and simplicity. Thus, viewing the *Monologion* as "composed of a chain of arguments," Anselm sought "unum argumentum"

---

[52] Cf. Cattin, "La prière de S. Anselme," pp. 381–83. Cattin tries to resolve this paradox by distinguishing between proof and conviction (which involves existential commitment). The two converge, he claims, when the object of speculation is wholly accessible to reason, but diverge where it is not (as in the case of God). Cattin says that Anselm inserted his reasoning into the context of prayer to bridge the gap between intellectual assent to the existence of God and existential commitment to Him. But this analysis seems to conflate the issues (i) of whether one can have a beatific vision of God apart from living faith that strives after God with will as well as intellect (and therefore involves "existential commitment"), (ii) whether there is anything question-begging about asking God's help in proving things about His existence and nature, (iii) of what bearing the ontological incommensuration between God and the rational soul has on either (i) or (ii). Presumably, mere intellectual assent to the existence of the teacher does not suffice for friendship, apart from some sort of "existential commitment" between the two (analogue of [i]), and this is so even though they are ontologically commensurate. My analogy with student-teacher collaboration in refuting solipsism or proving the existence of other minds shows that both ontological incommensuration and existential commitment are red herrings so far as (ii) is concerned.

that would imitate Divine self-sufficiency, for showing "that [i] God truly exists, that [ii] He is the highest good and needs no other, that [iii] all things need Him for their being and their well-being, and [iv] whatever [else] we believe about the Divine substance."[53] Key as this *unum argumentum* is to his view of the differences between the *Monologion* and the *Proslogion*, Anselm does not bother to identify it with precision.

The Ontological Argument?

Contemporary philosophers focused on the project of proving the *existence* of God are apt to understand by '*unum argumentum*' a reference to the so-called ontological argument, variously identified with the reasoning in c. ii or with cc. ii–iii taken together. This interpretation fits Anselm's note of contrast: whereas the *Monologion* argues from effects discernible by the senses or reason and requires the work of eighty chapters to conclude to the existence of God, *Proslogion* (cc. ii–iii) arrives at the (necessary) existence of God in fewer than three short pages.[54] Nevertheless, this interpretation is obviously mistaken, because c. ii establishes at most the existence, c. iii the inconceivability of nonexistence, of God, whereas Anselm was after results of broader scope: not only "that [i] God truly exists, and that [ii] He is the highest good and needs no other," but also "that [iii] all things need Him for their being and their well-being, and [iv] whatever [else] we believe about the Divine substance."[55]

A Reductio *Argument-Schema?*

Coloman Etienne Viola[56] identifies Anselm's *unum argumentum* not with a particular argument or arguments but with a *reductio* argument-schema based on his newfound formula that God is a being a greater than which cannot be conceived. In particular, Viola sees the reasoning

[53] *Proslogion*, Prooemium; S I.93.4–10; esp. S. I.93.7–9: "quia [i] deus vere est, et quia [ii] est summum bonum nullo alio indigens, et [iii] quo omnia indigent ut sint et ut bene sint, et [iv] quaecumque de divina credimus substantia . . ."

[54] Ibid., cc. ii–iii; S I.101.3–I.103.11.

[55] Ibid., Prooemium; S I.93.4–10; esp. S I.93.7–9. Cf. *Responsio editoris*, section X; S I.138.28–I.139.3. Cattin acknowledges this broad scope in the *Proslogion* ("La Prière de S. Anselme," pp. 383–84). Karl Barth already makes this argument in *Fides Quaerens Intellectum* (London: SCM Press, 1960), p. 113.

[56] Coloman Etienne Viola, "L'influence de la méthode anselmienne jugée par les historiens de son temps," *Analecta Anselmiana* IV, 2 (1975), 1–32.

of chapters ii–vii, ix, xi, xiii, xv, and xviii as instantiating the following argument form:[57]

(i)   God is a being a greater than which cannot be conceived.

(ii)   Either God is F or God is not-F.

(iii) If God is F (not-F), then not-(i).

(iv)   Therefore, God is not-F (F).[58]

This construal of '*unum argumentum*' allows it the requisite scope. More-over, it identifies a significant point of contrast between the *Monologion* and *Proslogion*. Viola contends that whereas (in all but two cases)[59] the *Monologion* mounts direct arguments, the *Proslogion* uses *reductio* argu-ments exclusively.[60] We might add, what Viola surely intends, that the *Proslogion*'s repeated deployment of the *same reductio* argument-schema would give it the simplicity and unity for which Anselm was seeking. Nonetheless, Viola's contrast is too sharply drawn, because Anselm of-fers direct arguments in at least five places in the *Proslogion*.[61] And

---

[57] See appendix to this essay.

[58] Thus, Viola characterizes the *Proslogion* argument as follows: "In effect, from a methodological point of view, one can summarize the *Proslogion* as follows: it is an effort to demonstrate the absurdity of any affirmation about God (including His existence, His essence, His attributes) that does not conform to the dialectical principle uniquely expressed by 'that than which nothing greater can be conceived' . . ." (in "L'influence de la méthode anselmienne," p. 15); and more precisely: "Let us try to reconstruct the 'unum argumentum' that encompasses our whole knowledge of God in the *Proslogion*. One could summarize this little work in a series of disjunctive syllogisms whose major is always given by 'And certainly we believe that you are a being greater than which cannot be conceived' and the minor by disjunctive propositions that express the disjunc-tion between two concepts or qualities that either are contradicting opposites or opposed as the more to the less perfect" (ibid., p. 15 n. 38). I "clean up" Viola's proposal a bit by not including the belief-operator in the major premiss.

[59] *Monologion*, c. iii; S I.15.30–I.16.6; c. iv; S I.17.3–8. But the *Monologion* contains other *reductio* arguments Viola does not notice, e.g., c. xviii; S I.33.15–23.

[60] Viola, "L'influence de la méthode anselmienne," pp. 13 n. 36; 15.

[61] (1) A direct argument is implicit in c. vi: (i) "Tu es . . . quidquid melius est esse quam non esse (from c. v) (ii) melius sit esse sensibilem, omnipotentem, misericordem, impassibilem quam non esse . . . (iii) tu . . . es sensibilis . . . omnipotens . . . misericors . . . impassibilis." (c. vi; S I.104.20–22). (2) In c. ix, regarding the compossibility of perfect goodness with both punishing and sparing the wicked, Anselm adds a direct proof: (iii) "melior est qui malis et puniendo et parcendo est bonus, quam qui puniendo tantum. (iv) ergo misericors es, quia, totus et summe bonus es." (S I.107.11–12). (3) Having dealt with the puzzles about the first conclusion of the direct argument implicit in c. vi, Anselm implicitly reasserts it, with a longer list of attributes, at the end of c. xi: (i) "Tu es . . . quidquid melius est esse quam non esse. (ii) Sic ergo vere es sensibilis, omnipotens,

although he could have used instantiations of the *reductio*-schema instead, the fact that he did not bother to do so contradicts Viola's generalization.

The Formula 'a Being a Greater than Which Cannot Be Conceived'?

Karl Barth concluded that Anselm's *unum argumentum* should be identified with the formula 'a being a greater than which cannot be conceived' itself.[62] The recognition of this formula as identifying the root from which the being, well-being, and independence of the Divine nature, as well as the dependence of anything else there may be, represents a conceptual advance over the *Monologion*, which argues from effects to a highest nature and then labors to show that the highest nature has the features to qualify as God. Given it, the premiss

(i)   God is a being a greater than which cannot be conceived

is available for use either in *reductio* arguments of the sort above or in direct arguments that continue in either of the following ways:

(iv)   What is F (not-F) is greater than what is not-F (F).

(v)   Therefore, God is F (not-F);

or

(vi)   What is F (not-F) is less than what is not-F (F).

(vii)   Therefore, God is not-F (F).

I favor this interpretation.

Modal Strength vs. Simplification

Viola contends that the predominance of the *reductio* schema makes the argumentation of the *Proslogion* more powerful than that of the

---

misericors et impassibilis, quemadmodum vivens, sapiens, bonus, beatus, aeternus, etc."
(S I.110.1–3). (4) Likewise, in c. xiii; S I.110.12–14: "Sed [i] omne quod clauditur aliquatenus loco aut tempore, minus est quam quod nulla lex loci aut temporis coercet. Quoniam ergo [ii] maius te nihil est, [iii] nullus locus aut tempus te cohibet, sed ubique et semper es" (5) Again, in c. xii; S I.110.6–8: "Sed certe (i) quidquid es, non per aliud es quam per teipsam. (ii) Tu es igitur ipsa vita qua vivis; et sapientia qua sapis, et bonitas ipsa qua bonis et malis bonus es; et ita de similibus."

[62] *Fides quaerens intellectum* (London: SCM Press, 1960), "Introduction," p. 13; c. ii, p. 73.

Monologion, where direct arguments predominate, because *reductio* arguments establish the necessity, whereas direct arguments prove only the truth, of their conclusions.[63] This claim is confused, however, because the demonstrated modal strength of the conclusion depends on that of the premises, not on whether the argument is direct or indirect. Both *Monologion* and *Proslogion* arguments purport to establish the necessity of most of their conclusions. The real advance in the *Proslogion* argumentation is the one Anselm advertises: that of unity and simplification.

Analogy and Thematic Congruence

Viola maintains that not only does the *reductio* replace direct argumentation in the *Proslogion,* it also displaces the extensive analogical reasoning the *Monologion* contains.[64] Once again, Viola thinks that *reductio* arguments are more powerful than analogical arguments or mere *rationes convenientiae.*

It is true that the *Proslogion* omits some analogical reasoning prominent in *Monologion.* (a) The *Proslogion* does not appeal to psychological, artist, and mental-speech analogies for an understanding of God's knowledge (cf. *Monologion,* cc. v, vii, ix, x, xii, xxix, xxx, xxxi, xxxvi) or self-love (cf. *Monologion,* c. xlix). (b) Neither does the *Proslogion* make use of psychological, mental-speech, and birth analogies to motivate language for talking about the Trinity (cf. *Monologion,* cc. xxxviii, xxxix, xlii, xliv–xlviii, liii–lx, lxii, lxiii), vocabulary for which Anselm claimed no more than suitability *("congruentius," "convenientissime," "magis convenit," "forsan . . . dici aptius").* But this is not because these matters receive a nonanalogical, simplifying justification by appeal to the *unum argumentum.* On the contrary, the *Proslogion* does not treat the *Monologion* puzzles about God's knowledge at all. Likewise, when Anselm finally introduces the Trinitarian talk about God—with the names 'Father', 'Son', and 'Holy Spirit'; the language of birth and speech—in *Proslogion,* c. xxiii, he simply takes it for granted, without making any attempt to justify it or to explain how God might be thought to be three. His

---

[63] Vida, "L'influence de la méthode anselmienne," p. 13: "The method of *reductio ad absurdum* is very powerful—demonstrating not only that such and such is true, but also that it can't be otherwise."

[64] Ibid.: "On all the evidence, it is not a matter here of a simple affirmative proof from positive reasons of *propriety or analogy,* or even of deduction from a certain premiss, but of demonstrating the impossibility and absurdity of the contradictory affirmation." (Italics mine.)

focus is to insist that whatever such threeness may be, it in no way compromises Divine unity or simplicity.[65] So far from replacing these *Monologion* analogies with considerations of greater theoretical simplicity and unity, the *unum argumentum* has no light to shed on these issues, and Anselm's *Proslogion* omits them altogether.

On the other hand, attention to the text shows (implicit and explicit) appeal to analogy to be by no means absent from the *Proslogion*. For example, it deploys without comment the *Monologion* analogies between space and time, between laws and natural regularities,[66] between speech and thought.[67] Again, the opening reasoning in c. ii advances its own analogy between a painter's preconception and the really extant picture to make the important distinction between a thing's existing in the intellect *(rem esse in intellectu)* and its existing in reality *(rem esse).*[68]

What the *Proslogion* evidences is not the abandonment of analogies but a shift in emphasis from Augustinian psychological models to an elaborate (and equally Augustinian) analogy between the corporeal and the spiritual. In the *Proslogion*, the theme of *sentire* ties the more affective spiritual exercises (of cc. i, xiv–xviii, xxiv–xxvi) with intellectual striving (of cc. ii–xiii, xviii–xxiii). Thus, Anselm includes *sensibilis* on his second list of Divine attributes,[69] explaining how it is appropriate to equate '*sentire*' with '*cognoscere*', and how God is *summe sensibilis*, while corporeal animal sensation is an inferior version.[70] Because that superior Divine *sentire* is compatible with impassibility, we "sense" the effect of His mercy, but He does not "sense" its affect.[71] Later on, Anselm insists that harmony, odor, flavor, and softness exist in God in an "ineffable way"; in creatures, in a sensible way.[72] Thus, he represents God as having both paradigm sensory capacities and sensible properties, where those in creatures are inferior imitations. The human senses, obstructed by sin, are incapable of sensing these Divine features.[73] And Anselm repeatedly laments that his striving enables him to understand

---

[65] *Proslogion*, c. xxiii; S I.117.10–20.

[66] Ibid., c. xiii; S I.110–11; c. xix; S I.115.6–15. Cf. *Monologion*, cc. xviii–xxii; S I.32–41.

[67] Ibid., c. iv; S I.103.14–16. Cf. *Monologion*, c. x; S I.25.10–27.

[68] Ibid., c. ii; S I.101.10.

[69] Ibid., c. vi; S I.104.20–21: "Verum cum melius sit esse sensibilem, omnipotentem, misericordem, impassibilem quam non esse . . ."

[70] Ibid., c. vi; S I.104.23–I.105.6.

[71] Ibid., c. viii; S I.106.11–12: "Etenim tu respicis nos miseros, nos sentimus misericordis effectum, tu non sentis affectum."

[72] Ibid., c. xvii; S I.113.6–7, 12–14.

[73] Ibid., c. xvii; S I.113.12–15.

God a little bit *(aliquatenus)* but not to "sense" Him.[74] God is Light and Truth,[75] which the eye of the soul would see more clearly were it not darkened by its weakness.[76] Like the *Monologion,* the *Proslogion* presupposes a comparison between spatial distance and cognitive inaccessibility,[77] between spatial size and ontological incommensuration,[78] between spatial and intellectual penetration.[79] *Proslogion* also uses bodily postures to express the soul's relation to God—now "bent over" hoping to "rise."[80] Sin is alternatively a heavy load,[81] an overwhelming flood,[82] or something into which the soul has fallen and with which it is entangled.[83] Anselm takes for granted an analogy between physical hunger and thirst and the soul's desire for God.[84] And his final commendation of God as the Good in c. xxv assumes an analogy between corporeal and spiritual delights sufficient to sustain the conclusion that God will satisfy all desires for the former.[85]

What is the meaning of these discrepancies between the *Monologion*'s and the *Proslogion*'s deployment of analogies? In my judgment, they reflect not doctrinal change but Anselm's attention to *thematic congruence*. The opening spiritual exercises of the *Proslogion* make use of the idea that God's image in human beings has been obscured by the Fall, to precipitate a sense of humility and motivate prayers for help.[86] For Anselm then to appeal—as he does in *Monologion* (c. lxvii ff.)—to the

[74] Ibid., c. xiv; S I.111.13–15: "Si vero invenisti: quid est, quod non sentis quod invenisti? Cur non te sentit, domine deus, anima mea, si invenit te?" Cf. c. xvi; S I.113.2–4: "Ubique es tota praesens, et non te video. In te moveor et in te sum, et ad te non possum accedere. Intra me et circa me es, et non te sentio."

[75] Ibid., c. i; S I.98.4–5; I.99.2, 17; I.100.8. C. ix; S I.107.4–5. C. xiv; S I.111.17–20, 25. C. xvi; S I.112.20, 27.

[76] Ibid., c. i; S I.98.3, 13–14. C. xiv; S I.111.13–15, 23–24; S I.114.2. C. xvi; S I.113.2–3. C. xviii; S I.114.11.

[77] Ibid., c. i; S I.98.8–9; S I.100.16. C. ix; S I.107.5.

[78] E.G., Anselm speaks of the soul's "brevitas" and "angustia" in contrast to God's "immensitas" and "amplitudo" (ibid., c. xiv; S I.122.3–9; cf. c. xvi; S.I.112.26–27; and c. xxi; S I.116.9).

[79] Ibid., c. i; S I.100.15–16. C. xvi; S I.112.20–21.

[80] Ibid., c. i; S I.100.4–5: "Domine, *incurvatus* non possum nisi deorsum aspeciere, *erige* me ut possum sursum intendere." (Italics mine.)

[81] Ibid., c. i; S I.100.6.

[82] Ibid., c. i; S I.100.5–6.

[83] Ibid., c. xviii; S I.114.3–6.

[84] Ibid., c. i; S I.98.20–21, 23. C. xviii; S I.113.19–I.114.2. C. xxvi; S I.121.24–I.122.1.

[85] Ibid., c. xxv; S I.118.20–I.119.3.

[86] Ibid., c. i; S I.100.12–19: "Fateor, domine, et gratias ago, quia creasti in me hanc imaginem tuam, ut tui memor te cagitem, te amem. Sed sic est abolita attritione vitiorum, sic est offuscata fumo peccatorum, ut non possit facere ad quod facta est, nisi tu renoves et reformes eam. Non tento, domine, penetrare alitudinem tuam, quia nullatenus com-

image of God in humans as grounds for confidence that his investigation of the Trinity will meet with some success would be thematically incongruous, jolt the soul out of the spiritual posture the opening exercise was meant to achieve. And this would be true, even though the damage sustained by the soul in the Fall is not such as to undermine the psychological analogies the *Monologion* actually uses in its discussion of the Trinity. After all, it is the *ante-mortem* face-to-face vision of God that the Fall has prevented (i.e., achieving the first, and higher, of Anselm's goals), not the lower goal reached by the *Monologion* ("to understand Your Truth a little bit").[87] On the other hand, imbedding the intellectual search (of cc. ii–xiii and xviii–xxiii) within the framework of such spiritual exercises makes the mystical analogy between the corporeal and spiritual highly appropriate.

Progressive Understanding *(Intelligere)*

Syllabi, Partially Overlapping

In the *Monologion,* Anselm treats an ambitious range of topics under the rubric "The Soul in Search of the Good": in particular, he tries to demonstrate by reason alone *(sola ratione)* (i) the existence of God, (ii) the dependence relations between God and creatures, (iii) what God is essentially *(substantialiter),* (iv) that God is three in one, and (v) what the end of human nature is and how it is rational for the human soul to seek God with all its powers. The syllabus of the *Proslogion* is controlled by the interaction of the *unum argumentum* with the themes of the spiritual exercises (cc. i, (i)–(iii) xiv–xviii, xxiv–xxvi) of the soul that seeks God's face. The *Proslogion* shares goals with the *Monologion,* because they are precisely what the *unum argumentum* illuminates best:[88] (i) the (necessary) existence of God is established in cc. ii–iii; (iii) the nature of God is unfolded in cc. v–xiii and xvii–xxiii; and (ii) that God is the independent source of all else is treated in cc. iii, v, xi, and xxii. As noted above, there is no *Proslogion* discussion of (iv), both because (iv) does not admit of simplified treatment via the *unum argumentum* and because repeating the *Monologion* case would be thematically incongruous. On the positive side, thematic congruence explains Anselm's relegation of (v) to the spiritual exercises of *Proslogion,* cc. i and xxiv–

---

paro illi intellectum meum; sed desidero aliquatenus intelligere veritatem tuam, quam credit et amat cor meum. Neque enim quaero intelligere ut credam, sed credo ut intelligam. Nam et hoc credo: quia 'nisi credidero, non intelligam'."

[87] Ibid., c. i; S I.100.17.

[88] Cf. ibid., Prooemium; S I.93.7–10; c. ii; S I.101.3–4.

xxvi,[89] and governs his selection of new attribute puzzles not considered in the *Monologion:* namely, between *sensibilis* and incorporeal or spirit;[90] between inconceivability of nonexistence (c. iii), truth (c. v), and justice (c. v), on the one hand, and omnipotence (c. vi), on the other;[91] between mercy and impassibility (c. vi);[92] and between justice (c. v) and mercy (c. vi).[93]

Excitatio mentis ad intelligendum

To stir up the mind to intellectual striving, Anselm turns the syllabus into a sequence of puzzles and problems. Having opened c. ii with a short prayer—"Therefore, Lord, You who give understanding to faith, grant me to understand, to the degree You know to be expedient, that You are as *we believe,* and You are what *we believe*"[94]—Anselm jars the reader with an apparent inconsistency in our beliefs: our belief that God exists, and our belief in Scripture, a verse of which reads "the fool has said in his heart, 'there is no God'" (Pss. 13:1; 52:1). Likewise, when Anselm turns to (iii) "whatever we believe about the Divine substance"[95] or "what, then, You are, Lord God,"[96] he articulates the *Monologion* criterion—"You are . . . whatever it is better to be than not to be"[97]— derives two attribute lists, and then confronts the reader with a row of prima facie inconsistencies in the results (cc. v–xi): between *sensibilis* and incorporeal or spirit;[98] between inconceivability of nonexistence (c. iii), truth (c. v), and justice (c. v), on the one hand, and omnipotence (c. vi), on the other;[99] between mercy and impassibility (c. vi);[100] and between justice (c. v) and mercy (c. vi).[101] Likewise, his addition of *aeternus* to the list in c. xi prompts first the *Monologion* reflection that

---

[89] Cf. ibid., c. i; S I.98.14–16, 18–19; S I.100.14–15, for mentions of the *ad quod factum est* of human nature, now theologically described as that of seeing God's face. Likewise, c. xxiv ("Excita nunc . . .") echoes c. i ("Excitatio mentis . . ." and "Eia nunc . . .") and introduces the commendation of God, the Good that satisfies, so that the work concludes with a resolve to seek God with all human powers.

[90] Ibid., c. vi; S I.104.23–25.

[91] Ibid., c. vi; S I.104.22; c. vii; S I.105.9–11.

[92] Ibid., c. vi; S I.104.22; c. viii; S I.106.5–8.

[93] Ibid., cc. ix–xi; S I.106.18–I.110.3.

[94] Ibid., c. ii; S I.101.4: "Ergo, domine, qui das fidei intellectum, da mihi, ut quantum scis expedire intelligam, quia es sicut *credimus,* et hoc es quod *credimus*." (Italics mine.)

[95] Ibid., c. ii; S I.93.9.

[96] Ibid., c. v; S I.104.11: "quid igitur es, domine deus . . ."

[97] Ibid., c. v; S I.104.15–16: "Tu es . . . quidquid melius est esse quam non esse."

[98] Ibid., c. vi; S I.104.23–25.

[99] Ibid., c. vi; S I.104.22; c. vii; S I.105.9–11.

[100] Ibid., c. vi; S I.104.22; c. viii; S I.106.5–8.

[101] Ibid., cc. ix–xi; S I.106.18–I.110.3.

God is not bound by the laws of space and time[102] and then a new question about how God's relation to space and time differs from that of other spirits.[103] Returning in c. xviii to the question, "quid es, domine,"[104] Anselm asks how the many attributes listed are related in God,[105] and cc. xix–xxi pursue further questions about God's relation to time and the meaning of terminology commonly applied to Him.[106]

Ec-static Progress

Already in the *Monologion*, Anselm has set his agenda of the mind overreaching itself. In particular, he finds, our language has to be stretched to express what the Highest Nature is *substantialiter;*[107] the Highest Nature's *manner* of thought and knowledge of creatures is fundamentally incomprehensible to us;[108] Its twoness and threeness transcend the human intellect.[109] Anselm's motto there is, that because the subject matter is too difficult for us, we must try, try again.[110]

Framed as it is with spiritual exercises aimed at the higher goal of seeing God's face, the *Proslogion* is even more dominated by this theme of ecstasy. But even within the parameters of the lower goal *(aliquatenus intelligere)*, the soul's attempt to understand (i)–(iii) mimics the movement of the opening spiritual exercises, as it rises from problems it can handle, through those that exceed its grasp, to a proof that God is "quiddam maius quam cogitari possit"[111] and a wider reflection on the ontological incommensuration between God and creatures (cc. xviii–xxiii).

Thus, the opening puzzle of c. ii is resolved by the famous arguments of cc. ii–iii, on the one hand; by observing that it is the fool who speaks in the scriptural quotation[112] and by appealing to the philosopher's distinction between various sorts of interior speech,[113] on the other. Likewise, Anselm "not unfittingly" *(non inconvenienter)* extends the use of *'sensibilis'* to make it equivalent to *'cognoscibilis'*, thereby rendering

---

[102] Ibid., c. xiii; S I.110.12–15.
[103] Ibid., c. xiii; S I.110.17–19.
[104] Ibid., c. xviii; S I.114.14.
[105] Ibid., c. xviii; S I.114.14–18.
[106] Ibid., cc. xix–xxi; S I.115.7–I.116.12.
[107] *Monologion*, c. xv; S I.28.3–7, 13, 16, 25.
[108] Ibid., c. xxxvi; S I.54.15–18.
[109] E.g., ibid., c. lxiv; S I.74.30–I.75.16.
[110] Ibid., c. xv; S I.28.5–8; c. xliii; S I.59.15–17.
[111] *Proslogion*, c. xv; S I.112.14–15.
[112] Ibid., c. iii; S I.103.9–11.
[113] Ibid., c. iv; S I.103.17–I.104.4. Cf. *Monologion*, c. x; S I.24.29–I.25.27.

'God is *sensibilis*' compatible with 'God is incorporeal'.[114] The philosopher's distinction between proper and improper uses of *'posse'* dissolves the apparent inconsistencies between omnipotence, necessary existence, truth, and justice.[115] Likewise, the implicit etymological understanding of *'misericors'* is explained away in terms of a distinction between we who "sense the *effect*" and God who "does not sense the *affect*."[116]

For Anselm, however, human intellectual capacity reaches its limits in the prima facie inconsistency between justice and mercy. No sooner does he pose the questions[117] than he begins to hint at the cognitive inaccessibility of Divine goodness—"Or, because Your Goodness is incomprehensible, is it hidden in the inaccessible light in which You dwell?"[118] This humble confession brings immediate insight, which articulates his original intuition in c. vi that mercy satisfies the attribute-criterion of c. v and thus can be predicated of God essentially *(substantialiter)* via the *unum argumentum:*

(T1) "the one who is good to the wicked by punishing and by sparing is better than the one who [is good to the wicked] by punishing alone."[119]

But if mercy thus finds its source in Divine goodness, Anselm laments that the precise reason of its arising is high and hidden.[120] He then proceeds to articulate the source of the apparent inconsistency: namely, that reason seems to postulate that

(T2) justice would always render goods to the good and evils to the evil.[121]

This clarification of the problem gives way, once again, to exclamations on the "immensity" of Divine goodness, as to intimations of its location

---

[114] Ibid., c. vi; S I.105.1–6.

[115] Ibid., c. vii; S I.105.16–I.106.2.

[116] Ibid., c. viii; S I.106.9–14.

[117] Ibid., c. ix; S I.106.18–I.107.3.

[118] Ibid., c. ix; S I.107.4–5: "An quia bonitas tua est incomprehensibilis, latet hoc in luce inaccessibili quam inhabitas?"

[119] Ibid., c. ix; S I.107.10–11: "melior est qui malis et puniendo et parcendo est bonus, quam qui puniendo tantum."

[120] Ibid., c. ix; S I.107.14–18: "O altitudo bonitatis tuae, deus! et videtur unde sis misericors, et non pervidetur. Cernitur unde flumen manat, et non perspeicitur fons unde nascatur. Nam et de plenitudine bonitas est quia peccatoribus tuis pius es, et in altitudine bonitatis latet *qua ratione* hoc es." (Italics mine.)

[121] Ibid., c. ix; S I.107.18–19.

beyond cognitive reach: "O the immensity of the goodness of God . . .
O immense goodness, You are thus beyond all understanding."[122] This
admission and prayer for aid issues in a methodological insight: "even
if it is difficult to understand *how* Your mercy does not take away from
Your justice, yet it is necessary to believe *that* it is not at all opposed to
Your justice."[123] Instead of taking (T2) as fixed, and combining it with
(T1) to infer that

(T3) mercy is opposed to justice,

Anselm will assume that because

(T4) Divine goodness is rooted in justice,

(T1) implies (not-T3) but rather

(T5) Divine mercy is rooted in Divine justice.[124]

He then prays for help to understand *how* this can be: "Then is Your
mercy born from Your justice? Then do you spare the wicked out of
justice? If so, Lord, if so, teach me *how* it is."[125] The beginning of an
answer comes in a gestalt shift: justice should be understood not via
(T2) but rather as signifying what befits a nature. But God's nature is
"to be so good, that You could not be understood [to be] better, and
to work so powerfully, that You could not be thought more powerful."
And God would not show Himself maximally good and powerful if He
made only the not-good good (by creating it) and not the evil good (by
sparing them). Hence to spare befits God's nature and so is just.[126]

Anselm seeks to penetrate further by posing another problem. Even
if (T2) errs in its universality,

(T2') it is just to render goods to the good and evils to the evil,

[122] Ibid., c. ix; S I.107.22–I.108.2: "O immensitas bonitatis dei . . . O immensa bonitas,
quae sic omnem intellectum excedis."
[123] Ibid., c. ix; S I.108.2–5: "etsi difficile sit intelligere, *quomodo* misericordia tua non
absit a tua iustitia, necessarium tamen est credere, *quia* nequaquam adversatur iustitiae."
[124] Ibid., c. ix; S I.108.5–7.
[125] Ibid., c. ix; S I.108.10–11: "Ergone misericordia tua nascitur ex iustitia tua? Ergone
parcis malis ex iustitia? Si sic est domine, si sic est, doce me *quomodo* est."
[126] Ibid., c. x; S I.108.11–20: "sic esse bonum, ut nequeas intelligi melior, et sic potenter
operari, ut non possis cogitari potius."

seems plausible. It follows *that* it is both just to spare and just to punish. Anselm wants to know *how* this can be. This question yields readily to a distinction between two measures of fittingness: the merits of the agent whose acts are judged, and the nature of the one who judges.[127] The next chapter goes a step further: since God "is so just that a more just cannot be conceived *(sic esse iustum, ut iustior nequeas cogitari),"* and since

(T6) "The one who renders both to the good and to the bad according to merits alone is more just than one who renders according to merits to the good alone."[128]

it follows that—given many guilty persons—God would both spare and punish.[129] But this result points to another question whose answer is permanently inaccessible: "certainly, no comprehensible reason can be given why—of those alike evil—You save these rather than those through Your goodness, and You condemn those rather than these through Your justice."[130]

Having thus reached the limits of human understanding, Anselm restates his answer to the c. v question, "what *(quid)* are You, Lord God?", reasserting the prima facie problematic c. vi list but adding some *Monologion,* c. xv, inclusions: living, wise, good, eternal.[131] After drawing the *Monologion,* c. xvi, conclusion that God is whatever He is *per se* and not *per aliud,*[132] which was identified there as a root of our troubles in adapting human language to talk about the Divine essence,[133] Anselm turns to the attribute of eternity,[134] which functioned in the *Monologion,* along with Divine simplicity, to precipitate a sense of the ontological incommensuration between God and creatures.[135] This theme carries over into the evaluation of results in c. xiv, where the Divine-human contrast culminates in the following exclamation: "What purity, what simplicity, what certainty and splendor is there!

---

[127] Ibid., c. x; S I.108.26–I.109.6.

[128] Ibid., c. xi; S I.109.13–14: (T6) "Iustior . . . est qui et bonis et malis, quam qui bonis tantum merita retribuit."

[129] Ibid., c. xi; S I.109.14–15.

[130] Ibid., c. xi; S I.109.22–24: "illud certe nulla ratione comprehendi potest, cur de similibus malis hos magis salves quam illos per summam bonitatem, et illos magis damnes quam istos per summam iustitiam."

[131] Ibid., c. xi; S I.110.2; cf. *Monologion,* c. xv; S I.20.30–31.

[132] Ibid., c. xii; S I.110.6–8; cf. *Monologion,* c. xvi; S I.30.12–13.

[133] *Monologion,* c. xvi; S I.30.5–I.31.8.

[134] *Proslogion,* c. xiii; S I.110.12–I.111.5.

[135] *Monologion,* c. xxviii; S I.46.2–3, 28–29.

Certainly more than what can be understood by a creature."[136] This conclusion is then consolidated in c. xv. where Anselm derives "You are something greater than could be thought" from the *unum argumentum*,[137] and laments in c. xvi, "This is the inaccessible light in which You dwell."[138] Thus, the attempt to understand God—His existence, nature, and relation to creatures—via the *unum argumentum* would have reduced itself to an absurdity were it not for the twin facts (a) that understanding comes in degrees[139] and (b) that only some human cognitive incapacity is metaphysically necessary, while some of it is a reversible consequence of the Fall. Thus, God's harmony, odor, flavor, softness, and beauty are by nature ineffable, but our inability to sense them is due to sin.[140] The remaining chapters, xviii, xxiii, return to the attributes—eternity, simplicity, and unity—that most contribute to the ontological contrast between God and creatures. But now these intellectual results make a positive contribution to the more ambitious project of seeking God's face, as they are used in c. xxiv to estimate the magnitude of the Good that God is, and hence in c. xxv its capacity to satisfy the soul. The consequent assurance of superabundant joy deepens humility and produces hope, both of which resolve (in c. xxvi) into the soul's acceptance of delayed gratification and into its determination to strive into God with all its powers.[141]

Fides Quaerens Intellectum vs. *Sola Ratione*

Anselm addresses his *Monologion* to a dual audience: to the brothers, he promises to proceed by the necessity of reason *(rationis necessitas)*,[142] to the *ignorantes*, by reason alone *(sola ratione)*.[143] By this, he intends to exclude (i) mere appeals to the authority of Scripture or the Church Fathers; to include both (ii) cogent deductive arguments and (iii) reasoning by analogy. His intention is that even one who begins from a

---

[136] *Proslogion*, c. xiv; S I.112.9–11: "Quid puritatis, quid simplicitatis, quid certitudinis, et splendoris ibi est! Certe plusquam a creatura valeat intelligi."

[137] Ibid., c. xv; S I.112.14–17.

[138] Ibid., c. xvi; S I.112.20.

[139] Ibid., c. i; S I.100.15–18; c. xiv; S I.111.20–21.

[140] Ibid., c. xvii; S I.113.12–15.

[141] Yves Cattin seems to imply that we are to understand the soul to have had a mystical experience of God that accounts for the transition from the compunction of despair to that of joyous desire ("Le prière de S. Anselme," pp. 392–93). In my view, this would amount to extreme eisegesis.

[142] *Monologion*, Prologus; S I.7.10.

[143] Ibid., c. i; S I.14.11.

posture of unbelief should arrive, by meditating the *Monologion*, at a knowledge of the existence of God and the truth of many other Christian doctrines, and at an appreciation of the rationality of seeking God, the Good that eternally satisfies, through a posture of living faith.[144]

By contrast, the *Proslogion* pattern of unfolding might look more like an exercise of (Carnapian internal) conceptual development than an attempt at rational proofs to outsiders. To begin with, (a) the *Proslogion* is an exercise for believers only. (b) The phrase 'sola ratione' never occurs in the *Proslogion*. (c) Even after Anselm has lowered his sights in c. i— from the goal of seeing God's face to that of understanding His truth to some extent *(aliquatenus)*—he declares, "For I do not seek to understand that I may believe, but I believe in order that I may understand. For *I believe that 'unless I believe, I shall not understand'*."[145] (d) Moreover, in c. ii, Anselm lets *Scripture* set the initial puzzle: "Or is there, then, no such nature, since 'the fool has said in his heart, "there is no God"'?"[146] And he spends some effort in cc. iii–iv in showing how that quotation from the Psalms is consistent with the unfolded implications of *'aliquid quo nihil maius cogitari possit'*, the *unum argumentum*.[147] The text of the *Proslogion* contains many allusions to Scripture.[148] Sometimes Anselm uses the language of Scripture to formulate his questions,[149] other times, to state his conclusion;[150] and he devotes the whole of c. xxi to expounding the meaning of a scriptural/liturgical phrase.[151]

These facts notwithstanding, the *Proslogion* observes the *Monologion* prohibition against supporting premises by mere appeals to Scripture or patristic authority. Most *Proslogion* references to Scripture occur in

[144] Ibid., cc. lxix–lxxi; c. lxxiv; S I.79.11–I.82.3; S I.82.20–I.83.8.

[145] *Proslogion*, c. i; S I.100.18–19: "Neque enim quaero intelligere ut credam, sed credo ut intelligam. Nam et hoc credo: quia 'nisi credidero, non intelligam'."

[146] Ibid., c. ii; S I.101.5–7: "An ergo non est aliqua talis natura, quia 'dixit insipiens in corde suo: non est deus'?"

[147] Ibid., cc. iii–iv; S I.103.9–I.104.4.

[148] Ibid., c. i; S I.97.7 (Matt. 6:6); S I.97.9–10 (Ps. 26:8); S I.98.4 (I Tim. 6:16); S I.98.9 (Ps. 50:13); S I.98.20–21 (Ps. 77:25; cf. Ps. 126:2); S I.99.10 (Ps. 121:9; Jer. 14:19); S I.99.11–12 (Ps. 114:3); S I.99.13 (Ps. 37:9); S I.99.15 (Ps. 6:4; Ps. 12:1); S I.99.16 (Ps. 12:4); S I.99.21 (Ps. 78:9); S I.100.3 (Job 3:24); S I 100.5–6 (Ps. 37:5); S I.100.7 (Ps. 68:16); S I.100.12–13 (Gen. 1:27); S I.100.19 (Isa. 7:9). C. xiv; S I.111.18 (Ps. 42:3); S I.111.21 (I John 3:2); S I.111.25 (I John 1:15). C. xvi; S I.112.20 (I Tim. 6:16); S I.113.3 (Acts 17:28). C. xviii; S I.114.3–4 (Ps. 50.7); S I.114.5–6 (Rom. 5:12); S I.114.9 (Ps. 24:7); S I.114.11 (Ps. 26:8–9; Cant. 6:12). C. xxvi; S I.120.23, 25; S I.121.4–6 (Matt. 25:21; cf. I Cor. 2:9). See also notes 149 and 150.

[149] Ibid., c.i.ii; S I.101.4–7 (Ps. 13:1; Ps. 52:1). C. xx; S I.115.19 (Ps. 89:2).

[150] Ibid., c. xi; S I.109.15–16 (Ps. 24:10; Ps. 144:17). C. xxiii; S I.117.20 (Luke 10:42). C. xxv; S I.120.17–18 (Matt. 22:37).

[151] Viz., 'saecula saeculi' and 'saecula saeculorum'; cf. ibid., c.xxi; S I.116.6–12.

the metalevel prayer and commentary.[152] Likewise, the *Monologion* uses the language of Scripture to (re)state its conclusions, in order to identify the philosophical results with doctrinal claims, and occasionally pauses to explain the language of Scripture—which means that such practices were in accord with Anselm's conception of *sola ratione*.[153]

Moreover, Anselm describes the intellectual search behind the *Proslogion* as that of discovering the *unum argumentum* through which to *prove* what he had established "by a chain of many arguments" in the *Monologion*.[154] Inasmuch as he presents the results of the latter as having been established by reason alone (*sola ratione*) or by the necessity of reason (*rationis necessitate*), he must surely regard the more powerful case (by virtue of theoretical simplification) of the *Proslogion* as doing the same. This impression is confirmed by Anselm's exclamation in c. iv, after he has stated and replied to an objection to the famous arguments: "Thank You, Good Lord, thank You. For what I believed earlier by Your gift, I now understand by Your illumination, in such a way that *even if I did not wish to believe, I could not not understand*."[155] Likewise, his replies to Gaunilo take for granted that even the unbeliever in the person of the fool should be convinced.[156]

---

[152] See note 148. Kurt Flasch is sensitive to this distinction when he observes that Anselm allows Scripture and doctrine to set the questions and determine the syllabus but not to provide the premises; rather, according to Flasch, Anselm looks for necessary reasons to support his conclusions: "Vernunft und Geschichte: Die Beitrag Johann Adam Mohlers zum philosophischen Verstandnis Anselm von Canturbury," *Analecta Anselmiana* I, (1970) 165–94, esp. 165.

[153] I defend this contention in my as yet unpublished paper "Method in the *Monologion*," section 5. Cf. *Monologion*, c. xxiv; S I.42.11–29, where Anselm pauses to explain what might be meant by speaking of the Highest Nature's age, or of its always existing.

[154] Cf. *Proslogion*, Prooemium; S I.93.1–10: "Postquam opusculum quoddam velut exemplum meditandi de ratione fidei cogentibus me precibus quorundam fratrum in persona alicuius tacite secum rationcinando quae nesciat investigantis edidi: considerans illud esse multorum concatenatione contextum argumentorum, coepi mecum quaerere, si forte posset inveniri *unum argumentum, quod nullo alio ad se probandum quam se solo indigeret*, et solum ad astruendum quia deus vere est, et quia est summum bonum nullo alio indigens, et quo omnia indigent ut sint et ut bene sint, et quaecumque de divina credimus substantia, sufficeret."

[155] Ibid., c. iv; S I.104.5–7: "Gratias tibi, bone domine, gratias tibi, quia quod prius credidi te donante, sic intelligo te illuminante, ut *si te esse nolim credere, non possim non intelligere*."

[156] *Responsio editoris;* S I.130.3–4. Cf. section VII; S I.137.3–5: "Non ergo irrationabiliter *contra insipientem ad probandum deum esse* attuli, quo maius cogitari non possit, cum illud nullo modo, istud aliquo modo intelligeret." Likewise, section VIII; S I.137.28–30: "Sic itaque facile *refelli potest insipiens* qui sacram auctoritatem non recipit, si negat quo maius cogitari non valet ex aliis rebus conici posse." Finally, section X; S I.138–39: "Puto quia *monstravi* me non infirma sed satis *necessaria argumentatione probasse* in praefato libello re ipsa existere aliquid, quo maius cogitari non possit; nec eam alicuius obiectionis infirmari firmitate. Tantam enim vim huius prolationis in se continent significatio, ut

As for Anselm's comment at the end of c. i—"'unless I believe, I shall not understand'"—It helps to observe first that this is a free quotation from Isaiah 7:9, within the context of a spiritual exercise designed to bring the soul to humility. Next, it is important to distinguish between discovering and following a given proof. Although the *Proslogion* invites its readers to recapitulate Anselm's exercise, it may be that Anselm takes the Isaiah quotation especially to himself. For, experience shows, it is more difficult to discover—in the method of *alloquium*, see and articulate for the first time—than to repeat the intellectual moves that someone else has already put into words. Anselm might reasonably think that *he* would not have been able to discover the *unum argumentum* apart from the multidimensional focus provided by living faith. Even if this were true, it would not follow that others—including unbelievers— would require as much or the same degree of focus to understand the reasoning he offers.

All the same, it is correct to say that Anselm was not *trying* in the *Proslogion* to convince the unbeliever. As already noted, the *Proslogion* is a prayer-exercise that could be undertaken by believers alone. Moreover, the compunction of desire drives Anselm to evaluate the results of its intellectual striving against his higher goal of seeing God's face. That his reasoning (in cc. ii–xiii, xviii–xxiii) enables the unbeliever to understand to some extent *(aliquatenus)* about the being and well-being of God and creatures, as well as about the utter dependence of the latter on the former, is—I submit—a genuine and foreseen, but incidental, effect of his *Proslogion* aims.

Anselm's method sees philosophizing as a way of praying, and praying as a way of philosophizing. His position is distinctive in the history of spirituality, because he rejects the apophatic's inference from the ontological "gap" to the *utter* cognitive inaccessibility of God to creatures. Instead, he insists that intellectual inquiry is one dimension of the soul's stretch for God; understanding a little bit, significant consolation, and interim joy. Again, Anselm's cognitive psychology contrasts with that of later medieval Aristotelians, because it denies the existence of "unaided natural reason" and treats all creative problem solving as essentially collaborative: the creature seeks, the Creator discloses, the creature articulates what it has seen. In the *Proslogion*, Anselm showed his monastic brothers how to make philosophy part of their prayer. At the same time, he invites contemporary Christian philosophers to make

---

hoc ipsum quod dicitur, ex necessitate eo ipso quod intelligitur vel cogitatur, et revera *probetur existere, et id ipsum esse quidquid de divina substantia oportet credere.*" (Italics mine.)

38

Marilyn McCord Adams

Divine partnership explicit by turning monologue-meditation into *Proslogion/ad-loquium,* by addressing our philosophical questions, puzzles, and thoughts directly to God in prayer.[157]

Appendix

Viola lists the putative instantiations as follows (in "L'influence de la méthode anselmienne," pp. 15–16 n. 38 continued):

A: esse in intellectu et in re
B: esse in solo intellectu (c. 2)

A: non posse cogitari non esse
B: posse cogitari non esse (c. 3)

A: summum omnium solum existens per seipsum
B: quidquid hoc non est (c. 5)
A: [quod] omnia alia fecit de nihilo
B: quidquid hoc non est (c. 5)
A: quidquid melius est esse quam non esse
B: contrarium (c. 5)
A: esse iustum
B: non esse iustum (c. 5)
A: esse beatum
B: non esse beatum (c. 5)

A: esse sensibilem
B: non esse sensibilem (c. 6)
A: esse omnipotentem
B: non esse omnipotentem (c. 6)
A: esse misericordem (c. 6)
B: non esse misericordem (c. 6)
A: esse impassibilem
B: non esse impassibilem (c. 6)
A: summus spiritus
B: corpus (c. 6)

A: sua omnipotentia facit aliud in se posse

[157] Research for this essay was funded by a University of California President's Humanities Fellowship and grants from the American Council of Learned Societies and the John Simon Guggenheim Foundation. I am grateful for this support.

B: ipse potest (c. 7)
A: nihil posse per impotentiam et nihil posse contra se
B: contrarium (c. 7)

A: esse bonum bonis et malis
B: esse bonum bonis tantum (c. 9)

A: et bonis et malis retribuere secundum merita
B: tantum bonis bona et non malis mala reddere (c. 11)

A: quod nulla lex loci aut temporis coercet
B: quod clauditur aliquatenus loco aut tempore (c. 13)

A: esse tantum id quo maius cogitari nequit
B: esse etiam quiddam maiusquam cogitari possit (c. 15)

A: esse totum quod est (esse omnino unum)
B: esse partibusiunctum (c. 18)

These are the alternatives posed by Anselm in the *Proslogion*. He repeatedly eliminates the second of the given pair as contradicting the
major premiss accepted by the fool *(aliquid quo nihil maius . . .)*. Because, if the fool accepts or prefers the second alternative (B), he
contradicts his major premiss. The unity of the *Proslogion*—the "unum
argumentum"—is thus achieved through the single major premiss. If
the interlocutor accepts it, it permits him necessarily and progressively
to eliminate the alternatives represented by (B). This is sufficient for
us to show the unitary structure of the *Proslogion*.

[2]

Can Philosophy Argue
God's Existence?

Brian Leftow

Many philosophers have tried to help warrant belief that God exists by arguing that God exists, that is, doing natural theology (henceforth NT). But to one strand of Western religion, all that NT says about God is in principle irrelevant. As some Western theists see it, NT cannot show the existence of the God of religious belief. NT argues that there is, for example, a "first cause" or a "perfect being." As these are distinctively philosophical descriptions, we can say that NT argues for a God of the Philosophers (henceforth GP). The theists I have mentioned hold that no GP can be the God in whom Western religion believes (henceforth God). So to them, the arguments of NT cannot lend warrant to belief that God exists.

Philosophers seldom consider religious objections to NT. Yet these objections are really of primary importance. The arguments of NT are just metaphysical arcana unless they do in fact help warrant belief that God exists. They do not do so if the GP they argue is not God. Proof of a GP is a proof of God only if God is identical with some GP. Again, if God is identical with no GP, then if one takes a proof of a GP to justify belief that God exists, one's purported justification for belief that God exists includes a falsehood, and so does not justify the belief. Further, if God is identical with no GP, that a GP exists may entail that God does not exist. After all, if God existed, why would He create or allow a GP distinct from Himself? Thus if the religious deny that God is a GP, NT threatens to undermine the religion it seeks to support.

Thus any argument of NT that purports to back the actual beliefs of actual Western theists must include some reason to think that God

[40]

is the GP to which it concludes. That is, NT can help to warrant belief that God exists only if NT at least implicitly overcomes religious objections to the Identity-Claim, that

(IC) God is identical with some GP.

Now the Christian tradition, in particular, has since its earliest days had a strand that rejects NT. Its luminaries include Tertullian, Jerome, Bernard of Clairvaux, Luther, Calvin, and Kierkegaard; in this century, its foremost figure has been Karl Barth. According to Barth, only revelation can deliver knowledge of God.[1] NT cannot. What NT can prove to exist, "whatever else it may be, is certainly not God."[2] That is, to Barth, "it cannot be denied that there are gods who in fact are knowable to us [in NT]. But it is very much to be denied that we have the right to identify any of them with the real God."[3] This is precisely a denial of IC, though as we shortly see, Barth more directly addresses IC's metalinguistic restatement,

(IC*) "God" and some distinctively philosophical description of a GP are coreferential.

NT can yield truths about God only if IC is true. So Barth attacks NT by attacking IC, or more specifically, IC*.

I want to defend NT against its theist foes, taking Barth as their champion. Barth makes two sorts of cases against IC*. One is based on his theory of religious language. I argue that this case fails. Barth's second challenge to IC* arises from an argument that it is morally or theologically inappropriate to use NT to argue God's existence or describe His nature.[4] I show that this raises interesting philosophical questions but argue that even so, the challenge fails.

The Problem of Reference

Barth had no ken of the philosophy of language or the ways it might interact with theology. But even so, he seems to want to question NT's references to God. Commenting on a psalm in which some theists find

[1] Karl Barth, *Church Dogmatics* II:1, trans. G. Bromiley and T. F. Torrance (Edinburgh: T. & T. Clark, 1957), p. 63.
[2] Ibid., p. 79.
[3] Ibid., p. 90.
[4] Ibid., pp. 63–95.

scriptural justification for NT, Barth notes that "in the Psalms . . . An audible call is made to all things to praise God. . . . But where is it all spoken about . . . otherwise than in such a way that it is quite clear . . . that the reference is . . . to the God of Israel, i.e. the God who acts toward and in Israel and reveals Himself in this action? He it is who, after He has made Himself visible in His action, now also . . . becomes visible in heaven and on earth."[5] Some arguments of NT contend that there is a cause of the universe, then claim that this cause is God. Barth asks NT whether we are "really speaking of the one true God if even provisionally we think of only one side of God—in this instance of God the [cause]. On what ground do we think we can speak . . . of only one side of God? . . . Scripture gives us no reason to think this . . . even when it speaks of . . . God the Creator, it also speaks of the one God of Abraham, Isaac and Jacob. . . . Is not the *Deus . . . creator* of [NT] the construct of human thinking . . . do we not have to ask what authority we have from the basis and essence of the Church to call it 'God'?"[6] Barth asks whether "the reference" is to Israel's God and whether we "really speak of" God. He wants, then, to question the reference of terms in the statements of NT which seem to denote God. Barth wants to call IC* into question.

As Barth sees it, Scripture always refers to God via names He dons in revealing Himself and descriptions drawn from the tradition founded on revelation. By so doing, it ensures that it is always dealing with the God revealed in that tradition. Only with God thus identified does Scripture adduce the universe or its character as subordinate evidence for God's existence and power. NT does not refer to God in this way. NT contends that there is a perfect being or a cause of the universe. It refers to this GP via these descriptions. Only later does it try to argue that this GP is the deity of a specific religious tradition.

Barth asks "what authority we have from the basis and essence of the Church," that is, God's revelation, to give the scriptural name "God" to the being NT proves. But this is a rhetorical question. Barth is sure that what NT can show to exist, "whatever else it may be, is certainly not God." He is sure that IC* is false. Let us now see just why Barth is so sure of this.

The Problem of Equivocity

Practitioners of NT often construct causal arguments that conclude that there is a cause for various states of affairs, for example, the uni-

[5] Ibid., p. 107.
[6] Ibid., p. 80.

verse's existence. They thus imply that a description we use of creatures, "cause," applies to God as well. Barth finds this problematic. He
thinks that "we know originators and causes. We can . . . extend their
series into the infinite. When we reach the point where we grow tired
of extending it, we can call that point 'god' or 'creator.' Within the series
we can talk . . . of creators and creations. But . . . we have no analogy
on the basis of which the nature and being of God as Creator can be
accessible to us. . . . What we can represent to ourselves lies in the
sphere of our own existence."[7] Barth holds, then, that God does not
really satisfy "cause" or other terms we employ. All the concepts we can
construct are drawn from the realm of creatures. They express what
creatures are like. As Barth sees it, God is wholly other than creatures.
There is no real, contentful likeness at all between God and creatures.[8]
According to Barth, then, no meanings we can give our terms apply
to God. If the words we use do apply to God, they apply only in a sense
wholly discrete from any sense we can give them. Nothing we can mean
by "cause" applies to God. Only in some other sense, which we do not
possess, is it correct to call God a cause. Our terms are *equivocal* when
used of God.

Let us suppose that Barth's equivocity claim is true and consider the
consequences. Suppose one has shown that

(1)   there is a cause of the universe.

In (1), "cause" presumably bears a sense rather like its ordinary sense.
Now (1) asserts God's existence (and so one has proved God's existence)
only if

(2)   God = the cause of the universe.

Now "cause" either does or does not bear in (2) the sense it bears in
(1). If it bears the sense it bears in (1) and if "cause" is equivocal *in
divinis*, (2) is false, and so (1) does not warrant belief that God exists.
On the other hand, it could be that in (2), "cause" bears a sense appropriate to God, and so (if Barth is right) a sense discrete from that in
(1). In this case, (2) may be true, but (1) and (2) do not jointly entail
that God exists. For if "cause" bears different senses in (1) and (2)
the inference fails by equivocation.[9] As parallel points apply to other

---

[7] Ibid., p. 76.
[8] Ibid., p. 188.
[9] This is not a new point. See, e.g., Aquinas, *Summa theologiae (ST)* Ia.13.5.

arguments of NT, if Barth's equivocity claim is true, NT cannot prove God's existence.

Further, if Barth is right about religious language, it is theologically incorrect to identify with God what a cosmological arguer proves to exist. (Again, parallel points apply to other arguments of NT.) To do so is either to treat God as a creature, applying to God descriptions that only a creature can satisfy, or to treat some actual or hypothetical creature as God. The latter, of course, is idolatry.

Barth frequently speaks of idolatry when discussing NT. He writes that "what is 'God' to the natural man . . . is a false god" and that through NT "this false god is known by him and is therefore knowable to him."[10] He insists that NT "means the introduction of a foreign god into the sphere of the Church."[11] Fleshing this out, Barth writes that the natural theologian's concept of God "is a construct which . . . derives from an attempt to unite Yahweh with Baal, the triune god . . . with the concept of being of Aristotelian and Stoic philosophy. The assertion that reason can know God from created things applies to the second and heathenish component of this concept of God, so that when we view the construct on this side we do not recognize God in it at all, nor can we accept it as a Christian concept of God."[12] Summing up, Barth notes that "man has . . . always had . . . the very 'natural' capacity to persuade himself and others of a higher and divine being. All idols spring from this capacity . . . To affirm that the true . . . God . . . can be knowable in this way is only possible if He has already been identified with that false god."[13] Barth's equivocity thesis about descriptions of God is the deepest philosophical root of this charge of idolatry. If only a creature can satisfy any description of deity that unaided human reason can construct, then since all philosophical concepts of God stem from human reason, to give the scriptural name "God" to a GP, that is, to identify it with the God of Abraham and Isaac, is to divinize an actual or hypothetical creature, to give a creature what is due God alone—in short, to treat a creature as an idol. To argue philosophically that God exists, then, is really to argue that there actually is an object for idolatrous worship, and recommend the worship of that object in place of God.

To meet Barth's challenge to NT, then, we must evaluate his view of

---

[10] Barth, Dogmatics II:1, p. 86.
[11] Ibid., p. 84.
[12] Ibid.
[13] Ibid.

theistic descriptions. First, though, let me show how Barth's claim that theistic descriptions are equivocal generates his skepticism about IC*.

Descriptivism

As we have seen, Barth holds that no description that unaided human reason constructs can apply to God. This leads him to reject IC*, I submit, in conjunction with an appropriately strong descriptivist theory of reference. For descriptivism, one can refer to an object O only by describing O or by using a term that one can explicate by describing O. We use definite descriptions and names to refer. To refer via definite descriptions is (obviously) to refer by describing. As to names, to descriptivism, a name is a term that one can explicate by describing O, for a name's meaning is a definite description that the name's tokener has in mind or at least can give if questioned—"Aristotle" *means* (say) "the teacher of Alexander." A term's meaning gives it the property of referring and determines its reference. So for descriptivism, even proper names like "Aristotle" refer only because Aristotle satisfies a definite description the referrer has in mind ("the teacher of Alexander") or can give if questioned. For descriptivism, then, one can refer only to objects one can describe, and what objects one refers to depends on how one does or would describe them.

Suppose, then, that as the strictest descriptivism would have it, only actually used descriptions determine reference. Suppose too that Barth is right that no description unaided human reason constructs applies to God. It then follows that no natural theologian, when acting as such, can refer to God. For to act as a natural theologian is precisely to rule out, at least while one is at work, any reference to God via descriptions founded on revelation. Further, on Barth's descriptivism, a natural theologian as such cannot refer to God even if he or she wants to do so. On the strictest descriptivism, if the speaker has an incorrect description in mind, the speaker's reference goes astray. Suppose that on a given occasion, a speaker means by "Aristotle" the teacher of Plato. Then on strict descriptivism, when the speaker says "Aristotle wrote the *Posterior Analytics*," the speaker actually refers to Socrates, who did not write this book, and so the statement is false rather than (as it seems) true. So too, on strict descriptivism, if a natural theologian identifies God as a GP, or tries to speak of God by speaking of a GP, the natural theologian refers to an idol, and not to God. I suggest, then, that Barth's rejection of IC* rests on two premises, his thesis that descriptions are equivocal *in divinis* and a strong descriptivist claim about reference.

If this is true, one might think to save IC* by arguing that a descriptivism strong enough to serve Barth's purposes is too strong to be credible. After all, surely even someone thinking falsely that Aristotle was Plato's teacher may mean by "Aristotle wrote the *Posterior Analytics*" that Aristotle did this. A weaker, more plausible descriptivism could say, for instance, that a token name's meaning on a given occasion is a *cluster* of descriptions the tokener actually has in view, or dispositionally possesses and would use to specify the token's reference if asked. This weaker descriptivism might then add that on a given occasion, a token refers to an object O if O satisfies most of these descriptions.[14] On such a view, one could argue, as long as most of the natural theologian's descriptions of God are appropriately tied to revelation, the natural theologian, acting as such, can refer to God.

I suggest, though, that even with descriptivism weakened in this way, if Barth's equivocity claim stands, one cannot rescue IC*. For suppose that a believer, most of whose descriptions for God stem from revelation, tries to refer to God on a given occasion via a GP-description (e.g., "first cause"). If the believer gives the GP-description any sense it bears in NT, this sense continues to be equivocal with any that applies to God. God still does not satisfy the description, and so IC* remains false. Weakening descriptivism may let a believer whose mind is "tainted" by the presence of GP-descriptions refer to God in the language of revelation. It does not rescue NT.

A Causal Theory of Theistic Reference

If our descriptions of God are purely equivocal, and none truly applies to God, no loosening of descriptivism can save the theistic reference of NT. To save NT, then, we must reject either descriptivism or the equivocity thesis.

Let us first consider an alternative to descriptivism. William Alston's "Referring to God" applies to talk of God the nondescriptivist, purely causal theory of reference recently argued by Saul Kripke and others.[15] On this account, what one refers to by using a referring term depends entirely on the causal history of one's possession of that term. Kripke describes his view this way:

[14] Tom Senor pointed this strategy out to me.

[15] William P. Alston, "Referring to God," in his *Divine Nature and Human Language: Essays in Philosophical Theology* (Ithaca: Cornell University Press, 1989), pp. 103–17.

Someone, let's say, a baby is born; his parents call him by a certain name. They talk about him to their friends. Other people meet him. Through various sorts of talk the name is spread from link to link as if by a chain. A speaker who is on the far end of this chain, who has heard about, say, Richard Feynman, in the market place or elsewhere, may be referring to Richard Feynman even though he can't remember from whom he first heard of Feynman or from whom he ever heard of Feynman. He knows that Feynman is a famous physicist. A certain passage of communication reaching ultimately to the man himself does reach the speaker. He then is referring to Feynman even though he can't identify him uniquely. . . . When the name is "passed from link to link," the receiver of the name must, I think, intend when he learns it to use it with the same reference as the man from whom he heard it.[16]

Alston adds to Kripke's theory the claim that when one refers via definite description, if the object which satisfies the description is not the object to which the causal chain links the description, the causal chain takes precedence: one is "really" talking about the object to which the causal chain is linked.[17] Thus (to use Alston's example), if Satan presents himself as the Creator to a community of humans and orders them to slaughter some innocents, then if a member of that community reports this and says, "The Creator ordered us to do it," that member makes a true claim about Satan, not a false claim about God.[18] So too, if a natural theologian uses a GP-description to refer to God, if the right sort of causal chain links God and this description, this description refers to God. The right sort of causal chain will be one in which the natural theologian's reference is parasitic on believers' references—for instance, one in which the natural theologian consciously means to refer to whatever it is to which believers refer. This sort of parasitism is possible only because of the distinctively causal element of Alston's view. On a descriptivist theory, the sense of the GP-description determines its reference, regardless of causal chain, and so a GP-description cannot climb onto the back of a believer's reference. On a causal theory, causal chain supersedes sense, and so even a GP-description can carry reference to God. So it can seem that on a causal view of reference, one cannot universally deny IC*.

---

[16] Saul Kripke, "Naming and Necessity," in Donald Davidson and Gilbert Harman, eds., *The Semantics of Natural Language* (Dordrecht: D. Reidel, 1972), pp. 298–99, 302, as quoted in Alston, "Referring," p. 106.

[17] Alston, "Referring," pp. 110, 112.

[18] Ibid., p. 110.

Still, the causal theory, on its own, may not rescue reference to God. The causal theory tells us that what all subsequent speakers refer to when they say "God" depends on what the one who "baptized" God as God (Adam?) referred to in the baptism. But what Adam referred to is determined by the description Adam gave what he referred to, or would have given if asked. The point is familiar from Wittgenstein's discussions of ostensive definition and naming. If one points at a pair of nuts and says "two," one might be naming one of the nuts, or both, or naming their color, or naming the volume of space one or both occupy, or not naming anything.[19] One resolves these ambiguities by describing what one means to point out. The descriptions show what semantic role one is giving the term—proper name, color name, or whatever. So only the way Adam did or would describe the thing he referred to in baptizing something as "God" made this reference determinate, and so made determinate the reference of all who inherited this reference via causal chain. Thus if all Adam had available to describe God were Barth's purely equivocal descriptions, we inherit from Adam (on Barth's terms) only an act of idolatry. We face the bizarre consequence that a semantic chain transmits original referential sin.

But this follows only if it was Adam who baptized God. Another alternative is to say that God baptized God. On the views of such mainline theists as Aquinas, God's thought does not take propositional form and does not move in the medium of language.[20] If this is true, God did not baptize Himself in His precreative eternity.[21] He named Himself, if at all, in speaking to His creatures, and only if His speaking was the first occasion on which anyone referred to God and was a literal direct production of physical sounds or else a causation of the relevant creaturely locutions. Presumably, God would get His self-reference right. So on these assumptions, a purely causal theory would let the creatures God addresses inherit God's own self-reference, and so avoid original referential sin.

This view would explain the importance the biblical tradition attaches to the *name* of God. On this view, God's naming Himself to us is an initial act of grace, an opening of Himself to our thought and language without which we could not think of Him or seek Him. To take that name in vain, then, is to dishonor a giver by failing to appreciate the worth of a valuable gift—rather like being given a Rembrandt

[19] Wittgenstein, *Investigations*, #28.
[20] See, e.g. *Summa contra gentiles (SCG)* I.57–58, and for a plausible contemporary defense, William P. Alston, "Does God Have Beliefs?" in his *Divine Nature and Human Language*, pp. 178–93.
[21] Of course, it would not affect the view to hold that He did.

and using it solely to cover a stain on a wall. More important in the present context, this view entails that and would explain why NT-references to God are parasitic on believers': on this view, it is to believers that God first spoke. Finally, as this view allows such parasitic references, it blocks the argument against IC*.

Explaining reference to God via a causal chain terminating in God's self-reference would be (to put it mildly) philosophically controversial. Yet this seems the only way to use the theory of reference to save IC*. Further, it saves IC* without rescuing NT as a whole, for it leaves philosophical descriptions of God equivocal, and so leaves NT unable to argue the existence or describe the nature of God. We can save NT, then, only by confronting Barth's equivocity thesis.

The Other Side of Equivocity

We have seen that for Barth, terms used to describe creatures are equivocal in application to God. To Barth, for any F that primarily describes creatures, God is not any sort of F we can conceive; He does not satisfy any sense we can give the term "F." Yet this does not mean that for Barth, for all F, God is not an F. Rather, it means that in some cases, God is an F and nothing else is.

Barth makes this line of thought explicit in dealing with God's existence: "How can this being which is the origin and boundary of all being, have only a part as we do in some being in general? . . . if we really encounter God in His being . . . will not this being of ours . . . be so questioned that we can be sure only of its not being? And then where is the comparability between His creator-being and our creature-being?"[22] To Barth, God truly exists, and when compared to God, the things we call existent hardly exist at all.[23] God's existence is so much more complete and stable than creatures' that only He is really what an existent is. Creatures are not truly beings. They are at best pale imitations of the one genuine being. Barth again illustrates this in discussing God's sovereignty: "We possess no analogy on the basis of which the nature and being of God as the Lord can be accessible to us. We certainly think we are acquainted with other lords and lordships. But it is not the case that we have only to extend our ideas of lord and lordship into the infinite and absolute and we will finally arrive at God

[22] Barth, *Dogmatics* II:1, p. 83.
[23] Thus Anselm in *Monologion* 28, a text Barth undoubtedly knew through his research for his early book on Anselm, *Fides Quaerens Intellectum* (London: SCM Press, 1960).

the Lord and His lordship. [Only] God is . . . really the Lord over all things. . . . Only as we know God's lordship will our own ideas of lordship have content."[24] Barth argues, then, that only God is in the full sense a being or a lord. Our concepts, including that of "lord," are drawn from the realm of creatures. Nothing we know in that realm is truly a lord, compared to God. This is why God is not a being, a lord, or the like in any sense we can give these terms, and we cannot ourselves construct the full sense of "lord" that applies to God, and yet God is truly a lord. Barth sums this up thus: "We use our words improperly . . . when we apply them . . . to . . . creatures. When we apply them to God they are not alienated from their original object and therefore from their truth, but . . . restored to it."[25] "If we apply these words to God, we do not withdraw them from their original meaning . . . we speak in the original truth of these words."[26]

Barth and Aquinas

There is a historical irony to Barth's treatment of equivocity, for the claims Barth makes to explain why no merely human descriptions apply to God are claims Aquinas makes to argue that some merely human descriptions *do* apply to God, albeit descriptions of an unusual sort. Aquinas writes that terms expressing perfections, such as "good," "apply primarily to God rather than to creatures, because these perfections flow from God to creatures. But as regards the imposition of the names, we primarily apply them to creatures which we know first. Hence they have a mode of signification which belongs to creatures."[27] Thomas means by this precisely that only God is "really" and properly what such terms "really" mean, and that the senses we ordinarily attach to these terms in speaking of creatures do not apply to God, but are at most related to senses that apply to God. Thus Thomas and Barth are at one on this. But Thomas suggests that if this much is true, our language about God is not purely equivocal.

As Aquinas sees it, when he calls God good, he is not at all treating God as a creature. Rather, he is saying that "whatever good we attribute to creatures, preexists in God, and in a more excellent and higher

[24] Barth, *Dogmatics* II:1, pp. 75–76.
[25] Ibid., p. 229.
[26] Ibid., p. 230.
[27] Aquinas, *ST* Ia.13.6.

way. . . . He causes goodness in things because He is good."[28] Now Aquinas's claim that effects preexist in their causes can be cashed in for two other claims, that causes causally suffice to produce their effects and that "what is made is like the maker, because every agent makes its like"[29]—that is, that effects resemble their causes in some significant way. So Aquinas claims that when we say God is good, what we assert is this: the things we call good are somehow relevantly like God.

Thus for Aquinas, the meaning of "good" in statements about God is quite discrete from its meaning in other uses. Our talk of God thus *is* equivocal. But because we comprehend the logic by which this use of "good" relates to other uses, we are using "good" analogously rather than purely equivocally: for Thomas, analogy is a kind of controlled equivocity.[30] More important, we can cash in an analogous use of "_____ is good" for a literal description of God, "_____ is such that good things are relevantly like Him."

This literal description speaks more of creatures than of God. It does not say just how creatures are like God. It also is highly abstract. So it says very little about God. But it does say something literally true about Him. Though Thomas thinks of analogy as controlled equivocity, as he *uses* the concept of analogy, he winds up holding that when we talk of God, our terms convey limited literal, nonanalogical information about Him: in particular, information about other things' relations to Him. As Thomas sees it, we can know of God literally "what He is not and how other things are related to Him."[31]

For Aquinas, then, one can literally paraphrase sentences of the form "God is F" into sentences of the form "Fs are, as Fs, relevantly like God" without loss of content. In the latter sentence, each term occurs with its ordinary meaning. (We can take "God" as a rigid designator for that which is identical with no creature.)[32] So for Aquinas, equivocity of nonrelational predicates or descriptions is compatible with the univocity of some relational predicates or descriptions. If Barth's view is in

[28] Ibid., Ia.13.2.

[29] Ibid., Ia.110.2.

[30] Ibid., Ia.13.6. For the claim that analogy is a sort of equivocity, Aristotle's *pros hen* equivocity, see G. E. L. Owen, "Aristotle on the Snares of Ontology," in Renford Bambrough, ed., *New Essays on Plato and Aristotle* (New York: Humanities Press, 1965), pp. 69–95, and "The Platonism of Aristotle," in P. F. Strawson, ed., *Studies in the Philosophy of Thought and Action* (London: Oxford University Press, 1968), pp. 147–74. For application to Aquinas, see David Burrell, *Analogy and Philosophical Language* (New Haven: Yale University Press, 1970).

[31] *SCG* I.30 (4).

[32] Aquinas favors a different move. See *ST* Ia.13.8–10.

effect Thomas's, then, it is not so complete an equivocity theory (I now argue) as to support a global rejection of IC*.

Natural Theology Redux

Consider the GP-description "first cause." One can circumvent Barth's equivocity objection rather as Thomas's limited-information strategy suggests. For the claim that something is a first cause asserts only that something *somehow* causally explains the universe's existence. It does not state the mode of causation involved. It does not say of any specific mode of causation that it is the one by which something causally explains the universe. So if we say that God = the first cause, we do not apply any supposed "purely creaturely" concept of causation to God. We leave room for the claim that God's mode of causation is unique and totally unlike creatures'.

Now Barth could respond to this Thomistic rejoinder in two ways. He could argue that it makes the cosmological argument vacuous. For to claim that something somehow explains the universe (he might say) does not at all really explain it. But Barth also could just reiterate his argument. I propose applying to God the concept of causally-explaining-in-some-way, henceforth the generic concept of causal explanation, or GCCE. This, Barth could argue, is as creaturely a concept as the concept of any specific mode of causal explanation.

I think NT could just concede the charge of vacuity. It is harmless, because the goal of NT is not really to explain the universe. It is to argue the existence of God. If an argument shows that the universe's existence *has* an explanation and that the explanation lies in God or a Godlike being, then this is enough for NT, even though it does not deliver the full concrete explanation of the universe's existence. In fact, NT should never try or claim to offer this full, concrete explanation. Someone doing NT presumably believes that the universe's explanation is this: God had a certain intention, and to realize that intention, He caused the universe to be. To give this explanation fully and concretely, then, NT would have to say what God intended in creating the universe, explain just how this intent led Him to action and why it led to the action it did, and back all this without appeal to religious tradition (since NT lies within the realm of purely philosophical argument). It would be folly to attempt these things.

Still, while NT *can* concede the vacuity charge, it need not. A general, abstract explanation *is* an explanation, albeit not as full an explanation as one might wish. Even an explanation that just points out whence the universe came, and says nothing at all about how it came thence, leaves us knowing more about the universe than we did before. If I ask you to explain your having a rabbit, and you tell me that a magician pulled it out of his hat and gave it to you, I know more about your having a rabbit than I did, even though many interesting questions remain unanswered.

The second Barthian charge would be that the GCCE is as tainted by its creaturely origins as the concepts of specific sorts of explanation. But I think this argument would understate the difference between the GCCE and specific concepts of explanation. The GCCE, I suggest, is not a concept of some indefinite kind of explanation, a sort of vague common denominator of the specific concepts of explanation we possess. If it *were* a common denominator, Barth's rejoinder might succeed. For it might be that all specific sorts of explanation share some trait that makes them unacceptably creaturely, and if they do, their common denominator will also have this trait. I suggest, though, that the GCCE is more like a purely formal concept. It is something like the concept of a kind of role a concept can play in our practices of making sense of the world. If the GCCE is the concept of a kind of linguistic role, then to apply it to God makes no claim at all about God's mode of being, acting, or explaining. To say that God stands in the GCCE to the universe is to claim only this:

> God's relation to the universe is such that there can in principle be a concept that can serve as a causelike explanation-relation linking God and the universe. The general linguistic role "cause" plays is appropriate for speaking of God's relation to the universe, even if we have no concrete concept able to express this relation.

This claim does not specify or use any particular causal concept. Thus it is not contentious, for that some concept instancing the GCCE can in principle apply to God is not a contentious claim. Even Barth concedes it, in granting that God *is* truly a cause. For were no such concept possible, we could not say even that while God is not a cause in any sense we can grasp, God is truly a cause. If we call God "truly a cause," we use a placemarker to fill a particular linguistic role, and use this placemarker to say that some concept playing that role applies to God.

Thus Barth's equivocity objection to NT fails. Even if our talk of God is as equivocal as Barth thinks, it may still involve literal though abstract truths about God. If these let us apply to God the conclusions of (e.g.) first-cause arguments, they validate IC*. We have seen that Barth's equivocity doctrine lies beneath his skepticism about NT's theistic references and his charge of idolatry. So if the equivocity objection fails, so do the reference challenge and the idolatry charge. Still, considering Barth's objections has clarified the limits of what NT can do or reasonably claim to do and the way we must interpret such conclusions of NT as "God is the universe's first cause."

The Natural Theologian's Motives

We have considered and rejected one Barthian attack on NT via IC*. Barth has another line of attack on NT and IC*. He dwells at length on the motives of natural theologians. He speculates that interest in NT betrays "an untheological type of thinking, i.e. a thinking which derives from some other source than gratitude and obedience."[33] He opines that NT "arises from . . . a dangerous curiosity which has an inquisitive desire to probe back behind [revelation] in order to assure itself from some superior position."[34] Barth finds in NT an urge to self-deification that lies close to the core of all sin.[35] He writes of NT that "we have to do here with the attempt of man to answer the riddle of his own existence and of that of the world, and in that way to master himself and the world."[36] "For the natural man, i.e. man as he thinks he can understand and rule himself without God, it is the meaning . . . of life to master himself and the world, and regard the goal . . . of this endeavor as . . . his god."[37] Again, to a Christian theologian, the desire for self-mastery without God is as such sinful, and indeed closely akin to the desire to be one's own god.[38]

These remarks are not (or not just) character assassination of natural theologians. For Barth descries a connection between a belief's moral or theological virtues and its epistemic virtues. It is a commonplace that motive can affect the moral properties of acts. Barth suggests that motive may also affect the epistemic properties of beliefs. To Chris-

[33] Barth, *Dogmatics* II:1, p. 64.
[34] Ibid.
[35] Ibid., p. 71.
[36] Ibid., p. 85.
[37] Ibid., p. 86.
[38] Casting about for a less reprehensible motive, Barth also fastens on the desire to do apologetics (ibid., p. 88). This, he argues, is self-defeating. The unbeliever will reject the apologist for insincerity if addressed with arguments on which believers do not actually base their belief (ibid., p. 93). If this insincerity is not found out, Barth adds, then either the arguments will be defeated, leaving the impression that there is no good case at all for Christian faith (ibid., p. 94), or the arguments may lead the unbeliever not to faith (ibid., p. 93) but merely to an arid philosophical theism that does not suffice for salvation.

tians, it is the pure in heart who see God (Matt. 5:8). So (thinks Barth) if a sort of belief must issue from an impure heart—a morally or spiritually tainted motive or inner state—it is ipso facto not knowledge of God. It is at most knowledge of an idol.[39] Thus Barth contends that as the belief-states NT induces are morally or theologically tainted, they cannot be states of knowing about the true God. This motive-based approach backs Barth's idolatry-claim by an argument independent of his equivocity doctrine.

Barth offers moral and religious considerations to defeat NT's claim to produce knowledge of God.[40] This raises two questions. One is simply whether Barth's move is legitimate—whether moral and religious considerations really can defeat knowledge-claims, or whether on the other hand Barth's argument is irrelevant or inappropriate.[41] The other is a narrower matter: *if* moral and religious considerations *are* legitimate defeaters, do they in fact defeat, for example, the claim that

[39] In what philosophers consider "the knowledge of God, man is . . . not occupied with God at all but only with himself, absolutising his own nature and being, projecting it into the infinite, setting up a reflection of his own glory" (ibid., p. 71).

[40] Though not (strangely enough) its claim to produce knowledge of *something:* as we saw earlier, Barth thinks that "it cannot be denied that there are gods who in fact are knowable to us [in NT]. But it is very much to be denied that we have the right to identify any of them with the real God" (ibid., p. 90). Barth does not actually claim that NT's arguments are invalid. He thinks he holds a complete equivocity theory of theistic predicates (though as we have seen, he really does not). We saw earlier that the invalidity of NT's arguments *would* follow from a complete equivocity theory. Yet to my knowledge, Barth nowhere actually draws this consequence. Nor does he claim that NT's arguments are unsound apart from such premisses as that God = the first cause. This leaves Barth in a puzzling position: he seems willing to allow that there are sound proofs of the existence of deities other than God. This needs explaining. One explanation would suggest that Barth cannot charge invalidity or unsoundness and still be consistent with his own view of the proper method for theology. Barth argues at length that Christian theology ought not so much to contest NT's claims as to abstain from even that much intercourse with NT, having seen that it is an inappropriate practice (ibid., pp. 162–70). To criticize NT is to do NT—and so publishers routinely list atheist philosophers' books against the "proofs" of NT as philosophy of religion or philosophical theology. Thus one who offered detailed philosophical critiques of NT's arguments would be mixing more with NT than Barth thinks advisable. Denying NT's identifying move seems the minimal dissent a Christian theologian can make. This is likely why Barth limits himself to this. So his attitude *may* be that NT's arguments are in fact invalid or unsound, but insofar as he writes as a Christian theologian, it is not appropriate for him to show this. Alternately, Barth may have in mind the Calvinist point that the human mind is a factory of idols, coupled with some Feuerbachian "projectivist" account of these idols' existence. That is, Barth's point in saying that "there really are such gods" may be that they exist because we create them, and (perhaps) create them in and with our attempts to prove philosophically that God exists.

[41] For argument pro, see Merold Westphal, "Taking St. Paul Seriously: Sin as an Epistemological Category," in Thomas Flint, ed., *Christian Philosophy* (Notre Dame: University of Notre Dame Press, 1990), pp. 200–226.

God = the first cause? If they do, they equally defeat all identity-claims linking God and a GP, and so defeat IC. I now turn to the first issue.

One can read Barth's claims about motives as claims that we do not understand why we want to or do believe IC or claims that imply IC. We think we want to believe or do believe these things because we think them true. But Barth's point may be that something altogether different really explains our inclination to believe them. For Barth, this is a desire for self-deification, which (I suggest) comes down to inordinate self-love. This etiology yields arguments against IC. I now develop and evaluate several of these.

Wishful Thinking

One claim Barth may be making is that we suffer a sort of wishful thinking in assenting to such beliefs as IC or that God = the first cause (call these sin-beliefs, or SBs). Barth's case might go this way: perhaps these beliefs seem true to us, and we affirm them because they seem true. All the same, they seem true only because the urges of our sinful nature mislead us. SBs seem true because we want them to be true, and not because they truly have the intellectual merits that are our best signs of truth. If this is so, then though they seem true to us and we adopt them for this reason, on another level we are wrong about why we hold SBs. On this level, we hold them because they satisfy our inordinate self-love. It might be, for instance, that our love of self makes us weigh the evidence about these beliefs unfairly. The deeper and more passionate our love of self, the more plausible it is that this love could make us radically misread the intellectual merits of beliefs appropriately connected with ourselves. Thus (Barth may say) this is a sort of wishful thinking: our desire that these things be true makes it seem to us that they *are* true.

Again, affection may make us exaggerate the merits of those we love, and malice may make us exaggerate the faults of those we hate. If we love ourselves inordinately, then, this self-love may be able to magnify the apparent intellectual virtues of a belief whose content flatters us in appropriate ways. It is core Christian belief that as sinners we hate God. So rejection of God could perhaps unconsciously lead us to minimize the evidence for a belief, or in some other way keep ourselves from assenting to it, if the belief's content presents God in ways we detest.

This argument is only as plausible as the claim that SBs really do so hook up with inordinate self-love as to be plausible candidates for wishful self-deceit. Barth's case about IC might be that we insist on IC to the extent that we are unwilling to wait on God to reveal Himself—a lack of patience and humility at the least, but more important a tacit judgment that our own desires are at least as important as God's. One could perhaps call this a form of self-deification.

The wish-fulfillment argument is an undermining defeater for SBs. Its point is to shake our confidence in the intuitions that favor SBs. But wish fulfillment also yields a rebutting defeater for SBs. That is, if (almost) all SBs arise from wish fulfillment, this generates an argument that (most) SBs are false.[42] For it is highly plausible that wish fulfillment is an unreliable mechanism of fixing belief, one that rarely delivers truth and even then does so only by accident. If all SBs are held only by wish fulfillment, and no belief held only by wish fulfillment is likely to be true, then no SB is likely to be true.

Whether one accepts that no belief held only by wish fulfillment is likely to be true depends on how likely one thinks it that a process with no intrinsic aim toward truth and no reliable method of generating it would nonetheless, by accident, yield truth much of the time. As I doubt this, I think that *if* the wish-fulfillment charge is correct, few if any SBs are true, and perhaps no SBs are. To the extent that one *suspects* wish fulfillment in SBs, then, one ought to reduce one's confidence in them.

Goals and Rationality

Plausibly, the goal of believing is to assent to truth and not assent to falsehood. If this is the goal of believing, then an act of believing is rationally justifiable qua believing only if it is truth-aimed, that is, only if its goal is to attain truth. In the same way, if the goal of playing chess is (say) winning, then a chess move is rationally justifiable qua chess move only if it is aimed at winning.[43] If one is in fact involved in a practice with a given goal, an action is rationally justifiable qua a move in that practice only if it is aimed at that practice's goal.

If this is true, it gives Barth a straightforward argument that we hold SBs irrationally, for he can argue that our assent to SBs is not actually truth-aimed.

If we want to believe the truth, one way a proposition can attract

---

[42] I owe this argument to Alvin Plantinga, "An Evolutionary Argument against Naturalism," *Logos* 12 (1991), 39–41.

[43] A move irrational qua chess move may be perfectly rational/justifiable in other respects. It may, for instance, be a perfectly rational way to shock your opponent.

belief is to appear true. But this is not the only way propositions can attract belief. Barth can suggest that SBs attract belief not because they appear true but because believing them satisfies our inordinate self-love. We are attracted to them, and we *think* the character of this attraction involves love of truth. But it is in fact love of something else.

This does not mean that we are somehow deceived about how these propositions seem to us. It is doubtful that we can be so. Consider a perceptual analogue: we can be wrong about whether an object *is* red, but we cannot be wrong about whether an object *seems* red to us. In the same way, we can be wrong about whether a proposition *is* true, but it is not even clear what it could mean to be wrong about whether it *seems* true. Rather than claiming error about how propositions seem, Barth's claim could be that if self-love and its allied wishful thinking account for a belief's seeming true to us, they are what "really" move us to assent to it. So too, were someone brainwashed into thinking that a certain proposition is plausible, one might say that even though on one level the believer assents because the proposition seems true, the "real" reason the believer assents is the brainwash.

Again, Barth can allege a sort of voluntary self-deception rather than a sort of wishful thinking. He *could* argue that we are on some level aware that what we want to believe attracts us by attracting our self-love, but we suppress this and channel the felt attraction of the belief into what we think of as the cognitive attraction of truth. But this idea of self-deception raises hard questions.[44] A less controversial reading of the voluntariness Barth might see in our self-deception might go thus: the complex of desires and attitudes we have determines how we weight evidence and the like. These desires and attitudes are voluntary to the extent that they are the result of our past voluntary actions and voluntary acceptances of "given" facets of our characters. Either way, the point of self-deception is to hide the truth from oneself. So an assent whose purpose is self-deception is ipso facto anything but truth-aimed.

If our assents to SBs are cases of wishful thinking or self-deception, and if a believing is rationally justifiable only if it is truth-aimed, we hold all SBs irrationally. This conclusion would let Barth reject IC without engaging NT in philosophical dispute. On this line of argument, Barth need not even claim that IC is false. He can settle for claiming that we have no right to believe it true, and perhaps add (via

---

[44] I cannot pursue these questions here. They are discussed in D. F. Pears, *Motivated Irrationality* (New York: Oxford University Press, 1974), and Brian McLaughlin and Amelie Rorty, eds., *Perspectives on Self-Deception* (Berkeley: University of California Press, 1988).

a general claim that one ought not to hold beliefs irrationally) that we ought to reject it.

A Falsity Argument

Barth can use his etiology to argue not only that SBs are unwarranted but that they are outright false. For one strand in Christian theology understands improper self-love as in part a rejection of and desire to avoid the truth about God and goodness.[45] As Barth might put it, someone who wants to be God (in effect) does not want to know the truth about who really is God.

If this strand of Christian theology is correct, then, inordinate self-love is at odds with attaining the truth about God. So if Barth is right about what desire inclines us to adopt SBs, this is some reason to think these claims false.[46] That SBs arise in part from desires that directly oppose attaining the truth is reason to think that the beliefs in question are true, if at all, by happy accident. For the beliefs' very appeal lies in the signs they give to our hidden desires that they are not true, or that they have other qualities that in fact they are likely to have only if they are not true. The better we are at finding what satisfies our hidden desires, then, the more likely it is that beliefs that seem to have a quality that satisfies these desires really do have that quality. Barth and Christian theologians generally would argue that we are *very* adept at satisfying the hidden desires of our sinful natures, and in particular at hiding from truths about God that might impede these satisfactions. It follows that a belief's appealing to our sinful nature either directly suggests that it is not true or suggests that it has other qualities it is likely to have only if not true.

Truth-aimed Mechanisms and Happy Accidents

That SBs are true by happy accident if at all yields an undermining argument against them. Suppose for the nonce that a belief is adequately justified only if the mechanism producing it is reliable. One strand in the concept of reliability is statistical: a belief-producing mechanism is reliable only if it usually produces true beliefs. Another

---

[45] See John Calvin, *Institutes of the Christian Religion*, trans. Henry Beveridge (Philadelphia: Westminster Press, 1960), bk. 1, chap. 3, pp. 43–44.

[46] This is also reason to deny these beliefs the status of knowledge even if they are true, if one holds that beliefs count as knowledge only if they are reliably generated.

aspect of cognitive reliability is teleological: a belief-producing mechanism is reliable only if our assents to the beliefs it produces are truth-aimed. For a belief is adequately justified only if it is one we can hold rationally, and (as we have suggested) we can hold rationally only beliefs our assents to which are truth-aimed. If this is so, and if SBs do in fact issue from a process (that of believing what satisfies our self-love) that yields non-truth-aimed assents, we have an argument that SBs are inadequately justified and unreliably produced.

Still another strand in the notion of reliability is what one might call "Gettier reliability."[47] Suppose I see an animal in a field. It looks just like a sheep, so I form the belief that there is a sheep in the field. Now as it happens, the animal is really an unusually large poodle. But behind a bush in the field, hidden from my view, there is in fact a sheep. In this case, my belief that there is a sheep in the field is true. But it is true by lucky chance. The reason I take it to be true (that the animal I see is a sheep) is not the reason it *is* true (that the hidden animal is a sheep). In this sense, the belief is *true* by accident, by the lucky chance that a sheep was hidden in the field. Now suppose this *regularly* occurred with our visual beliefs.[48] Then vision would regularly produce accidentally true beliefs. It would be accidental that vision produced true beliefs, even if it regularly or always did so. Vision would do so only subject to the continuation of a series of happy accidents.

I submit that in this case, intuitively, vision would not be a reliable faculty. Though statistically reliable (i.e., usually producing truth), it would be Gettier-unreliable, and this would be reason to call vision unreliable *simpliciter*. For in this case, vision *of itself* would be unreliable—that is, such as to get the facts wrong in the absence of external correction—although the complex of vision plus coincidence would be statistically reliable. (Gettier reliability, then, is a completely nonstatisti-

---

[47] The sort of problem I now raise is related to what philosophers call the Gettier problem—hence the name. But the example I use is actually from Roderick Chisholm, *Theory of Knowledge*, 1st ed. (Englewood Cliffs, N.J.: Prentice-Hall, 1966), p. 23 n. 22.

[48] One could easily sketch some science-fiction scenario for this. More interesting, at least one major philosopher has held just this. Suppose I see a sheep and form the belief that there is a sheep present. According to Plato, the animal my eyes see is *not* a true sheep. It is just an imitation of the true sheep, the Form of Sheep. Though it is not visible, however, the Form of Sheep *is* present in a way where the material imitation sheep is, and so my belief that a sheep is present is accidentally true. Now one might reply that for Plato, it is hardly an accident that the Form of Sheep is present wherever a material imitation sheep is present: in fact, that there are material imitation sheep just is the fact that the Form of Sheep is present in certain ways to areas of the *Timaeus*'s "Receptacle." This is true, but it is irrelevant to the sense of "accident" I employ. Even if it is necessarily the case that where a sheep is, The Sheep also is, still if the sheep and not The Sheep causes my belief, the belief is accidentally true.

cal notion. A belief-forming mechanism can be Gettier-unreliable even if it always yields the truth.) To put it a perhaps better way, in this case, the process of forming beliefs based on vision would not really be truth-aimed, even if it always yielded truth. Rather, this process would systematically miss the truth, but something external to the process would ensure in each case that error is corrected. This process would be truth-aimed in a statistical sense, that of usually producing truth, but intrinsically non-truth-aimed.

To an externalist about justification, at least, it is plausible that a belief is adequately justified only if it issues from a truth-aimed process. If a process is Gettier-unreliable, it is *not* truth-aimed, strictly speaking, even if it is statistically reliable. If this suggestion is correct, it gives Barth an undermining argument. For if SBs are true only by happy accident, then even if all our SBs are true, the process leading us to them is non-truth-aimed (in the Gettier sense). This entails not that SBs are false but that we have no good reason to think them true.[49]

A Reference-failure Argument

The arguments so far developed suggest that a consideration of motives that may figure in the adopting of a certain belief *can* provide legitimate defeaters for that belief. But the fact that an SB appeals to our sinful nature can also take us in another direction altogether. It can suggest that SBs involve a failure of reference—that SBs are not about what we think they are. Thus it can provide Barth with reason to reject IC*.

As we shortly see, Barth thinks that any true belief about God, as such, tends to move us toward God (i.e., toward likeness of and friendship with God). That is, he ascribes spiritual fruits to such beliefs. I suggest below that Barth's reason to believe this is confused. But one can offer this claim another rationale.

I suggest below that God may have made us with a natural desire to be in personal relation with Him. If this is true, then knowing more about God might always inflame this desire. This is not so in human personal relations. Some things I learn about someone I want to meet may make me want this all the more. Others may completely turn me off on that person—the truth about human beings is often disappointing. In God's case (so theists say), the truth cannot disappoint. God is

---

[49] That a belief's generator is *statistically* unreliable, on the other hand, is reason to doubt the belief's truth.

wholly perfect, and so all truths about Him are such as to make us want to know Him. Thus one can base an argument that true beliefs about God, as such, tend to move one toward God, on God's perfection and the claim that God has made us to know Him. The claim that true beliefs about God, as such, tend to move one toward God may seem obviously false, given, for example, James 2:19 ("You believe that there is one God. Good! Even the demons believe that—and shudder.") But it can be true both that any true belief about God, as such, tends to move the believer toward God, and that in the case of demons and others, this movement is checked and counteracted by other factors. Theists might say, for instance, that one effect of sin is precisely that this tendency is always checked unless God graciously removes the impediments. This is why I say that true beliefs about God *tend to* move one toward God rather than that they *do* move one toward God.

Suppose, then, that in fact, SBs are an epistemic outgrowth of sin. Nothing that arises distinctively from sin tends toward God. Sin and its fruits are precisely what separate us from God. Now true beliefs about God should tend to unite us with God, that is, should bear spiritual fruit. Suppose, then, that a given belief, apparently about God, arises from sin. If it does, that belief stems from an underlying process that tends to separate us from God, and so the belief *accompanies* separation from God. If in addition it is true that not only sin but its fruits tend to separate us from God, then if this belief is a fruit of sin, it tends of itself to separate us from God rather than bring us closer to Him. It follows, then, that that belief either is not true or is not about God. As I have suggested, for reasons of general theological method, Barth prefers the latter conclusion.

Barth's point, then, may be that sincere true beliefs truly about the Christian God—or at least some sets of these, which overlap significantly with sets of beliefs NT claims to warrant—would be accompanied by distinctive virtues that beliefs founded on NT do not have.[50] It may be that among the benefits of faith in the Christian God is that this God graciously removes impediments to these virtues, thus ensuring that these beliefs' powers to affect behavior are not blocked.

Given his thoughts about natural theologians' motives, we might speculate that for Barth, these associated virtues include gratitude and obedience to God, contentment with religious beliefs accepted on faith,

[50] Similar criteria are often invoked in distinguishing veridical from nonveridical apparent mystical experiences of God. See Nelson Pike, "On Mystic Visions as Sources of Knowledge," in Steven Katz, ed., *Mysticism and Philosophical Analysis* (New York: Oxford University Press, 1978), pp. 214–34, and George Mavrodes, "Real vs. Deceptive Mystical Experiences," in Katz, *Mysticism*, pp. 235–58.

and a ceasing of the quest to deify oneself. We might sum them up by saying that such beliefs would produce love of God, replacing love of self. To avoid gratuitous slurs on individual natural theologians, we might put Barth's argument this way: certain sets of beliefs about God, sincerely adopted, tend strongly to produce love of God. NT can warrant what appear to be significant subsets of these beliefs. But beliefs adopted on these grounds do not tend to produce love of God. So the beliefs NT warrants must be distinct from the genuine beliefs about God. The two sets of beliefs involve the same predicates, such as "———— caused the universe to exist." (As we have seen, even if we grant Barth all that he means by claiming that predicates are equivocal *in divinis,* one can still say this, at least by using the GCCE.) So they must differ in subject. If they do, the beliefs NT warrants do not concern the true God.

The Spiritual-fruit Argument Parried

One obvious response to this spiritual-fruit argument is that NT and Christian faith may deal with the same subject but under different descriptions. Difference in description can be relevant to producing love of God. It is not surprising if "a non-spatiotemporal explainer caused the universe to exist" and "a loving God who intends your good caused the universe to exist" induce different affective or volitional responses. So perhaps claims of NT and Christian faith refer to the same being, and the difference in the way they describe them accounts for the (alleged) difference in accompanying spiritual fruit.

Barth could block this response by shifting to the sort of causal theory of theistic reference Alston commends. For Barth could then perhaps argue that beliefs' ability to produce love of God depends not on how their contents describe Him but on whether they are about Him, *whatever* the description by which the contents refer to Him. Alston has suggested that perhaps many religions are founded on some direct experiential contact with God, however badly they conceive of Him or report that contact.[51] If so, then sentences expressing these religions' theological beliefs may be *about* God, may pick Him out, via a causal chain of reference, and regardless of how they describe Him. If something like this were true, a Christian theologian might reasonably explain these religions' producing genuine saints and/or genuine love of God in virtue of their beliefs' *in fact* producing a cognitive relation

[51] Alston, "Referring," pp. 115–16.

to God, regardless of any misdescription they involve. Thus adopting a causal theory of reference for beliefs that produce spiritual fruits lets us understand the presence of spiritual fruits in other religions. But on this sort of causal-theoretic view, NT's failure to produce significant affective or volitional response to God might indeed count heavily against its referring to Him.

Still, even if Barth moves to a causal theory of theistic reference, his spiritual-fruit argument faces at least one problem. For if in fact acceptance of truths of NT does not often accompany love of God, this might be because NT does not of itself produce any tendency to love God, or it might instead be because even though such acceptances do generate such a tendency, where a belief is accepted only on NT's grounds, God does not remove the impediments that keep this tendency from flowering. So to speak, there is no observable difference between NT's producing an ever-checked tendency toward God and NT's producing no tendency toward God at all. Thus it seems that we have no warrant to say that NT does not in fact produce a tendency to love God.

Barth might have an answer to this. We have already suggested that one benefit of Christian faith may be that God removes impediments that otherwise would prevent our loving Him. Barth might therefore reply with this dilemma: either NT produces no tendency to love God, or it yields only a checked tendency. If it produces no tendency, we have the argument as before. If it produces only a checked tendency, this is because if one's belief is founded on NT, God does not graciously remove the impediments to loving Him. If one asks why God would not do this, the answer can only be that God wills to be known not in this way but only through revelation. If this is so, NT, the attempt to know God apart from revelation, is a rebellion against God's own will about how to know Him. Thus it is a sinful pursuit, and so (Barth might conclude) NT still stands condemned.

I shortly address the question of whether NT *does* thus stand condemned. For now, though, I note that this rejoinder, whatever it does to NT, leaves IC* standing. For all Barth has shown, NT can refer to God and therefore can argue God's existence.

Theological Reliabilism

Still, even if we have not been able to give Barth a successful argument against IC* and NT, a general worry remains. For Barth, to count as a knowing of or about God, a cognitive state must have not just epistemic but moral or theological virtues—it must, for instance, be a case of what he calls "grateful and obedient" thinking. NT is as such a faithless pursuit, Barth thinks. Those who adopt it, while they adopt it, are not taking the standpoint of faithful, grateful receivers of revelation. But only the eyes of faith see God. So whatever NT sees is not God. Barth implicitly endorses a sort of theological reliabilism. Belief in a proposition, he seems to think, can constitute knowledge about God only if the belief emerges from a belief-generating process that is reliable not just in general but also in the specific context of theology. Barth's appeal to motives is in effect an argument that metaphysical argument, even if reliable in other contexts, is not reliable in theology. Any process rising from and shot through with self-deification, to Barth, cannot be trusted to issue in claims both true and about God. More generally, insofar as sin consists in rejection of God and (partly) a desire not to know the truth about Him, it seems reasonable that if a certain way of obtaining beliefs is peculiarly an outgrowth of sin, it is not dependable as a source of knowledge about God. One might speculate that only belief-generating processes rooted ultimately in love of God would be reliable in theology. So even without an airtight argument against NT, Barth raises a general worry that a friend of NT needs to address.

Can the Natural Theologian Be Saved?

Drawing general morals from the last few sections' arguments, we seem to have at least some religious or moral reason to doubt a claim if

(3)   the faculty that suggests it is morally or religiously impaired,

(4)   the process that leads to this belief is morally or religiously unreliable in either a statistical or a Gettier sense,

(5)   the desire that inclines us to it neither is nor connects appropriately with the desire for truth (this raises the question of Gettier reliability),

(6)   the desire that inclines us to it opposes the desire for truth,

(7)   the desire that inclines us to it neither is nor connects appropriately with the love of God,

(8) the state of believing it is not appropriately connected to a state of loving God, or

(9) true beliefs about God should tend to unite us with God, and this belief is about God but does not have this tendency.

Let us begin by asking why Barth is so sure that NT is as such a faithless endeavor and so runs afoul of (7). As Barth sees it, if the arguments of NT yield knowledge of God, humans have a "relationship with God . . . not founded by God's election and therefore not determined by the grace of God."[52] Christianity claims that human beings are related to God only through God's grace (i.e., through unmerited divine action). As Barth sees it, a successful proof of God's existence would be a human work, not an act of divine grace, and a human work establishing from our side a relation to God. Thus Barth concludes that any theistic proof either fails as an argument or, if it succeeds, relates us to something other than God. Moreover, if a successful theistic proof would be a human work establishing a relation to God, to seek a theistic proof is to seek a relationship with God not founded on grace. It is therefore to reject the grace God offers. To reject divine grace just is to refuse to have faith in God, in the Christian sense of "faith." This, I suggest, is the theological root of Barth's animus against NT.

But it is not clear that Christian theology must evaluate NT as Barth does. A Christian theologian can legitimately argue that God's very creation of the universe is an act of grace. It is, after all, the giving of a great good entirely without desert—if no creature yet exists, no creature yet deserves anything. This act of grace might extend to the creating of a creature able without further divine help to attain some knowledge of God. Perhaps the very creating of a creature to which knowledge of God is naturally available counts as an act of grace to that creature. For that matter, might not the execution of a theistic proof depend on gracious divine help, and might the prover not acknowledge this? Anselm, after all, prayed for the insight to find and execute the ontological argument of *Proslogion* 2.

Barth might reply that "NT is the doctrine of a union of man with God existing outside God's revelation in Jesus Christ. It works out the knowledge of God that is possible and real on the basis of this independent union."[53] Barth's point might be this. Suppose that the crea-

---

[52] Barth, *Dogmatics* II:1, p. 103.
[53] Ibid., p. 168.

tion of beings capable of NT or empowerment to do NT *would* be acts of grace. Such acts would detract from the centrality of God's act in Christ. If this is so, then a proper Christian emphasis on the primacy of Christ (Barth may think) requires belief that God has not performed this particular sort of gracious act. Thus it requires the rejection of NT, or the conclusion that its God is not the God of Christianity.

Barth insists that there is no "knowledge of God" outside Christ. There is an important ambiguity in the biblical locution "knowledge of God." For "knowledge of God" can consist of knowing *about* God or of knowing God. The former is a matter of believing propositions. The latter is a form of personal relationship, including some sort of personal acquaintance. Barth's argument depends, I think, on a failure to make this distinction. For once we have the distinction in hand, we can see that there might well be knowledge about God that does not suffice to let one know God, that is, be His acquaintance or have some other personal relation to Him.

If there is such knowledge about God, then even if NT provides it, NT does not unite God with humanity apart from Christ (i.e., provide a second way to gain personal relationship with God) or dilute the message that salvation is through Christ, and it is not the case that to pursue NT is ipso facto to reject grace or to reject the personal relationship God offers. Once we distinguish knowing about God from knowing God, there is just no reason to consider the pursuit of NT incompatible with faith or to be sure that God has not given humanity the grace needed to prove His existence.

Barth might legitimately ask why God would make nonsalvific knowledge *about* Himself available. God is all-wise, doing nothing without good reason. But what reason could there be to provide a nonsalvific, nonpersonal knowledge of Himself, particularly if (as Christians believe) God's reason to create at all involved a desire to share Himself in personal communion with creatures? One possible reason might arise precisely from God's desire to share Himself.

If God wants personal communion with creatures, He would increase His chance of achieving this by creating creatures with a natural desire for communion with Him. Often a desire is the more intense for having a clearly defined object: the more one knows about it, the more one wants it. Again, it is easier to pursue intensely a single, known goal than to pursue intensely a vague, general plan whose goal is uncertain. So too a lonely person's desire for friendship grows keener if that person comes to focus on one specific person as a desired friend. Thus one effective way to create a creature with a strong natural desire for God could be to create a creature naturally able to gain some knowledge about God, enough perhaps to inflame desire, allow someone to want God for a friend, and help in taking definite steps to be God's friend. Now if the psychological claims I have made are true at all, they are true only of creatures constituted as we are. God could have made psychologically different creatures, for whom these might not have been true. So the most I can suggest is that if God wants for other reasons to create creatures with psychological makeups broadly like ours, *then* these truths *might* yield a reason for God to make natural-theological knowledge available. But this is enough. For in fact, God *has* wanted to create creatures with our psychological makeup.

Barth also might legitimately ask why someone who does not reject divine grace or refuse faith *would* seek additional nonsalvific knowledge about God. But this question is answerable. If the possibility of NT exists because God has made us naturally to desire Him, NT can arise precisely from this desire for God. Desire for God is a form of love of God. Some who are not believers, then, may pursue NT from the form of love of God appropriate to those who do not yet know Him personally. These have not yet accepted grace. But this does not mean that they have rejected it. So here we see one reason why a lover of God who has not rejected and does not reject grace might pursue NT.

It also seems conceivable that a believer's pursuit of NT arise precisely from the *believer's* love of God. For instance, it seems compatible with faith for a believer to want to display for skeptics the rationality of some of what the believer believes. Again, one way to disparage God, surely, is to deny that He exists. It is a loving thing to defend one's friends when others disparage them. There is also such a thing as loving and delighting in the truth. One way to express this love is to display how powerful the evidence is that shows that it *is* the truth, rather as someone proud of a strong friend might want him to show how much stronger he is than others.

If the love of God can inspire NT, religious arguments cannot defeat IC. Those who pursue NT may or may not be moved ultimately by the love of God. One cannot generalize about their motives. Thus one cannot generally prohibit identifying God and a GP.

Let us now consider (3)–(9) in light of this possible etiology of NT. If a Christian theologian can maintain that empowerment to do NT is a gift of grace, NT will find no difficulty in (3) and (4). In the case of (5) and (6), there is certainly no opposition between desire for God and desire for truth. The Old Testament, common property of Jews and Christians and well regarded in Islam, depicts God as strongly valuing truth and the knowledge of it (see, e.g., Proverbs 2:1–8). Loving someone tends to make one love what that person loves, for loving someone involves identifying with that person's interests and concerns. So love of God should tend to foster (inter alia) love of truth, if truth is itself a good God favors. The New Testament (John 14:6) goes so far as to suggest that at some deep level, the love of God and the love of truth are identical, and such writers as Augustine and Anselm develop this thought.[54] Thus even if the love of God drives NT, (5) and (6) are no bar to accepting, for example, that God = the universe's first cause.

Let us now consider (7)–(9). We have seen that the cognitive states NT involves or induces may have an appropriate connection to the love of God. For we have seen that love of God can inspire and express itself in the pursuit of NT, and these are surely forms of appropriate connection to the love of God. Further, given this, one can suggest that *success* in pursuing NT might heighten love of God. Thus any individual's belief in IC, or acceptance that an argument proves God's existence, may well pass the set of tests (7)–(9). These tests cannot rule out IC. To the extent that our alternate etiology of NT is plausible, then, NT seems a defensible practice, even for the faithful Christian. Barth can pursue this matter further only by arguing that his etiology of NT is in some way superior to this section's. Whether and how he might try to do so are matters for another essay.

Morals of the Story

By examining Barth, we have seen that moral or religious factors can provide legitimate undermining or rebutting defeaters, in at least some contexts. In particular, one can licitly use them to defeat claims to knowledge about God. (One finds this sort of move in the New Testament. Thus I John 2:4 reasons that "the man who says 'I know [God]' but does not do what He commands is a liar, and the truth is not in him.") For at least some of the arguments I have sketched above are plausible. Further, we have seen that Barth can reasonably use his view of SBs' genesis to back his rejection of IC*. In fact, a reference-failure argument is another way this etiology can undermine an SB. If one thinks a sentence S expresses a proposition P, and finds it warranted to believe what S expresses, then if one finds out S really expresses P*, not P, it follows that the warrant one thought one had for P is really warrant for P*, and that one has no warrant for P after all. Apparently, then, consideration of moral or religious state can have a legitimate place in epistemology.

[54] See Augustine, *Confessions* X.24, and Anselm, *De veritate*.

This has fascinating implications. For instance, if there are moral and religious defeaters, there are also moral and religious *requirements* for having knowledge of God. For claims to this sort of knowledge must at least be able to survive the offering of moral and religious defeaters. I think one could show this to apply to moral knowledge as well. One may wonder, then, whether some noncognitive factors can actually confer epistemic merit. For instance, might the love of God that is active in faith be an epistemic as well as a theological virtue?[55] Again, might there be legitimate moral and religious requirements on knowledge not directly involving God and the good? For instance, might proper love of truth be a moral or affective prerequisite for having adequate justification for a belief? After all, the less one loves truth, the less (ceteris paribus) the pains one will take to seek it, and so perhaps evidence that a person does not sufficiently love the truth is reason to doubt that that person has inquired long or well enough to justify adequately that belief. Similarly, one might legitimately doubt a scholar or scientist's conclusions if one knows this person to have the moral flaw of laziness. For a lazy person may well be disinclined to do adequate research.

These, though are avenues to travel another day. This essay suggests two conclusions. One is that moral and religious criteria may be relevant in assessing some claims to knowledge. The other is that these criteria do not defeat NT's claim to argue or even "prove" the existence of God. The grounds Barth surveys support no blanket rejection of IC. If this is so, one can hope that no other distinctively religious objection to IC will succeed. The religious, then, can grant that NT can argue, and a sound argument of NT can prove, the existence of their God.[56]

[55] For the role of love in faith, see Aquinas, *ST* II–IIa.4.3–4.

[56] I wrote this essay during the tenure of a grant from the Evangelical Scholarship Initiative of the Pew Charitable Trust. I thank ESI for making this work possible.

[3]

William Alston on
the Problem of Evil

WILLIAM ROWE

William Alston is in the forefront of prominent philosophers who support and defend the rationality of belief in the God of traditional theism: an omnipotent, omniscient, perfectly good being who is the creator of the world. His project includes *positive* attempts to show that belief in theism can be rationally grounded in ordinary religious experiences, as well as *negative* attempts to show that there are no good reasons for rejecting theism. In 1991, Alston published a major essay in defense of theism against the charge that the facts about evil in our world constitute a strong prima facie case for atheism.[1] I propose here to evaluate the strengths and weaknesses of this essay.

Noting that attempts to argue for the logical inconsistency of God and evil have largely been abandoned, Alston focuses on the inductive (probabilistic, evidential) argument from evil, adopting the following formulation of that argument:

1. There exist instances of intense suffering that an omnipotent, omniscient being could have prevented without thereby losing some greater good or permitting some evil equally bad or worse.
2. An omniscient, wholly good being would prevent the occurrence of any intense suffering it could, unless it could not do so without thereby losing some greater good or permitting some evil equally bad or worse.

---

[1] William P. Alston, "The Inductive Argument from Evil," *Philosophical Perspectives, 5, Philosophy of Religion* (Atascadero, Calif.: Ridgeview, 1991), pp. 29–67. Page references appear in parentheses in the text.

3. There does not exist an omnipotent, omniscient, wholly good being.[2]

Alston uses the term 'gratuitous suffering' for any case of intense suffering E that satisfies premise 1 or—to avoid some inadequacies in 1—that an omnipotent, omniscient, wholly good being would have no sufficient reason to permit. Having thus characterized gratuitous suffering, Alston writes: "E's being gratuitous, then, is the contradictory of the *possibility* of God's having a sufficient reason to permit it, and equivalent to the *impossibility* of God's having a sufficient reason for permitting it" (p. 30; italics mine). Although the quoted remark seems to play no vital role in the argument he develops, to forestall misunderstanding it is important to note that if the modal term 'possible' is taken in either its logical or epistemic sense, the remark is false. For E to be gratuitous, all that is required is that there be no sufficient reason for God's permitting E. It is not required that there be no sufficient reason for God's permitting E in every possible world in which E occurs. For in some possible world, E occurs in circumstances such that had God prevented E a worse world would have obtained. The point is that some evil in the actual world may be such that God would have no sufficient reason for permitting it without that evil being *necessarily* such that God would have no sufficient reason for permitting it. And, as for the epistemic use of 'possible', it's clear that the question whether a certain evil is gratuitous has nothing to do with what any human being knows or is (isn't) justified in believing.

To justify accepting premise 1 (that gratuitous evil exists), all one need do is justify the belief that some particular evil that occurs is gratuitous. Alston notes two particular examples of evils that I've held are reasonably believed to be gratuitous.

In (1979) and subsequent papers Rowe focuses on the case of a fawn trapped in a forest fire and undergoing several days of terrible agony before dying (hereinafter 'Bambi'). In (1988) he adds to this a (real life) case introduced by Bruce Russell (1989), a case of the rape, beating, and murder by strangulation of a five-year old girl ('Sue') by her mother's boyfriend. Since I am specifically interested in criticizing Rowe's argument I will argue that we are not justified, and cannot be justified, in judging these evils to be gratuitous. (p. 32)

[2] This is how I put the argument in "The Problem of Evil and Some Varieties of Atheism," *American Philosophical Quarterly* 16 (1979), 335–41.

Alston accepts the task of establishing that no one is or can be justified in believing that the sufferings of Bambi and Sue are such that an omnipotent, omniscient being could have prevented them without thereby losing some greater good or permitting some evil equally bad or worse.[3] Indeed, Alston undertakes to show we cannot be justified in asserting any instantiations of "E is such that an omnipotent, omniscient being could have prevented it without thereby losing some greater good or permitting some evil equally bad or worse (pp. 30–31)."

It is, of course, one thing to argue that no one can be rationally justified in accepting premise 1 and another thing to argue that we are justified in accepting the denial of premise 1. It seems clear that apart from appealing to a rationally justified belief in the existence of God and inferring the denial of 1 from that belief, it would be quite incredible to suppose that any human being is justified in accepting the denial of 1.[4] Alston seems to agree with this. "To sum up: I think that examining the interconnections of good and evil in the world by our natural powers cannot suffice to establish either 1. or its negation. For particular cases of suffering we might conceivably be able to establish non-gratuitousness in this way, but what I shall argue in this paper is that no one can justifiably assert gratuitousness for any case" (p. 31).

Alston notes the growing body of literature devoted to answering the

---

[3] Alston later shows that it is not quite right to imply (as I have) that God could have no other reason for permitting a certain evil except that preventing it would involve losing a greater good or permitting some equally bad or worse evil (pp. 33–35). The corrections needed in the formulation of premise 1 are not directly relevant to the central argument of his essay. So, for the purpose of evaluating Alston's argument, we can continue to think of God's reason for permitting an instance of intense suffering as the securing of a greater good or the prevention of some evil that is equally bad or worse.

[4] In an endnote Alston says that "Rowe proceeds as if he supposed that the only alternatives are (a) its being reasonable to believe 1 and (b) its being reasonable to believe not-1" (p. 62). He then quotes a passage in which I claim that not-1 is unlikely and conclude that "although we cannot *prove* that (1) is true, it is, nevertheless, altogether *reasonable* to believe that (1) is true, that (1) is a *rational* belief." I am a bit puzzled by the charge that I have overlooked the possibility that it may be rational to believe neither 1 nor its denial. For in a footnote to the very passage Alston quotes, I am careful to remind the reader that "it is one thing to argue that it is unreasonable to think that (1) is false and another thing to conclude that we are therefore justified in accepting (1) as true." I then point out that "there are propositions such that believing them is much more reasonable than disbelieving them, and yet are such that *withholding judgment* about them is more reasonable than believing them." After citing an example from Chisholm, I note that "it might be objected that while we've shown that believing (1) is more reasonable than disbelieving (1), we haven't shown that believing (1) is more reasonable than withholding belief" ("The Problem of Evil," p. 338). These do not strike me as the remarks of someone who supposes that the only alternatives are rationally believing 1 or rationally believing not-1. The lesson, I suppose, is that anything really important to the text should be in the text and not relegated to a footnote.

inductive argument from evil. Much of this literature focuses on the cognitive disparity between the human mind and an omniscient mind. Being omniscient, the theistic God would know many propositions we don't know. Presumably, some of these propositions would be about various goods and their interconnections with horrendous evils like Bambi and Sue.[5] Starting from the disparity between God's knowledge and ours, recent critics of the problem of evil have argued that we cannot have a good reason to believe that Bambi and Sue serve no good that would justify an omnipotent, omniscient being in permitting their occurrence. For, so they claim, given all that God would know that we don't know, it is reasonable to believe that the goods, if such there be, that would justify God in permitting Bambi and Sue would be *beyond our ken*. While indicating some sympathy with these critics,[6] Alston proposes to focus less on the cognitive distance between the human mind and the divine and more on the numerous considerations one would have to be justified in excluding as God's reason(s) for permitting Bambi and Sue, if one is to be justified in making the "universal negative" claim that there is *no sufficient reason* a divine being would have for permitting these evils. Starting from the fact that this universal negative claim excludes any sufficient divine reason for permitting Bambi and Sue, Alston argues that given our limited perspective, we cannot be justified in ruling out all such potential divine reasons and, therefore, cannot be justified in believing that an omnipotent, omniscient, morally perfect being would not permit Bambi and Sue.

What potential divine reasons for permitting Bambi and Sue are we unjustified in ruling out? A major part of Alston's project is to consider familiar Christian theodicies and to explore their possible application to Bambi and Sue. These theodicies divide into those proposing divine reasons for suffering that are concerned with possible goods to those who endure the suffering and those proposing divine reasons for suffering concerned with possible goods not restricted to the sufferers. His examples of the first sort are punishment for sin, soul making, and having a vision of the inner life of God. His examples of the second sort are the value of free will, benefits to those who cause or witness the suffering, and the value generated by a lawlike, natural order.

[5] For brevity, we can think of God's permitting Bambi and Sue as God's permitting the particular *sufferings* of Bambi and Sue that were earlier described. Sometimes I use 'Bambi' and 'Sue' to refer to the individuals Bambi and Sue. At other times, I use the names to refer to their particular sufferings.

[6] In correspondence Alston has indicated that he *doesn't agree* with these critics in holding that "given all that God would know that we don't know, it is reasonable to believe that the goods, if such there be, that would justify God in permitting Bambi and Sue would be *beyond our ken*."

The goods delineated in Christian theodicies are among the class of *goods we know about*. Within this class there also are goods that do not figure prominently in Christian theodicies. In addition, we may presume that there is a class of *goods we do not know about*, goods beyond our ken. In what follows, we look first at Alston's efforts to find a partial divine reason for Bambi and Sue among the goods we know about, particularly those goods that figure in certain Christian theodicies. Later we critically evaluate his claim that we cannot possibly be justified in ruling out potential divine reasons for Bambi and Sue that concern goods beyond our ken.

Alston emphasizes that he is considering Christian theodicies only as *live possibilities* for divine reasons for permitting evil. He is not undertaking to show that any of these theodicies is correct (p. 36). Since he does not spell out what he means by a live possibility in this context, I shall take a live possibility here to be something that we have no good reason to believe would not wholly or partially justify an omniscient, omnipotent, wholly good being in permitting some evil.[7] The question then becomes whether any or all of the theodicies are live possibilities *for Bambi and Sue*. If they are not live possibilities, if they are implausible suggestions as to what might justify an omnipotent, omniscient being in permitting Bambi and Sue, then, insofar as his use of Christian theodicies is concerned, Alston will have failed to make his case, that is, he will have failed to show that no one is justified in believing premise 1 of the inductive argument from evil.

Do Christian theodicies provide live possibilities for divine reason to permit Bambi and Sue? Alston admits that theodicies that focus on some good for the sufferer do not seem of much help here.

> I am, naturally, most interested in suggestions that constitute live possibilities for divine reasons for permitting Bambi's and Sue's suffering. And many familiar theodicies do not pass this test. . . . Bambi's suffering, and presumably Sue's as well, could hardly be put down to punishment for sin, and neither case could seriously be supposed to be allowed by God for the sake of character building. (p. 37)

Nor does Marilyn Adams's suggestion that "temporal suffering itself is a vision into the inner life of God" look promising for either Bambi or Sue. But Alston thinks it has a some chance of success.

---

[7] In correspondence Alston has indicated that he would explain a live possibility in terms of what we have no *sufficient reason* to believe would not wholly or partially justify an omniscient, omnipotent, wholly good being in permitting some evil.

The only real chance for an exception is Adams's suggestion that the experience of suffering constitutes a vision of the inner life of God. Since this is not confined to those who identify it as such, it could apply to Sue, and perhaps to Bambi as well, though presumably only Sue would have a chance to recognize it and rejoice in it, retrospectively, in the light of the beatific vision. However, I don't want to insist on this exception. Let us say that a consideration of the theodicies thus far canvassed does nothing to show that we can't be justified in affirming an instantiation of 1. for Bambi and Sue. (p. 44)

Expressions such as "I don't want to insist on this exception" and "Let us say" sound a bit like concessions to the proponent of the argument from evil. It's as though, if all else were to fail, one could make one's stand on the possibility that the suffering of Bambi and Sue are permitted because they are visions of God. But since there are livelier possibilities down the road, we can afford not to insist on this possibility. Nevertheless, consider how utterly implausible this "exception" is. Can anyone seriously entertain the idea that Bambi's excruciating suffering on being burned in the forest fire constitutes a vision *by Bambi* of the inner life of God? And even if one could bring oneself seriously to entertain this idea, could one believe that such a vision would justify God in permitting Bambi's excruciating suffering? After all, Bambi is acutely aware of the suffering but totally unaware that the suffering is a vision of God, as Alston is careful to note. If Alston is willing to countenance this theodical suggestion as a potential divine reason for Bambi's suffering, we can, I think, rightfully complain that he is not sticking to his intended plan of presenting us with real live possibilities for God's reasons for permitting Bambi and Sue. For this suggestion, whatever merit it may have when applied to the suffering of the Christian martyrs, is surely a dead option for a divine reason for permitting Bambi.

One might overlook this particular deviation from Alston's avowed intention to present only live possibilities for divine reasons to permit Bambi and Sue if it were the only such lapse in his essay. But after agreeing that the theodicies of the first sort (those concerned with possible goods to those who endure the suffering) do "nothing to show that we can't be justified in affirming an instantiation of 1. for Bambi or Sue," Alston argues that for all we know, the sufferings of Bambi and Sue are necessary, "in ways we cannot grasp, for some outweighing good of a sort with which we are familiar, e.g., supreme fulfillment of one's deepest nature" (p. 44). It is, I think, difficult to square this judgment with Alston's earlier rejection of the idea that the soul-making theodicy of John Hick provides a live possibility for a divine reason to permit Sue's suffering. For Alston notes that it "strains credulity" to suggest that Sue's moral and spiritual development in an afterlife would justify God in permitting Sue's suffering. I agree that Hick's suggestion when applied to Sue's suffering "strains credulity," and I also agree with Alston's judgment that the proponent of the argument from evil is justified in rejecting the soul-making theodicy as a live possibility for a divine reason to permit Sue's suffering. But isn't it just as much a strain on our credulity to suggest that the torture, rape, and strangulation of a five-year-old child (or God's permission of it) is necessary in order for her to attain the supreme fulfillment of her nature? (What, after all, is the supreme fulfillment of one's nature from the Christian perspective if not, as Hick's theodicy supposes, a life of eternal fellowship with God?) And what does Bambi's suffering and death have to do with the supreme fulfillment of Bambi's nature? Alston suggests that the suffering and death may be "necessary in ways we cannot understand" for the supreme fulfillment of Bambi's nature. And, for my part, I have to admit that I have no *proof* that this isn't so. But since Alston is here considering a good (supreme fulfillment of one's nature) with which we are familiar, I think we do know enough to be entitled to view with considerable skepticism the suggestion that Bambi's excruciating suffering and death are so related to the supreme fulfillment of Bambi's nature that even an omnipotent being could not enable Bambi to achieve the latter without permitting the former.

At this point I might as well lay my cards on the table concerning the two examples I've given that strike me as falling short of Alston's goal of providing *live possibilities* for divine reasons for Bambi and Sue. A live possibility for a divine reason for Bambi and Sue is something that we have *no good reason* to believe would not justify an omniscient, omnipotent being in permitting Bambi and Sue. In rejecting the suggestions Alston makes of Bambi's suffering as a vision of God (which he doesn't insist on) or as necessary (in ways we don't or can't comprehend) for the supreme fulfillment of Bambi's nature, I am of course contending that they are not *live possibilities* for divine reasons to permit Bambi's excruciating suffering and death as a result of being severely burned in the forest fire. That is, I am contending that it is rational to believe that if the goods in question are obtainable at all, an omnipotent, omniscient being could obtain them without having to permit Bambi's excruciating suffering and death (or something equally bad or worse). Now we've already seen that Alston needs to *establish* that there are live possibilities for Bambi and Sue if he is to show that no one is justified in believing premise 1 of the inductive argument by appealing to the cases of Bambi and Sue. And here I want to expose what I believe are two fallacious lines of argument that someone might employ in an effort to establish that either of the goods we've been discussing is a live possibility for a divine reason to permit Bambi and Sue. First, one may point out that p is logically possible—or that we don't know that it isn't logically possible—and conclude that p is, therefore, a live possibility. Second, one may note that we don't know with certainty that not-p—or that no one can prove that not-p—and conclude that p is, therefore, a live possibility. It is obvious that both lines of argument are fallacious. Many things we know to be false are, nevertheless, logically possible and known to be logically possible. But if p is known to be false, p is not a live possibility. And although one may not know that not-p or be able to prove that not-p, one may have good reasons to believe that not-p. So the fact that we don't know or can't prove not-p doesn't entitle us to conclude that p is a live possibility.

It would be a mistake to think that Alston is explicitly or intentionally engaging in either form of fallacious inference. For he is at times quite explicit in rejecting as live possibilities considerations that he and I agree are logical possibilities that no one can claim to know for certain to be false. My point in mentioning these two fallacious inferences is both to note their seductive charm and to emphasize the necessity of moving beyond mere logical possibility and inability to disprove as grounds for taking various goods as potential live possibilities for Bambi and Sue. It is important to bear in mind that something more than this needs to be done if we are to be persuaded that something is a genuine live possibility for a divine reason to permit Bambi and Sue.

So far as goods for the sufferer are concerned, what we've seen is that Alston believes that the prominent Christian theodicies *fail* to provide live possibilities for the cases of Bambi and Sue. But, as we've also seen, he thinks that he can establish that some goods we are familiar with (for example, the supreme fulfillment of one's nature) are such that we have no good reason to think that an omnipotent, omniscient being can obtain them without having to permit Bambi's and Sue's sufferings. And he also holds that it is in principle impossible for us to be justified in precluding patient-centered *goods we do not know about* as providing an omnipotent, omniscient being with a morally sufficient reason to permit those sufferings.

As for my part, I've indicated that aside from logical possibility an inability to disprove Alston does little or nothing by way of "establishing" that we are not justified in precluding familiar goods like the supreme fulfillment of Bambi's nature or Bambi's having a vision of God from providing an omnipotent, omniscient being with a morally sufficient reason to permit Bambi's excruciating torment and death. As for goods beyond our ken, we treat this matter later, once we have considered Alston's discussion of theodical suggestions for divine reasons that extend beyond benefit to the sufferer.

The other theodicies Alston explores concern goods that are not restricted to the sufferer. An initial problem with such theodicies is that they seem to suggest that it is permissible for God to allow a creature to undergo severe suffering so that He may bring a benefit to others—either other creatures or Himself. But this strikes many as unjust.[8] Alston partially agrees with their judgment. He thinks it would be unjust for God to permit someone to suffer for the welfare of others if the suffering resulted in the person's life as a whole being less than good. But if the person's life as a whole is on balance good and the person so sees it, then, in Alston's judgment, it may be permissible for God to allow the person to suffer so as to bring a benefit to others.

> A perfectly good God would not wholly sacrifice the welfare of one of His intelligent creatures simply in order to achieve a good for others, or for Himself. This would be incompatible with His concern for the welfare of each of His creatures. Any plan that God would implement will include provision for each of us having a life that is, on balance, a good thing, and one in which the person reaches the point of being able to see that his life as a whole is a good for him. . . . Nevertheless, this is compatible with God having as part of his reason for permitting a given case of suffering that it contributes to results that extend beyond the sufferer. So long as the sufferer is amply taken care of, I can't see that this violates any demands of divine justice, compassion, or love. (p. 48)

It's difficult to determine whether Alston intends to include Bambi in the position he here takes. In the passage quoted it first looks as though he does so intend. For he talks of *intelligent creatures* and God's concerns for the welfare of each of *His creatures*. But in the next sentence he talks only of *persons* and makes remarks that could scarcely apply to Bambi. In any case, if he does intend to be making a point about any plan that God would implement for all his intelligent creatures, including Bambi, then he must be supposing that there is an afterlife for Bambi as well as Sue. For it is evident that some of God's creatures do not have an earthly life that is as a whole good for them.

---

[8] Alston quotes Eleonore Stump on this point and observes that many theists and atheists concur with her judgment.

It also seems clear that Alston is opposing the dominant Christian conviction that there is an eternal hell as well as an eternal heaven. For on the doctrine of an eternal hell, it is exceedingly unlikely that its inhabitants will all come to see their lives as "good on balance" and "joyfully endorse" what they have endured.[9]

Alston begins his discussion of particular goods that extend beyond the sufferer with an examination of the free will theodicy. According to this theodicy, God is justified in permitting evil actions and their consequences because He has bestowed on some of His creatures genuine freedom in a range of actions, and it is a conceptual impossibility for God to crate a free agent with respect to some action and also determine the agent to choose (not choose) to perform the action. So, according to this theodicy, God permits certain horrors to occur because to prevent them would be to prevent a certain degree of freedom in His creatures. Against this theodicy, Alston notes that it has been argued (1) that God could have created free creatures who always choose to do what is right, and (2) that permitting free will with respect to certain actions at certain times isn't worth the horrendous evils (for example, Sue's suffering) that result from the use of that freedom. Concerning the first objection, Alston points out that if we set aside middle knowledge, as he does in the essay, God would not be able to create beings with genuine freedom and "guarantee" that they will always choose to do what is right. And he further notes that even if we grant middle knowledge, Plantinga "has established the *possibility* that God could not actualize a world containing free creatures that always do the right thing" (p. 49).

Before considering his response to the second objection, we should note two points. First, to conduct his case on the *assumption* that there is no middle knowledge considerably weakens Alston's argument. For there is no consensus on whether middle knowledge is possible. And if middle knowledge is possible, then we have reason to think that an omnipotent, omniscient being could have created a world with less evil, but as much good, as our world contains.[10] Nor will it do to emphasize that Plantinga has established the *possibility* that even with middle

---

[9] Alston avoids rejecting the Christian doctrine of an eternal hell by supposing that God's plan might simply ensure that each person has ample opportunity to choose freely so as to have a life that is on balance a good to them. But since, presumably, Bambi lacks free will, it would seem (1) that an afterlife for such sentient creatures must be postulated in order to ensure that their lives are on balance a good for them, and (2) that no such creatures can be assigned to an eternal hell.

[10] For a brief discussion of this point, see my essay, "Ruminations about Evil," in Tomberlin, *Philosophical Perspectives, 5, Philosophy of Religion*, pp. 74–76.

knowledge God could not have created a world with free creatures that always do the right thing. For Alston needs to show that even with middle knowledge it remains a *live possibility* that God could not have created a world with free creatures who always do what is right. But all that Plantinga has shown is that it is a *logical possibility* that such would be the case. Here again, I'm afraid, we have a slide from what is a logical possibility to what is a live possibility, from what is broadly logically possible to what we have no good reason for thinking isn't so. Indeed, that such a slide has occurred is indicated by the sentence with which Alston begins his very next paragraph. "Thus we may take it to be a *live possibility* that the maintenance of creaturely free will is at least part of God's reason for permitting wrongdoing and its consequences" (p. 50; italics mine).

Suppose we endeavor to apply the free will theodicy to the case of Sue's suffering on being beaten, raped, and strangled by her mother's boyfriend. The first question we need to ask is whether the possession of free will is something that is *in itself* of such great value as to merit God's permission of the horrendous moral evils in the world. I think the answer must be no. We should distinguish the intrinsic value of possessing free will from its extrinsic value. The mere possession of free will does not strike me as itself having much in the way of intrinsic value.[11] But the possession of free will does seem necessary to attaining states that are of great intrinsic value. Thus, if we can agree that free will is necessary for the existence of things of great intrinsic value, we can agree that an omnipotent, omniscient, perfectly good being would likely endow His creatures (or some of them) with free will, providing that it does result to a sufficient degree in the things of great intrinsic value for which its possession is necessary. But, of course, our free will is limited; there are many things to which it does not extend. Moreover, it is sometimes right to curtail a particular exercise of free will when one foresees or predicts that its exercise is evil and or will result in considerable suffering. Since curtailing a particular exercise of free will does not significantly diminish a person's overall degree of freedom, the question at hand is whether it is rational to believe that an omnipotent, omniscient, perfectly good being would have prevented the particular exercise of free will (if that is what it was) the mother's boyfriend engaged in when he beat, raped, and strangled the five-year-old child. As Alston put the issue:

[11] Thus, it seems to me that the free will theodicy needs to be included within something like Hick's soul-making theodicy, a theodicy that stresses some intrinsic goods for which free will is a necessary condition.

Presumably a tiny additional constriction such as would be involved in God's preventing Sue's attacker from committing that atrocity would not render things radically different, free-will-wise, from what they would have been without that. So God could have prevented this without losing the good emphasized by this theodicy. Hence we can be sure that this does not constitute a sufficient reason for His not preventing it. (p. 50)

Alston thinks, however, that the preservation of Sue's attacker's free will is a *live possibility* for at least part of God's reason for permitting the suffering Sue undergoes at the hands of her attacker. For he reasons that the value of free will is such that God can intervene in only a small proportion of cases.

Rowe's claim would then have to be that Sue's murder was so horrible that it would qualify for the class of exceptions. But that is precisely where the critic's claims far outrun his justification. How can we tell that Sue falls within the most damaging n% of what would be cases of human wrongdoing apart from divine intervention. To be in a position to make such a judgment we would have to survey the full range of such cases and make reliable assessments of the deleterious consequences of each. Both tasks are far beyond our powers. (p. 51)

Alston's point seems to be this. God cannot intervene in all cases of the use of free will in doing evil that results in suffering, for this would severely limit human capacity to choose between good and evil. God, then, would intervene only in a certain percentage (n) of such cases. The cases in which God intervenes would be selected so as to minimize human suffering overall or to maximize human welfare. And we simply don't know enough about what would be cases of human wickedness (past, present, and future) apart from divine intervention to determine whether or not Sue's case would be included among the percentage of cases God would select to eliminate.

Hence, by the nature of the case, we are simply not in a position to make a warranted judgment that Sue's case is among the n% worst cases of wrongdoing in the history of the universe. No doubt, it strikes us as incomparably horrible on hearing about it, but so would innumerable others. Therefore, the critic is not in a position to set aside the value of free will as at least part of God's reason for permitting Sue's murder. (p. 51)

Does this argument *establish* that we aren't justified in excluding the value of human free will as part of God's reason for permitting Sue's suffering? Well, if the basic premise of Alston's argument is correct, the argument does establish just that. For to be so justified, Alston requires that we compare the episode involving Sue with the whole range of cases of human wrongdoing in the universe (past, present, and future) that would occur apart from divine intervention in order to determine whether Sue's case is sufficiently bad to warrant God in setting aside the value of free will in that case. And of course, no human being knows enough to engage in such a comparison. But I do not think this knowledge is required. The free will theodicy is built around the idea that the possession of freedom to do good and evil is a good *in each person* that God creates. What is important, therefore, is that each person have some measure of freedom to do good and evil. Now, as Alston will readily admit, (1) we don't possess unlimited freedom, and (2) it is sometimes right to curtail someone's freedom in order to prevent some horrendous evil act that results in considerable suffering to an innocent person. But if God were to select some person and effectively prevent that person from ever choosing to do an evil deed that results in suffering to an innocent person, we can agree that this might severely diminish the value of that person's freedom to do good and evil. So God has a reason to permit each person effectively to engage in doing good and evil acts. Of course, God would be able to intervene in some of those acts without significantly diminishing the person's general freedom to do good and evil. What, then, do we have to make a judgment about in order to determine whether the prevention of Sue's attacker's freedom to beat, rape, and strangle Sue would have diminished entirely the value of that person's freedom to do good and evil? Do we have to compare it with all the cases of human wrongdoing, past, present, and future, as Alston claims? Clearly not. What is at issue here is not some sort of amount of freedom to do good and evil in the entire universe, past, present, and future. What is at issue is the degree and value of Sue's attacker's freedom to do good and evil. Would this particular intervention severely diminish the value of that individual's overall degree of freedom to do good and evil? And if it would, is the value of that individual's overall degree of freedom to do good and evil worth the price of permitting the act in question? Perhaps some rational judgments are required about these questions in order for us to be justified in taking Sue's suffering as an instance of gratuitous suffering. But this is a far cry from having to do a survey of all human acts of wickedness in the universe, past, present, and future.[12]

What strikes me as the most promising suggestion of a live possibility for a divine reason to permit *natural* evils like Bambi is the last theodicy Alston considers: "the appeal to the benefits of a lawlike natural order, and the claim that suffering will be an inevitable byproduct of any such order" (p. 52). Clearly, if human beings are to make meaningful free choices concerning good and evil, they must be able to anticipate the consequences of their choices, and this is possible only if things happen (in relation to their choices) in a lawlike manner. Instances of suffering like Bambi are the inevitable by-product of the system of laws that enables us to anticipate the consequences of our choices.

The standard objections to this theodicy are two. First, God may intervene to prevent various cases of natural evils without significantly weakening our confidence in what will happen as a result of our choices. Second, it has seemed to some critics that God could have instituted a set of laws of nature that would result in far less disastrous natural evils than actually occur in our world.[13] Alston develops formidable replies to each of these objections. I consider only the first standard objection and his response to it.

Alston agrees that a natural order can be regular enough to enable us to anticipate consequences of our choices, even if there are exceptions to the regularities.

So long as God doesn't do this too often, we will still have ample basis for suppositions as to what we can reasonably expect to follow what. But note that by the same line of reasoning God cannot do this too often, or the desired predictability will not be forthcoming. Hence, though any one naturally caused suffering could have been miraculously prevented, God certainly has a strong prima facie reason in each case to refrain from doing this; for if He didn't He would have no reason for letting nature usually take its course. And so He has a possible reason for allowing nature to take its course in the Bambi case, a reason that would have to be overridden by stronger contrary considerations. (p. 53)

[12] One might argue that were God to intervene in Sue's case, He would have to intervene in every similar case, with the result that no human being would be free to do evil acts of the kind represented by Sue. I respond to an argument of this sort below in connection with the theodicy that rests on the need for the world to operate in accordance with relatively stable laws of nature.

[13] See, for example, Quentin Smith, "An Atheogical Argument from Evil Natural Laws," *International Journal for Philosophy of Religion* 29 (1991), 154–74.

Alston concludes that to be justified in believing God has no sufficient reason for not intervening to prevent Bambi, we would have to be justified in supposing God has a sufficient reason to make Bambi an exception to His general policy of letting nature take its course.

> And how could we be justified in supposing that? We would need an adequate grasp of the full range of cases from which God would have to choose whatever exceptions He is going to make, if any, to the general policy of letting nature take its course. Without that we would not be in a position to judge that Bambi is among the n% of the cases most worthy of being miraculously prevented. And it is abundantly clear that we have and can have no such grasp of this territory as a whole. We are quite unable, by our natural powers, of determining just what cases, or even what kinds of cases, of suffering there would be throughout the history of the universe if nature took its course. We just don't know enough about the constituents of the universe even at present, much less throughout the past and future, to make any such catalogue.... Hence we are in no position to judge that God does not have sufficient reason for refraining from interfering in the Bambi case. (p. 53)

Alston claims that in order to be justified in believing God would have no sufficient reason for permitting Bambi, we would first have to compare Bambi with the entire range of cases of suffering there would be in the universe, past, present, and future, if nature took its course. For since only n percent exceptions could be made to the general policy of letting nature take its course, we would need to make such a comparison in order to be justified in judging that Bambi falls within the percentage of allowable exceptions. Since we cannot make any such comparison, we cannot be justified in believing that God would not have a sufficient reason to refrain from interfering in the Bambi case.

Again, I don't think Alston is right in what he insists we must know if we are to make such a judgment in the Bambi case. In the first place, he gives a poor argument for the conclusion that God has a strong prima facie reason in each case to let natural regularities obtain. The only reason given in the theodicy under examination for letting natural regularities obtain is that human beings need to be able to anticipate the consequences of their choices. Consider, then, far-off regions of the universe where events would take millions of years to register any impact upon human beings. So far as this theodicy is concerned, God may have no reason at all to impose regularities on those regions. Moreover, if He were to impose them, He would have no reason at all (so far as this theodicy is concerned) to interfere in those regions in only a small percentage of cases. For all Alston has said, God might be interfering quite frequently in those regions. And, coming closer to home, it is clear that the cases in which God's interference must be measured and kept to a certain percentage distributed over time are not global in the way Alston suggests. They are in fact limited to cases in which divine intervention *could interfere with our human ability to antici-pate the consequences of our choices.* Thus, if we were supposing that God would change bullets into butter on certain occasions when they are fired at innocent persons, we might well run afoul of the theodicy we are examining. But the Bambi case could easily be resolved without any effect at all on our ability to anticipate the consequences of our choices. God might have arranged for the lightning to strike harmlessly some high ground, rather than a tree; thus forestalling the forest fire. Or, lightning having struck the tree, God might have prevented the tree from bursting into flames. Or, the tree having burst into flames, God might have put out the flames by causing a quick rainfall, and so on. An important feature of the Bambi case is that the sorts of interference required to prevent Bambi's excruciating pain and slow death over several days are those that likely would have no influence at all on our ability to anticipate the consequences of our choices. Alston's mistake here is to neglect to distinguish cases where interference with the usual course of nature would weaken our ability to anticipate the consequences of our choices from cases where interference with the usual course of nature would quite likely not weaken our ability to anticipate the consequences of our choices. His argument does have some validity for cases of the first sort: occasionally turning bullets into butter when they are fired at an innocent person, bringing some well-known person back to life after it is established that the person has been dead for four days, and the like. It is with respect to cases of this sort that God might have a strong prima facie reason not to interfere. But no such prima facie reason has been established for cases of the latter sort, cases that include Bambi.

It might be argued that if God had interfered in Bambi, then He would have had to interfere in every case where, unnoticed by humans, some sentient animal was about to be injured and subjected to excruciating pain while slowly dying. And, so the argument might go, if this were so, it is rather likely that human beings eventually would become aware of this interference and cease to be morally concerned for the supposed suffering of animals due to natural forces. The answer to this is that there would be a threshold beyond which further massive interference by God would perhaps have such an untoward effect. But

it seems eminently clear that we are far away from any such supposed
threshold. I conclude, therefore, that Alston's appeal to the theodicy
based on the human need for a natural order so as to be able to anticipate the consequences of human choices does not succeed in *establishing*
that we cannot be justified in thinking that an omnipotent, omniscient
being would have no morally sufficient reason for permitting Bambi.

I've now completed my examination of Alston's efforts to identify
among the goods we know a live possibility for a divine reason to permit
Bambi and Sue. As we've seen, his strategy was to search for such a
reason among various Christian theodicies, both those that emphasize
a good primarily to the sufferer and those that do not. My judgment
has been that his efforts in both sorts of theodicies have failed. Oddly
enough, this judgment is only slightly different from Alston's own conclusion. Alston allows that none of the reasons offered by the sufferer-
centered theodicies "could be any part of God's reasons for permitting
the Bambi and Sue cases" (p. 58). (We should remember here, however,
that he concedes this only "for the sake of argument".) He does claim
that reasons offered by the non-sufferer-centered theodicies could be
a part, but *only a part,* of God's reasons for allowing any case of suffering (p. 58). So Alston agrees with me that the reasons presented in the
theodicies he has examined do not constitute a live possibility for a
sufficient reason for God to permit Bambi and Sue.[14] Our only main
difference thus far is over the question of whether the reasons presented in the non-sufferer-centered theodicies could constitute a part
of God's sufficient reason for permitting Bambi and Sue. Alston sums
up his situation with respect to finding a reason for Bambi and Sue
among Christian theodicies.

> This left me without any specific suggestions as to what might be a
> fully sufficient reason for God to permit those cases. And hence show-
> ing that no one can be justified in supposing that reasons of the sort
> considered are not at least part of God's reason for one or another
> case of suffering does not suffice to show that no one can be justified
> in supposing that God could have no sufficient reason for permitting
> the Bambi and Sue cases. And hence it does not suffice to show that
> Rowe cannot be justified in asserting 1. (p. 58)

How then does Alston propose to make up the difference, to establish that we cannot be justified in believing that there is no sufficient

---

[14] I should emphasize here another area of agreement with Alston. Although I have
rejected Christian theodicies as live possibilities for Bambi and Sue, I agree with him
that these theodicies may well provide live possibilities for other cases of suffering that

divine reason for permitting Bambi and Sue? His reply is to claim that we are not justified in ruling out *goods we are not aware of* as constituting a sufficient divine reason for Bambi and Sue.

> Even if we were fully entitled to dismiss all the alleged reasons for permitting suffering that have been suggested, we would still have to consider whether there are further possibilities that are undreamt of in our theodicies. . . . Since it is in principle impossible for us to be justified in supposing that God does not have sufficient reasons for permitting E that are unknown to us, and perhaps unknowable by us, no one can be justified in holding that God could have no reasons for permitting the Bambi and Sue cases, or any other particular cases of suffering. (pp. 58–59)

Indeed, Alston claims that even if everything else he has argued were in vain and his opponent could rule out all the theodical suggestions he has put forward, "she would still face the insurmountable task of *showing herself to be justified* in supposing that there are no further possibilities for sufficient divine reasons. That point by itself would be decisive" (p. 59; italics mine).

Before turning to consider Alston's appeal to goods beyond our ken as the real source for God's sufficient reason for Bambi and Sue, I want to enter a slight protest in the "who has to show what" category. The critic claims to be *justified in believing* that there is no sufficient divine reason to permit Bambi and Sue. Alston explicitly accepts the task of *establishing* that the critic is *not justified in believing* that there is no sufficient divine reason to permit Bambi and Sue. Fair enough. But in the remark quoted just above, we are told that the critic is now faced with the task of *proving* (showing) that she is justified in believing that there are no sufficient divine reasons for Bambi and Sue. As things started out, Alston was going to prove that the critic is not and cannot be justified in believing that there are no sufficient divine reasons for Bambi and Sue. Now we are told that the burden is on the critic to prove that she is justified in so believing. Isn't it enough for it to be true that the critic is justified in this belief? Why is the burden now placed on the critic to provide justification for being justified in believing that there are no sufficient divine reasons for Bambi and Sue? Surely Alston doesn't think that in order to be justified in believing p,

---

occur in our world. Much of what Alston argues on this score strikes me as important and correct.

one must prove that she is justified in believing p.[15] So I think we can safely put to one side the point that the critic must *show* that she is justified in believing that Bambi and Sue are gratuitous. Instead, let us concentrate on Alston's argument to establish that the critic is not justified in believing that Bambi and Sue are gratuitous because she cannot be justified in ruling out the securing of certain goods *beyond our ken* as constituting God's sufficient reason for permitting Bambi and Sue.

Alston gives both a positive and a negative argument on this matter. The positive argument is intended to establish that our present *knowledge about values* is insufficient to merit any judgment about what future goods might justify God in permitting Bambi and Sue. The negative argument is intended to refute an argument I have given for the conclusion that it is likely that no good state of affairs is such that an omnipotent, omniscient being's obtaining it would morally justify that being in permitting Bambi or Sue. Let's look first at Alston's attack on this argument.

I have endeavored to support the proposition

(Q)   No good state of affairs is such that an omnipotent, omniscient being's obtaining it would morally justify that being in permitting Bambi and Sue.

by giving as a reason for it the proposition

(P)   No good state of affairs we know of is such that an omnipotent, omniscient being's obtaining it would morally justify that being's permitting Bambi or Sue.[16]

Of course, as we've seen, Alston does not think I am justified in holding (P) to be true. But his point here is that even if we are fully justified in accepting (P), we are not justified in accepting (Q) on the basis of (P). In support of the inference, I have said that it is simply one more instance of our common practice of making inferences from the known to the unknown, that if we've observed many A's and found them all to be B's, we have some reason to believe that the A's we haven't observed will likely be B's as well. I went on to note that this reason is subject to defeat by having some reason to think that were some A's not B's, they would likely not be found among the A's we encounter or

---

[15] For proof of this, see his elegant essay, "Level Confusions in Epistemology," in his *Epistemic Justification: Essays in the Theory of Knowledge* (Ithaca: Cornell University Press, 1989), pp. 164–65.

[16] See "Evil and Theodicy," *Philosophical Topics* 12 (1988), 119–32.

know about.[17] But barring having some such defeater, I claimed that (P) gives us a reason to believe (Q).

Alston raises an important objection to taking (P) as a reason in support of (Q). His point is that the *epistemic worth* of any such inference depends on our having some background knowledge that the characteristic in question (being such that obtaining it would not justify an omnipotent, omniscient being in permitting Bambi or Sue) "can reasonably be expected to be present in all or most goods if it is found in a considerable sample" (p. 46). Sometimes we do have such background knowledge. We know, for example, that *being a good watchdog* is a characteristic that can be expected to be present in all or most dogs of a given breed if it is found in a considerable sample of that breed. Sometimes we have the opposite background knowledge. If we observe a considerable sample of a given breed of dog and note that each dog in the sample has the characteristic of *being female,* we know that this characteristic can reasonably be expected *not* to be found in all or a very large percentage of the breed. The inference of (Q) from (P) is, Alston contends, like neither of these. We simply have no background knowledge to go on here. So he concludes that we cannot be justified in holding (Q) by virtue of inferring it from our justified belief in (P).

This is, as I've said, an important objection to the argument I've given in support of the inference from (P) to (Q). Although I continue to hold that (P) is a good reason for (Q) both in the sense of (a) making (Q) more likely than it otherwise would be and in the sense of (b) making (Q) more probable than not, I now recognize that the argument I gave, and which Alston criticizes, is sufficient to establish *only* that (P) is a good reason for (Q) in the sense of (a) making (Q) more likely than it would otherwise be. The fact that one has observed many A's and have found all of them to be B's does make the proposition that all A's are B's more likely than it would otherwise be. (Alston would not deny this.) But one proposition may make another proposition more likely than it would otherwise be without making it *more probable than not.* And it is the latter, and not just the former, that must be true if one is to be justified in believing (Q) by virtue of inferring it from (P). So the argument I have used to support the inference from (P) to (Q) is inadequate for something like the reason Alston gives. To shore it up we would need some reason to believe that the goods we know of (the A's we've observed) are representative of the goods there are (the A's there are). Noting the variety of goods we know of would be relevant to the task of providing such a reason. Having a good argument to

---

[17] See ibid., p. 124.

think that most goods are known to us would also be relevant.[18] But quite apart from trying to shore up the argument I gave in support of the inference from (P) to (Q), I believe a different, more effective argument can be given to show that (P) is a good reason for (Q) in sense (b), as well as sense (a). But I don't have space here to spell out that argument.[19]

Alston's positive argument for why we aren't justified in believing that no *good beyond our ken* is such that obtaining it would morally justify an omnipotent, omniscient being in permitting Bambi or Sue rests on the idea that our knowledge of values and the conditions of their realization is analogous to our knowledge of physical science.

The development of physical science has made us aware of a myriad of things hitherto undreamed of, and developed the concepts with which to grasp them—gravitation, electricity, electro-magnetic fields, space-time curvature, irrational numbers, and so on. It is an irresistible induction from this that we have not reached the final term of this process, and that more realities, aspects, properties, structures remain to be discerned and conceptualized. And why should values, and the conditions of their realization, be any exception to this generalization? A history of the apprehension of values could undoubtedly be written, parallel to the history just adumbrated, though the archeology would be a more difficult and delicate task. (p. 45)

Later in his essay, Alston again stresses what he takes to be an analogy between scientific knowledge and our knowledge of values.

Why should we suppose that the theodicies thus far excogitated, however brilliant and learned their authors, exhaust the field. The points made in the earlier discussion about the impossibility of anticipating future developments in human thought can be applied here. Just as we can never repose confidence in any alleged limits of future human theoretical and conceptual developments in science, so it is here, even more so if possible. It is surely reasonable to suppose that God, if such there be, has more tricks up His sleeve than we can envisage. (pp. 58–59)

[18] Michael Tooley has advanced such an argument in "The Argument from Evil," in Tomberlin, *Philosophical Perspectives, 5, Philosophy of Religion*, pp. 114–15.

[19] I present this argument in "The Evidential Argument from Evil: A Second Look," forthcoming in Daniel Howard-Snyder, ed., *The Evidential Argument from Evil* (Bloomington: Indiana University Press, 1996).

What are we to make of this argument? Is there a history of values to be written that would parallel the history of physical science? I really don't think so. The reason is that the development of physical science concerns empirical matters the determination of which depends greatly on technological advances. In the area of values, however, the question of whether a given state of affairs is *intrinsically good* is not an empirical matter at all. Indeed, that something is intrinsically good, evil, or neutral is a matter of necessity and to be discerned by the comprehending intellect. And so it is that many of the things that are intrinsically good were as clearly known by the ancients as by us. Of course, the knowledge of how to bring it about that certain intrinsic goods obtain is akin to scientific knowledge. But, strictly speaking, this is not a matter of knowledge of values at all. So as long as we are discussing intrinsic values and our knowledge of them, Alston's claim that the development of our knowledge of values parallels the development of our knowledge of physical science is implausible. Of course, we do have to allow that there are possible states of affairs that have great intrinsic value and are unknown to us. But, as Michael Tooley has pointed out, basic moral truths that we do know place limits on what intrinsic values could justify a perfectly good being to permit innocents to suffer. For example, according to Tooley, our moral truths about justice imply "that an omnipotent and omniscient person would be justified in allowing an innocent individual to suffer only if the individual in question benefitted from that suffering."[20] So, no matter how grand and glorious an unknown good might be, we know that God would not be justified in permitting Sue's suffering solely in order to obtain that good, if Sue were not to share in that good (or have the freedom to share in it). Moreover, when we take fully into account what an omnipotent, omniscient being would be able to bring into existence without permitting Bambi and Sue, it becomes doubtful, I believe, that intrinsic goods we do not know are any more likely to justify such a being in permitting Bambi or Sue than are the goods within our ken. Thus, the mere fact that God would know a lot more than we know doesn't seem a sufficient basis for holding, as Alston does, that it is *in principle impossible* for any human being to be justified in believing that there are any gratuitous evils.

Although I do not think Alston has succeeded in his principal aim of establishing that the inductive argument from evil is a failure, I

[20] Tooley, "Argument from Evil," p. 127. We should note that Tooley thinks this moral truth need not apply in the case of a being that is not omnipotent and omniscient (see pp. 112–13). Even with this emendation, some would object to his claim. Perhaps it may be strengthened by restricting it to cases of *involuntary* suffering by innocent persons.

William Alston on the Problem of Evil

cannot deny that he has raised significant doubts about the argument that I have not laid to rest.[21] I believe that the points he has brought up in this important, thoughtful essay will be discussed for some time to come.[22]

[21] In particular, as I noted earlier, he has shown that the reason I gave in support of the inference from (P) to (Q) is inadequate.

[22] I am grateful to Martin Curd, Paul Draper, William Hasker, David O'Connor, Daniel Howard-Snyder, Jeff Jordan, Bruce Russell, and Eleonore Stump for helpful comments on an earlier draft of this essay. I am also indebted to William Alston for his incisive comments on the penultimate draft.

[4]

God's Knowledge and
Its Causal Efficacy

ELEONORE STUMP AND NORMAN KRETZMANN

Problems

Most people agree that any being that could count as God would have to know everything there is to know. But *how* is God supposed to know what he knows? Obviously, not by beginning with sensations, the way human beings generally do, since, as perhaps even more people agree, God isn't corporeal and so can't have sensations. Conceivably, material objects might make some other sort of cognitively effective causal impression on an incorporeal God, but it's not easy to imagine what that might be. Besides, any account of such an impression would face the apparently insuperable obstacle of the absolute impassibility that is often included among standard divine attributes. Still, if a person's moving her hand from here to there can't causally affect the mind of God, how does he know that she is moving her hand? 'He just does!' has some appeal as a response on behalf of an omnipotent being, but it's no answer.

Thomas Aquinas worked hard at providing answers to questions about how God knows, but the explanation he developed seems to add to the difficulties. Not only is his account of God's knowledge perplexing in its own right; it also seems inconsistent with positions Aquinas takes elsewhere regarding the nature of God and human free will.

A representative exposition of Aquinas's account of God's knowledge can be found in a recent book by Leo Elders, *The Philosophical Theology of St. Thomas Aquinas.*[1] Elders says that according to Aquinas, God

---

[1] Leo Elders, *The Philosophical Theology of St. Thomas Aquinas*, Studien und Texte zur Geistesgeschichte des Mittelalters (New York: E. J. Brill, 1990).

knows "all things which exist at any time, whether past, present or future. . . . [He] knows whatever will come to be in the succession of time.[2] But "God's knowledge of things other than himself can only be based on his causality. He knows things because he is their cause and he knows them in and through his causality."[3] And in discussing Aquinas's views of God's causality, Elders claims, "It is manifest that God causes things by his intellect. . . . [Of course,] an intelligible form alone is not a principle of action unless there is an inclination to produce this effect. Hence God's intellect must be determined to precisely this effect by his will."[4]

One problem with this familiar exposition is that it apparently commits Aquinas to a determinism that leaves no room for human free will. According to Elders, Aquinas maintains that God knows everything that occurs in time, but his knowing is "in and through" his causing the things and events he knows, and his causing is a function of his will. As Elders describes it, then, Aquinas's position is that the basis for God's knowing everything that happens is that he wills it and thereby causes it to happen. But all human actions, sinful as well as virtuous, are among the events that "come to be in the succession of time." And so Elders's traditional interpretation attributes to Aquinas a position that is not only contrary to what most medieval Christians believed but also explicitly inconsistent with much that Aquinas himself says about the freedom of the human will and God's relation to sin.[5]

Furthermore, this familiar exposition of Aquinas has some odd epistemological implications. Strictly speaking, human beings can't know a contingent thing or state of affairs unless it first exists or obtains, but, on Aquinas's account as Elders expounds it, for God the converse is the case: strictly speaking, no thing can exist, no state of affairs can obtain, unless God first knows it. Where God is concerned, knowledge is supposed to be logically prior to and causally efficacious of the reality of what is known.

The sort of Thomistic interpretation represented in Elders's exposition draws its main support from a claim Aquinas makes repeatedly. In *Summa theologiae*, for example, Aquinas asks whether God's knowledge is the cause of things, and his answer is a resounding affirmative: "It must be said that God's knowledge is the cause of things. For God's knowledge is related to all created things as a craftsman's knowledge

---

[2] Ibid., p. 234.
[3] Ibid., p. 230.
[4] Ibid., p. 234.
[5] Notice that this epistemic determinism is *causal* and therefore not to be confused with the much-discussed incompatibility of divine foreknowledge and human freedom.

is related to the things he crafts, but a craftsman's knowledge is the cause of the things he crafts.[6] In *Summa contra gentiles*, too, Aquinas maintains that "God knows things other than himself insofar as he is the cause of them,"[7] and in arguing for this claim he says that "one has adequate cognition of an effect through the cognition of its cause. . . . But God himself is, through his essence, the cause of being for other things. And so, since he has the fullest possible cognition of his essence, we must hold that he has cognition of other things as well."[8]

This last passage hints at a further difficulty in Aquinas's account of God's knowledge. For Aquinas, all cognition requires an assimilation between the cognizer and what is cognized,[9] and for there to be such an assimilation there must be in the cognizer a likeness or form of the thing being cognized. And so Aquinas says that "everything that is understood is understood through some likeness *(similtudo)* of it in the one who understands"; and "cognizers are distinguished from noncognizing things in this respect, that noncognizing things have only their own form, but a cognizer is naturally suited to have a form of something else as well, for a form *(species)* of what is cognized is in the cognizer."[10] Human beings acquire the forms necessary for cognition from extramental reality. So, in a person who is cognizing a cup, who understands that the thing she sees is a cup, the epistemically requisite form of *cup* has its immediately operative stimulus in that cup itself, present before her and causally affecting her vision. Or when a person smells bread baking or hears a car crash outside her window or feels an insect running across her arm, she normally has those cognitions because something in extramental reality is causally affecting her senses and providing her intellect with raw material from which it abstracts the requisite recognizable forms.

---

[6] *Summa theologiae* (ST) Ia.14.8c: "dicendum quod scientia Dei est causa rerum. Sic enim scientia Dei se habet ad omnes res creatas, sicut scientia artificis se habet ad artificiata. Scientia autem artificis est causa artificiatorum."

[7] *Summa contra gentiles* (SCG) I. 65.530: "Deus cognoscit alia inquantum est causa eis."

[8] SCG I.49.412: "Effectus enim cognitio sufficienter habetur per cognitionem suae causae: . . . Ipse autem Deus est per suam essentiam causa essendi aliis. Cum igitur suam essentiam plenissime cognoscat, oportet ponere quod etiam alia cognoscat."

[9] See, e.g., SCG I.63.521: "omnis cognitio per quandam assimilationem fiat"; and *Quaestiones disputatae de veritate* (QDV) 10.4, obj. 5: "omnis cognitio est per assimilationem."

[10] ST Ia.55.2, obj. 1: "Omne enim quod intelligitur, per aliquam sui similitudinem in intelligente intelligitur"; ST Ia.14.1c: "considerandum est quod cognoscentia a non cognoscentibus in hoc distinguuntur, quia non cognoscentia nihil habent nisi formam suam tantum; sed cognoscens natum est habere formam etiam rei alterius, nam species est in cognoscente." 'Understand' is a standard translation of *'intelligere'*, but it can be misleading. As Aquinas uses *'intelligere'*, even a case of your recognizing that something you see is a tree counts as understanding (that is a tree).

It's different for God. Divine cognition does require an intelligible form, but in God's cognition of something other than himself the requisite intelligible form is *not* drawn from the thing cognized. Instead, the form through which God cognizes any and all created things is just his own nature, so that it seems that God cognizes creatures solely in virtue of cognizing himself. "There are two ways in which something is cognized: one, in itself; the other, in something else. . . . [A thing is cognized] in something else, . . . for example, when a man is seen in a mirror through a form belonging to the mirror. . . . Now [God] sees things other than himself not in themselves but in himself, insofar as his essence contains a likeness of things other than himself."[11] So God, unlike human cognizers, does not acquire an intelligible form of a cognized created thing from the thing cognized. Rather, he has cognition of himself and of all things other than himself through just one intelligible form, which is his own nature: "The only intelligible form by which the divine intellect has intellective cognition is God's own essence."[12]

Furthermore, the single intelligible form through which God knows is an all-encompassing, perfectly universal form. "To the extent to which an intellect is higher," Aquinas says, "it can with a single [form] cognize several things, to which a lower intellect can attain only through many [forms]."[13] Therefore, for God's intellect, the greatest possible, there is just one perfectly universal intelligible form.

Finally, this feature of Aquinas's account raises an especially difficult form of the criticism commonly leveled against dualism: how could an immaterial mind interact with matter?[14] The question has special force against Aquinas because even in his discussions of human cognition he emphatically denies that the immaterial human intellect can know material things directly. What the immaterial intellect can know directly

---

[11] ST. Ia. 14.5c: "considerandum est quod dupliciter aliquid cognoscitur: uno modo, in seipso; alio modo, in altero. In seipso quidem cognoscitur aliquid, quando cognoscitur per speciem propriam adaequatam ipsi cognoscibili: sicut cum oculus videt hominem per speciem hominis. In alio autem videtur id quod videtur per speciem continentis: sicut cum pars videtur in toto per speciem totius, vel cum homo videtur in speculo per speciem speculi, vel quocumque alio modo contingat aliquid in alio videri. . . . Alia autem a se videt non in ipsis, sed in seipso, inquantum essentia sua continet similitudinem aliorum ab ipso."

[12] SCG I.46.389: "intellectus divinus nulla alia speci intelligibili intelligat quam sua essentia."

[13] SCG I.31.281: "Intellectus etiam, quanto fuerit altior, tanto aliquo uno plura cognoscere potest, ad quae cognoscenda intellectus inferior non pertingit nisi per multa." See also, e.g., QDV 8.10 and ST Ia.55.3.

[14] For a brief but representative instance of this complaint, see Daniel Dennett, *Consciousness Explained* (Boston: Little, Brown, 1991), pp. 33–37.

is only immaterial universals abstracted from the particular material things that instantiate them. The human intellect does know material things, he thinks, but only in virtue of attending to the "phantasms," likenesses acquired through corporeal external senses and processed by corporeal internal senses but accessible to incorporeal intellect.[15] Extrapolating from this feature of his account of human cognition, one can see how an entirely immaterial God might know universals or natures. But it offers no apparent help for seeing how God could know material particulars themselves, since, among other considerations, there are no divine corporeal senses through which the divine intellect could be put in touch with particulars.

On the one hand, then, his account of God's knowledge appears to commit Aquinas to a causal form of epistemic determinism, in which God's knowing anything other than himself is his causing it to exist or occur. And, on the other hand, it seems that Aquinas's account is a species of Averroism, in which God can know his own nature and all universals or creaturely natures but cannot know individuals—or at least not material individuals, such as human beings. Epistemic determinism and an Averroistic account of God's knowledge present problems of their own, and each of them is contrary to Aquinas's explicit, characteristic positions on human freedom and God's knowledge of particulars. Worse yet, epistemic determinism and Averroism are apparently incompatible with each other.

Sed contra

We are convinced that this picture of Aquinas, drawn from the traditional interpretation of his account of God's knowledge, is distorted. We can't solve all the problems his account raises, but we can show that it involves neither epistemic determinism nor Averroism, and that it does not conflict with considerations of impassibility. In the process, we touch on some generally perplexing features of human cognition.

There are reasons for being immediately skeptical about any interpretation of Aquinas's account that makes it look Averroistic—most obviously because Aquinas in expressly opposing Averroism claims, of course, that God does know material individuals. What's more, he insists, God knows them with "*proper* cognition." That is, God knows material individuals *as* individuals, and not just the natures they instantiate or the species they belong to. In summing up his argument to this effect in *Summa theologiae*, Aquinas says, "Consequently, we must

[15] See, e.g., ST Ia.85.1 and 86.1, and *In Aristotelis librum De anima commentarium* (In DA), III.12 and 13.

say that God cognizes things other than himself with proper cognition: not only insofar as they share in the nature of being but insofar as each one is distinguished from another."[16] Again, "God's knowledge must extend all the way to particular things that are individuated by matter."[17] Aquinas thinks that material individuals must be among the objects of God's knowledge because he takes God to be the creator of material individuals initially and to exercise direct providential governance over all of them always,[18] and how could God create or directly govern embodied individuals if he couldn't know them individually?

So either Aquinas's account of God's knowledge does not entail Averroism, or it is incompatible with other claims Aquinas makes about God.

There are also obvious reasons for distrusting an exposition that has Aquinas holding, as Elders says, that "God's knowledge is a *causal* knowledge so that God knows things because he makes them."[19] Aquinas does associate God's knowing with his creating, but he himself can hardly have construed that association as making God's knowledge always and only causative. He argues, for example, that although God knows human evil, he does not cause it.[20] Evil, then, must be known by God even though not with a "*causal* knowledge."

Furthermore, God is supposed to know all nonactual possible things. As Aquinas puts it, God knows all the things that never were, or are, or will be, but that nonetheless could be.[21] And yet, of course, it can't be "because he makes them" that God knows such things, since by definition those are the very things God chooses not to make.[22]

Finally, and most important, Aquinas holds that God knows future contingents but that the way he knows them is essentially dependent on his eternality, his atemporal mode of existence, because of which they are not future with respect to him. Elders, whose interpretation here, too, is typical of recent discussions, offers this explanation. Future

---

[16] ST Ia.14.6c: "Oportet igitur dicere quod alia a se cognoscat propria cognitione; non solum secundum quod communicant in ratione entis, sed secundum quod unum ab alio distinguitur." See also, e.g., SCG I.65; QDV 2.5; *Quaestiones disputatae de potentia* (QDP) 6.1; and *Scriptum super Sententiis magistri Petri Lombardi* (In Sent) I.36.1.1.

[17] ST Ia.14.11c: "necesse est quod scientia Dei usque ad singularia se extendat, quae per materiam individuantur."

[18] See, e.g., SCG III.76.

[19] Elders, *Theology of Aquinas*, p. 238.

[20] See, e.g., QDV 2.15.

[21] See, e.g., SCG I.66.

[22] Someone might object that although God obviously does not make things that are never actual, he might nonetheless have created the possibilities they represent. Some scholars take Descartes to have held such a position, for example. It is not a position Aquinas would accept, however, since he does not suppose that modality is created by God.

contingents, he says, "can be considered . . . in their causes; [but] since these are not determined to one effect, they cannot give certitudinal knowledge."[23] Instead, Elders argues, in order for God to know contingent states of affairs that are future with respect to us, they must be really present to God in eternity: "Without their being present, God cannot know them with certitude."[24] And the reason Elders gives for this claim is that God "knows these things as they exist in reality. There is no science [i.e., full-fledged, "certitudinal" knowledge] without existing things as its object."[25] But if God knows things only insofar as he causes them, then to hold that a consideration of future contingent things in their *causes* is insufficient to provide God's sort of knowledge of them is tantamount to saying that God *cannot* have knowledge of future contingents. Furthermore, as we've already pointed out, if divine knowledge is always causative, God's knowledge of anything other than himself is logically prior to and causative of the existence of its object. By Elders's own lights, then, it must count as a mistake to say, as he does, that "without their being present, God cannot know them with certitude." Rather, on his view, without God's first knowing them, future contingent things and events cannot be at all.

So, if God's all-encompassing knowledge is always and only causative, then not only is God's consideration of future contingents in their causes *sufficient* for his knowledge of them, but, in fact, knowledge of them in their causes (or in their primary, divine cause) is the *only* way God can know them. In that case invoking the doctrine of divine eternity to explain the atemporal presence of temporal objects to God's cognition would be simply irrelevant to an explanation of God's knowledge of future contingents: in order to have knowledge of them, God wouldn't need the presence of things that are future with respect to us. But Aquinas certainly does hold that divine knowledge of future contingents must be explained in terms of their atemporal presence to God as objects of his cognition.[26] In Aquinas's view, then, God's knowledge of future contingents is *not* just a function of his causing them.

It should now be clear that either Aquinas's account of God's knowledge is inconsistent or he does not present it as exclusively causative.

The Analogy of Angelic Cognition

In constructing what we believe to be a more accurate presentation of Aquinas's account of God's knowledge, we found it helpful to work

[23] Elders, *Theology of Aquinas*, p. 237.
[24] Ibid., p. 239.
[25] Ibid., p. 238.
[26] See, e.g., ST Ia.14.13.

through his theory of angelic cognition. Since Aquinas takes angels to be purely spiritual and superhuman but nonomniscient beings, and since his understanding of all superhuman cognition is to a considerable extent extrapolated from his understanding of human cognition, his treatment of angelic cognition provides an intermediate account that illuminates what he has to say about divine cognition.

In the first place, angels, like all other intellective beings, have cognition through intelligible forms; but they are supposed to be like God and unlike human beings in cognizing through forms that are *not* taken from objects of cognition. "The lower intellective substances, human souls, have intellective power that is not complete by nature but is completed in them successively, in virtue of the fact that they get intelligible forms from things. But intellective power in higher spiritual substances—in angels, that is—is complete by nature through intelligible forms, insofar as they have, along with their natures, intelligible forms for understanding all the things they can by nature cognize."[27] "An angel doesn't cognize individuals through an acquired form at all, because it doesn't cognize [anything] through a form it gets from a thing; for in that case things would act on its intellect, which is impossible. Nor does it cognize [an individual] through some form newly infused by God, newly revealing something to the angel. For the forms the angel has in it, which were created along with it, are sufficient [for it] to cognize everything cognizable [by it]."[28] So, unlike a human being, who normally has cognition of a cup in front of her through an intelligible form of *cup* that she acquires in consequence of having been causally affected by a cup, an angel is supposed to cognize whatever it cognizes through intelligible forms provided at its creation along with its nature—its concreated, or innate, intelligible forms. Like God, then, an angel is said to cognize anything other than itself solely through an aspect of itself.

Second, like God and unlike human beings, angels are absolutely immaterial knowers. For that reason, angelic cognition, like divine cog-

---

[27] ST Ia.55.2c: "inferiores substantiae intellectivae, scilicet animae humanae, habent potentiam intellectivam non completam naturaliter; sed completur in eis successive, per hoc quod accipiunt species intelligibiles a rebus. Potentia vero intellectiva in substantiis spiritualibus superioribus, idest in angelis, naturaliter completa est per species intelligibiles, inquantum habent species intelligibiles connaturales ad omnia intelligenda quae naturaliter cognoscere possunt." See also ST Ia.54.4, ad 1; and QDV 8.9.

[28] *Quaestiones quodlibetales* (QQ) 7.1.3, ad 1: "dicendum quod angelus nullo modo cognoscit singularia per speciem acquisitam: quia nec per speciem acceptam a re, sic enim res agerent in intellectum eius, quod est impossibile; neque per aliquam speciem de novo influxam a Deo revelante ipsi angelo aliquid de novo, quia species quas angelus habet apud se concreatas, sufficiunt ad omnia cognoscibilia cognoscenda."

nition, is entirely intellective, surpassing human intellective cognition in the degree of universality and the consequently elegant fewness of the intelligible forms it needs in order to cognize things. "God understands all things through his one essence. But the higher intellective substances, although they do understand through more than one form, [in comparison with lower intellective substances] they understand through fewer and more universal forms, more powerful for comprehending things, because of the efficacy of the intellective power that is in them. In the lower [intellective substances], however, there are more forms, which are less universal and less efficacious for comprehending things, to the extent to which [these lower substances] fall short of the intellective power of the higher ones."[29] And so Aquinas says that "an angelic mind's cognition is more universal than a human mind's cognition, because it extends to more things using fewer means."[30]

So far, then, it looks as if some of the problems in Aquinas's account of divine cognition affect his account of angelic cognition as well. Since angels are absolutely immaterial cognizers, without corporeal senses, it is, again, hard to see how they could cognize embodied individuals as such. And, as we've just seen, Aquinas does emphasize the universality of their knowledge. Consequently, a kind of Averroism seems to threaten his theory of angelic knowledge, too.

Furthermore, angels are supposed to know things other than themselves through intelligible forms built into their natures, not through forms acquired from such things. So, like God, angels seem, mysteriously, to cognize things other than themselves solely by way of a kind of introspection. But how could beings whose cognition depends on innate intelligible forms know material particulars at all unless the existence and behavior of those particulars were predetermined?

Despite these similarities between angelic cognition and divine cognition, Aquinas of course denies that angels know what they know in virtue of knowing what they will, or that angelic cognition is causative at all.[31] So although an intelligible form in an angelic intellect functions as a means of cognition (as does a form in a human intellect or, in

[29] ST Ia.89.1c: "Deus per unam suam essentiam omnia intelligit; superiores autem intellectualium substantiarum, etsi per plures formas intelligant, tamen intelligunt per pauciores, et magis universales, et virtuosiores ad comprehensionem rerum, propter efficaciam virtutis intellectivae quae est in eis; in inferioribus autem sunt formae plures, et minus universales, et minus efficaces ad comprehensionem rerum, inquantum deficiunt a virtute intellectiva superiorum." See also ST Ia.55.3.

[30] QDV 10.5, ad 6: "cognitio mentis angelicae est universalior quam cognitio mentis humanae, quia ad plura se extendit paucioribus mediis utens."

[31] See, e.g., QDV 10.4: "Et similiter formae intellectus angelici, . . . sunt similes formis mentis divinae, quamvis non sint causa rerum."

God's case, the divine essence itself), angelic intelligible forms do not cause the things angels cognize and are not drawn from them either.

Aquinas is equally explicit in his denial of any sort of Averroism with regard to angelic cognition. Angels, he reasons, must know singular, embodied things: "no one can guard something he isn't cognizant of. But angels guard individual human beings. . . . And therefore angels cognize individuals."[32]

But if it is a mistake to interpret Aquinas's view of angelic cognition as entailing causal determinism or Averroism, then the formal similarities between his accounts of angelic and divine cognition provide the beginning of a basis for supposing that it may also be a mistake to see either of those difficulties as entailed by his views of God's knowledge. If we can see how angelic cognition is supposed to work without running into causal determinism or Averroism, we may also gain some insight into the proper interpretation of Aquinas's account of God's knowledge.

In approaching problems of divine cognition via a consideration of Aquinas's account of angelic cognition, the following three questions are perhaps the most useful. (1) How could an angel cognize individuals, given that it cognizes only universally? And (2) how could an angel cognize individuals other than itself without acquiring forms from them? Finally, (3) how could intelligible forms built into an angel's nature at its creation enable it to cognize individuals other than itself unless the existence and behavior of those individuals were predetermined? Considering these questions will put us on the right track for interpreting Aquinas's account of God's cognition.[33]

Cognizing Universally

To see how the first question should be answered, it's essential to be clear about what Aquinas means by cognizing universally. In discussing

[32] ST Ia.57.2, s.c.: "nullus potest custodire quod non cognoscit. Sed angeli custodiant homines singulares. . . . Ergo angeli cognoscunt singularia."

[33] Another helpful analogue to God's knowledge is the knowledge the separated human soul is supposed to have after death but before the resurrection of the body. The separated soul also knows embodied individuals although it lacks corporeal senses; and Aquinas holds that after death it can cognize, as angels do, through forms that are *not* acquired from the cognized things. (See, e.g., ST Ia.89.1.3 and 4; and QQ 3.9.1.) The discussion we're about to develop could, therefore, have been based on the separated soul's cognition rather than on angelic cognition. But special problems in Aquinas's discussion of the knowledge separated souls are supposed to have make it more appropriate in this connection to focus on his account of angelic cognition.

angelic cognition, Aquinas provides this explanation. "The expression 'cognizing something universally' is used in two ways. In one way, as regards the thing cognized, as [when] one cognizes *only* the universal nature of a thing. And in this way cognizing something universally is cognizing it more imperfectly, for a person who knew of a human being only that it is animal would cognize it imperfectly. In the other way, as regards the medium of cognizing. And cognizing something universally in this way is cognizing it more perfectly, for the intellect that can have proper cognition of individuals through one universal medium is more perfect than an intellect that cannot do so."[34] In other words, when Aquinas maintains that angels cognize universally, he does not mean that *what* they cognize is always a universal, as if angels were supposed to have only common natures as objects of their cognition. But what, exactly, is the other sense of 'cognizing universally', the sense in which he does mean to claim that angels cognize universally?

We get some help toward an answer when we recognize that he thinks that even the human intellect cognizes individuals universally in this other sense. In cognizing anything, the human intellect standardly and primarily apprehends the quiddity, or the *quod quid est* of the thing.[35] (By '*quod quid est*' here Aquinas means the kind to which something belongs, considered in an unanalyzed way—that is, in medieval terms, the species as distinct from the definition.[36]) Yet, Aquinas claims, the human intellect does cognize material particulars: "just as we could not sense the difference between sweet and white unless there were one common [internal] sensory power that had cognition of both, so, too, we could not cognize the relation of universal to particular unless there were one power that cognized them both." But, he goes on to say, the human intellect cognizes material individuals *through* their shared universal: "Intellect, therefore, has cognition of both [the universal and the individual], but in different ways. For it has cognition of the nature of the species, or of the *quod quid est*, by extending [to it] directly; it

[34] ST Ia.55.3, ad 2: "dicendum quod cognoscere aliquid in universali, dicitur dupliciter. Uno modo, ex parte rei cognitae, ut scilicet cognoscatur solum universalis natura rei. Et sic cognoscere aliquid in universali est imperfectius: imperfecte enim cognosceret hominem, qui cognosceret de eo solum quod est animal. Alio modo, ex parte medii cognoscendi. Et sic perfectius est cognoscere aliquid in univerali: perfectior enim est intellectus qui per unum universale medium potest singula propria cognoscere, quam qui non potest."

[35] See, e.g., ST Ia.57.1; 85.1 and 5; and In DA III.8. See also Norman Kretzmann, "Infallibility, Error, and Ignorance," in Richard Bosley and Martin Tweedale, eds., *Aristotle and His Medieval Interpreters* (*Canadian Journal of Philosophy*, supplementary volume 17 [1991]), pp. 159–94.

[36] See, e.g., in DA III.8.705, 706, 712, 713.

has cognition of the individual itself, however, by a kind of reflection, insofar as it turns back to the phantasms from which the intelligible forms are abstracted."[37] The intellect, in other words, uses an abstract intelligible form—the intellectively abstracted quiddity of a material particular—as the means by which to cognize the particular picked out by the phantasm. But when it does so, the intelligible form is only the medium through or by which the intellect knows the material particular, not *what* it knows: "the intelligible forms by which the possible intellect is actualized are not the intellect's object. For they are related to the intellect not as *what* is understood, but rather as *that by which* it understands."[38]

What Aquinas has in mind here may be elucidated by recent neurobiological work. As a result of neurological deficits brought about by injury or disease, certain patients manifest various kinds of agnosia. A patient who has a visual agnosia, for example, has normally functioning visual channels and is in possession of ordinary concepts but cannot use visual data for cognition just because he can't associate the data with the appropriate concepts in his possession. In Oliver Sacks's popular presentation of agnosia, a visual agnosia patient who had the concept *glove* and who could identify a glove as such if he could touch it was shown a glove by Sacks who held it up and asked him, "What is this?" "A continuous surface with five outpouchings," the patient promptly replied. When Sacks asked again, "Yes, but *what* is it?" the patient made an effort, using the unreliable method of inferring (as Aquinas would say) from a thing's accidents to its *quod quid est*, and guessed, "A coin dispenser?"[39] The patient could sense the material individual pre-

---

[37] In DA III.8.712–13: "Sicut enim supra dictum est, quia non possemus sentire differentiam dulcis et albi, nisi esset una potentia sensitiva communis quae cognosceret utrumque, ita etiam non possemus cognoscere comparationem universalis ad particulare, nisi essset una potentia quae cognosceret utrumque. Intellectus igitur utrumque cognoscit, sed alio et alio modo. Cognoscit enim naturam speciei, sive quod quid est, directe extendendo seipsum, ipsum autem singulare per quandam reflexionem, inquantum redit super phantasmata, a quibus species intelligibiles abstrahuntur." See also, e.g., ST Ia.86.1 and 85.1.

[38] In DA III.8.718: "Manifestum est etiam, quod species intelligibiles, quibus intellectus possibilis fit in actu, non sunt obiectum intellectus. Non enim se habent ad intellectum sicut quod intelligitur, sed sicut quo intelligit." See also ST Ia.85.2.

[39] Oliver Sacks, *The Man Who Mistook His Wife for a Hat* (New York: Summit Books, 1985), p. 13. For an excellent recent neurobiological study of agnosias, see Martha J. Farah, *Visual Agnosia* (Cambridge, Mass.: MIT Press, 1990). In *Principles of Neural Science* (Eric Kandel, James Schwartz, and Thomas Jessell; New York: Elsevier, 1991), agnosia is defined as "the inability to perceive objects through otherwise normally functioning sensory channels" (p. 831). Not all agnosias are visual. For example, astereognosia, which is caused by damage to the parietal cortex, is "an inability to recognize the form of objects by touch even though there is no pronounced loss of somatosensory sensitivity" (ibid).

sented to his sight but could not cognize it precisely because he could not get at the *quod quid est* of what he saw. Sacks, on the other hand, who does recognize a glove when he sees one, does not on that occasion have its *quod quid est* as the *object* of his cognition. Rather, as Aquinas would say, Sacks has cognition of this material individual, understands it to be a glove, *through* the appropriate universal intelligible form, by associating the visual data with the concept *glove*.[40]

So, cognizing universally in the relevant sense in which Aquinas thinks angels and humans cognize universally is cognizing a thing by means of a common nature under which it is subsumed. And the cognition of particulars requires cognizing universally in this way; even consciously seeing a cup involves recognizing under some description what one is being visually affected by. Cognition is more than sensation.

Aquinas also thinks that more powerful intellects are able to cognize particulars as subsumed under fewer, higher universals. A little boy may be able to cognize his mother's disposable coffee cup in virtue of being able to apply to it the universal *cup*. But (other things being equal) a chemist who knows the nature of Styrofoam, and a physicist who understands the basic constituents of matter, are equipped to have deeper, fuller cognitions of the same object. They, too, cognize through the universal *cup*, but that universal is subsumed under other universals, which are themselves subsumed under other universals, and so on until we come to the highest universal available to the cognizer in question—perhaps, in the case of the physicist, the nature of matter itself. Their cognition of the particular locates it within the grand scheme of things. This feature of cognition seems to be what Aquinas has in mind in reasoning that higher angels must know by subsuming things under fewer universals than lower angels do. "The higher the

---

[40] For the sake of brevity, we are glossing over many complications here, but two of them should be at least noted. In the first place, agnosia is a puzzling phenomenon. We introduce it here as an illuminating example, but if the example were pressed, it would raise more questions than it answers. For instance, one odd feature of agnosia is that the patient plainly *can* identify *some* genus to which the thing he sees belongs. To cognize a glove as a continuous surface is to cognize that particular universally, but the universal serving as the medium of cognition in that case is very abstract, nothing like the thing's proximate genus, let alone its species. Second, although we present our discussion here in terms of the *quod quid est* of whatever is being cognized, what is at issue in cognizing a particular universally cannot be only the genera and species to which the cognized thing belongs. For the medievals, universals consist not only in genera and species but also in the rest of the predicables, including differentiae, propria, and accidents. Therefore, in recognizing that the thing he sees has five outpouchings, the agnosia patient is also cognizing a particular through the medium of a universal. And so any conscious awareness of any shareable characteristic of any thing presented to the senses counts as cognizing that particular universally.

angel, the fewer the forms through which it can apprehend the whole realm of intelligible things. We can recognize a kind of instance of this among ourselves, for there are some people who cannot grasp an intelligible truth unless it is laid out for them in particulars, individual case by individual case. And this, of course, is a result of the weakness of their intellects. But there are others, whose intellects are stronger, who can grasp many things on the basis of a few."[41]

So, when we see both of Aquinas's senses of 'cognizing universally', it is clear how an intellect that is in epistemic contact with individuals cognizes them in virtue of cognizing universally.[42]

Cognizing through Concreated Intelligible Forms

This way of answering the first question about angelic cognition seems to make the second and third questions harder. How could an angel cognize other created things without acquiring intelligible forms from them? A human being cognizes a particular cup through the intelligible form *cup*, and human beings typically get their intelligible forms of cognized objects from the objects themselves.[43] How could

[41] ST Ia. 55.3c: "quanto angelus fuerit superior, tanto per pauciores species universitatem intelligibilium apprehendere poterit. Et ideo oportet quod eius formae sint universaliores, quasi ad plura se extendentes unaquaeque earum. Et de hoc exemplum aliqualiter in nobis perspici potest. Sunt enim quidam, qui veritatem intelligibilem capere non possunt, nisi eis particulatim per singula explicetur: et hoc quidem ex debilitate intellectus eorum contingit. Alii vero, qui sunt fortioris intellectus, ex paucis multa capere possunt."

[42] We understand epistemic contact as a component in perception or in divine analogues to perception. Though we don't have a set of necessary and sufficient conditions for it, we can say roughly what we mean by 'epistemic contact'. According to contemporary neurobiological theories of perception, after incoming sensory data have been processed at low levels, they are processed further by various other "modules" or "systems," including one that connects sensory data to conscious awareness and one that matches sensory data to information stored in associative memory. (For a clear, simple discussion of the connections between, for example, visual sensory data and associative memory, see Stephen Kosslyn and Oliver Koenig, *Wet Mind: The New Cognitive Neuroscience* [New York: Macmillan, 1992], pp. 52–58.) By 'epistemic contact' we mean the result of the central nervous system's processing of sensory data that does not include the matching of the data to information stored in associative memory. We take this description of epistemic contact to be roughly equivalent to the following description in Aquinas's terms: the apprehension of the accidents of some extramental thing without any apprehension of that thing's *quod quid est*.

[43] Since the prerequisite sensory experience in the case we're discussing would typically be experience of cups, it may seem that our representations have to be acquired from the things cognized in order for there to be cognition of things outside the mind. But, of course, by purely linguistic means we can be and sometime are equipped ahead of time with an intelligible form we need in order to recognize something the first time we

intelligible forms built into an angel's nature at its creation enable it to cognize individuals other than itself without acquiring forms from them? Aquinas puts the problem pointedly: "if through a form concreated along with it [an angel] could cognize some particular when it is present, then [the angel] would have cognized it from the beginning of [the angel's] own existence, while the cognized thing was still future. But that could not be, because cognizing future things belongs only to God."[44]

The solution here depends, first, on recognizing, as before, that in the cognition of a particular the intelligible form is not what is cognized but rather only the medium through which cognition takes place. "Intelligible forms are related to intellect as sensible forms are related to sense. But a sensible form isn't what is sensed; rather, it is that by which a sense senses. Consequently, an intelligible form isn't what is actually understood, but [only] that by which the intellect understands."[45] Except in atypical cases of introspectively attending to one's concepts themselves, then, the intelligible form of a particular is not the object of cognition but something like a representation of it by means of which the particular is cognized.[46]

---

encounter it. The acquisition of intelligible forms can be carried out conceptually; it need not depend on close encounters with the relevant objects.

[44] QQ 7.1.3: "si per speciem concreatam posset aliquod particulare cognosci dum est praesens, a principio creationis suae illud cognovisset quando adhuc erat futurum; quod non posset esse, quia futura cognoscere solius Dei est."

[45] ST Ia.85.2, s.c.: "species intelligibilis se habet ad intellectum, sicut species sensibilis ad sensum. Sed species sensibilis non est illud quod sentitur, sed magis id quo sensus sentit. Ergo species intelligibilis non est quod intelligitur actu, sed id quo intelligit intellectus." See also In DA III.8.

[46] In many passages, Aquinas is concerned to rule out the possibility that the intelligible form is itself the object of cognition in ordinary cases of cognition, in which people take themselves to be cognizing external particulars. In his recent book *Cognition: An Epistemological Inquiry* (Houston, Tex.: Center for Thomistic Studies, 1992), Joseph Owens is similarly concerned to show that the direct object of the intellect is not an intelligible form but some extramental object. He is so concerned to rule out the possibility of skepticism, however, that he goes to the other extreme and maintains that for Aquinas there is unmediated awareness of things in the world. Aquinas's position seems to stand somewhere between the position Owens ascribes to him and the position Aquinas himself is ruling out. Owens is right to hold that the object of ordinary intellective cognition is part of extramental reality and not some internal state of the intellect's. But, on the other hand, it takes a process on the part of the intellect to reach the state in which it has cognition of some extramental object, and that process is mediated by intelligible forms. Pace Owens, then, an intelligible form is, therefore, the medium between the cognizer and the thing cognized. The nature of Aquinas's position can be seen clearly, for example, in QQ 7.1.1: "sciendum est quod in visione intellectiva triplex medium contingit esse. . . . Aliud [that is, the second] medium est quo videt; et hoc est species intelligibilis, quae intellectum possibilem determinat, et habet se ad intellectum possibilem, sicut species lapidis ad oculum. . . . Primum ergo medium et secundum non faciunt mediatam

It's also helpful to recognize here that the direct, immediate cognition of things outside the mind involves, among other things, these three components. There is (a) being in epistemic contact with something, as when a human being with normal vision receives and initially processes visual data stemming from something present to her. Then there is also the higher processing of the visual input, which itself has two components: (b) possessing the representations, concepts, or intelligible forms through which what one is in contact with can be rendered intelligible, and (c) applying those appropriate representations to what one is in contact with. The agnosia patient is characterized by components (a) and (b) but is unable to achieve (c): he can't apply his appropriate concept *glove* to his visual input. He receives visual input from the glove, and he has the concept of a glove; but his agnosia prevents his having proper cognition of that particular glove because he is unable to apply his stored representation *glove* to the thing with which he is in visual epistemic contact.

The outlines of this analysis show up in Aquinas's explanation of angelic cognition. Angels can't have any new cognitions, an objector says, just because they have all their representations built into them at their creation. Aquinas replies that although angels don't acquire any new intelligible forms, they are capable of new cognitions because they can newly *apply* the intelligible forms naturally inherent in them to things that are newly present to them.[47]

So the intelligible forms, the media of angelic *or* human cognition, are something like conceptual lenses. The angelic or human intellect might be thought of as looking through them in order to cognize or render intelligible the things with which the cognizer is in epistemic contact. On this interpretation of Aquinas's notion of intelligible forms, it doesn't much matter whether the conceptual lenses are acquired through experience, human-fashion, or come as part of the cognizer's original equipment. It's easy to suppose that the media of cognition must be acquired from extramental things because it's easy to conflate the different components of the cognitive process and to think of the possession of intelligible forms as the sole means of simultaneously making epistemic contact and rendering intelligible the things with

---

visionem: immediate enim dicitur aliquis videre lapidem, quamvis eum per speciem eius in oculo receptam et per lumen videat: quia visus non fertur in haec media tamquam in visibilia, sed per haec media fertur in unum visibile, quod est extra oculum."

[47] QQ 7.1.3, obj. 3: "quamvis nihil recipiat, tamen formam quam apud se habebat prius, applicat ad particulare quod de novo fit"; ad 3: "applicatio illa est intelligenda per modum illum quo Deus ideas ad res cognoscendas applicat, non sicut medium cognoscibile ad aliud, sed sicut modus cognoscendi ad rem cognitam."

which the cognizer is in contact. But that these are distinct components is clearly indicated by the case of the agnosia patient. When he moves from a bizarre but acceptable general characterization to an incorrect specific characterization despite his possession of the appropriate representation *glove,* he shows that he is in command of only some of those components. Aquinas's account also requires distinguishing these three components, and his discussion of angelic cognition is most helpfully understood as concerned with only components (b) and (c).

So the claim that angels must cognize universally doesn't mean that universals are the only objects of angelic cognition. Instead, Aquinas's idea is that naturally inherent, universal intelligible forms are the media through which angels render intelligible particular objects with which they come into epistemic contact. And at least some of the perplexing features of his account of angelic cognition can be cleared up by recognizing that Aquinas is primarily concerned to explain the nature of angelic representations, rather than the way angels make epistemic contact with the particular objects of their cognition.

God's Cognition of Creatures

These clarifications of Aquinas's theory of angelic cognition help us understand his account of God's knowledge. Among the things perplexing about it are his claims that God cognizes things other than himself in himself, "insofar as his essence contains a likeness of things other than himself," and that God cognizes by means of just one, perfectly universal intelligible form.[48] Both these claims can now be seen as logical extensions of Aquinas's claims about angelic cognition.

Because Aquinas thinks of God as being itself, God's nature is for Aquinas the most universal form, through which all beings can be cognized. The grandest unified *metaphysical* Theory of Everything would explain all creatures not in terms of their fundamental particles and forces but in terms of their participation in subsistent being. So for God to cognize created things in himself, through his own nature, through the intelligible form *subsistent being,* is to cognize them as deeply and understand them as fully as possible.[49] Nothing in this line entails that *what* God knows is only universal, or that he knows only common natures and not particulars, any more than the physicist's

---

[48] See notes 8, 12, and 13.

[49] In putting the point this way, we are simplifying for the sake of brevity. Aquinas's account has an additional complexity we can't examine here. For some idea of the complexity, see QDV 2.3 and 4; also QQ 7.1.1.

deeper understanding of matter entails that he can't know ordinary material individuals like this cup.

Similarly, the claim that the only intelligible form for God is his own nature does not entail that God can't cognize individuals, because for present purposes that unique intelligible form is simply *the medium through which* he cognizes individuals: "God cognizes his effects through his essence in the same way as a thing itself is cognized through a likeness of the thing."[50] As the human intellect cognizes a corporeal individual such as this cup through an intelligible form *cup*, so God's essence serves as the intelligible form through which he cognizes each and every created individual. There is, however, this relevant difference between the human intellect and the divine mind. Except in relatively rare cases of introspection, for a human intellect an intelligible form is the medium through which the intellect cognizes and not *what* it cognizes. But God not only cognizes eternally through his essence; he also eternally cognizes his essence itself, since he knows himself primarily, and other things as well. And that's why Aquinas says that "God cognizes himself and other things in one cognition."[51]

So in the case of divine cognition, too, some of what is perplexing in Aquinas's account is cleared up if we take it as an account of the nature of God's representations and the way divine representation renders intelligible everything with which God is in epistemic contact, rather than as a theory about how God is in epistemic contact with creatures or how the one divine representation is applied to objects of God's cognition.

Intellective Cognition of Material Particulars

There is, of course, still a problem about how Aquinas thinks an immaterial cognizer—God, or an angel, or the human intellect—can cognize *material* particulars, since in discussing human intellects he insists that only the sensory soul can cognize material objects as such, through the bodily senses. But on Aquinas's view is there any difficulty in an immaterial intellect's cognizing a material object? And why should he think that direct human cognition of material particulars can be had only by the senses?

In the introduction to this essay, when we were pointing out difficult-

---

[50] QDV 2.3: "Hoc modo autem Deus per essentiam suam effectus suos cognoscit, sicut per similitudinem rei cognoscitur res ipsa." See also notes 8 and 13 above.

[51] QDV 2.3: "una cognitione se et alia cognoscit."

ies for any account of divine cognition, we remarked that philosophers who raise objections to dualism standardly see a problem in an immaterial knower's knowing a material object, because they suppose that knowledge requires the one thing known to act causally on the knower, and they cannot imagine how an immaterial knower could be affected by the causal action of a material thing. But Aquinas wouldn't see the problem in quite those terms, because he would agree that the intellective cognition of a material particular cannot be explained in terms of the immaterial mind's being directly affected by the causal action of the material object.

He does suppose that a material object of cognition exercises efficient causation in the cognitive process, but only to the point in the process at which he locates the phantasms, the processed deliverances of the senses.[52] At that point, the direction of efficient causation is reversed. The phantasms do not act on the intellect to produce abstract likenesses of themselves.[53] Rather, in order for the intellect to cognize anything, it must abstract an intelligible form from phantasms.[54] So where intellect becomes active in the cognitive process, at the threshold of intellective cognition, the only causal relationship running *from* the direction of the material object is the *formal* causation through which its form persists in the abstraction produced when the intellect strips away the individuating characteristics retained in the phantasm.[55]

[52] ST Ia.84.6c: "Sed quia phantasmata non sufficiunt immutare intellectum possibilem, sed oportet quod fiant intelligibilia actu per intellectum agentem; non potest dici quod sensibilis cognitio sit totalis et perfecta causa intellectualis cognitionis, sed magis quodammodo est materia causae."

[53] See, e.g., In DA III.7.694: "Id enim cuius similitudo est species, in virtute aliqua cognoscitiva existens, non ex hoc fit cognoscens, sed cognitum. . . . Per hoc igitur quod species intelligibilis, quae est in intellectu possibili, est similtudo quaedam phantasmatum, non sequitur quod nos sumus intelligentes, sed quod nos, vel potius phantasmata nostra, sint intellecta ab illa substantia separata."

[54] See, e.g., ST Ia.85.1c: "necesse est dicere quod intellectus noster intelligit materialia abstrahendo a phantasmatibus"; also ad 1: "Et hoc est abstrahere universale a particulari, vel speciem intelligibilem a phantasmatibus, considerare scilicet naturam speciei absque consideratione individualium principiorum, quae per phantasmata repraesentantur."

[55] If Aquinas's view here seems odd, it might be reassuring to notice that a somewhat similar claim is made by modern neurobiology. A recent text, for example, reports that "the occipital lobe receives input from the eyes, and hence it processes visual information." The seen object acts on the eyes to produce "input," but that input is itself acted upon by the occipital lobe, which "processes" it. And, from a neurophysiological point of view, the efficient causation exercised by extramental things underdetermines cognition: "the same information is treated in different ways in different parts of the brain. . . . Thus, although the kind of information sent to a network restricts what it can do, the input alone does not determine what a network computes." Kosslyn and Koenig, *Wet Mind,* p. 33.

God's Knowledge and Its Causal Efficacy

At any rate, it seems unlikely that Aquinas is formulating the difficulty here simply as a problem regarding an immaterial intellect's being causally acted on by a material object.[56] Instead, we think, the problem for Aquinas can be formulated in this way. In the first place, the issue as he sees it has to do not with matter in a twentieth-century sense— every instance of which he would characterize as a composite of matter and form—but rather with matter apart from any forms, including those that constitute subatomic particles. And, second, it arises in consequence of Aquinas's theory about how human cognition works. Cognition requires that a form or likeness of what is cognized be in the cognizer, and cognition on the part of the immaterial human intellect requires that the forms of things it cognizes be abstracted from those things. But any form or likeness of any material object is distinct from the object's matter. So, in abstracting and acquiring an intelligible form of a material object, the intellect is coming into epistemic contact only with something nonmaterial. It is not directly connected with the matter of the cognized object.

The real problem here is not that an immaterial intellect can't be affected by the causal action of a material thing but that in the nature of the case the immaterial intellect can acquire only immaterial aspects of material particulars. Aquinas says that "every form as such is universal, and so the addition of a form to a form cannot be the cause of individuation [for corporeal individuals], because however many forms are gathered together at once, . . . they do not constitute a particular. . . . Rather, the individuation of a form depends on the matter through which the form is limited to this or that determinate [thing]."[57]

Another way of seeing the problem for human cognizers is to review the mode of human cognition. Human beings acquire the intelligible forms through which they have cognition from things they cognize. But formless matter is utterly inert because it is pure potentiality; it cannot act on anything. Consequently, matter considered just as such can't act on the mind so as to produce an intelligible form of itself. "Because of the weakness of its being, since it is being only in potentiality, matter [by itself, apart from form] cannot be a source of action.

---

[56] There is, of course, a parallel problem regarding the way an immaterial entity can causally affect a material entity. But this is unlikely to have seemed problematic to a traditional theist such as Aquinas, who believes that an immaterial God causally affects his creation.

[57] QQ 7.1.3: "Omnis autem forma de se communis est: unde additio formae ad formam non potest esse causa individuationis: quia quotcumque formae simul aggregentur, ut album, bicubitum, et crispum, et huiusmodi, non constituunt particulare, quia haec omnia simul sunt in uno, et ita in pluribus potentiis est possibile invenire; sed individuatio formae est ex materia, per quam forma contrahitur ad hoc determinatum."

And therefore a thing that acts on our soul acts only through form. And so the likeness of a thing imprinted on a sense and purified through several stages until it gets to the intellect is a likeness of a form only."[58] Therefore, the human intellect cannot directly cognize the individuating material component in the composites of matter and form that are ordinary corporeal individuals.

The problem is solved as regards human beings because their senses are corporeal and receive corporeal impressions of the material particulars being sensed. "A sense is a power of a corporeal organ. . . . Now anything whatever is received in something in keeping with the recipient's mode [of being]. . . . And, therefore, a sense has to receive corporeally and materially a likeness of the thing it senses."[59] Moreover, "the object of any sensory power is a form insofar as it is in corporeal matter. Because matter of this sort is the source of individuation, every power of the sensory part [of the soul] cognizes particulars only."[60] In other words, the senses, unlike the intellect, can be in contact with the matter of what is cognized—at least in this respect, that they are corporeally affected by the qualities of the things being sensed. By reflecting on, or "processing," the input that has its source in corporeal impressions on the corporeal senses, the immaterial intellect itself can cognize matter indirectly in turning to the phantasms. And so, Aquinas says, "the intellect cognizes both [universals and particulars], although not in the same way."[61]

But, of course, this way of resolving the problem as regards human intellective cognition is not available for divine or angelic cognition, since God and angels don't have corporeal senses. How, then, are they

[58] QDV 2.5: "materia autem, propter debilitatem sui esse, quia est ens in potentia tantum, non potest esse principium agendi; et ideo res quae agit in animam nostram, agit solum per formam. Unde similitudo rei quae imprimitur in sensum, et per quosdam gradus depurata, usque ad intellectum pertingit, est tantum similitudo formae." See also QDV 10.4: "In mente enim accipiente scientiam a rebus, formae existunt per quamdam actionem rerum in animam; omnis autem actio est per formam; unde formae quae sunt in mente nostra, primo et principaliter respiciunt res extra animam existentes quantum ad formas earum."

[59] In DA II.12.377: "sensus est virtus in organo corporali; intellectus vero est virtus immaterialis, quae non est actus alicuius organi corporalis. Unumquodque autem recipitur in aliquo per modum sui. Cognitio autem omnis fit per hoc, quod cognitum est aliquo modo in cognoscente, scilicet secundum similtudinem. Nam cognoscens in actu, est ipsum cognitum in actu. Oportet igitur quod sensus corporaliter et materialiter recipiat similtudinem rei quae sentitur."

[60] ST Ia.85.1c: "et ideo obiectum cuiuslibet sensitivae potentiae est forma prout in materia corporali existit. Et quia huiusmodi materia est individuationis principium, ideo omnis potentia sensitivae partis est cognoscitiva particularium tantum."

[61] See note 37 above.

supposed to cognize corporeal individuals—human beings, for instance? Or, to put the question more precisely, how do they cognize the individuating matter in the corporeal individuals they know?

The difficulty for human cognizers is that they receive from cognized things themselves the representations through which they cognize such things. But matter considered as such cannot act on the cognizer; anything that acts in any way acts through a form of some sort. So, since human cognizers have to acquire the representations through which they know, the best they can get is an *indirect* representation of the matter in the composites of form and matter they cognize.

God and angels, on the other hand, do not have to get intelligible forms from external things they cognize. Angels have their representations of things built into them at their creation by God, and God cognizes all the things he makes through the universal intelligible form that is his own nature. Now one of the things he makes is precisely matter itself. That is, God not only makes composites of matter and form, as any craftsman or inventor does, but also creates the formless matter that underlies the forms of any material object. It is this aspect of his creative activity that earns it the designation *ex nihilo*. As the "inventor" of matter, God cognizes it under the perfectly universal intelligible form that is his nature, and so of course he does not acquire his cognition from matter. Instead, he creates matter to instantiate the cognition of it he already has. And by means of this "inventor's" cognition of matter, God cognizes matter *itself,* as human knowers cannot do. "The being of things, which is common to [their] form and matter, flows from the forms of things in the divine mind, and so these forms are related immediately to both form and matter [in created things]. . . . And in this way our mind has immaterial cognition of material things, but the divine mind and an angelic mind cognize material things more immaterially and yet [also] more perfectly."[62]

So in this case, too, the difficulty raised by Aquinas's account is considerably diminished once we recognize that Aquinas is explaining just how it is that the objects with which God is in epistemic contact are intelligible to him, rather than how God is in epistemic contact with them.

The Causative Character of God's Knowledge

We are now in a position to consider the problems stemming from Aquinas's claim that God's knowledge is causative. Contemporary read-

---

[62] QDV 10.4: "Sed formae rerum in mente divina existentes sunt, ex quibus fluit esse rerum, quod est commune formae et materiae; unde formae illae respiciunt et formam et materiam immediate, et non unum per alterum. . . . Et sic mens nostra de rebus

ers of such a claim are likely to interpret it as meaning that God knows everything he knows in virtue of his causing it to be the case. As a result, it seems that this claim about God's knowledge commits Aquinas to causal epistemic determinism: our knowing that Brutus is one of Caesar's assassins depends on Brutus's action; God's knowing that Brutus is one of Caesar's assassins accounts for his action.

Three assumptions lie behind this interpretation of Aquinas's claim. The first is that God's act of cognition (with or without an accompanying act of will) brings about what God cognizes; the second is that the causation in question is efficient causation; and the third is that what gets caused is events or states of affairs. We think all three assumptions are false.

As we've seen, Aquinas identifies God's own nature as the intelligible form through which God cognizes everything. "God cognizes his own nature perfectly, and so he cognizes it in every way in which it can be cognized. But it can be cognized not only as it is in itself, but [also] insofar as it can be participated in by creatures in some mode of likeness."[63] When God's nature is considered as the intelligible form through which God knows other things, it is helpfully understood in terms of what Aquinas calls the divine ideas.[64] These ideas are forms or likenesses[65] representing ways in which God's nature might be imitated, and Aquinas says that they play a part in all of God's cognition of things other than himself.[66] The ideas do not put God into epistemic contact with creatures. Rather, Aquinas likes to say, they are analogous to the ideas a craftsman has; they are like the pattern the craftsman has in mind before he begins to make anything.[67] The divine ideas, then, are exemplars: any thing God creates has the form it has in imitation of the form that is the divine idea representative of that thing. It is for this reason and in this respect that the divine ideas constitute causes of the things created in accordance with them. But then they

---

materialibus immaterialem cognitionem habet; mens vero divina et angelica materialia immaterialius, et tamen perfectius, cognoscit." See also QDV 10.5; also 2.5 and 6.

[63] ST Ia.15.2c: "Ipse enim essentiam suam perfecte cognoscit: unde cognoscit eam secundum omnem modum quo cognoscibilis est. Potest autem cognosci non solum secundum quod in se est, sed secundum quod est participabilis secundum aliquem modum similitudinis a creaturis."

[64] ST Ia.15.1, ad 2. See also QDV 3.2: "Dico ergo, quod Deus per intellectum omnia operans, omnia ad similitudinem essentiae suae producit; unde essentia sua est idea rerum; non quidem ut essentia, sed ut est intellectus."

[65] See, e.g., QDV 3.1: "ideas latine possumus dicere species vel formas." See also QDV 3.3: "idea est ratio rei, vel similitudo."

[66] QDV 3.3 See also ST Ia.15.3,s.c.: "omnium quae cognoscit, Deus habet proprias rationes. Ergo omnium quae cognoscit, habet ideam."

[67] ST Ia.15.1.

are, of course, *formal* causes, not efficient causes: "A form is, in a certain respect, a cause of that which is formed in accordance with it, whether the forming takes place by way of the form's inhering, as in the case of intrinsic forms, or by way of imitation [of it], as in the case of exemplar forms."[68]

So when Aquinas says that God's knowledge is causative, he does not mean that God's act of cognition efficiently causes the events and states of affairs God knows. He means that the divine ideas are formal rather than efficient causes, and what they are causes of is not events or states of affairs in creation but rather just created things themselves. His favorite analogy to illustrate what he means by a divine idea is the pattern a builder has in mind as he begins to build a house.[69] That mental pattern of the house is the formal cause of the house; and it is the formal cause simply of the existence of that house, not of any particular contingent events associated with it, such as its deteriorating or burning down. Aquinas says that "in order for an individual thing to be cognized, the cognitive power must contain a likeness of it in its particularity. . . . Now the likeness of a cognized thing is in a cognizer in two ways. In one way, [it is in the cognizer] as caused by the thing, as in the case of those things that are cognized through a form abstracted from the things. In the other way, [it is the cognizer] as a cause of the thing [cognized], as is evident in the case of an artisan who cognizes an artifact through the form through which he makes it."[70]

In our view this understanding of Aquinas's claim that God's knowledge is causative rebuts the objection that his claim entails causal epistemic determinism.

Epistemic Contact

We have now dispelled the two main worries we originally raised about Aquinas's account of God's knowledge—namely, that it consti-

---

[68] QDV 3.3: "Est enim forma quodammodo causa eius quod secundum ipsam formatur; sive formatio fiat per modum inhaerentiae, sicut in formis intrinsecis, sive per modum imitationis, ut in formis exemplaribus." See also QDV 3.1: "Haec ergo videtur esse ratio ideae, quod idea sit forma quam aliquid imitatur ex intentione agentis, qui determinat sibi finem."

[69] See, e.g., ST Ia.15.2.

[70] QQ 7.1.3: "sciendum est, quod ad hoc quod singulare aliquod cogoscatur, oportet quod in potentia cognoscitiva sit similitudo eius, in quantum particulare est. . . . Similitudo autem rei cognitae dupliciter est in cognoscente: uno modo sicut causata a re, sicut in his quae cognoscuntur per speciem abstractam a rebus; alio modo sicut causa rei, ut patet in artifice, qui cognoscit artificiatum per illam formam per quam ipsum facit."

tutes a species of Averroism and that it entails determinism—but important problems remain. We began with a question about the way an omniscient God knows, and we've been expounding Aquinas's account of God's knowledge because it seems to offer a detailed, defensible answer to the question. But at least part of what that question seeks is an explanation of the way God might make epistemic contact with creatures, and nothing we have looked at in Aquinas's theory so far addresses that issue. His theory of God's knowledge is primarily an attempt to present a plausible explanation of the way the mind of God renders intelligible to itself everything with which it *is*, somehow, in epistemic contact. As such, it is the theological analogue to a neurobiological description of those processing mechanisms that enable a normal human cognizer to do what the agnosia patient can't do, namely, cognize the things with which he is in epistemic contact. This much of Aquinas's account is rich, complicated, and sophisticated. But how, on his view, does God make epistemic contact with the created things he cognizes?

It sometimes looks as if Aquinas's response to this question isn't very different from the blank reply, "He just does!"[71] In replying to questions about God's epistemic contact with corporeal individuals, Aquinas has a tendency to say such things as this: "God does cognize individuals. For all the perfections found in creatures preexist in God in a higher way. . . . But cognizing individuals is a feature of our perfection, and so it is necessary that God cognize individuals. For even the Philosopher considered it absurd to suppose that there is something that is cognized

---

[71] In a discussion of this essay Alvin Plantinga suggested that it is a mistake to look for a mechanism by means of which God knows. He pointed out that we don't look for a mechanism by means of which God exercises his omnipotence. In the case of divine power we are content just to note that omnipotence enables God to do whatever is at issue, without investigating the means by which an omnipotent being could do what he does. This line is not unattractive. It might even explain some of the peculiar slant of Aquinas's discussion of God's knowledge. Aquinas, too, might think there is nothing to discuss regarding the mechanism by means of which God knows, but that what must be discussed is how a simple God could know anything if knowledge requires representations of intelligible forms. If that is Aquinas's view, we should expect to find virtually nothing in his texts on how God applies his representations or makes epistemic contact with things but quite a lot on how a simple God can have intelligible forms in his intellect. So Plantinga's suggestion has some plausibility as the basis for an interpretation of Aquinas's approach. On the other hand, it also looks like a better line with which to end an investigation of God's knowledge than one with which to cancel any such investigation. If it turns out that reason's investigation can't come up with an account of how God knows what he knows, then Plantinga's suggestion can help explain why reason comes up empty. But beginning with Plantinga's suggestion will preclude reason's investigation entirely.

by us but not by God.[72] Blank as this standard reply is, however, it does express the leading idea in his approach to an account of God's nature via an extrapolation from human nature: anything we can do (that involves no human imperfection), God can do better.

But a more forthcoming response can also be found in his writings. Aquinas divides all knowledge into two sorts: "one sort is called the knowledge of vision, through which things that are, or will be, or were, are cognized. The other is the knowledge of simple awareness, through which one cognizes things that neither are, nor will be, nor were, but can be."[73] And he supposes God must have both these sorts of knowledge. Possibilities that are never actualized are cognized by God "in accordance with the awareness of simple intellection [i.e., the knowledge of simple awareness]. On the other hand, God cognizes things that are present, past, or future with respect to us insofar as they are in his power, in their own causes, and in themselves. And [his] cognition of them is called awareness [i.e., knowledge] of vision."[74] There are many other places where Aquinas talks about God's intellective observation,[75] God's view,[76] God's vision,[77] and God's gaze.[78] So the things with which God is in epistemic contact he renders intelligible through the intelligible form that is his essence and that is reflected and particu-

---

[72] ST Ia.14.11c: "dicendum quod Deus cognoscit singularia. Omnes enim perfectiones in creaturis inventae, in Deo praeexistunt secundum altiorem modum, ut ex dictis patet. Cognoscere autem singularia pertinet ad perfectionem nostram. Unde necesse est quod Deus singularia cognoscat. Nam et Philosophus pro inconvenienti habet, quod aliquid cognoscatur a nobis, quod non cognoscatur a Deo." See also ST Ia.57.1 and 84.1.

[73] QQ 3.2.3: "una dicitur scientia visionis, per quam cognoscuntur ea quae sunt, erunt, vel fuerunt. Alia simplicis notitiae, per quam cognoscuntur ea quae nec sunt, nec erunt, nec fuerunt, sed esse possunt."

[74] SCG I.66.550–51: "Quae quidem a quibusdam dicuntur a Deo cognosci secundum notitiam simplicis intelligentiae. Ea vero quae sunt praesentia, praeterita, vel futura nobis, cognoscit Deus secundum quod sunt in sua potentia, et in propriis causis, et in seipsis. Et horum cognitio dicitur notitia visionis."

[75] See, e.g., SCG I.67.557: "Divini autem intellectus intuitus ab aeterno fertur in unumquodque eorum quae temporis cursu peraguntur prout praesens est." See also *Compendium theologiae* I.133; ST Ia.14.13.

[76] QDP 16.7: "totus decursus temporis, et ea quae per totum tempus aguntur, praesentialiter et conformiter eius aspectui subduntur."

[77] See, e.g., ST Ia.14.9 and 12; also QDV 2.12: "unde, cum visio divinae scientiae aeternitate mensuretur, . . . sequitur ut quidquid in tempore geritur, non ut futurum, sed ut praesens videat: hoc enim quod a Deo visum est, futurum est rei alteri, cui succedit in tempore; sed ipsi divinae visioni, quae non in tempore, sed extra tempus est, non est futurum, sed praesens."

[78] See, e.g., ST Ia.14.13: "Unde manifestum est quod contingentia et infallibiliter a Deo cognoscuntur, inquantum subduntur divino conspectui secundum suam prasentialitatem."

larized in the divine ideas that are the formal causes of created things. But it looks very much as if Aquinas takes God to be in epistemic contact with creatures in virtue of metaphorically "seeing" them.

The claim that God's epistemic contact with creatures is a kind of "seeing" helps explain an otherwise puzzling feature of Aquinas's account, one that we noted at the beginning of this essay. In considering God's knowledge of future contingents, Aquinas takes the line that it requires that they be present to God, as they can be if God is eternal and thus atemporal. So he applies the doctrine of divine eternity as required to account for God's knowledge of future contingents and indeed, of all things temporal.[79] But it's hard to understand why God's mode of cognition would require its objects' presence, until we're told that God's epistemic contact with creatures consists in "seeing" them. As we've already noted, if God's knowledge of future contingents were simply a matter of God's consulting his acts of causation or otherwise engaging in introspection, the doctrine of eternity would be entirely irrelevant to an explanation of it.

If God's epistemic contact with creatures consists in "seeing" them atemporally, then his cognizing them and their doings does not compromise divine immutability. But that can't be the whole story. As Aquinas himself would agree, any process that could count as cognition of contingents must also involve reception.[80] And since receiving is a kind of undergoing, it seems that God's cognition of creatures must be incompatible with his impassibility.

Although we haven't found Aquinas directly addressing the issue of impassibility in his account of God's knowledge, we think his understanding of it can be inferred from other things he says. Among the kinds of receiving or undergoing he recognizes, some involve deterioration or improvement—for instance, getting sick and getting better— and those are most obviously the kinds that divine impassibility must rule out. But often enough reception is simply a component of completion, the actualization of a subject's natural potentialities.[81] A cognitive faculty's reception of its data is that kind of reception: "'undergoing' is [sometimes] used generally for any change, even if it pertains to the perfecting of a nature—as when understanding or sensing is said to be a kind of undergoing."[82] Of course, God's perfect intellect couldn't

---

[79] See note 85 below and the text to which it is attached.

[80] For this a priori truth, he also has Aristotelian authority: *De anima* II.11.423b26–424a10 and III.4.429a13–18.

[81] See, e.g., ST IaIIae.22.1; Ia.79.2.

[82] ST Ia.97.2c: "Alio modo, dicitur passio communiter, secundum quamcumque mutationem, etiam si pertineat ad perfectionem naturae; sicut intelligere vel sentire dicitur pati quoddam."

get perfected—most fundamentally because "the divine intellect is not in potentiality but is pure actuality,"[83] but also because God cognizes even temporal things not successively but all at once, timelessly, and real potentiality is time-bound: "Intellect . . . is said to undergo insofar as it is somehow in potentiality to intelligible things . . . *before* it understands."[84] All the same, God's intellect wouldn't *be perfect* if it weren't somehow timelessly in receipt of·what its "seeing" discloses, aware of information without first having been without it.

It's also worth noticing here that Aquinas seems to be presupposing the distinction we drew earlier between being in epistemic contact with something and rendering intelligible what one is in epistemic contact with. God renders temporal things intelligible in cognizing them through the intelligible form that is his essence, but he is in epistemic contact with them because all temporal things are atemporally present to him: "the whole course of time and the things that happen throughout all time are within his view as present and as suited to it."[85]

What's more, in his account of God's knowledge Aquinas also seems to be presupposing what we identified as the third element in the cognitive process, applying a representation to what one is in epistemic contact with. For example, Aquinas draws this closely related distinction: "every cognition is in accordance with some form, which is the source of cognition in the cognizer. But this sort of form can be considered in two ways. In one way, in keeping with the being that it has in the cognizer; in the other way, in keeping with the relation it bears to the thing whose likeness it is. Considered in the first relationship, it makes the cognizer actually cognizant. Considered in the second relationship, however, it determines the cognition to some determinate cognizable thing."[86] The intelligible form through which God cognizes— his own nature—makes him actually cognizant of everything he is in epistemic contact with. But, as Aquinas indicates, there also has to be

---

[83] ST Ia.79.2c: "intellectus divinus non est in potentia, sed est actus purus."

[84] In DA III.9.722: "Intellectus igitur dicitur pati, inquantum est quoddammodo in potentia ad intelligibilia, et nihil est actu eorum antequam intelligat." See also SCG I.16.133: "quod est potentia, nondum est."

[85] QDP 16.7 (note 76 above). In our article "Eternity, Awareness, and Action" (*Faith and Philosophy* 9 [1992], 463–82), we discuss some of the problems associated with epistemic and causal relationships between an eternal being and temporal beings.

[86] QDV 10.4: "omnis cognitio est secundum aliquam formam, quae est in cognoscente principium cognitionis. Forma autem huiusmodi potest considerari dupliciter: uno modo secundum esse quod habet in cognoscente; alio modo secundum respectum quem habet ad rem cuius est similitudo. Secundum quidem primum respectum facit cognoscentem actu cognoscere; sed secundum secundum respectum determinat cognitionem ad aliquod cognoscibile determinatum." See also QDV 3.1.

a certain relationship between the intelligible form and what is cognized, a relationship that "determine[s] the cognition to some determinate cognizable thing."

An explicit example of this distinction occurs in Aquinas's discussion of angelic cognition. As we've seen, Aquinas argues that when an angel has a new cognition of something, it does not acquire a new representation or intelligible form; instead, it merely makes a new application of an intelligible form it has always had. Aquinas explains that "this applying should be understood in accordance with the way God applies the [divine] ideas to cognize things. [God does] not [apply a divine idea] to something else as a medium [of cognition] that is [itself] cognizable; rather, [he applies it] to the thing cognized as the mode of cognizing [it]."[87] So Aquinas recognizes that the cognitive process involves more than possessing a representation or intelligible form, and here he identifies what else is needed as applying the intelligible form to the cognized thing.

On Aquinas's account of God's knowledge, then, for God, too, direct and immediate cognition of things outside his mind involves at least three elements: (a*) God's being in epistemic contact with everything he cognizes, (b*) God's possessing a representation of what he cognizes, and (c*) God's applying that representation to what he is in epistemic contact with. Virtually all Aquinas's discussion of God's knowledge is an explanation of (b*), an attempt to say how God has adequate representations of all things other than himself. His understanding of the other two elements of God's cognition has to be extracted from the little he says about them in his account of divine knowledge, his speculation about angelic cognition, and his general discussions of intellect. Given the preeminence of the doctrine of God's absolute simplicity in Aquinas's philosophical theology and the difficulty of accounting for ideas of things in a simple God, the focus of Aquinas's attention is perhaps understandable. But it leaves us with problems, and one of them is the problem of God's epistemic contact with creatures.

There is a long-standing view of how epistemic contact is typically established when a human being cognizes an external object: the thing being cognized has an effect on the cognizer's senses, and that causal connection constitutes the epistemic contact. But, of course, this kind of explanation can't be what accounts for God's epistemic contact with creatures. As far as we can see, however, Aquinas provides no further

---

[87] QQ 7.1.3, ad 3: "applicatio illa est intelligenda per modum illum quo Deus ideas ad res cognoscendas applicat, non sicut medium cognoscibile ad aliud, sed sicut modus cognoscendi ad rem cognitam."

help in analyzing God's epistemic contact than to hold that God applies his ideas to what he cognizes and that God atemporally "sees" all things other than himself. In this respect, then, Aquinas's account is just incomplete.

It's worth noticing, however, that currently standard accounts of human cognition are also incomplete in analogous respects, contrary to what one might suppose. Although it's clear that representations have to be applied to what the cognizer is in epistemic contact with, no one has more than a rudimentary idea of what such application consists in or of what has gone wrong in agnosia patients who are no longer capable of it. Furthermore, although it's true that what is cognized acts causally on the cognizer's senses, for that causal connection to count as *epistemic* contact at all, the sensory data produced in that way must undergo some processing by the central nervous system. Causal contact between some object and say, an eye in a vat would not constitute epistemic contact. But sensory input by itself underdetermines the result of the central nervous system's processing.[88] How is the result of that processing related to the thing cognized, then? Or, to put it another way, how is it that the result of the processing constitutes epistemic contact with the extramental things that generated the sensory input? The straight truth seems to be that nobody knows.[89] The incompleteness of Aquinas's account of God's knowledge looks less surprising when we recognize that contemporary accounts of human knowledge are incomplete in the same way.

We have presented an interpretation of Aquinas's account of God's knowledge as an answer to the question, How does God know what he knows? We've shown some of the misinterpretations to which the account is liable, and we've argued that when his account is properly understood, it commits Aquinas to neither determinism nor Averroism. Insofar as the question about God's knowledge with which we started this essay tacitly included a question about God's epistemic contact with what he knows, Aquinas's account will not give us a complete answer. But if, as we have suggested, this is a question that has not yet been answered regarding human cognition, it should not be surprising that

---

[88] See note 55 above.

[89] It is, of course, possible to suppose that evolution or God has constructed human beings in such a way that their cognitive processing yields reliable information about the world around them. For a critical discussion of such a claim about evolution, see Alvin Plantinga, *Warrant and Proper Function* (Oxford: Oxford University Press, 1993). But attempts to solve the puzzle by pointing to evolution or God's creative activity don't seem to get us very far if what we are interested in is the mechanism by which human cognitive processing is reliably related to what it cognizes.

Aquinas provides no answer for it with regard to divine cognition, and all the more so because his approach to that topic is founded on his understanding of human cognition. Furthermore, as his rich, complicated account of divine cognition indicates, he fully realizes that there is a lot more to cognition, divine or human, than epistemic contact. For the aspects of cognition beyond epistemic contact, Aquinas's account of God's knowledge seems to us not only consistent with and illuminating of the rest of his monumental philosophical theology but also insightful as regards human cognition. In fact, the wonder is that without the data of contemporary neurobiology or the imaginative stimulus of computer analogies, Aquinas was able to produce as sophisticated an account of cognition as he does.[90]

[90] We're grateful to Scott MacDonald, Timothy O'Connor, and Robert Pasnau for detailed written comments, to Norris Clarke, William Hasker, Peter van Inwagen, and Alvin Plantinga for comments in discussion, to Thérèse Druart for a helpful correction, and to audiences at the American Catholic Philosophical Association, the Society of Christian Philosophers, the University of Notre Dame, McGill University, Duke University, and the University of Western Washington.

THE EPISTEMOLOGY OF
RELIGIOUS EXPERIENCE

[5]

Religious Experience and the Practice Conception of Justification

ROBERT AUDI

There are at least two possible kinds of justification for theistic beliefs. One is evidential and is exemplified by the kind of justification supposed to be provided by the traditional arguments for the existence of God; the other is experiential and is supposed to be provided by certain religious experiences. Since the early 1980s, philosophical discussions of possible justifications for theistic beliefs have tended to focus more on the experiential routes to justification of these beliefs than on the evidential routes.[1]

This essay continues that line of inquiry and explores some of the justificatory resources of religious experience. Its special concern is to consider those resources from the point of view of the practice conception of justification—roughly, the position that justification is to be understood in terms of socially established patterns of appraising belief—and to offer a partial appraisal of that position by comparing it with some other leading conceptions of justification. The point of departure is an influential view of justification presented by William James in his classic work, *The Varieties of Religious Experience.*

The Jamesian View of the Epistemic Status of Religious Experience

To understand James's view on the justificatory power of religious experience, we should first consider what kind of experiences he had

[1] See, e.g., C. F. Delaney, ed., *Rationality and Religious Belief* (Notre Dame: University of Notre Dame Press, 1979); Alvin Plantinga and Nicholas Wolterstorff, eds., *Faith and*

in mind. He describes the cases he takes as paradigms of religious experience as having in common what he calls mystical states. These states he characterizes as always (in the subject's eyes) ineffable and noetic, and as *usually* transitory and passive, where by 'passive' he means 'occurring involuntarily' and, by implication, 'dominating the subject's consciousness'.[2] (The passivity, I believe, really belongs to the subject, not the experience.) Here are two samples, the first from John of the Cross, the second from St. Theresa:

> We receive this mystical knowledge of God clothed in none of the sensible representations, which our mind makes use of in other circumstances. Accordingly in this knowledge, since the senses and the imagination are not employed, we get neither form nor impression, nor can we give any account or furnish any likeness, although the mysterious and sweet-tasting wisdom comes home so clearly. . . . The soul then feels as if placed in a vast and profound solitude.[3]

> In the orison of union, the soul is fully awake as regards God, but wholly asleep as regards things of this world and in respect to itself. During the short time the union lasts, she is as it were deprived of every feeling. . . . In short, she is utterly dead to the things of the world and lives solely in God.[4]

James comments that "the deliciousness of some of these states . . . evidently involves organic sensibilities, for it is spoken of as too extreme to be borne. . . . But it is too subtle and piercing a delight for ordinary words to denote."[5] He does not, however, attempt, as some have done,[6] to argue that this suggests a physical cause in virtue of which the experiences seem devoid of evidential value.

Rationality: Reason and Belief in God (Notre Dame: University of Notre Dame Press, 1983); Robert Audi and William J. Wainwright, eds., *Rationality and Religious Belief: New Essays in the Philosophy of Religion* (Ithaca: Cornell University Press, 1986); and William P. Alston, *Perceiving God: The Epistemology of Religious Experience* (Ithaca: Cornell University Press, 1991).

[2] See William James, *The Varieties of Religious Experience* (1902; New York: Longmans, Green, 1925), esp. Lecture XVI, which introduces these four marks (pp. 300–302). The involuntariness of such experiences does not imply that the will has no *influence* on them, but James is suggesting they cannot be produced at will.

[3] Ibid., p. 407.

[4] Ibid., pp. 408–9.

[5] Ibid., p. 412.

[6] For discussion of this undermining possibility, see, e.g., Huston Smith, "Do Drugs Have Religious Import?" *Journal of Philosophy* 61 (1964).

The heart of James's view on the justificatory resources of religious experience is set forth in three statements:

(1) Mystical states, when well developed, usually are, and have the right to be, absolutely authoritative over those who have them.

(2) No authority emanates from them which should make it a duty for those who stand outside of them to accept their revelations uncritically.

(3) They break down the authority of nonmystical or rationalistic consciousness, based upon the understanding and the senses alone. . . . They open out the possibility of other orders of truth.[7]

In clarifying (1), James sets forth a strong parity thesis: "Our own more 'rational' beliefs are based on evidence exactly similar in nature to that which mystics quote for theirs. Our senses, namely, have assured us of certain states of fact; but mystical experiences are as direct perceptions of fact for those who have them as any sensations ever were for us."[8] In commenting on (2), he says that the mystical feeling of "enlargement, union, and emancipation" that he has described "has no specific intellectual content of its own. It is capable of forming matrimonial alliances with the most diverse philosophies and theologies. . . . We have no right, therefore, to invoke its prestige as distinctively in favor of any special belief, such as that in the . . . absolute goodness of the world. . . . I repeat that nonmystics are under no obligation to acknowledge in mystical states a superior authority conferred upon them by their intrinsic nature."[9] And regarding (3), James says, "As a rule, mystical states merely add a supersensuous meaning to the ordinary outward data of consciousness. They are excitements like the emotions of love or ambition, gifts to our spirit by means of which facts already objectively before us fall into a new expressiveness. . . . They do not contradict these facts as such or deny anything that our senses have immediately seized."[10]

In the light of James's overall discussion, I would suggest the following by way of interpretation. First, James maintains that certain mystical experiences—including paradigms of what are commonly called reli-

---

[7] James *Varieties*, pp. 422–23. He goes on to discuss each of these in his next three subsections.

[8] Ibid., pp. 423–24.

[9] Ibid., pp. 425–26.

[10] Ibid., p. 427. It is somewhat puzzling that James here talks as if the subject were perceiving the mystical object *via* perceiving something ordinary; he does indeed mean to allow for this, but it is not the main kind of case he discusses—or cites from the literature. But there is certainly no inconsistency: what is perceived (the "data" of consciousness) is one thing; its adding meaning to ordinary objects is another.

gious experiences—usually produce justified beliefs about their apparent object.[11] Although he does not explicitly say it, I believe he means to include theistic propositions among those for which one might acquire justification, for instance the propositions that God is reaching through to one, that God's power is present in the world, and that divine love surrounds us. Second, despite the strong parity claim in his elaboration of point (1), James is surely implying that those who do not have mystical experience would be justified in withholding belief from the same propositions that, for the subjects of those experiences, are justified.

What is not quite clear is whether James intends here a contrast with ordinary beliefs justified by the senses. I suspect he does. For one thing, we can suppose he notices that it is standard practice to require a special reason for disbelieving testimony based on experience that comes to one through the five senses: if you have been in an interior room all day and after entering the building I tell you that it is rainy outside, then, given my superior epistemic position, you need a reason to reject my statement, say that I was not in a position to judge or have some reason to lie. A second point is that in noting the epistemic worth of mystical experience, James says that mystical states do not yield beliefs contradicting facts "our senses have seized," as if to suggest that one epistemic liability they might have may be ruled out. Third, it is noteworthy that in "The Will to Believe," he limits the scope of the doxastic freedom he there affirms by stipulating that "the freedom to believe can only cover options which the intellect of the individual cannot by itself resolve; and living options never seem absurdities to him who has them to consider."[12] This restriction to options not resolvable by the intellect does not significantly limit his third point about religious experience. Even if such experience justifies only what is not, or does not seem to the individual subject to be, inconsistent with what is shown by ordinary sensory experience or by reason, it can still open a window on "other orders of truth." This is, of course, a cleverly vague metaphor: it leaves open whether those who have such experiences *do* see other orders of truth or simply *can* see them, say through sufficiently careful observation.

Two broader questions of interpretation should also be noted. Is James's approach here mainly pragmatic, as is suggested by remarks like his rhetorical question, "If the mystical truth that comes to a man

[11] Though in point (1) he does not use 'justification' or any similar term, like 'warrant', in saying that these experiences [usually?] "have the right to be" authoritative over the subject, he is presumably implying that they provide justification for the relevant beliefs.

[12] See *Essays in Pragmatism by William James*, ed. Alburey Castell (New York: Haffner, 1948), p. 106.

proves to be a force that he can live by, what mandate have we of the majority to order him to live in another way?"[13] This point is clearly harmonious with a pragmatic approach; but when James stresses, in the same paragraph, the equal *directness* of mystical and ordinary experiences as sources of belief, he sounds not like the pragmatist he officially is but more like an epistemologist who is not a pragmatist and is simply comparing justificational credentials on their purely evidential merits. A pragmatist can make this comparison, of course, but this parity move by itself would yield James's positive conclusion *if,* as is normally granted by nonskeptics, direct experiences tend to be justificatory. For one might then hold that the mystic's justification (at least in these instances of noninferential belief-formation) is simply a special case of the justification that arises from any sensory experience, or at least any direct experience, that is unopposed by conflicting experience or, say, by good reasons to think one is hallucinating.

On this interpretation, then, James was, on the one hand, a pragmatist in cases in which we have evenly divided evidence (or can get no evidence at all yet also have no counterevidence), allowing here that we may justifiably "will to believe," but, on the other hand, less pragmatic, if a pragmatist at all, about justified belief in the usual cases of direct experiential grounding. It may seem puzzling that James might hold a pragmatic theory of truth yet not (at least unqualifiedly) a pragmatic theory of justification. But surely truth can be pragmatically understood as what "works," even if justification is taken to emerge only from certain sources, such as sense experience. Indeed, the idea that truth is what works seems most plausible when truth is posited on the basis of justification from such sources—which are apparently reliable in producing beliefs true in a *non*pragmatic sense—and working is understood in terms of confirmation through the sorts of experiences they yield, above all, perception that corresponds to justified expectations about the future.[14]

One other reading of James should be considered. Even if James is quite pragmatic about the status of beliefs formed in cases of evenly divided evidence, his view could be not that the belief one adopts in such a case is, qua belief, justified but that willing to believe the relevant proposition is, qua action, justified. The pragmatism, on this reading, is not a thesis about doxastic justification—justification for *holding* be-

---

[13] Ibid.

[14] I see no way to prove that these sources are reliable in this sense, but a case can be made that it is at least not unreasonable to think so. That no noncircular proof is to be found is powerfully argued by William P. Alston in *The Reliability of Sense Perception* (Ithaca: Cornell University Press, 1993).

liefs—but applies to behavioral justification, in this case for *producing* beliefs. On either reading of Jamesian pragmatism, we have a contrast to the other approaches to justification I want to consider in relation to religious experience.

The Practice Conception of Justification

If James's conception of justification—or of justification in certain important cases—is largely pragmatic, the dominant approach in epistemology at least since Aquinas has been realist and foundationalist.[15] Within this approach, however, there are many options. It remains possible, for example, to be a rationalist or an empiricist and, in either framework, to accord greater or lesser degrees of recognition to the epistemic relevance of social and linguistic contexts. The practice conception of justification is not usually considered a candidate to be foundationalist, in part because the social or psychological or other foundations it may posit are not normally taken to yield the high epistemic status—such as indubitability—associated with historically most prominent foundationalist views, particularly Descartes's. But once moderate versions of foundationalism are understood, it is apparent that the position is readily adaptable to a practice framework.[16]

The practice conception of justification derives in part from Thomas Reid, who stressed our natural (perhaps innately determined) ways of forming beliefs, and in part from Ludwig Wittgenstein, who gave great weight to social and linguistic factors important in accounting for justification. The basic idea of the practice conception—in the rather generic form in which I want to consider it—is that beliefs are justified in terms of a social practice in which certain modes of belief-formation are recognized as conferring justification on the beliefs they generate, provided that there are no undermining factors, such a high degree of mutual inconsistency among the beliefs coming from these recognized

[15] Nicholas Wolterstorff puts it even more strongly: calling foundationalism the "*classic theory of theorizing in the Western world*," he takes it to say that "we must begin with a firm foundation of certitude and build the house of theory on it by methods of whose reliability we are equally certain." See *Reason within the Bounds of Religion* (Grand Rapids, Mich.: William B. Eerdmans, 1984), p. 28.

[16] For an account of moderate foundationalism, with discussion of the extent to which the view can accommodate considerations of coherence, see my *Structure of Justification* (Cambridge: Cambridge University Press, 1993), esp. chap. 8.

sources.[17] The remainder of this section clarifies the practice conception, particularly as applied to theistic beliefs.

On the practice conception, we can speak of a justificatory practice in terms of larger or smaller segments of human behavior, for instance of the standard *perceptual* practice, meaning the framework of belief-forming mechanisms and responses to them in virtue of which we (who stand inside the practice) do not normally demand a reason for beliefs formed noninferentially on the basis of sense-experience. Instead, we tend to expect such beliefs to be true, and we expect normal people to guide their lives by beliefs of this sort; we do not expect to find the senses regularly contradicting one another (or themselves); and so forth. Such beliefs are, in this respect, foundational. Coherentist versions of the practice view are also possible, but they have been less commonly developed in this tradition and need not be considered here. It should be stressed, however, that although the absence of contradictions of the kinds just mentioned does imply that, for any plausible practice conception, *incoherence* is a negative constraint on noninferential justification, it does not imply that coherence is a positive condition for justification, particularly if that status is taken to imply that coherence is a ground.[18]

Perceptual practices are not the only kind. We might also speak of an analogous *logical* practice, referring to our inferential behavior and our critical standards governing inferences; and there is also an overall social pattern of justificatory discourse encompassing both perceptual and logical practices. Religious justificatory practices are yet another kind, but they may incorporate elements in our everyday non-religious practices. Since it is the possibility of experiential religious justification that is of special concern here, it is the comparison of religious practices to our perceptual practice that is most relevant.

---

[17] My paradigm here is the view of Alston; see esp. his *Perceiving God.* As he says in the introduction, a doxastic practice is "a way of forming beliefs and epistemically evaluating them . . . it is rational to engage in any socially established doxastic practice that we do not have sufficient reasons for regarding as *unreliable*" (p. 6). Alston's views are too extensive and subtle to permit detailed treatment, and some of the points that emerge concerning such practices may not as they stand apply to his position. But I hope they will apply nearly enough to raise useful questions about the nature and justificatory resources of his position.

[18] This point can be seen by reflection on why incoherence is not the mere absence of coherence. I have developed and defended the point in chaps. 3 and 4 of *Structure of Justification.* Among the points noted there is that coherence might be necessary for justification because it is a *consequence* of something else that produces justification, rather than itself a *ground* of justification.

The terminology of engaging in a practice may suggest a kind of doxastic voluntarism that is inappropriate to the most plausible forms of the practice conception. To engage in our everyday practice of forming beliefs perceptually does not require forming them at will or even consciously monitoring their formation with a view to controlling them indirectly, for instance by exposing oneself to influences, such as "social conditioning," that will change one's belief system. Participation in the practice is above all a matter of employing certain norms socially accepted among those who form the community sharing the practice. For example, we accept as justified most of the beliefs that attribute to people's environment observable properties we take to be manifested in their perceptual experience; we tend to criticize people for harboring beliefs attributing observable properties to environments they have neither experienced nor in any way been told about; and we expect them, at least by indirect means, to disabuse themselves of these beliefs. If I look out the window and report that it is raining, normally I will be taken to express a justified belief; and if I believe there are bears in the suburbs, but lack even secondhand evidence, I will not be considered to be justified and will be expected either to gather evidence for my belief or to revise my view. The perceptual practice is, then, doxastic in the sense that it centrally concerns formation and appraisal of belief, but its voluntary aspects are not acts of belief-formation; they are, chiefly, the range of actions exhibiting adherence to certain critical standards.

The practice approach permits endorsing all three of James's main points cited above. There can be a mystical practice analogous to our standard perceptual one, at least on the assumption that the relevant mystical or religious experiences produce the beliefs in question—for our purposes, mainly theistic beliefs—noninferentially.[19] If such practices are possible, then on the practice conception (1) there can be justified beliefs of the kinds that James says mystics can have and (2) these might be *true* and thus might realize the possibility that the mode of experience grounding them is, as James puts it, a window on a wider reality. As to James's point that those who lack the religious experiences may justifiably reject their evidential authority, this too is compatible with the practice conception: grounds that provide sufficient justification for one person within a practice need not be recognized as doing so by others in the practice or, certainly, by those outside the practice.

[19] This is a somewhat problematic assumption, but I intend to grant it for the sake of argument. For some of the problems, see my "Direct Justification, Evidential Dependence, and Theistic Belief," in Audi and Wainwright, *Rationality and Religious Belief,* pp. 139–67.

In at least one important respect, however, the social practice view is broader than James's. For it counts as religious a wider range of experiences than those James had in mind. As William P. Alston puts it in one place:

> If God can appear to me as loving or powerful or glorious when I am not sensorily aware of a field of oats or the words of the Bible or a sermon, why shouldn't He also appear to me as loving or powerful or glorious when that appearance comes *through* my sense perception of the field of oats or whatever? . . . I have nothing to say against this possibility, and hence no reason to discredit those who report their cognition of God in these terms rather than in terms of indirect perceptual recognition.[20]

Using the terminology illustrated here, we can say that whereas James was speaking chiefly about direct mystical experience (and mainly such experience of God), Alston is talking about both direct and indirect theistic perception (and distinguishes various cases of each). Moreover, Alston sets out his view in the context of an account of perception that subsumes theistic perception, whether direct or indirect, as a special case,[21] whereas James conceives the relevant experiences mainly as "states" and, though he also uses perceptual terminology in some places, seems uncommitted about whether they may be unqualifiedly perceptual.

Indirect mystical experiences have an epistemologically important property that deserves special comment. At least in the common sorts of cases suggested here, the indirect experiences have what I shall call a *naturalistic base,* in the sense that God is perceived through—or perhaps in—some natural object or set of events. The direct experiences, by contrast, are meant to be seen as *perceptually autonomous:* God appears to the subject but not in or through any natural guise.[22] This would account at least in part for the ineffability of such experiences. The practice conception, then, not only countenances the possibility of

[20] Alston, *Perceiving God,* p. 8.

[21] See esp. ibid., chap. 1, in which the theory of appearing is given perhaps the most extensive defense it has received in recent decades.

[22] The 'in' and 'through' need not be taken as equivalent. There are varieties of theistic perception we must largely ignore here; e.g., what Alston cites as a case of indirect perception may be conceived instead as one in which a perceptual experience, instead of being, say, a seeing of God through an intermediary, facilitates a direct perception of God. I have discussed some of the possibilities, in relation to Alston's view, in "Perceptual Experience, Doxastic Practice, and the Rationality of Religious Commitment," *Journal of Philosophical Research* 20 (1994), 1–18.

many kinds of theistic perception; it also leaves open that the less dramatic, perhaps more common, naturally based religious experiences are as strongly justificatory as the autonomous kinds, or at any rate sufficiently so to warrant the subject in holding certain theistic beliefs. Given that many who have the naturally based experiences may never have (or never be aware of having) the autonomous kinds, this is an epistemologically significant point.

It should not go unnoticed that countenancing religious doxastic practices as sources of justified theistic beliefs leaves one free to limit their parity with ordinary sense experience. Parity comes in degrees and may apply to only one aspect of a set of practices. It does not entail epistemic equality; it implies epistemic credentials of the same kind, perhaps, but not necessarily of the same breadth or strength. Consider James: he took mystical experience and ordinary perceptual experience to be on a par in terms of directness (by which he apparently meant noninferentiality), yet he apparently regarded the former as different from the latter in the strength of the epistemic claims it makes on those who lack the relevant grounds of justification. This could apply to practice (whether or not James would have so applied it) as follows: in the perceptual practice the grounds of justification, such as perceptions of the weather outside one's window, are interpersonally binding in a way that the grounds of justification in a mystical practice are not.[23] The two differ, then, in their internal structure, as opposed to their relations to other practices (though they may differ there too). This is an *intrapractice* difference, not an *interpractice* one.

The point that parity does not imply epistemic equality might seem to go against the idea that justification is rooted in practices, but it need not. For one thing, some practices are more comprehensive than others, for example in the diversity and number of beliefs they yield, and also more basic, in producing beliefs of a kind *required* for the success of one or more other practices that do not, in turn, yield beliefs required for the success of the former. Our standard perceptual practice seems, in these senses, both more comprehensive and more basic than any well-established mystical practice, particularly if the latter pro-

---

[23] Since James, in the relevant passage, is epistemically comparing not practices but (by implication, at least) experiences, I am speculating on how his view applies to the practices. He may, however, be doing something akin to comparing practices when he compares the evidential situations of mystics and "nonmystics," as he does in *Varieties*, pp. 425–26. A further question is what his view implies for someone who does not use the perceptual practice and is confronted with a perceptual report. This cannot be answered in the abstract; much depends on the standards governing the practice from which the report is being judged.

ceeds in many instances from naturalistic grounds and, to that extent, apparently relies on the perceptual practice. Some practices might also achieve more self-support than others, in the sense that people engaging in them achieve, through participating in them over time, stronger confirmation of the expectations generated by participation in the practice than is achieved by people similarly engaging in another practice over a comparable time span.[24]

Furthermore, if one already engages in our perceptual practice, then relative to the justification one achieves from so doing, the capacity of any further practice to yield justification may be limited, particularly if it produces beliefs irreconcilable with those acquired through the perceptual practice. Production of these beliefs would illustrate a *normative* limitation: given commitment to the perceptual practice, the new irreconcilable beliefs would be prima facie unjustified and so should (prima facie) be given up. But a quite pervasive *psychological* limitation is also likely: the perceptual practice (or it together with other common-sense practices such as those involving memory, introspection, and logic) would simply prevent the formation of a whole range of beliefs that might otherwise be formed through engaging in a different practice, such as a mystical one. This two-sided limitation exercised by the standard practice on other practices gives the former a kind of strong de facto priority, even if in principle it may be on a par with any other comparable coherent practice.

As James may have seen, some such de facto priority does appear to characterize the relation between the perceptual practice and the religious one. First, the former is more comprehensive and more basic in the sense just illustrated: producing a wider range of beliefs, considered in terms of diversity of content, and generating beliefs (such as perceptual ones) required for the justification of at least some arising in the religious practice. Second, it may also receive more self-support (for example, in confirmation of beliefs it leads one to form about the future), at least for most people who engage in both. There could thus be structural parity and epistemic inequality. Each practice is socially grounded, but one practice is at once more pervasive and an element in the other, in such a way that at least the following asymmetries hold: first, some of the justification generated in the theistic practice depends on perceptual justification, as where justified beliefs about God depend on justification regarding the natural objects through which God is seen; and second, the defeating role of the former practice relative to

---

[24] Alston emphasizes this dimension of practices. See *Perceiving God*, esp. chap. 6; its last section is devoted to the degree of self-support of the relevant Christian practice.

the latter is stronger, for instance because perceptual justification for believing that one is not speaking to a person can outweigh theistic justification for believing one is doing so, more readily than conversely. These points do not, of course, imply that there are or will be any conflicts between the two sets of justified beliefs.

Parity may be in any case a double-edged advantage for most theists. For it is entirely possible that there are alternative and mutually inconsistent doxastic practices among different religious groups and that their equal claim to ground justification detracts from the epistemic achievements of any. Perhaps the traditional project of natural theology can be seen as in part a way of avoiding this problem, at least for those religious truths sufficiently general to be established by premises available through the basic sources of justification. If someone who sees God as having properties incompatible with those I attribute to God can be equally justified, should I not wonder whether I am well justified at all? This is the (epistemic) problem of religious pluralism, and natural theology might be conceived as offering at least a partial solution to it.

One response is that as long as our grounds are different, we may in fact be equally well justified with respect to mutually incompatible propositions.[25] But it is possible that someone grounded in a different religious practice could claim to have a similar experience phenomenally speaking and still emerge from it with an incompatible belief about what it represents. This may be rare as a matter of fact, but it is possible. For reasons of these sorts, it may well seem that an account of justification that can give so much to opponents is not one whose standards one should be intellectually satisfied to have met.[26] At this point, however, we should remember that, on the social practice view, this is a kind of problem that can beset *any* justificatory scheme. Compare the case of different physical theories accounting for the same perceptual data. It is arguable that unless we become skeptical in scientific matters, too, disallowing justification in either case, we are judging

[25] Alston notes this, esp. in ibid., chap. 7.

[26] Alston is aware of this issue and responds to it. He says, e.g., that given the "fruits of the spirit" enjoyed by many Christians, their religious practice possesses a kind of self-support that "markedly changes the picture. In the face of this self-support it is no longer the case that the most reasonable hypothesis is that none of the competing practices provide an effective cognitive access to the Ultimate . . . one may quite reasonably continue to hold that CMP [the Christian mystical practice] does serve as a genuine cognitive access to ultimate Reality . . . even if one can't see how to solve the problem of religious pluralism, even if one can't show from a neutral standpoint that Christianity is right and the others are wrong on those points on which they disagree" (*Perceiving God*, p. 276).

the religious practice by a double standard.[27] There are, of course, disanalogies between competing scientific views and competing religious outlooks; but whatever we make of the disanalogies, the analogy in question remains important: in either case, justification for a view, unlike its truth, can apparently be evenly divided between opposing sides.

The Intuitionist Conception of Justification

Proponents of both the pragmatic and the practice approaches to justification can grant that in fact experience and reason, as usually understood in terms of consciousness ("inner sense"), the five senses, memory, and "logical" (especially deductive and inductive) intuition—the standard *basic sources* of justification, as I shall call them[28]—are a universal practice, or perhaps a set of constituent practices in a common-sense justificatory practice. (The individuation of practices is a difficult matter that I leave aside in this essay.) But pragmatists and social practice theorists do not accord this universality any special status or take it as a sign of any noncontingent truths. By contrast, in the intuitionist tradition the relevant justificational principles, such as the principle that beliefs noninferentially grounded in sense-experience are prima facie justified, are a priori and necessary.[29]

Since intuitionism may be the leading conception of justification that contrasts with both the pragmatic and practice conceptions, and since the basic sources of justification it tends to recognize may be considered fundamental even by nonintuitionist views, such as reliabilism, it is appropriate to consider it here.[30] Moreover, far from taking justification to be *unrelated* to justificatory practices, or holding that there cannot

[27] Alston deals with this double-standard problem in (among other places) ibid., chap. 6. In the next section I explore some further apparent differences between the perceptual and other practices.

[28] These are described in detail in my *Belief, Justification, and Knowledge* (Belmont, Calif.: Wadsworth, 1988), chaps. 1–4, and widely discussed in the literature. I should note that in my view memory differs from the other cases in not being a basic source of knowledge, as it is of justification. For further discussion of this issue, see Carl Ginet, *Knowledge, Perception, and Memory* (Dordrecht: D. Reidel, 1983), and Thomas D. Senor, "Internalistic Foundationalism and the Justification of Memory Beliefs," *Synthese* 94 (1994), 413–76.

[29] For a discussion of this approach and references to some leading proponents, see my "Justification, Truth, and Reliability," *Philosophy and Phenomenological Research* 49 (1988).

[30] Reliabilism is a major approach to justification, but since one can incorporate it into the practice conception, as Alston does, I do not separately consider it here. See esp. his *Perceiving God*.

be, at least within a certain range, alternative practices in which justification arises, intuitionism is quite compatible with the existence of social practices in which belief-forming mechanisms and justificatory norms regarding beliefs are central. The point is that the practice embodying the basic sources as justificationally fundamental—which intuitionists have tended to regard as a universal common-sense practice—reflects epistemic truths that transcend the commitments or conventions peculiar to any particular culture or community.

There is no space here for a detailed account of intuitionism, but the idea, in part, is that these justificational principles are constitutive of the concept of justification around which epistemological discussion of justification revolves. Roughly, for a belief to be justified is for it to conform to these principles, in a sense implying that understanding the concept of justification is closely tied to understanding them. Alternative ways to judge beliefs are possible, for an alternative way of judging beliefs can *derive* epistemic authority from the basic sources—for instance by developing correlations between deliverances of its sources, such as mystical experience, and beliefs resting on perceptual sources—but no other way of judging the justification of beliefs has the same kind of claim to this authority as is conferred by the basic sources. These are taken to be basic in the sense that their justificational authority does not derive from that of any other source. The intuitionist position is not, then, a parity view, allowing that there might be competing practices with as good a claim to ground justification.

An intuitionist view does not imply, however, that there are a priori limits on what sources *derivatively* justify; it is only nonderivative justification that is apparently exhausted by the constitutive sources in experience and reason. Indeed, though intuitionism as described here posits no other basic sources, it need not deny that there *could* be additional basic sources, but if there are, then those unaware of them could not have a full understanding of the concept of justification. Intuitionism would certainly not take the possibility of undiscovered basic sources to be inconsistent with the fundamental conception of justification as determined by constitutive a priori principles: the basic source theory referred to above is not the only form an intuitionist view can take. On even that basic source theory, however, religious experience can be a (derivative) source not only of justified belief but of noninferential belief. The point would be that, even when noninferentially *formed*, the beliefs are not directly *justified:* they are justified by appropriate relations to considerations grounded in the standard sources. *Knowledge,* it should be noted, need not be treated in the same way, since it is arguable that knowledge does not require justification.

But this is not a possibility to be pursued here, in part because, if one had theistic knowledge without justification for the relevant outlook, then, whatever one's religious status, one would lack something that is of great epistemological importance.[31]

Is the intuitionist view positing just four basic sources of justification really a kind of epistemic imperialism? If it seems so, notice four points. First, the domain of experience and reason is universal, and all human beings are its citizens. Second, it is only the range of basic sources that is, on the intuitionist view, apparently limited; the range of possible nonbasic sources is unlimited. Third, no substantive idea about the world (including theistic views, of course) is automatically ruled out by so conceiving justification. And fourth, when we consider all the other practices having a serious claim to provide distinct basic sources, it appears that they lack a certain *epistemic autonomy:* either they incorporate the standard basic sources, as where religious experience with a naturalistic base is rooted in a certain *way* of seeing or hearing elements in nature, or at least it is not possible for human beings to engage in those practices without also engaging in the standard one. The other practices do not, for example, have an independent vocabulary and independent epistemic standards for the appraisal of beliefs and inferences.

These points do not fully meet the charge of imperialism, but perhaps enough has been said to make it reasonable to suppose for the sake of argument that there are no basic sources of justification beyond the four in question. This is in any case an important supposition to explore. For even those who reject the intuitionist conception may, for other reasons, believe that there are in fact no other basic sources—or even fewer than four since some philosophers will follow Mill in construing even our logical and mathematical beliefs as very general kinds of empirical belief.[32] Moreover, there are those who, quite apart from any explicit epistemology, are simply unable to take seriously any claims about the world that they cannot see as somehow confirmable through sensory experience more or less as usually understood. This attitude can stem from a naturalistic world-view with or without an empiricist

---

[31] For examinations of the relation between justification and knowledge see William P. Alston, "Justification and Knowledge," in his *Epistemic Justification: Essays in the Theory of Knowledge* (Ithaca: Cornell University Press, 1989); and my "Justification, Truth, and Reliability."

[32] W. V. Quine (in some of his writings) and some of his followers come to mind here. For the empiricism, see, e.g., Quine, "Two Dogmas of Empiricism," in his *From a Logical Point of View* (New York: Harper and Row, 1953); and for an indication of a foundationalist conception of sources, see, e.g., W. V. Quine and Joseph Ullian, *The Web of Belief* (New York: Random House, 1979), esp. chap. 2.

epistemology. If it is assumed that there are no other basic sources—or alternatively, that the only "reasonable" justificational practice is the one built around them—what may be said to accommodate religious experiences, whether richly mystical or of some other form, as possible grounds of theistic beliefs?

Much depends on what kinds of experiences we are talking about, for instance on how vivid and steadfast they are and whether their content is appropriate to their being, say, produced by God. Much also depends on the degree of experiential confirmation received for the beliefs formed through these experience and on the degree of support those beliefs receive from other considerations, such as arguments for the existence of earthly activity of God. And much depends on what kinds of grounds we are speaking of. There are grounds for knowledge, for justification, and for rationality, and all of these are important for the question of the epistemic resources of religious experience. I have already said that I take knowledge of God to be possible even without justification. I now want to suggest that rationality is possible without justification. The next section develops this idea and shows how it is significant for the general issue of the status of the religious experience regardless of one's specific conception of justification, including particularly the practice conception but also the other two major views of justification we have considered as foils for it.

Belief, Faith, and Reason

The problem of faith and reason is perhaps the most general category in which the question of the rationality of theistic belief is considered. Yet discussions of the problem in recent years have often focused on the justification of theistic beliefs, as if it could be assumed to be equivalent to their rationality. Even apart from these discussions, rationality is commonly thought to be roughly equivalent to justification. I take it, however, that although a justified belief must be rational, a rational belief, though it perhaps cannot be patently unjustified, need not be positively justified.[33] This is consistent with what theistic proponents of the practice conception of justification, as well as James and others, have said. The practice theorist, and certainly also James, can be seen as maintaining, in effect, that the point of view of rationality does not entail that only beliefs grounded in the standard basic sources

[33] I have compared and contrasted justification and rationality in "Faith, Belief, and Rationality," *Philosophical Perspectives* 5 (1991), 213–39.

be countenanced as rational. I think this view may be sound. Indeed, it may be that it is a constitutive principle of rationality (even if not of justification) that a belief arising noninferentially from experience, at least within the context of a doxastic practice that there is no reason to think unreliable, is prima facie rational, provided it does not conflict with beliefs well grounded in the standard basic sources.

Another point of contrast between rationality and justification is this: where a belief is justified, there is a ground we may call *a* justification of it whether experiential or inferential, that is, something that produces the justification. But for rationality, there need be no precise analogue of such a ground, something (of an evidential kind) that produces the rationality of the belief in question in the same way. We do not speak of *a* rationality for a belief; there are doubtless grounds of its rationality, constituting a basis for that (perhaps a supervenience base for it), but the rationality here, unlike justification, does not take its name, as it were, from any specific grounds for it or, I think, from what might be called a practice of rationality on analogy with the practice of justification. There may be a rationalization for a given rational belief, but a rationalization is not what is wanted for this grounding role, and providing a rationalization for a belief may in fact suggest that the belief is *neither* rational nor well grounded.[34] The notion of a rationale might be thought analogous to that of a justifying ground, but even if, as I doubt, something we might plausibly call a rationale is present for every rational belief, it need not amount to something producing the rationality of that belief. For one thing, a belief need not be based on a rationale one has for it; the rationale might be available but, for instance, simply a retrospective defense of what was believed on a hasty impression.

It may be, then, that rationality is a focus that is more receptive than justification to what we might call the *practice conception of normative adequacy*—the wider view about normative status of which the practice conception of justification may be considered a special case.[35] For justification seems tied more to specific justifiers than rationality is to any analogue of a justifier. Even apart from this contrast, the notion of rationality is a weaker concept. It is, however, strong enough to make its possession by theistic beliefs sufficient to place the believer above certain criticisms, for instance the charge of intellectual laxity. If a rational person may be religious, or (more narrowly) may even hold

[34] This is a complicated matter, which I have tried to sort out in "Rationalization and Rationality," *Synthese* 65 (1985), 311–34.

[35] Here, then, I am trying to extend the sort of practice conception of justification Alston has so plausibly developed.

theistic beliefs that are permissible from the point of view of rationality, that is highly significant for the problem of assessing the relation between faith and reason.

If it turns out, then, that the practice conception of justification is too latitudinarian to account for justification, or otherwise fails to do so, it may still provide a good account of rationality. Rationality may be, more than justification, a matter of being in line with a social standard—at least where that standard meets certain negative constraints, such as consistency and accord with (some appropriate degree of) epistemic authority for the basic sources. If I lack a justification for a belief, I may be, for instance, unable to defend it and unwarranted in regarding it as representing knowledge; yet I need not be irrational in holding it, and if, in general terms, I meet criteria for being a rational *person*, my belief derives therefrom a presumption, however slight, of rationality, in a way it does not acquire such a presumption of justification. Rationality belongs for the most part to beliefs that are not irrational,[36] whereas justification seems always to trace to some kind of specific, adequate ground. Mere absence of conditions that would make a belief *un*justified imply not that it is justified but at most that one may withhold its negation as opposed to being justified in disbelieving the proposition in question, i.e., believing that it is false. But absence of conditions that would make a belief irrational, together, at least, with certain experiential or social patterns favoring it, does tend to imply that it is rational.

Why should rationality differ from justification in this way? One possible explanation is that, unlike justification, it is a *virtue concept*, roughly in the sense that its primary application is in reference to persons and its use to describe other things, such as beliefs, actions, and desires, derives from its primary use. On this view, rather as a just action is one characteristic of a just person (one with the virtue of justice) and is not to be defined in terms of conformity to a rule,[37] a rational belief is not one conforming to an epistemic rationality principle but one characteristic of a rational person, or at least of such a person in the relevant context, say, of physical (including biological) and social factors. Indeed, a virtue-theoretic approach may well work *better* for rationality than for the moral concepts, because, unlike them, the notion of rationality is far less constrained by specific requirements

---

[36] Bernard Gert has defended in detail the stronger view that rationality is simply the contradictory of irrationality, which he takes as the prior notion. He might not accept, however, the use I make of a similar view here. See esp. *Morality* (Oxford: Oxford University Press, 1988).

[37] As is suggested in, e.g., some passages in Aristotle's *Nicomachean Ethics* 1105b5 ff.

on the appropriate content of belief or desire or, correspondingly, on the appropriate kind of action. Even if a rational person must believe certain self-evident propositions—at least upon considering them— still, given different experiences, there will be scarcely any limit to the differences in beliefs about the world we may find among rational persons. Rational persons must take their experiences seriously in determining or appraising their outlook on the world, but rationality imposes precious few constraints on what their experiences will be like. It certainly does not preclude rational persons from having religious experiences or require them to give a skeptical interpretation of unfamiliar experiences they have that are religious.

There is surely something to be said for the virtue-theoretic conception of rationality. But it must be qualified to take account of the fact that a justified belief is ipso facto rational. If, for example, my belief that a bush is burning before me is perceptually justified, it is also rational. If there is a virtue element in the notion of rational belief, this is not its only element. The notion seems to reflect the confluence of at least two sources: the general concept of a rational person and the notion of a justified belief. It may be argued, of course, that the notion of a justified belief is *also* a virtue concept. But although there is no doubt a coherent notion of an epistemically virtuous person, surely a fundamental ingredient in epistemic virtue is a tendency to hold beliefs of the kind grounded in the basic sources whenever one has the appropriate experiences, such as visual impressions of a burning bush.[38]

As this last point suggests, it may turn out that a rational person must be understood partly in terms of a well-groundedness conception of justified belief, but that once people meet this and other rationality standards, their beliefs that are not *ir*rational by well-groundedness criteria (for example, not such that one has readily available a strong justification for believing a contrary proposition) are rational. It seems that the virtue element in rationality does not "kick in" until the person is already rational, to some degree, by the well-groundedness standard. That standard, however, does not impose highly specific content on our

---

[38] This is not the place to argue for so large a thesis. But I have done so implicitly in some of the works already cited, including *Belief, Justification, and Knowledge* and "Justification, Truth, and Reliability." For accounts of virtue epistemology, see Ernest Sosa, "Knowledge and Intellectual Virtue," *The Monist* 68 (1985), 226–45; Jonathan Kvanvig, *The Intellectual Virtues and the Life of the Mind* (Lanham, Md.: Roman and Littlefield, 1991); and James Montmarquet, *Epistemic Virtue and Doxastic Responsibility* (Lanham: Rowman and Littlefield, 1993).

belief systems and certainly seems to permit religious experiences to count as at least derivative justificatory grounds.

People differ greatly, of course, in the extent to which their lives apparently render a theistic outlook rational. Some dwell in the House of the Lord: they love and are loved; they feel at one with nature; they flourish at home and at work; and their lives from sunup to sundown are felt to be blessed. The losses they face, far from bespeaking a God-less world, evoke love and compassion from others. They either know nothing of the atheistic argument from evil or feel immune to it. Other people are always beclouded: evil and failure befall them, and even their successes are felt as a mere temporary relief from unhappiness and are never taken as reasons to view the world more positively or to think they might be beneficiaries of divine love. Their thinking is dominated by a sense of the fortuitous, or even the malign, in the world, and they find neither nature nor people nor art to be sacred. A theistic outlook tends to be more likely to seem rational in a blessed and sunny life than in a life of frustration and darkness.

Even if rationality is not as liberally interpretable as I am suggesting and lacks the virtue element just sketched, the concept might still operate in a way that yields results equivalent to those I am imagining. A belief rational by the practice conception, for instance, might be equally so by an intuitionist conception of rationality. Such a conception need not take rationality to be always grounded in the basic sources, even if it takes justified beliefs that are so grounded to be rational. It might simply treat socially recognized kinds of experiences as, in generally rational persons (the kind with, for one thing, predominantly justified beliefs), grounds of the prima facie rationality of beliefs. Each standard can be made more or less strict, and their results can coincide. In any case, whether we hold a intuitionist view or a practice view, or indeed various other kinds of positions on normative status, it matters greatly whether our main focus is justification or rationality.

So far in this section, my strategy has been to move from justification to rationality as a major normative focus in the treatment of faith and reason. It remains important to consider justification (and knowledge) as well; but given the magnitude of the task of reconciling faith and reason,[39] and the importance of rationality as a minimal normative standard that we should generally like to meet, if anything is to be

---

[39] One reason I have not emphasized for the magnitude of this task is the problem of evil, which, at least for many philosophers, seems to provide good reason for atheism. Rigorous defenses of the argument from evil have been developed by William L. Rowe, e.g. in his "The Empirical Argument from Evil," in Audi and Wainwright, *Rationality and Religious Belief*, 227–47. Responses to this essay and further developments in the debate can be found in *Faith and Philosophy* from the middle 1980s to the present.

gained by focusing on rationality as contrasted with justification, it should be attempted. This is a broadly epistemological move. What I now want to suggest is that we may also make some progress by a related move in the philosophy of mind.

If our problem concerns reason in relation to *faith*, it should not be simply assumed that the fiduciary notions we must use are various kinds of religious beliefs. Among kinds of belief, the main candidates for fiduciary centrality are, of course, belief *in*, which might be called attitudinal faith, and (religious) belief *that*, which might be called propositional faith provided the proposition in question has appropriate content, say that God is sovereign in the universe. These two notions are of central importance in the philosophy of religion, but it may still be fruitful to shift from belief to some other fiduciary attitude as—for at least one stage of our inquiry—our chief psychological focus.

It has been widely acknowledged that there are many kinds of faith and I am convinced that there is a nondoxastic kind. One might, for instance, have faith that God will ultimately see to our every need, without believing—or, of course, disbelieving—this, just as one can have faith that a war in the Middle East can be avoided, without believing that.[40] One's faith here is cognitively stronger than mere hope, for instance in being incompatible with the degree of doubt possible for a proposition one hopes is true. Nondoxastic faith, as compared with hope that has the very same propositional content, is also attitudinally positive in a different way. One cannot, for instance, merely want the occurrence of what one has faith will take place: there must be a conception of the thing in question as positive, in a way an object of hope need not be conceived. Granted, if we specify that the hope is religious, then there presumably must, as with faith, be a positive attitude. But whereas a kind of positive attitude is intrinsic to faith as such, it is not intrinsic to hope as such.

Nondoxastic faith is capable of being behaviorally influential enough to govern huge segments of one's life by motivating actions of a definite kind, and this capacity is stronger, other things being equal, than the corresponding capacity of religious hope. But nondoxastic faith is not reducible to any kind of belief. This is not to imply that either belief *in*, attitudinal faith, or belief *that*, propositional faith, is reducible to nondoxastic (propositional) faith; the suggestion is only that the propositional fiduciary component of attitudinal faith can be constituted by nondoxastic propositional faith if that is sufficiently rich and properly

[40] See, e.g., my "The Dimensions of Faith and the Demands of Reason," in Eleonore Stump, ed., *Reasoned Faith* (Ithaca: Cornell University Press, 1993), pp. 70–89, which also contrasts faith and hope and other related notions.

integrated into the person's life.[41] Thus, if nondoxastic faith is weaker than belief in what we might call its cognitive commitment, it may yet be strong enough motivationally and attitudinally to sustain a religious life. Let us ask, then, whether there might be experiences sufficient to render it rational (or even justify it) that are not sufficient to render the corresponding belief rational (or justify it). I believe there might be; the epistemic standards for rational nondoxasic faith seem to me weaker than those for belief.

If this epistemic view is correct, as I believe it is, it implies that the prospects for showing religious experience to have a positive role in rendering rational a religious outlook on the world are considerably better than they would be if we spoke only of belief as our central attitude and only of justification as our main normative category. This comparative point is independent of whether a pragmatic or practice or intuitionist conception of justification is sound. But the point seems to me to go well with the practice conception, which appears so much more permissive than many views of justification as to make it especially interesting to view that conception in terms of rationality rather than justification. Rationality is a broad feature of persons, and it is significantly more global than justification, which does not even apply to persons as opposed to their behavior, cognition, and motivation. There is much to be said for the idea that there are as many kinds of rationality as there are coherent doxastic practices that have sufficient social realization and are consistent with the epistemic authority of the basic sources.

The latitude and pluralism that rationality allows must not be thought to imply that it is too weak to be a substantive constraint on a world-view. Rationality as I conceive it remains a normative status sufficiently strong to make its possession by theistic attitudes quite significant. Similarly, nondoxastic faith, if weaker than belief in its implicit cognitive commitment, may be conceptually quite rich and volitionally very strong: the richness of the content of faith is unaffected by the degree of cognitive commitment the faithful have to that content. One can have faith regarding as many things—indeed more, since nondoxastic faith is in a way more "permissive." There are surely some people who might withhold belief in cases where they might comfortably hold nondoxastic faith. Moreover, the volitional commitment of the faithful to, for instance, the ways of God that they have faith are required of them can be unlimitedly strong regardless of how good their justifying grounds for the religious propositions that form the content of their

---

[41] I have partially explicated this and briefly defended it in "Dimensions of Faith."

faith. There may even be more or deeper faith, in one use of the term, expressed by devoting one's life to divinely inspired ways regarding which one has nondoxastic faith, than in devoting it to ways one unqualifiedly believes are thus inspired.

Rational persons will in some sense tend to be confident in proportion to the felt strength of their grounds, and what begins as minimally rational nondoxastic faith can become both more rational and, ultimately, pass into rational doxastic faith. By contrast, rational doxastic faith, given certain cognitive or psychological counterforces, may be replaced (even if temporarily) by a rational nondoxastic faith less vulnerable to those pressures. Nondoxastic faith need not be an ideal of the theist, and those for whom justified belief or knowledge is an ideal may reasonably seek progressively stronger grounds for their faith. Nothing said here implies that these are not reasonable ideals, but even those who hold them may want to recognize nondoxastic faith as a fiduciary position that may be available to them or others when those ideals cannot be met. Nondoxastic faith provides for the possibility of significant religious ideals that can be achieved even when obstacles prevent realizing the more demanding ideals that philosophers have often defended or attacked.

Religious rationality, seen in this light, arises, and is embodied, in some of the most pervasive, coherent, and rewarding human practices. I see no cogent ground for denying that religious justification, for theistic beliefs a well as for nondoxastic faith, could also arise from the kinds of experiences that certain religious practices take as warranting them. Such justification is indeed readily viewed as a further stage in the same progression of experiences and other kinds of grounds of cognition that lead first to rational nondoxastic faith. But the thesis that there is justified doxastic faith, faith entailing justified theistic beliefs, is substantially stronger than the thesis that there is rational nondoxastic faith, and has had far more attention, especially in the past two decades. The latter thesis, and the corresponding case for religious rationality, whether of faith or of belief, is more readily defended: the rationality of a cognitive element, whether doxastic or not, tends to be more readily achieved than its justification. If this is, as it appears, a distinct position on the perennial problem of the reconciliation between faith and reason, it may provide for both some new directions in philosophical reflection and some new space for the exercise of faith.[42]

[42] This essay is dedicated to William P. Alston, whose work has been indispensable in developing the position suggested here and in many other epistemological projects I have done. Earlier versions were presented at Mercer University and the University of Nebraska, and for helpful comments I thank the faculty and students in those audiences, an anonymous reader for Cornell University Press, and, especially, Thomas Senor.

[6]

The Epistemic Value of Religious Experience: Perceptual and Explanatory Models

WILLIAM HASKER

I

It is coming to be widely agreed among philosophers of religion that religious experience has an important role to play in justifying religious belief. Just what that role is, and how we may best conceptualize the contribution of religious experience to the rationality of religious belief, remain very much in question. But I believe it can safely be said that two of the leading candidates for this task are the approaches I shall label the *perceptual model* and the *explanatory model.*

The perceptual model views religious experience, at least in favorable cases, as strongly analogous to sense-perception and as playing a comparable role in the justification of belief.[1] In the words of William Alston, "the experience or, as I shall say, the *perception* of God plays an epistemic role with respect to beliefs about God importantly analogous to that played by sense perception with respect to beliefs about the physical world".[2] Since sense-perception is universally regarded as one of our best-accredited modes of belief-acquisition, it is clear that the

---

[1] For purposes of this essay, we shall understand a person's being justified in a belief as the person's being reasonable or rational in accepting that belief; for something (fact, event, belief, experience, etc.) to justify a belief is simply for it to make it reasonable for some person to hold that belief. In the case of beliefs justified by experience, to be sure, it can make an important difference whether we are thinking of the justification of the belief *for the experiencer* or for someone else; in general, which one is intended should be clear from the context. Many additional questions are raised by the concept of justification, as Alston has shown in great detail (see his *Epistemic Justification: Essays in the Theory of Knowledge* [Ithaca: Cornell University Press, 1989]). But to pursue these issues further lies beyond the scope of this essay.

[2] William P. Alston, "Perceiving God," *Journal of Philosophy* 83 (1986), 655.

perceptual model, provided its claims can be made good, promises important benefits for the rationality of religious belief.

The alternative view regards systems of religious belief as, in effect, large-scale explanatory hypotheses, somewhat similar to large-scale scientific theories. Religious experience is seen to function as one item among others in a cumulative case that if successful, will show the religious hypothesis in question to be superior to competing hypotheses. The specific role of religious experience is as a *datum for explanation*—a datum that, it is alleged, cannot equally well be explained by nonreligious hypotheses and perhaps not by alternative religious hypotheses. It is because of this role of religious experience that I have labeled this the explanatory model.[3]

Both the perceptual model and the explanatory model have been developed with considerable care and philosophical sophistication.[4] In general, however, similar levels of effort do not seem to have been invested in the comparative evaluation of these models. Now it is certainly welcome to have as candidates two alternative ways of conceptualizing the epistemic value of religious experience. And it is not to be taken for granted that the two models will ultimately prove incompatible. Indeed, there is a way in which they can readily be combined: One can construct a "cumulative case" argument for one's religious hypothesis, relying heavily on explanatory considerations, and then invoke the perception of God as an additional source of support for one's cumulative case.[5] Some exponents of the explanatory model, how-

---

[3] The term 'confirmation model' may suggest itself as an alternative. But in the kind of view I have in mind, religious experience is viewed not as the fulfillment of a *prediction* made by the hypothesis in question but rather as a *datum for explanation*, and this feature is better captured by the term 'explanatory model'.

[4] For the perceptual model, see Richard Swinburne, *The Existence of God* (Oxford: Oxford University Press, 1979), chap. 13 (but see the following note for more on Swinburne); Carolyn Franks Davis, *The Evidential Force of Religious Experience* (Oxford: Oxford University Press, 1989); and the following works by William Alston: "Christian Experience and Christian Belief," in Alvin Plantinga and Nicholas Wolterstorff, eds., *Faith and Rationality: Reason and Belief in God* (Notre Dame: University of Notre Dame Press 1983), pp. 103–34; "Perceiving God," *Journal of Philosophy* 83 (1986), 655–65; "Religious Diversity and Perceptual Knowledge of God," *Faith and Philosophy* 5 (1988), 433–48; and *Perceiving God: The Epistemology of Religious Experience* (Ithaca: Cornell University Press, 1991). (*Perceiving God* became available about the time work on this essay was completed. The book is not appealed to in the body of the essay, but I believe all the views ascribed to Alston here are consistent with the book). For the explanatory model, see Basil Mitchell, *The Justification of Religious Belief* (New York: Oxford University Press, 1981); William J. Abraham, *An Introduction to the Philosophy of Religion* (Englewood Cliffs, N. J.: Prentice-Hall, 1985); and Nancey Murphy, *Theology in the Age of Scientific Reasoning* (Ithaca: Cornell University Press, 1990).

[5] This is essentially the strategy Swinburne follows, which is the reason for classifying him with the perceptual model.

ever, have specifically rejected perceptual categories as inappropriate to religious experience. So in the interest of focusing sharply the difference between the models, it will be helpful to frame the issue in terms of a comparison between the perceptual model and a version of the explanatory model that rejects the view that experience of God can be well understood in perceptual terms.

I have claimed that direct, explicit comparison of the two models has been somewhat lacking, but an exception must be made for an extremely interesting article by William J. Abraham.[6] In this article Abraham not only emphasizes the crucial epistemic role of religious experience—specifically, of the "inner witness of the Holy Spirit"—but deals explicitly with several alternative ways of conceptualizing this role. I, in turn, take Abraham's essay as a foil against which to develop my own discussion of this question. Although I finally arrive at conclusions different from his, I want to say at the outset that Abraham has performed an important service in calling attention to the issue and in providing both data and insights that can contribute to its resolution.

Abraham begins by pointing to some features of the cognitive life of "mature Christian believers" which go largely unrecognized in philosophical discussions of the rationality of belief. First, the primary religious intellectual concerns of such believers center not on "mere theism" but rather on much more specific beliefs "about the person of Christ, about the mysterious reality of the Holy Trinity, about the presence of the Holy Spirit in one's life, about the possibility and reality of forgiveness, about the existence of one, holy, catholic, and apostolic church, and the like" (p. 435). These beliefs "not only matter enormously to the religious believer, but . . . are often held with a high degree of certainty" (p. 435). Philosophical discussions, on the other hand, usually focus on the "very fundamentals of theistic belief," treating more specific doctrines such as those mentioned above as "secondary and peripheral" (pp. 434–35). Furthermore, such discussions usually proceed according to "standard inductive and deductive arguments," and by these standards specific religious doctrines can't possess anything like the degree of certainty believers often take them to have. The upshot is that these more specific religious beliefs are regarded, in effect, as optional "over-beliefs" that are not subject to rigorous intellectual standards, so that "one can believe anything in this arena and get by without scrutiny" (p. 436).

---

[6] William J. Abraham, "The Epistemological Significance of the Inner Witness of the Holy Spirit," *Faith and Philosophy* 7 (1990), 434–50. Page references appear in parentheses in the text.

Abraham's emphasis on the *certainty* that typifies the mature Christian believer is extremely important both for his article and for the present discussion. Because of this it may be helpful for me to state explicitly how I think his talk about certainty is to be understood. Abraham is sharply critical of the tendency among philosophers of religion to dismiss the believer's certainty by invoking "the standard distinction between a *person feeling* certain, understood as a psychological state of no cognitive significance, and a *proposition being* certain, understood as a proper cognitive proposal" (p. 435). A bit later, he criticizes the tendency of fideists to make a switch "from an account of the rationality of belief to a vision of the causes of believing . . . located in the action of God in the human heart" (p. 436). It seems clear from this, then, that Abraham does want to give "an account of the rationality of belief," that he wants the doctrines of the faith to be understood as "proper cognitive proposals." And he wants to show that believers can be fully rational—epistemically and not merely pragmatically rational—in having the very high degree of confidence in these doctrines that many of them exhibit. This requires, I take it, that the degree of confidence in the doctrines is matched by the strength of the grounds on which they are held. Understood in this way, one who is *certain* concerning her beliefs is fully rational only if she has grounds for those beliefs which suffice to make it extremely improbable that the beliefs are false.

Abraham, then, deplores the dissonance between the actual phenomena of religious belief and the account given of it by philosophers. In the interests of bridging the gap, he directs our attention to a specific form of religious experience, namely, the "inner witness of the Holy Spirit." He alludes to several persons who exemplify this experience, citing in some detail accounts from the Methodist Hester Ann Rogers, the Quaker Robert Barclay, and the Orthodox St. Seraphim of Sarov, as recounted by Nicholas Motovilov. He then summarizes in a half-dozen points the central features of this experience. I won't at this point rehearse either the narratives or Abraham's summary, but will have occasion to return to both later in our discussion.

At this point Abraham moves into the issue that is of main concern here, namely, the proper epistemological description and evaluation of the experience. I have claimed that the perceptual model and the explanatory model are the two leading contenders, but Abraham also discusses three other approaches that deserve at least passing mention. He considers the idea that the Spirit's witness is "a form of religious intuition" but dismisses this because such appeals to intuition are vacuous, obscure, and in general philosophically unenlightening. He also rejects the proposal that this experience should be seen as a case of mystical experience.[7] For one thing, most examples of the witness of the Holy Spirit don't fit the standard criteria for mystical experience. Furthermore, "we have no agreed upon account of how to read the cognitive value of mystical experience" (p. 444), which means that such a classification even if accepted, would not aid us greatly in our task of epistemological assessment.

A third[8] way of conceptualizing the epistemic value of the Spirit's witness is found in Alvin Plantinga's claim that religious beliefs grounded in such experiences are "properly basic"—that is, are appropriately accepted without having to be inferred from other beliefs that one holds. This approach deserves to be taken seriously; indeed, Abraham seems to find it more promising than the approach I am calling the perceptual model. Nevertheless, I do not pursue Plantinga's view here, mainly for reasons given by Abraham:

> It would be helpful if Reformed epistemologists would spell out more clearly the relation between talk of the inner witness of the Holy Spirit and their epistemological proposals. . . . As it stands we have to rest content with rather vague talk about a feeling of being forgiven or a scattered reference here and there to Calvin and Barth. We need a much richer account of the theological concepts being deployed by the Reformed epistemologists and a much deeper account of their meaning and history. (p. 440)

I believe this is essentially correct. Plantinga's contributions to the epistemology of religion are extremely important, but he has not yet given (or claimed to give) anything like a comprehensive account of the epistemology of religious belief, and the result is that many questions that are important for a study like the present one remain unanswered. William Alston, on the other hand, has been more explicit on at least some of the crucial points and so his version of Reformed epistemology (or, as he will have it, "Anglican epistemology"!) provides a better focus for our discussion. (It should be noted, however, that Plantinga's approach is *consistent with* the perceptual model on all im-

[7] Abraham has in mind here introvertive mysticism, in which "the human agent characteristically enters a state of consciousness which is devoid of its ordinary contents, which involves an experience of oneness with the divine, which appears to have an eminently real object that is perceived as divine, which is accompanied by complete bliss and peace, and in which there is no awareness of the passage of time" (p. 444).

[8] In Abraham's ordering, this is the *fourth* way, coming after his discussion of the perceptual model.

portant points; Alston's and Plantinga's respective epistemological projects are complementary rather than in competition with each other.)

II

We now turn to the discussion Abraham provides of the perceptual
model, which he characterizes as follows:

> A third way to handle the appeal to the work of the Holy Spirit in
> bringing certainty would involve appealing to some basic perceptual
> principle, say, the principle of initial credulity, and applying it to the
> kind of experiences cited. According to this principle, things are as
> they seem to be unless we can give good reason to believe other-
> wise. . . . On this analysis, we would be perfectly within our intellectual
> rights to take an apparent experience of the Holy Spirit as an experi-
> ence of the Holy Spirit unless we had good reason to think otherwise.
> (pp. 444–45)

Abraham's critique of the perceptual model is crucial to our present
undertaking, so it is quoted here in full:

> Two considerations should make one reluctant to accept this analysis.
> First, apparent experiences of the Holy Spirit are not generally al-
> lowed to stand alone in the Christian tradition. It is always appropriate
> to look for additional confirmation such as we saw in the case of Mo-
> tovilov. St. Seraphim treated Motovilov's request for further evidence
> as entirely acceptable. In addition, cases involving self-deceit or involv-
> ing lack of spiritual discernment are treated differently from our
> normal perceptual procedures. Appeal is made to moral and spiritual
> transformation as a further witness to the indwelling presence of the
> Holy Spirit. More generally, it is common for the saints to insist that
> the very capacities needed to perceive the presence of the Holy Spirit
> have to be drastically overhauled by divine grace or even supplied by
> God to the human subject. It is only the pure in heart who see God,
> hence one's experience of God depends crucially on repentance and
> on waiting on God in the liturgical acts of the church. Hence further
> ancillary claims of both an ontological and epistemic nature are de-
> ployed to flesh out what is at issue. All these elements add dimensions
> to the experience which suggest that it cannot be dealt with in terms
> of common perceptual capacities and principles.
> Secondly, it is exaggerated to claim that an apparent experience of

William Hasker

the Holy Spirit could by itself underwrite the rationality of, say, belief in the existence of the Holy Spirit. What this analysis ignores is the fact that talk about the work of the Holy Spirit is intimately related to a wider tradition which embodies at certain points appeal to special revelation. It is not as if we can know that the Holy Spirit exists and acts simply because we have had certain kinds of religious experiences. Expressed more summarily, we cannot see the Holy Spirit in the way that we can see tables and trees. Yet this is what a simple application of the principle of initial credulity asks of us. They [sic] suggest that the existence of the Holy Spirit or the activity of the Holy Spirit can be established by recourse to conventional perceptual capacities and conventions. (p. 445)

Clearly, this critique is both subtle and highly compressed. (And as a result it contains some things that I, at least, find rather obscure.) It seems to be something of an understatement, furthermore, to say that the critique involves only "two considerations." The critique really consists of a series of points in which Abraham alleges that the epistemic role of the Spirit's witness is dissimilar to that of perceptual experience; I shall argue in each case either that there is no dissimilarity or that, if it does exist, it is not sufficient to undermine the analogy between the two types of experience.

Abraham's first point may be stated summarily thus: Religious experience both admits and (in many cases) requires supplementation by other types of evidence, whereas perceptual experience does not.[9] A significant point here is that it is not at all clear that the example of Motovilov supports Abraham's claim. Motovilov asks, to be sure, "how he himself can recognize the Holy Spirit's true manifestation" (p. 439). But this occurs *before* he has experienced the Spirit for himself. And St. Seraphim's own statements strongly suggest that this experience is *not* in need of further confirmation:

It is very simple, my son, wherefore the Lord says: All things are simple to them that get understanding. Being in that understanding, the Apostles perceive whether the spirit of God abideth in them or not; and, being filled with understanding and seeing the presence of God's spirit within them, they affirmed that their work was holy and

---

[9] One might well choose to separate "admits" and "requires" as distinct points in the argument. But it simplifies the exposition to treat both of them together.

pleasing to God. . . . Thus the Holy Apostles were consciously aware of the presence in themselves of God's Spirit.[10]

Later on, after Motovilov and St. Seraphim have together experienced the Spirit's manifestation, there is no thought of a need for additional evidence; as Abraham himself notes, "St. Seraphim expects Motovilov's doubts about the presence of the Holy Spirit to be fully answered. There is no more need to ask how a person may be sure that he or she is in the grace of the Holy Spirit. This has been experienced firsthand; Motovilov has experienced the Holy Spirit for himself" (p. 440).[11]

So Abraham's own example seems to show that the Spirit's witness is *not* always in need of further confirmation. And on the other hand, it simply is not true that perceptual experience does not admit or require further confirming evidence. In the simplest cases, to be sure, where familiar, easily recognizable objects are identified at close range under good conditions ("This is a ball, that is a dog, and over there is a tree"), there may be little or no sense in talking about confirming evidence. (And some of the remarks Abraham makes, here and elsewhere, suggest that he may be relying too heavily on such simple examples.) But if the objects experienced are rare or difficult to identify, or if for some other reason there are questions about perceptual reports, confirming evidence may be crucial. Jurists, for example, strongly prefer that eyewitness testimony concerning crimes or accidents be supplemented by physical evidence, because experience teaches that even sincere and apparently confident witnesses fairly often get things wrong. Examples could easily be multiplied; in general, it is clear that this does *not* constitute a disanalogy between religious and perceptual experience.

Additional questions may be raised, to be sure, by the *kind* of confirming evidence that is thought to be relevant—thus, Abraham's reference to "moral and spiritual transformation." This does place us at some distance from everyday perceptual experience; still, analogies are not entirely lacking. It's clear that in some cases the presence or absence of an appropriate *affective response* to an object one claims to have perceived may strongly affect the credibility of the claim. ("If he had really

[10] From George P. Fedodov, ed., *A Treasury of Russian Spirituality* (Belmont, Mass.: Nordland, 1975), p. 273; quoted by Abraham on p. 439.

[11] It is true, to be sure, that Motovilov "was confronted with a miracle wherein he was aware, for example, of the bodily transfiguration of both St. Seraphim and himself, and he was also aware of a warmth which did not melt the snow" (p. 442). But if this is essential to the epistemic value of the experience, then the example is of extremely limited applicability!

seen a bear in the bushes, he'd be a lot more scared than he is.") And it is not out of the question that a person's claim, for instance, to have studied art or music under a renowned master should be judged, in part, by whether the person gives evidence of having learned the sorts of things one would be expected to have learned under such tuition.[12] I am prepared to admit, all the same, that there is at this point a certain dissimilarity between the witness of the Spirit and ordinary perceptual evidence. But I don't think the difference is so severe as to undermine the analogy between the two.

The second paragraph of Abraham's critique continues the theme of the need for further evidence but adds to that a new consideration, namely, the involvement of the experience of the Spirit in a "wider tradition which embodies at certain points appeal to special revelation" and which cannot, therefore, be established simply on the basis of an experience one has had. Now it is quite true that "we cannot see the Holy Spirit in the way that we can see tables and trees." (Note again the reliance on overly simple examples.) And it is also true that speaking of the inner witness of the Holy Spirit involves the application of a rather extensive conceptual scheme. If, for instance, the Holy Spirit is conceived of as the third Person of the Nicene Trinity, consubstantial with and proceeding from the Father and the Son, then it's clear that this involves assertions going far beyond what could be attested by the experience itself.

What Abraham seems to have overlooked is that perceptual experience also involves appeal to "wider conceptual schemes" that go beyond what is given phenomenally in the experience itself.[13] This is not always obvious in familiar cases such as perceiving tables and trees, because the conceptual schemes employed are so familiar that we take them almost entirely for granted. But consider the quite familiar experience of looking up and seeing that a jet airliner is beginning its landing approach. There is already quite a bit of conceptual sophistication (though taken for granted by moderns) in seeing that the object in the sky is an *airplane*—as opposed, for instance, to a very large bird or a chariot of the gods. That it is a *jet* airplane involves the further distinction between jet- and propeller-driven aircraft. Still further knowledge is presupposed in the identification of the plane as an airliner and in

---

[12] Admittedly, such considerations would likely be applied *by another person* seeking to evaluate the veracity of a claim; the subject herself probably would not be in need of such confirmation. And in general, it is probably more common for persons to come to have doubts about their own religious experiences than about their perceptual experiences.

[13] For an extensive discussion of this point, see Alston, *Perceiving God*, chap. 2.

the knowledge of airport procedures implied in the description of it as "beginning its landing approach." All this is entirely uncontroversial, but it does involve a great deal more than one can see by just looking up in the sky. For another example, consider a scientist looking at a bubble-chamber photograph and identifying a certain trace as the track of a particular kind of elementary particle. Here large amounts of extremely abstruse theory are involved, and some of it may remain controversial. So far, then, the analogy between religious experience and perceptual experience remains undisturbed.

There remains, to be sure, Abraham's point that, insofar as the description of the experience involves this kind of broad conceptual scheme, the experience cannot "stand on its own" epistemically. This is certainly true, as is illustrated both by the witness of the Spirit and by the interpretation of cloud-chamber photographs. In the perceptual situation there is a ready way around this difficulty, a retreat to a more restrained description of the experience in which the questionable theoretical commitments no longer appear. (Thus, we may go from "this negative pion track" to "this trace.")[14] Is a similar move available in the case of religious experience? Certainly it is; it's for this reason Alston speaks of *M-beliefs* (for "manifestation"); these are beliefs about "what God is doing, or how God is 'situated', vis-à-vis that subject at that moment. Thus by experiencing the presence and activity of God *S* can come to know (justifiably believe) that God is sustaining her in being, filling her with His love, strengthening her, or communicating a certain message to her".[15] Alston explicitly distinguishes these M-beliefs from beliefs involving a greater degree of theological elaboration that can't be justified directly by experience. So, presumably, one could redescribe the witness of the Holy Spirit in terms that do not presuppose a developed trinitarian theology.[16]

Almost certainly Abraham would not accept this; he writes, "The proposed experience, if it is to be identified, surely require the kind of specificity enshrined minimally in talk of the inner witness of the Holy Spirit" (p. 447). If this is taken as an objection to Alston's sort of procedure, it may be misdirected. Certainly a full, rich, and adequate

[14] There is no need to strip the description of *all* theoretical commitments—say, down to "pure sense-datum language." It is sufficient to strip away the commitments that in the given context are seriously controversial.

[15] "Perceiving God," p. 655; see also "Christian Experience and Christian Belief," pp. 104–5.

[16] There remains, to be sure, the question about *how much* of the content implied in the description of the experience can reasonably be ascribed to the experience itself. This is a difficult question that is not pursued further here. In any case, the same sort of question arises for perceptual experience generally.

description of this experience requires that the full resources of the Christian conceptual scheme be applied to it. (That, after all, is what elaborate conceptual schemes are *for*—cf. the bubble-chamber example.) But there is no reason to doubt that the witness of the Spirit may have been experienced quite fully by persons unfamiliar with the Nicene doctrine of the Trinity—for example, by the Apostle Paul himself! A description of the experience in general theistic terms that suppresses any explicit reference to the Holy Spirit might well be considered impoverished; it does not follow that such a description would be vacuous or lacking in epistemological significance.[17] I believe, therefore, that throughout this discussion the parallel between the Spirit's witness and perceptual experience remains unscathed.

Yet another line of argument is introduced by Abraham's reference to the special conditions required for one to experience the Spirit's witness: only the pure in heart shall see God; God himself must "overhaul" the faculties by which the Spirit is perceived; it is necessary to repent and to wait on God, and so on. Now all this would come as no surprise to Alston; he explicitly suggests that "God has decreed that a human being will be aware of His presence in any clear and unmistakable fashion only when certain special and difficult conditions are satisfied".[18] But does all this destroy the parallel with perceptual experience? I don't think so; admittedly, the most usual kinds of perceptual experience don't involve such special conditions, but parallels do exist. The need for a divine "overhaul" of the faculties involved corresponds pretty closely with familiar cases in which (for example) one's visual or auditory faculties have become impaired because of illness or injury.[19] Certainly, also, there are many cases in which prolonged and difficult cultivation and training are required for one to perceive aright: con-

---

[17] Consider the following description of her experience by Simone Weil: "In a moment of intense physical suffering, when I was forcing myself to feel love, but without desiring to give a name to that love, I felt, without being in any way prepared for it (for I had never read the mystical writers) a presence more personal, more certain, more real than that of a human being, though inaccessible to the senses and the imagination" (Simone Weil, *Waiting for God*, trans. Emma Crawford [New York: Harper and Row, 1973], p. 24). Here the lack of conceptual elaboration in the report of the experience actually serves to intensify the impact of the report, showing as it does that the experience was not the result of a preestablished conceptual "set" that might have induced it.

[18] "Christian Experience and Christian Belief," p. 129.

[19] If, on the other hand, it is insisted that the capacities involved must literally be "supplied by God to the human subject," so that no "normal" human capacities are involved at all, then the gap between perceptual experience and the witness of the Spirit becomes pretty wide. But this would seem to be a somewhat extreme theological interpretation of the Spirit's witness, one that an adherent of the perceptual model need not accept.

sider the oenologist's ability to identify by taste and smell a particular vintage, or the conductor's ability to perceive what is happening in an instrumental part buried in a complex symphonic texture. Cases in which special qualities of mind and spirit are required are perhaps less common (except in moral "perception," which is itself highly controversial). But consider the attention with which a skilled therapist listens to a patient, prepared to hear not only what is said but what is *not* said. Consider, also, the receptivity with which a skilled art critic looks at a painting and seeks to discern the presence (or absence) of an authentic Rembrandt. In both these cases, intensive training has to be coupled with a particular sort of openness and receptivity in order to secure the desired results. I conclude, then, that considerations such as these may put some strain on the analogy between perceptual and religious experience but don't come anywhere close to invalidating that analogy.

At a later point in his article, Abraham offers a further criticism of the perceptual model that deserves mention here; he writes:

> The perceptual model becomes immediately implausible when the details are pressed. Those who have explored its possibilities find themselves in the awkward position of having to develop an elaborate anthropology where the soul has to have senses to match the eyes and ears of our normal perceptual equipment. So the inner witness of the Holy Spirit not only has to underwrite the rationality of belief in the Holy Spirit but also the rationality of an overloaded theological anthropology. (pp. 447–48)

Abraham may have in mind here that aspect of the mystical tradition set forth (for example) in chapter 6 of Anton Poulain's *The Graces of Interior Prayer*,[20] where Poulain speaks of "intellectual spiritual senses" corresponding to each of the five senses of normal perception. I believe, however, that this material is best understood as an account of the *phenomenology* of the experience of God, as reported by the mystics; nothing in this requires the sort of "overloaded anthropology" Abraham complains of.[21] Seen in this light, his objection is without force against the perceptual model.

This concludes my discussion of Abraham's criticisms of the percep-

---

[20] Anton Poulain, *The Graces of Interior Prayer: A Treatise on Mystical Theology*, enlarged ed., trans. L. Smith (St. Louis: Herder, 1950). (I owe the reference to Poulain to William Alston, who in turn owes it to Nelson Pike.)

[21] In correspondence, Abraham informs me that he was thinking here of Jonathan Edwards and John Wesley. I would suppose that their accounts also can be dealt with as suggested in the text.

tual model. It is important to see what has and what has not been done. My claim is that none of Abraham's criticisms damages the analogy between perceptual experience and religious experience sufficiently that one rationally ought to give up the perceptual model.[22] I have not argued, nor do I know how to argue, that no other dissimilarities between the two types of experience can be adduced in the future which might compel the abandonment of the model. But pending such an eventuality, the perceptual model remains a viable option for interpreting the epistemic value of religious experience.

III

We now turn to the model Abraham himself favors, which is a version of what we are calling the explanatory model.[23] He explains this approach as follows:

A fifth alternative is to see the appeal to the internal witness of the Holy Spirit as helping to render plausible a large scale, integrative system of belief. On this analysis one would construe the claim about the presence of the Holy Spirit in the believer's inner life as intimately related to a wider narrative of the activity of God in creation, in human experience generally, and in history, which in turn would be linked to a web of beliefs about the nature of God, other spiritual experiences, human nature, ethical commitment, life after death, and the like.

The specific experience of the Holy Spirit would not in itself underwrite the rationality of belief in the complex vision from which the very language of the inner witness of the Holy Spirit is derived and gains its meaning. Rather, taken with a host of other considerations, and integrated into a judgement governed by tacit and largely implicit conventions of explanation, it would lend its own weight to the total evidence adduced. (p. 447)

[22] I have not dealt with Abraham's remark about "cases involving self-deceit or involving lack of spiritual discernment." I find this statement of his rather obscure, and I prefer not to speculate about his meaning. If this sentence is meant to introduce an important point distinct from those already considered, then I can only ask that Abraham make his meaning more explicit.

[23] Further light on Abraham's approach to these matters may be found in chap. 9, "Soft Rationalism," of his *Introduction to the Philosophy of Religion*. The emphasis on the witness of the Holy Spirit does not appear in this chapter, but most of the other themes of the present discussion are touched upon.

Abraham proceeds to cite four considerations in favor of this model. Three of the four, however, can be dealt with rather briefly, since they are in effect mirror images of his criticisms of the perceptual model. He says, "One of the obvious merits of this approach is that it recognizes the theologically laden character of the description of the experience at issue" (p. 447). This is indeed a merit of the model, but (as we have seen) this aspect of the situation is readily accommodated by the perceptual model, so it offers little in the way of comparative advantage for the explanatory model.

"Another merit of this position," Abraham continues, "is that it does not claim too much merely on the basis of experience. Hence it does not claim that somehow the believer has proved for himself or herself that the Holy Spirit really exists" (p. 447). Now the question of *how much* justificatory weight should be attributed to religious experience is central to the entire discussion and will certainly not be resolved by the present essay. I have already said some things relevant to this in the discussion of the perceptual model, and I return to the topic later in the discussion of the explanatory model. So we move on to Abraham's next argument, which is that "a further merit of this position is that it allows corroborative evidence to be used without strain" (p. 448). As we've seen, this is also true of the perceptual model, so it is of no help in deciding between the two.

We are now ready for Abraham's final argument, which he states as follows:

The most important merit of this proposal is that it makes adequate sense of the certainty attributed to this kind of experience. It is this that makes this kind of experience so interesting philosophically. In the view currently under consideration this feature is captured in this fashion. Christian theism according to this analysis is an elaborate liturgical, theological, and metaphysical vision whose centre is found in a personal God who has made human agents not only in his own image but with a destiny to love God and enjoy him for ever. Human agents are made to know God in a way analogous to the way they know each other. Knowledge of other persons can clearly be of two sorts. We can know others indirectly, that is, through narratives, biographies, descriptions of their activity and character, and the like. And we can know others directly, that is, we can know them for ourselves by acquaintance, by encountering them and getting to know them intimately. The latter kind of knowledge clearly brings with it much greater certainty than the former. We generally value direct, person-to-person encounter with others over against indirect knowledge of others. Likewise with God. Encountering God, coming into an experience with God where his Holy Spirit comes to dwell in the depths of our hearts, experiences which embody this element naturally bring with them a sense of certainty analogous to coming to know someone personally, who heretofore was known by description or hearsay. This is why people emerge from this kind of experience so convinced. And so they should, if they have their epistemological wits about them. Taken with the evidence of all the accumulated signs and marks of God's presence in the world, they permit precisely the kind of certainty one finds in the saints and martyrs. (pp. 448–49)

The first, and most obvious, reply to this is to ask how it is that this "person-to-person encounter" with God does not involve *perceiving* God. In ordinary parlance, "meeting someone personally" involves our seeing and hearing him, perhaps touching his hand, and the like. We do not generally think we have "encountered" someone by way of an explanatory scheme, even if such a scheme has a strong "cumulative case argument" in its favor! The least that can be said here is that Abraham owes us an explanation—an explanation he has not provided—of how we "come to know God personally" without this in any way involving *perceptual knowledge* of God.

But suppose we set this aside for the moment and assume there is some viable concept of "encountering God personally" that does not involve *perceiving* God. What, then, of the other claims made by Abraham? It is undeniably true, as he says, that we value intimate personal knowledge of others more than knowledge by description and hearsay. But Abraham's claim about the superior certainty possessed by the former kind of knowledge just does not seem to me to be true. It happens that I have seen both President Harry S. Truman and Queen Elizabeth II "in the flesh," but I do not find that I believe in their existence any more firmly than in that, say, of Abraham Lincoln and Queen Victoria. If I come to be seriously in doubt about the existence of some individual who has been described to me, a personal meeting will not necessarily settle the question: the possibility of imposture must also be eliminated. (Only *very* young children believe in Santa Claus because they have talked to him at the shopping mall.) Nor does direct acquaintance have decisive advantages in learning the characteristics of a person. Biographers can sometimes unearth aspects of a subject's personality and character that were unknown even to close associates—and I would by no means support the proposal that my college, in filling faculty vacancies, should disregard written evidence and rely entirely on the impression made in a face-to-face interview. In all these cases, direct acquaintance seems to be one way of gaining knowledge among others—not inferior to indirect methods, but not necessarily superior to them either.

There is, I must confess, one exception to this, (at least) one respect in which direct acquaintance *is* cognitively superior to indirect knowledge. But before taking this up, I wish to explore a difficulty in Abraham's proposal that has so far gone unremarked. Abraham seems to be committed to the following three propositions:

(1) In identifying an experience as the inner witness of the Holy Spirit, we are invoking a complex system of Christian beliefs.

(2) The judgment that one is experiencing the inner witness of the Holy Spirit is both noninferential (see p. 444) and certain (see, e.g., p. 440).

(3) The experience of the inner witness of the Holy Spirit plays a crucial role in conferring epistemological certainty on the Christian beliefs involved in the description of the experience (see pp. 435–37, 448–49).[24]

These three propositions are certainly not formally inconsistent; indeed, they might very well all be true—especially if one construes the witness of the Spirit in terms of the perceptual model. But I do not think all three propositions can be true if we also accept certain other views embraced by Abraham. The first assertion is certainly true, and in typical cases the second is surely true as well. The judgment that one has the Spirit's witness, as Abraham says, "is not a matter of inferring the causes of one['s] experience from the phenomenological features of that experience; it is more a matter of learning how to apply a rich network of concepts derived from Christian scripture and tradition to one's experience" (p. 444). Now, if in judging that one has the Spirit's witness one is applying a "rich network of concepts," then that judgment cannot be true unless the doctrines from which the concepts receive their meaning are also substantially true.[25] Certainly the experi-

---

[24] In fairness it should be stated that Abraham does not claim that this third proposition has been established by his argument (see p. 449). Pretty clearly, though, he believes that it is true and hopes that its truth could be established by the full argument of which his paper forms one part.

[25] The doctrines need not be true *in every detail;* there is no reason to suppose (for example) that Western Christians, who affirm the *filioque,* and Eastern Christians, who reject it, are not both speaking about the same Holy Spirit. But if the doctrines concern-

ence by itself can't *prove* the doctrines are true; this is a point Abraham himself frequently insists on (see pp. 445, 447). So we must ask, *What grounds the certainty of this experience?* To be sure, we can readily see that one who has such an experience might *feel certain* about doctrines concerning which she was formerly undecided. But Abraham has nothing but scorn for proposals that would sunder the subject's *feeling* of certainty from the epistemological certainty of the propositions believed (see pp. 435–36). And nothing in our account thus far gives any clue as to how the doctrines in question could acquire this kind of certainty.

What am I saying here? Am I claiming that Motovilov was deluded in being certain that he had experienced the Spirit's presence, or that Hester Ann Rogers was excessive in her confidence that her sins had been forgiven? Not necessarily. There is nothing in the account given of these cases[26] that suggests that the "background beliefs" appealed to in interpreting their experience were in question at all. Motovilov is not wondering whether or not there is a Holy Spirit; he is concerned about whether he himself can enter into an experience of the Spirit. And Hester Rogers was not wondering whether there is a God, whether he holds us accountable before his law, whether he offers us salvation in Jesus Christ, and the like; rather, she was "in great distress about the state of her standing before God" (pp. 437–38). In each case, the broader theological background for the experience is taken as already sufficiently established. What is lacking, and what the experience supplies, is assurance about the subject's own personal relationship to salvation and to the Spirit of God.

And this brings us back to the point about the cognitive merits of direct acquaintance with persons. I've said that, in general, direct acquaintance is not necessarily superior to other modes of knowledge acquisition. But there is one clear exception to this, and that is where what needs to be known concerns *the attitude of the person known toward the knowing subject.* Suppose I have done something that, I reasonably fear, may have deeply offended you. It is little comfort to me to infer, from my past knowledge of your character, that you are not likely to hold a grudge over the incident. It may be only a little better if some

---

ing the Holy Spirit are substantially false, then one cannot correctly identify a certain experience as "the witness of the Holy Spirit."

[26] Throughout this essay I am relying on the accounts of these experiences given by Abraham. Clearly, an authoritative study would require both a wider induction and a deeper study of individual cases, but this exceeds the scope of the present paper. In any case, Abraham has done an outstanding job of assembling and illuminating some very instructive examples.

third party, even a trusted mutual acquaintance, assures me of your continued goodwill. What I need is for you, personally, to look me in the face and assure me with evident sincerity that my fault is forgiven and our relationship is unbroken. And this is not simply a matter of my psychological need for reassurance; it is also the case that in such matters there really is no other equally satisfactory way of acquiring the knowledge of your present attitude toward me.

But this, of course, is just the sort of knowledge Motovilov and Hester Rogers were in need of. The question about one's relation to the Holy Spirit is met by the actual presence of the Spirit; the question of one's standing before God is met by God himself, through the Holy Spirit, assuring one of his love and forgiveness. That such experiences should bring certainty is anything but surprising.

But, of course, this still leaves the epistemological certainty of the background theological beliefs unaccounted for. These beliefs are not themselves "proved" by the experiences; rather, they are *presupposed* and *applied* to the experiences. How as a matter of fact Motovilov or Hester Rogers arrived at their acceptance of the respective background beliefs could be determined only (if at all) by a study of their biographies. So in these cases, Abraham's proposition (3) is not vindicated. Indeed, how could it be?

IV

Of necessity, many of the conclusions of this essay are provisional. I have argued that Abraham's criticisms of the perceptual model do not seriously damage it and that his reasons for preferring the explanatory model have little weight. This does not exclude the possibility that other arguments may be produced that succeed where his have failed.[27] Nor do I wish to rule out the possibility that some other model may be identified that will be superior to either of those discussed here. But there is one conclusion I am confident will survive future discussion of these topics: I believe it is clear that the perceptual model will ascribe a great deal more epistemic value to religious experience than the explanatory model is able to do.[28] This, I think, is what ought to have

[27] A large number of arguments against the perceptual model are discussed by Alston in *Perceiving God.*

[28] Abraham himself seems ambivalent about this: on the one hand, he praises the explanatory model for not claiming too much on the basis of experience alone; on the other, he extols its ability to show how religious experience justifies the strong claims of certainty often made for religious beliefs. These claims don't look as though they can be

been expected all along; perceptual evidence is just stronger than inference to the best explanation, which is the principal mode of justification employed in the explanatory model.[29] It's true, of course, as Abraham says, that experiences of the inner witness of the Spirit with their attendant claims of certainty are "one of the subtle pieces of data which an adequate phenomenology of religious belief must accommodate and explain" (p. 449). But naturalistic explanations of religious experience are neither difficult to produce nor obviously highly implausible, so that an argument to the best explanation in this instance has only limited force.

The explanatory model will no doubt recognize that judgments that one is experiencing God, has the Spirit's witness, and the like are typically immediate and noninferential. But if perceptual categories are ruled out, the best available alternative construal is probably the one employed by Abraham: the judgment is made by applying "a rich network of concepts derived from Christian scripture and tradition to one's experience" (p. 444). But these concepts presuppose complex theological doctrines that cannot plausibly be thought of as immediately justified by the experience; thus it turns out that crucial Christian beliefs are *presupposed* by the experience as interpreted rather than *justified* by the experience. To be sure, the successful application of the network of concepts to one's experience may in some sense offer a confirmation of the presupposed beliefs. But such confirmation is relatively weak in its epistemic force, especially in view of the fact that the doctrinal system is only weakly predictive. It's clear that by far the greater part of the burden of justification will have to be borne by factors other than experience.

How much justificatory weight will the perceptual model ascribe to religious experience? A full answer to this must await further development and analysis of that model, but I think it is clear that the epistemic value ascribed to experience will be a great deal more than for the explanatory model. Now of course it could be that the modest estimate on this point which derives from the explanatory model is the correct one, and that attempts to ascribe greater value to these experiences represent overreaching. But philosophers who are initially inclined to ascribe a high epistemic value to religious experience, as well as those

---

easily reconciled with each other—and as we have seen, the latter claim simply does not withstand examination.

[29] It may be of interest here to note that Basil Mitchell, a leading proponent of the explanatory model, is willing to speak of "direct awareness" of God, though he doesn't want to call this perception. Mitchell, however, eschews the strong claims of certainty that Abraham is concerned to explicate and defend (see *Justification of Religious Belief,* chap. 6).

who suspect that without an important contribution from experience it will be difficult to construct a satisfactory justification of religious belief, have good reason to pursue the perceptual model, to develop it, and to hope for its success.[30]

[30] I would like to express my appreciation to William Alston, William Abraham, Tom Senor, and the participants in the philosophy of religion reading group at Notre Dame for valuable comments on an earlier draft of this essay.

[7]

Religious Language, Religious Experience, and Religious Pluralism

WILLIAM J. WAINWRIGHT

N o one's contribution to the resurgence in the philosophy of religion is greater than William Alston's. His discussions of the divine attributes, religious language, and religious experience are rich and rewarding. They are also, in my opinion, largely correct. This essay, though, focuses on two strands in Alston's thought that need further examination: his defense of the possibility of literally ascribing personalistic predicates to God, and his response to the problem incompatible religious experiential practices create for his account of religious experience. I shall argue that in both cases difficulties emerge that can be satisfactorily met only by showing that the theistic worldview is superior to its rivals.

I

Alston's most important contribution to the analysis of religious language is his demonstration that we can speak literally of God. The class of personalistic predicates ("P-predicates") is central to theistic life and thought. Alston shows that if we construe mentalistic terms functionally, then at least part of what we mean when we ascribe such predicates as "wants," "intends," and "believes" to human beings can be literally ascribed to God. "Wants," for instance, can be defined by a set of lawlike generalizations that links wanting with other mental states and with appropriate behavioral outputs. An example of such a generalization would be "If S wants that p and believes that doing A will bring about p, then S has a tendency to do A".[1] Although God's mental states are very different from ours, the generalization is literally true of both.

Alston's alternative to "wholesale univocity"[2] and "pan-symbolism"[3] has been neglected in previous literature. On this view, divine and human intellection and volition share certain abstract features (those identified in the functional analysis). The *ways* in which God and human beings realize these features differ radically, however. Indeed (supernatural assistance apart), we have no idea precisely *how* they are realized in the divine nature; the intrinsic nature of God's mental states necessarily eludes us. This account respects God's transcendence but also permits literal and univocal predication. We can form concepts of these abstract features, find terms for them, and then apply the terms literally to Him. Since the *same* abstract features are displayed by both God and human beings, our (literal) terms also apply univocally.

Alston acknowledges that these predicates are thin. "All we have are concepts of positions in a structure of mutual dependence". God's being favorably disposed toward a goal, for example, and His doing A to bring it about "are the sorts of things that are related to each other and to other states and activities" in functional relations specified by conditionals like "If the agent has a pro-attitude toward a goal and a cognition that doing A is the way to realize it, the agent will have a tendency to do A". "Virtually nothing" has been said "as to what it is that stands in these relations". Nor is it clear how the concepts could be filled out (pp. 97–99).

In the human case, we can fall back on "our own first-person sense of what it is like to want something . . . to believe that something will occur, . . . to feel that we ought to do something, to intend to do something, and so on". We have no "such insight into what it is like to be God". In addition, "our concepts of human motivational factors are enriched by aspects that must be absent" in God's case. Our conception of intention or willing, for example, is "partly constituted by our understanding of the way in which the . . . intention holds fast through a variety of changing circumstances" and "our awareness of effort of will in struggles against temptation". Neither is relevant to a timeless and

---

[1] William P. Alston, *Divine Nature and Human Language: Essays in Philosophical Theology* (Ithaca: Cornell University Press, 1989), p. 74. Subsequent page references appear in parentheses in the text.

[2] Wholesale univocity is the view that "ordinary terms" are "used in the same ordinary senses of God and human beings" (p. 65).

[3] Pan-symbolism is the view that all God-language (or at least all substantive God-language) is symbolic. Formal predicates like "being the referent of a term" or "being such that no substantive predicates apply to it" can be literally applied to God, but substantive predicates cannot.

perfect being. "Indeed", says Alston, "there is some question as to whether our account even entails that the system constitutes a distinctively *personal* agent", although he suggests that the fact that "the 'output' of the system" is construed "in rich, intentionalistic *action* terms . . . may suffice to dispel the doubts" (pp. 99–100).

It isn't clear to me that it does. For the system's "outputs" can be construed as actions only if they are caused by the right kind of psychological states, and the question is, *Are* they? Any doubts that the system is distinctively personal carry over to its outputs. For if the *system* isn't personal, then its outputs aren't those of a personal agent, that is, they aren't *actions*. What is at issue, in short, is whether we are entitled to *call* the system's outputs "actions."[4]

Alston's picture of God is uncomfortably reminiscent of some others. Anselm, for example, claimed that God is compassionate in the sense that He acts as if He felt compassion although He doesn't actually do so. God acts as we do when we act compassionately (the effects are the same), but He doesn't experience the feeling. Charles Hartshorne rightly objects that a compassion without feeling isn't real compassion. Or consider Maimonides' contention that literal predications about God should be taken negatively or construed as claims that God brings about certain effects. Interpretations like these protect God's transcendence. But, as Aquinas points out, we seem to mean *more* than this, namely, that God intrinsically possesses *analogues* of such human properties as "loving the good," "being compassionate," and so on, and possesses them in some richer sense than having states that play the same functional role. "God is good," for example, means more than that God causes goodness or that God isn't evil;[5] it means that "whatever good we attribute to creatures pre-exists in God, and in a more excel-

---

[4] When I made this charge in an earlier version of this essay, Alston responded by arguing that God's mental states have the right propositional content to ensure that the system is personal. "Thus when states of the subject with propositional content of the form *bringing about A is the best way of realizing B* regularly interact with states with the propositional content *realizing B* to result in the realizing of A, we have ample grounds for taking states of the first sort to be cognitive propositional attitudes (belief or knowledge that p, where p is the proposition in question), states of the second sort to be pro-attitudes toward realizing B . . . , and the resultant bringing about A to be an intentional action" ("Reply to My Critics," *American Philosophical Association*, Chicago, 1991). Perhaps this is sufficient to show that God's "mental" system is personal in some sense. (Though note that on some accounts of having propositional content, similar considerations would show that sufficiently sophisticated computers or robots are personal systems.) I am not fully convinced that it disposes of the objection in the next paragraph.

[5] Or that God has states that underlie His disposition to cause goodness and that make it true that He isn't evil.

lent and higher way." Anything less "is against the intention of those who speak of God."[6]

Does it matter that these "concepts of the divine psyche and . . . activity" are "quite sparse"? Alston concedes that it does. Although "we do not need more for theoretical purposes", concrete representations are required for "guidance, direction, inspiration, assistance in attaining salvation," and so on. These concrete pictures, though, do not literally apply to God. We must, therefore, launch ourselves "into the still not sufficiently charted seas of the figurative and the symbolic" (pp. 100–102).

I believe that great deal may hang on the success of this voyage. There are two possibilities. One is that our metaphor's cognitive meaning is exhausted by (something like) Alston's austere functional account. Those portions of our metaphors that can't be understood in this way are rhetorical devices for stirring hearts and enlisting wills; they are psychologically important but lack cognitive significance. The other is that (some of) the aspects of our metaphors that escape the functional analysis also have cognitive force.

The second possibility appears to me to be correct. Our representations of God as father, compassionate, Lord, and the like function as *warrants* for a variety of religious actions and responses; we use them to *justify* certain attitudes and patterns of conduct.[7] We must implicitly believe, then, that in deploying these representations we are making true assertions about God. Alston clearly agrees.

Could the portion of our metaphor's cognitive meaning that escapes Alston's functional analysis be irreducibly metaphorical?

Alston distinguishes two strata of truth-claims in metaphorical statements. "First, there is the very unspecific claim that the exemplar [the sort of thing the predicate literally applies to] is sufficiently similar to the subject [what the statement is about] . . . to make the former a useful model of the latter. (Call this M-similarity.) Second, there is some more specific attribution that is derived from one or more particular points of resemblance" (p. 27). "Achilles is a lion," for instance, implicitly asserts that a lion is a useful model for Achilles, and (in the right context) that it is a useful model in virtue of the lion's valor. The statement that x is M-similar to y is literally true if true at all. Can the second stratum also be expressed literally?

---

[6] Aquinas, *Summa theologiae* I. Q 13. A2.

[7] Note that the claim that God has the appropriate functional states doesn't clearly warrant or justify our *loving* Him, for example.

Alston has an argument that implies that it can. Suppose I say "God is my rock," meaning to attribute a property, P, to God.

(1)   I cannot do this unless I have P in mind. But

(2)   If I have P in mind, I must have a concept of P. And, if I do,

(3)   "I can associate an element of the language with P in such a way as to use that element to attribute P to something". Now

(4)   If P is cognitively accessible to me, "it will be, in principle, cognitively accessible to any other human being". Hence,

(5) · Others, too, can (in principle) associate an element of the language with P.

So, assuming that these meanings can be shared,

(6)   "It is in principle possible that a language should contain words that have the meanings required for the literal expression of" the content of "God is my rock." (pp. 28–29)

Now what holds for metaphors as a whole should also hold for the cognitively meaningful portion of them that isn't captured by the functional analysis. In asserting more than that some state of God stands in the requisite functional relationships, I presumably intend to attribute some property P' to Him. I can't do this, however, unless I have P' in mind. And the argument goes through as before.

Yet how much does it really establish? When a predicate is used metaphorically, what the predicate literally applies to (the "exemplar") functions as a model of the metaphorical sentence's subject. Now I would agree that the speaker in these cases typically has certain features of the exemplar (vaguely) in mind, and that it is because of these features that he believes the exemplar to be like the subject. He means to be asserting, in other words, not just that God is like a rock but that God is like a rock with respect to some property(s) Q that the rock has. I also agree that the speaker has a concept of the relevant divine property P. I suspect, however, that the concept of P often amounts to nothing more then that of "a property like Q." This property can, of course, be predicated literally.

Nevertheless, I think it is quite possible that the portion of our metaphor's cognitive meaning that can't be articulated by the functional

analysis can *only* be expressed by these likeness claims. We must therefore consider Alston's contention that likeness statements can't capture
what we are after.

It isn't helpful to be told that God is like so-and-so, since any two
things are like each other in some respect. Are any two things *significantly* like each other in some way? The answer isn't entirely clear, but
"it seems plausible to suppose that, with sufficient ingenuity, virtually
any metaphorical predicate can be elaborated in a theologically plausible way" (p. 32). If it can, then anything we can metaphorically say
about God will be true.

In addition, metaphorically irreducible theological statements won't
stand in "the desired logical relations" to other statements. "God is
loving", for example, will be compatible with "God is cruel." For both
a "loving and merciful" and "an arbitrarily cruel and bloodthirsty"
human being might be "suitable model[s] for God (in some respect or
other)" (p. 33). Nor will entailment hold. For consider the following
argument.

(1)   A perfectly loving being will forgive those who repent.

(2)   God is perfectly loving. Therefore,

(3)   God will forgive those who repent.

The premises can be true and the conclusion false, since "it is . . .
logically possible that both a perfectly loving human being and an unforgiving human being are useful models of God in some respect(s) or
other" (pp. 33–34).

Finally, assertions of significant likeness are too indeterminate to warrant predictions, or conclusions "concerning how we ought to act and
feel, or what attitudes we should have". That God's purpose is for
human beings to "enjoy eternal blessedness," that God is able to carry
out His purposes, and that His "purposes are unchanging" doesn't
imply that human beings will enjoy it, since the respects in which God
is like "a human being that unvaryingly has a certain purpose he is
able to carry out" may not be the right ones. For similar reasons, that
God commands us to love one another doesn't entail that we *should* do
so (pp. 34–35).

I do not find these arguments compelling, although I would agree
that the last set of considerations shows that traditional theists will want
to apply *some* predicates to God literally that can't be analyzed as disguised
comparisons. In particular, they will want to ascribe predicates like

"brings it about that some or all human beings enjoy eternal blessedness" and "has a property(s) that makes loving behavior mandatory."[8]
What isn't clear to me is that the remainder of what we wish to ascribe
to God couldn't be such that it can be expressed only by likeness
statements.

Likeness statements have more content that Alston ascribes to them.
A contradictory of any likeness statement can be obtained by prefacing
it with "It is not the case that." If metaphors are implicit likeness statements, then metaphors too have contradictories. There is also a less
trivial sense in which they do so. Core theological metaphors are typically (disguised) comparisons. God is a craftsman, for example, implicitly asserts that His relation to the world is more like that of a craftsman
to his product than that of an acorn to the oak or of the sun to the
heat and light it emits. The terms of the implicit comparison are determined by context. In practice, less favored models are typically drawn
from rival religious traditions or doctrinal rivals within one's own
tradition.

If this is correct, some metaphorical theological assertions will contradict others. "God is a craftsman" contradicts "God is the world egg
(seed)," since the first implicitly asserts that God is (*überhaupt*) more
like a craftsman than a seed whereas the second implicitly asserts the
opposite.

(Not all religious metaphors, of course, are comparative. If a śakta
says "God is our mother," his assertion implies that the divine is more
like a mother than a father [or, more precisely, more like a mother
than the masculine figures that signify Viṣnu or Śiva]. But when Julian
of Norwich addresses God [or Jesus] as Mother, her assertion implies
only that God's [or Jesus'] relation to us is significantly like that of
a mother's.)

Nor is it clear that (all) familiar entailments must be rejected. Consider Alston's sample entailment. The second premise can be construed
as "God is more like a perfectly loving human being than a human
being who isn't" and the denial of its conclusion as "Either God is more
like an unforgiving human being than a human being who isn't or God
is exactly as much like an unforgiving human being as He is like a
forgiving one." It isn't clear that these statements (and [1]) are
consistent.

Even if the statements aren't interpreted as comparisons, something
like the inference from (1) and (2) to (3) might still be legitimate. For

[8] Notice, however, that predicates like these are even "thinner" than our functional
predicates.

another way of interpreting (or perhaps reconstructing) Alston's argument is this:

(1) A perfectly loving human being is very different from one who won't forgive others.

(2) God is very much like a perfectly loving human being. Hence,

(3) God is very different from a human being who won't forgive others.

The inference pattern is:

A is very different from B.
C is very much like A. Hence,
C is very different from B.

The pattern, of course, is invalid. That Bob is very much like his mother and that his mother is very different from his father doesn't entail that *Bob* is very different from his father. As different as his father and mother are from each other, he may be very much like both. I suggest, however, that even though our premises don't *entail* the conclusion, they contextually imply it. That they do is implied by the fact that we must take special precautions to prevent people from drawing the conclusion. (By saying, for example, that in spite of the fact that Bob is very much like his mother and she is very different from his father, he is also very much like his father.) While the premises don't entail the conclusion, they *warrant* it in the absence of a disclaimer. I suggest, then, that in the absence of disclaimers, something like Alston's premises justify our concluding that God is very different from a human being who won't forgive others.

Finally, one might interpret our nonliteral predicates analogically. One way of drawing the distinction between metaphor and analogy is this.[9] In the case of analogy (but not metaphor), x is implicitly said to be like y with respect to *all* of y's entailed properties. Hence, if the similarity between God and a perfectly loving human being is analogical, God will also exhibit a property similar to forgiveness. If so, the inference goes through.

My argument to this point can be summarized as follows. If, for

---

[9] Up to this point, I have followed Alston's practice and used "metaphor" to cover what various writers speak of as analogy, symbol, parable, model, and so forth.

example, Christian theological statements *justify* Christian life and practice, then their cognitive significance isn't exhausted by a functional analysis or by statements about God's causal relations to other things. For these are too thin to justify them. Is the remainder irreducibly metaphorical? Strictly speaking, it isn't. If I am correct, the remainder can be captured by likeness statements,[10] and likeness statements are literally true if true at all. This victory over pan-symbolism is hollow, however, for few pan-symbolists would object to a reduction of this kind. If the only way in which metaphorical statements can be translated literally is by employing likeness statements, then pan-symbolists have just about what they wanted. Of course, if Alston is correct, statements of significant likeness are even thinner than our austere functional or causal statements, and, if they are, it is doubtful that they can furnish the guidance or justification provided by (some) religious metaphors. I believe I have shown, though, that these statements can have more content than he allows.

Nevertheless, in spite of this disagreement, I believe Alston has shown that some P-predicates can be literally applied to God. In particular, I

---

[10] Lynne Tirrell ("Reductive and Nonreductive Simile Theories of Metaphor," *Journal of Philosophy* 88 [July 1991], 337–58) contends that similes must be distinguished from (literal) comparisons. "The engine of my boat is like the engine of my car" can be justified (explicated) "with a long tedious list of properties both have—in the same literal sense" (p. 343). "Juliet is like the sun" cannot. The inferences the latter sanctions ("Juliet is warm, she is bright and dazzling, she is the center of Romeo's world, his day begins with her, and so on" [p. 341]) are as figurative as the simile itself. Tirrell concludes that similes aren't literal comparisons since they can't "be explained in purely literal terms" (p. 341). One might therefore argue as follows. Even if metaphors can be translated by similes, they can't be translated by straightforward likeness statements. I am accordingly mistaken in thinking that religious metaphors can be explicated by likeness statements that are literally true if they are true at all.

I am not convinced that this argument is sound. Although similes may differ from ordinary likeness statements in the way Tirrell suggests, this isn't sufficient to show that they aren't literal comparisons. Tirrell seems to assume that a comparison is literal only if the points of resemblance can be literally expressed. This is false. Consider "The taste of oysters is like the taste of clams" or "Scarlet is like crimson." We can't specify a common property that grounds the likeness that scarlet and crimson, or the two tastes, literally have. The assertions, nonetheless, are literally true. (We *can* specify the class of comparison, viz., colors or tastes. But doing so doesn't explicate the nature of the similarity we are calling attention to; blue and scarlet are also colors, and the taste of oysters and the taste of sugar are also tastes.) Nor is the use of figurative language decisive. The fact that we use figurative language to explicate the points of likeness may distinguish similes from straightforward comparisons. It doesn't show that similes aren't literally true. Suppose I say that my love for one of my daughters differs from my love for the other (although it is neither greater nor less). I may need figurative language to explicate the difference. It doesn't follow that my statement isn't literally true. Similarly here. The fact that I have to use figurative language to explicate the nature of a likeness between x and y doesn't entail that "x is like y" isn't literally true.

believe he has shown that part of what we mean when we apply mental terms to persons can be defined functionally and that that part can be literally (and univocally) applied to God.

But suppose it can. *Should* it be? The plurality of religions confronts us with a different and potentially more serious problem. The most compelling argument for "pan-symbolism" is based not on God's transcendence or the limits of our conceptual resources but on the contingent fact (or alleged fact) that He has revealed Himself in diverse and equally valid ways. This argument has been effectively presented by John Hick. Hick believes that we can "reasonably claim that our own form of religious experience . . . is veridical."[11] Because there are no epistemically relevant differences between our form of religious experience and those embedded in other traditions, we must assign them the same validity. Yet the phenomenological objects of the various forms of religious experience are different. To preserve the experiences' validity, we must postulate the Real-in-itself of which God, Brahman, Nibbāna, and the like are phenomenal manifestations. Hick doesn't think literal predication is impossible. Certain formal concepts apply to God. Although Hick denies it, his position also commits him to ascribing literally some substantive predicates to the Real, namely, goodness and being a cause or necessary condition of finite substances and events.[12] But his argument does preclude the possibility of literally ascribing P-predicates to the divine. For suppose that P' is a P-predicate ("loves being in general," for example, or "knows every true proposition") and that non-P' is its complement. If the divine is veridically experienced as P' and also as non-P',[13] then God can't literally be either. (It is logically impossible for the divine literally to be P' and at the same time literally to be non-P'. If the Real is literally P' [or non-P'] but only symbolically non-P' [or P'], then the experience of the divine as non-P' [or P'] is less veridical than the experience of the divine as P' [or non-P']. This is contrary to our hypothesis. Hence, if both experiences are [equally] veridical, then the Real isn't literally P' and it isn't literally non-P'.)

Alston must defuse this argument if he is to show that true literal predication of P-predicates is a *real* (and not merely logical) possibility for theists. I doubt that he can do this without showing that theistic religious experiences are more veridical than the experiences of Buddhists, Advaitins, Taoists, and other nontheists. I am suggesting, in

---

[11] John Hick, *An Interpretation of Religion* (New Haven: Yale University Press, 1989), p. 235.

[12] See my review of Hick's book in *Faith and Philosophy* 9 (April 1992), 259–65.

[13] I suspect that a more accurate description of what actually occurs is that theists experience the Real as P and nontheists experience it as Q where Q (e.g., "a naked unity devoid of distinctions" or "emptiness") at least appears to entail non-P.

other words, that in order to show that the true literal predication of
P-predicates is a real possibility, Alston must show that theistic ways of
experiencing and thinking about the Real are cognitively superior to
nontheistic ways of doing so. I argue in the next section, however, that
the cognitive superiority of theistic religious experiences can be defended only by establishing the superiority of theistic metaphysics—a
task Alston has so far been reluctant to undertake.

II

Alston's account of religious experience lies at the center of his
defense of Christian theism. Alston believes we can't establish the reliability of sense-perception, induction, rational intuition, or any basic
doxastic practice without relying on what we learn from engaging in
the practice. Why, then, trust them? (1) The practices are socially established. (2) They are self-supporting; their outputs support their claim
to reliability. (3) They are internally consistent. (4) Their outputs are
also consistent with the outputs of other well-established doxastic practices. Similar considerations show that we are justified in engaging in
Christian mystical practices.

In my opinion, Alston's defense succeeds in defusing the standard
objections to the veridicality of Christian mystical experience. One objection, however, can't be set aside so easily. "An apparent experiential
presentation of God as Ø will provide only *prima facie* justification of
the belief that God is Ø . . . But the concept of prima facie justification
has application only where there is a system of knowledge or justified
belief about the relevant subject matter, against which a particular
prima facie justified belief can be checked". Our "religious perceptual
doxastic practices" must therefore be construed as including within
them "at least the main lines of the body of beliefs of the religion[s]
within which" they "flourish". But these belief systems "are, as wholes,
seriously incompatible with each . . . other".[14] The mystical practices
that incorporate them are thus also incompatible. It follows that at
most one is reliable. "Now why should I suppose that CMP [Christian
mystical practice] is the one that is reliable (if any are)?" Although
each tradition can produce internal reasons for thinking its practice is
reliable, there seem to be no *external* reasons for doing so. "Hence, it

---

[14] William P. Alston, *Perceiving God: The Epistemology of Religious Experience* (Ithaca:
Cornell University Press, 1991), p. 262. Subsequent page references appear in parentheses in the text.

cannot be rational to engage in CMP; and by the same reasoning it cannot be rational to engage in any other particular form of MP [mystical practice]" (p. 269).

Alston addresses this issue in "Religious Diversity and Perceptual Knowledge of God"[15] and, more fully, in chapter 7 of *Perceiving God*. His discussion is interesting and helpful. I doubt whether it is sufficient.

He begins by inviting us to consider situations in which "different people give conflicting sense perceptual reports [about an accident, for example] . . . and in which there is no neutral ground" for resolving the conflict, or to consider various "ways of predicting the weather" where there is "no non-question begging reason for supposing that [one] method is more reliable than the others". In cases like these one has "no sufficient rational basis" for confidence in one's report or in one's method. But there is "a crucial difference" between these cases and the religious situation. In the former, "it is clear what would constitute non-circular grounds for supposing one of the contestants to be superior to the others even if we do not have such grounds". (The accident might have been videotaped. More accurate statistical data could show that one method is more successful than the other.) "It is because the absence of such reasons . . . is the absence of something there is a live possibility of one's having, and that one knows how to go about getting, that this lack so clearly has negative epistemic consequences. But precisely this condition is lacking in the religious diversity case". "We have no idea of what non-circular proof of the reliability of CMP would look like, *even if it is as reliable as you please.* Hence why should we take the absence of such a proof to nullify, or even sharply diminish, the justification I have for my Christian M-beliefs?"[16] (pp. 270–72).

Or consider "the methodological opposition between psychoanalysts and behaviorists". The dispute hinges on whether "clinical 'insight' and 'interpretation'" counts as evidence. "There is no common ground on which the dispute can be resolved". It is not, however, "irrational for the psychoanalyst to continue to form clinical beliefs in the way he does". Similar considerations apply, mutatis mutandis, to our continued use of a mystical practice (pp. 272–73).

Or imagine "a diversity of sense perceptual doxastic practices"—an Aristotelian one in which we see what is visually perceived "as made up

---

[15] *Faith and Philosophy* 5 (October 1988), 433–48.

[16] An M-belief (manifestation belief) is a belief about God or the Real acquired on the basis of one's religious experience.

of more or less discrete objects scattered about in space", "a Cartesian practice of seeing" it "as an indefinitely extended medium that is more or less concentrated at various points", and a Whiteheadian practice of seeing "the visual field . . . as made up of momentary events growing out of each other in a continuous process. . . . Let's further suppose that each of these practices serves its practitioners equally well in their dealings with the environment". Finally, suppose "that we are as firmly wedded to our 'Aristotelian' form of SP [sense-perceptual practice] as we are in fact". "In such a situation" it is not "irrational" for us to continue to form perceptual beliefs in the way we do. "By parity of reasoning, the rational thing for a practitioner of CP to do is to continue to form Christian M-beliefs" in the way she does (pp. 273–74).

Note finally that the very possibility of alternative sense-perceptual practices "gives rise to the same problem". For their mere "possibility raises[s] the question of why we should suppose that it is rational" to form sense-perceptual beliefs as we do, "given that we have no reason to suppose" that our practice is "more reliable than these other possibilities". Yet, of course, it *is* "rational to engage in [our] SP, despite the lack of any non-circular reason for regarding our Aristotelian SP as more reliable than its *possible* alternatives". A similar conclusion follows for CMP (p. 274).

In my opinion, Alston's defense is only partly successful. Suppose I am not already engaged in a mystical practice. Has Alston provided me with reasons for accepting the outputs of CMP? He believes he has. I am justified in believing p provided that "X is justified in believing that p . . . X tells me that p", and "I am justified in supposing that X is justified in believing p". Since Alston believes he has shown not only that "CMP endows its products with prima facie justification" but also that "mystical perceivers can be justified, all things considered, in their perceptual beliefs", he concludes that I (who do not engage in the practice) can have good reasons for accepting these perceivers' testimony and hence for believing their claims (pp. 280–81; cf. p. 283).

I am not sure this will do. For I have similar reasons for believing that Buddhist mystical practice (BMP) or Hindu mystical practice (HMP) "endows its products with prima facie justification", and so on. Since I do, I have similar reasons for accepting the testimony of those who engage in these practices. But these practices and their products are, by hypothesis, incompatible with CMP. Hence, whatever reasons I have for assenting to the products of BMP are reasons *against* assenting to the products of CMP (and vice versa). And this seems to be a good reason for withholding assent altogether. The existence of incompatible mystical practices seems to provide the religiously uncommitted with a rather decisive reason for suspending judgment.

Alston's discussion, however, is primarily addressed to those who are already engaged in CMP (or some other mystical practice). Has Alston shown that it is reasonable for Christians (or Buddhists) to retain their commitments? I am not sure he has.

Consider his examples. In the case of conflicting perceptual reports or rival meteorological methods, we can specify in concrete detail precisely what sorts of evidence would settle the issue—tape from a suitably situated video camera, the testimony of better-placed witnesses, statistical information about the comparative success of rival forecasting methods, and so on. We cannot do this in the religious case. Yet why should this matter?

It might matter if the religious dispute *couldn't* be resolved, for, in that case, we could argue as follows. Our conflicting perceptual reports and rival meteorological methods lack positive epistemic features that they *might have had*. Our competing mystical practices do not. (For *no* evidence could resolve the issue.) Now nothing can properly be faulted for failing to exhibit a good-making feature that things of that kind can't have. Hence, the existence of unresolved disputes matters in the first case but not in the second.

But this can't be Alston's argument. In the first place, we *do* know how the religious dispute *could* be resolved. As Alston recognizes, it could be resolved by historical and metaphysical arguments based on neutral premises that show that the overrider systems and doxastic outputs of some mystical practices are closer to the truth than those of others.[17] In the second place, Alston thinks that the plurality of mystical practices should diminish (though not destroy) our confidence in our practice's reliability and hence in its epistemic rationality. It shouldn't (or so I have just argued) if the dispute *couldn't* be resolved.

The difference, at most, comes to this. We know exactly what sort of evidence would settle the issue in the nonreligious cases and can describe it in some detail. In the religious case, we have a general idea of the kind of evidence we are looking for (neutral metaphysical or empirical arguments) but can't specify it with any precision. And even this isn't clear. For can't we describe (a series of) miracles that would be rationally conclusive? (Cf. the story of Elijah and the priests of Baal.) Although it may be *unreasonable* to expect this sort of evidence to be forthcoming in the foreseeable future, expectations of this kind can

---

[17] The situation would be different if we knew that proofs of this kind were impossible, but Alston hasn't attempted to establish this.

also be unreasonable when perceptual reports or meteorological methods conflict.[18]

The difference, then, seems to be a difference in degree, not in kind. I fail to see how it justifies treating these cases differently.

There are other reasons for according more weight to the diversity objection than Alston does.

Many traditions contain doctrines that (if developed in certain directions) imply that other mystical practices are (at least) partly reliable. Examples are that God is love, the universality of the eternal Buddha nature, and so on. Alston thinks the problems these doctrines create are primarily theological and not epistemic (see pp. 257 and 266 n. 13). I am not sure this is true. For any reason for believing that an incompatible doxastic practice is reliable is a prima facie reason for thinking one's own is not. (This problem does not arise with respect to sense-perception. Our Aristotelian perceptual practice provides no reasons for thinking that a Cartesian perceptual practice is reliable [and vice versa].) It is always possible, of course, for Christians or Buddhists to accommodate the claim that other mystical practices are partly reliable by accepting products of those practices that are consistent with Christian or Buddhist doctrine and discounting the rest. They can also accommodate it by reinterpreting the products of other practices so as to *make* them consistent with the products of their own. The more worth one ascribes to competing practices, however, and the more one respects their integrity by refusing to edit them selectively or reinterpret them radically, the less confident one can be about the reliability of one's own. The degree of tension will be determined by *how* reliable one thinks alternative mystical practices are. If God really is loving, however, or the Buddha nature *is* universally accessible, they must be reliable enough to provide adequate opportunities for salvation.

One reason why it is rational for me to continue to engage in CMP (if I do) is that it seems to work; the practice is self-supporting (cf. pp. 275–76). Hick has argued that other mystical practices also work. Not only does each provide a payoff, truthfully assuring its adherents that engaging in it will yield certain fruits; but the payoffs are essentially the same, namely, "the transformation of human existence from self-centredness to Reality-centredness"—a transformation expressed in lives exemplifying "the ethical ideal, common to all the great traditions of agape/karuna (love/compassion)."[19] If Hick is right, our situation is

---

[18] For example, we sometimes have compelling reasons for believing that a dispute between witnesses will never be resolved. (We know that there were no other witnesses, that the event wasn't videotaped, etc.)

[19] *Interpretation of Religion*, pp. 14 and 36.

similar to that of someone confronted with alternative sense-perceptual practices where "each . . . serves its practitioners equally well in their dealings with the environment" (*Perceiving God*, p. 273). It would be unreasonable for a person in this situation to abandon her Aristotelian perceptual practice, for she has no reason to think the alternatives are better.

But I think she *does* have a reason for doubting that what Aristotelian practitioners have conceptually "added" to what is visually presented has more purchase on (is more firmly grounded in) reality than the conceptual contributions of those engaged in Cartesian or White-headian practices. Wouldn't the most reasonable attitude for her to take toward her perceptual reports,[20] then, be "acceptance" rather than belief? (I have in mind something like Van Fraassen's account of the right attitude toward empirically equivalent scientific theories.)[21] Muta-tis mutandis, shouldn't Christians or Buddhists (only) *accept* rather than believe reports that have been structured by specifically Christian or Buddhist concepts—perceptual reports like "God spoke to me," for example, or "I entered into Nibbāna"?

Alston has argued that in spite of the inability of the psychoanalyst to show that psychoanalysis is superior to behaviorism, it is rational for him to continue to form his clinical beliefs in the way he does. The Christian's (or Buddhist's) situation is similar. CMP (or BMP) is not only "a socially established doxastic practice that has not been shown to be unreliable"; it is also significantly self-supporting (pp. 275–76). It is thus as rational for the Christian (or Buddhist) to adhere to her views as it once was for an advocate of Aristotelian, Galilean, or Cartesian physics and chemistry to adhere to his. But *why* was it rational for (e.g.) the Cartesian to stick to his guns, given that there was, at the time, no neutral way of resolving the conflict between him and his opponents? For the same reason it is rational for the psychoanalyst to stick to his. Because it is unreasonable to abandon a research project that is still promising.[22] But what follows? Clearly, that it is reasonable

---

[20] With the exception, if any, of reports about perceptions that aren't structured in specifically Aristotelian or Cartesian or Whiteheadian ways. (Would "'Red' is instantiated over there" be an example?)

[21] Acceptance, however, involves more than using a theory for "important purposes" like prediction. One also uses it "as a source of explanations, as a means of formulating questions and pursuing answers," and so on. (Richard Miller, *Fact and Method* [Princeton: Princeton University Press, 1987], pp 158–59.)

[22] I think that *this* is why the psychoanalyst's continued commitment is reasonable and not (as Alston seems to suggest) because we have no idea how to resolve his dispute with the behaviorists.

to *engage* in the project or to continue to act *as if* one's favorite theory were true. It *isn't* clear that it is reasonable to *believe* it.

There is, however, a significant difference between *theories* like Aristotelian, Cartesian, and Galilean science, or psychoanalysis and behaviorism, and *doxastic practices.* According to Alston, engaging in a doxastic practice involves thinking it reliable and, hence, accepting its outputs as (for the most part) *true,* that is, *believing* them.[23] If so, one can't engage in a doxastic practice by merely acting *as if* it were reliable. Engaging in CMP, for example, involves thinking it reliable and thus believing (most of) its outputs. The distinction I have tried to draw between accepting and believing, or acting as if and believing, collapses.

I think this is right. Nevertheless, I believe one can, from time to time, step back from one's doxastic practices and ask whether there are independent reasons for or against their epistemic rationality. A person who does this might (without making any obvious errors) come to the conclusion that although it is pragmatically rational to engage in the practice, it isn't epistemically reasonable to do so. If the pragmatic reasons are strong enough, he might further conclude that he should suppress any doubts he may have and continue to engage in the practice, or that he should try, as it were, to live on two planes of consciousness at once—engaging in the practice on one level and hence trusting in its reliability while, on another, doubting it. Something like this appears to have been the goal of some ancient skeptics with respect to believing in general. Alston's defense of the pragmatic rationality of continuing to engage in CMP thus seems compatible with certain forms of epistemic skepticism. Whether the latter is *reasonable* is another matter. But the considerations that implied that "acceptance" might be the most rational attitude suggest that it may be.

How strongly does diversity count against CMP's reliability? I have argued that the answer partly depends on whether we are already engaged in a mystical practice or not.

Those of us who aren't are confronted with an analogue of one of Hume's arguments against miracles. Since miracles support incompatible religious systems, cases for miracles destroy one another. There are two ways of undercutting Hume's argument. One can show that the alleged conflicts between religious systems aren't real or one can show that the cases for miracles aren't equally strong. Similarly here. Now Alston thinks that overrider systems and hence the practices that incorporate them really do conflict. Hence, the first avenue of escape isn't open to him. He must therefore show that the practices aren't

[23] See *Perceiving God,* chap. 4, sec. ix.

equally well founded. It is difficult to see how he could do this without introducing empirical and metaphysical arguments that establish the superiority of (e.g.) the Christian world-view.

Yet what about people who *are* engaged in CMP or some other mystical practice? It is epistemically rational to engage in a doxastic practice if there are good reasons for regarding it as reliable.[24] It is epistemically irrational to engage in it if there are good reasons for thinking it unreliable. In the absence of good reasons either for or against a doxastic practice's reliability, it is epistemically nonrational to participate in it.[25] Alston believes that the fact that CMP is socially established and significantly self-supporting, and that it hasn't been shown to be unreliable, is a good reason for regarding it as prima facie reliable. This seems right. But whether it is a good reason for regarding it as rational *überhaupt* depends on the strength of whatever overriders there may happen to be. In the case of CMP, the most significant overrider is the diversity of mystical practices.

Are there good reasons for regarding CMP as *unreliable*? There are; the prima facie reliability of incompatible mystical practices is a good reason for thinking that CMP is prima facie unreliable. Whether it is a good reason for regarding it as unreliable *überhaupt* depends once again on how much weight should be placed on diversity.

Alston has offered reasons for thinking that the diversity of mystical practices doesn't override the evidence for CMP's reliability. I have argued that these reasons aren't as compelling as he thinks and that the overrider is therefore stronger than he allows. Is it or is it not, then, epistemically rational to engage in CMP? This question is difficult to answer, because, as Alston says, we lack "the conceptual resources to quantify degrees of rationality" (p. 275). I am skeptical, however, of the possibility of a completely successful defense of the epistemic rationality of a mystical practice on what Alston calls a "worst case scenario" (p. 270). If the metaphysical and empirical arguments for a Christian (or Buddhist) world-view really are no better than those for its rivals,

---

[24] I am using "rationality" in an "objective" rather than "subjective" sense. A belief is objectively rational if a fully informed and properly functioning agent would hold it. An action or policy is objectively rational if an agent of this kind would endorse it. But we often aren't fully informed and aren't ideal epistemic agents. Hence, beliefs, actions, and policies that are objectively rational aren't always rational *for us*.

[25] One might suggest that it is epistemically irrational to engage in a doxastic practice if there is *no* reason to believe that it is reliable even if there is also no reason to believe that it is *un*reliable. I think, however, that an analogue of the Principle of Credulity is true of doxastic practices. Apparent perceptions and established doxastic practices are both innocent until proven guilty. The fact that a doxastic practice is engaged in is thus *a* reason for trusting it. (Although one that can, of course, be overridden.)

then I doubt whether his remarks are sufficient to show that it is rational to regard CMP or BMP as reliable. If it isn't, then it isn't epistemically rational to engage in it. Whether it is epistemically *ir*rational to do so depends on whether the diversity of mystical practices overrides the reasons for regarding CMP as reliable or simply offsets them. If (as I suspect) it simply offsets them, it isn't irrational.

So where do we stand? Suppose there really were well-established non-Aristotelian perceptual practices. In the absence of arguments showing that an Aristotelian framework is preferable to its rivals, I doubt that it would be epistemically rational for me to continue to engage in my practice, although it *would* be pragmatically rational for me to regard it as reliable and might not be epistemically *ir*rational for me to do so. Similarly here; on the "worst case scenario", the most that follows is that it is pragmatically rational, and not epistemically irrational, to engage in CMP. Whether one can establish more than this depends on the prospects for Christian metaphysics.

My conclusion, then, is this. Whether one is committed to a mystical practice or not, metaphysical and empirical argumentation of a familiar sort (arguments for God's or Nibbāna's existence, Christian or Buddhist "evidences," etc.) is probably needed to show that commitment to an MP is fully rational. Alston's defense of CMP is impressive and, on the whole, convincing. To be fully successful, however, I believe it must form part of a persuasive cumulative case argument for the Christian world-view.[26]

[26] The same is true of other mystical practices. Most of what Alston says in defense of CMP could be adapted to justify (e.g.) BMP. Commitment to BMP is fully rational only if one has good reasons for thinking that the Buddhist world-view is superior to its rivals.

An earlier version of this essay was presented at the 1991 Central Division meeting of the American Philosophical Association. I wish to thank William Rowe, who commented on an early draft, and my respondent, William Alston. My essay has benefited from their criticisms.

PART

III

RELIGIOUS PLURALISM

[8]

Pluralism: A Defense of
Religious Exclusivism

ALVIN PLANTINGA

When I was a graduate student at Yale, the philosophy department prided itself on diversity: and it was indeed diverse. There were idealists, pragmatists, phenomenologists, existentialists, Whiteheadians, historians of philosophy, a token positivist, and what could only be described as observers of the passing intellectual scene. In some ways, this was indeed something to take pride in; a student could behold and encounter real live representatives of many of the main traditions in philosophy. It also had an unintended and unhappy side effect, however. If anyone raised a philosophical question inside, but particularly outside, class, the typical response would be a catalog of some of the various different answers the world has seen: there is the Aristotelian answer, the existentialist answer, the Cartesian answer, Heidegger's answer, perhaps the Buddhist answer, and so on. But the question 'what is the truth about this matter?' was often greeted with disdain as unduly naive. There are all these different answers, all endorsed by people of great intellectual power and great dedication to philosophy; for every argument *for* one of these positions, there is another *against* it; would it not be excessively naive, or perhaps arbitrary, to suppose that one of these is in fact *true*, the others being false? Or, if there really is a truth of the matter, so that one of them is true and conflicting ones false, wouldn't it be merely arbitrary, in the face of this embarrassment of riches, to *endorse* one of them as the truth, consigning the others to falsehood? How could you possibly know which was true?

Some urge a similar attitude with respect to the impressive variety of religions the world displays. There are theistic religions but also at least some nontheistic religions (or perhaps nontheistic strands of religion) among the enormous variety of religions going under the names 'Hinduism' and 'Buddhism'; among the theistic religions, there are strands of Hinduism and Buddhism and American Indian religion as well as Islam, Judaism, and Christianity; and all these differ significantly from one another. Isn't it somehow arbitrary, or irrational, or unjustified, or unwarranted, or even oppressive and imperialistic to endorse one of these as opposed to all the others? According to Jean Bodin, "each is refuted by all";[1] must we not agree? It is in this neighborhood that the so-called problem of pluralism arises. Of course, many concerns and problems can come under this rubric; the specific problem I mean to discuss can be thought of as follows. To put it in an internal and personal way, I find myself with religious beliefs, and religious beliefs that I realize aren't shared by nearly everyone else. For example, I believe both

(1)   The world was created by God, an almighty, all-knowing, and perfectly good personal being (one that holds beliefs; has aims, plans, and intentions; and can act to accomplish these aims)

and

(2)   Human beings require salvation, and God has provided a unique way of salvation through the incarnation, life, sacrificial death, and resurrection of his divine son.

Now there are many who do not believe these things. First, there are those who agree with me on (1) but not (2): there are non-Christian theistic religions. Second, there are those who don't accept either (1) or (2) but nonetheless do believe that there is something beyond the natural world, a something such that human well-being and salvation depend upon standing in a right relation to it. And third, in the West and since the Enlightenment, anyway, there are people—*naturalists*, we may call them—who don't believe any of these three things. And my problem is this: when I become really aware of these other ways of looking at the world, these other ways of responding religiously to the world, what must or should I do? What is the right sort of attitude to take? What sort of impact should this awareness have on the beliefs I

---

[1] *Colloquium Heptaplomeres de rerum sublimium arcanis abditis*, written by 1593 but first published in 1857. English translation by Marion Kuntz (Princeton: Princeton University Press, 1975). The quotation is from the Kuntz translation, p. 256.

hold and the strength with which I hold them? My question is this: how should I think about the great religious diversity the world in fact displays? Can I sensibly remain an adherent of just one of these religions, rejecting the others? And here I am thinking specifically of *beliefs*. Of course, there is a great deal more to any religion or religious practice than just belief, and I don't for a moment mean to deny it. But belief is a crucially important part of most religions; it is a crucially important part of *my* religion; and the question I mean to ask here is what the awareness of religious diversity means or should mean for my religious beliefs.

Some speak here of a *new* awareness of religious diversity, and speak of this new awareness as constituting (for us in the West) a crisis, a revolution, an intellectual development of the same magnitude as the Copernican revolution of the sixteenth century and the alleged discovery of evolution and our animal origins in the nineteenth.[2] No doubt there is at least some truth to this. Of course, the fact is all along many Western Christians and Jews have known that there are other religions and that not nearly everyone shares *their* religion.[3] The ancient Israelites—some of the prophets, say—were clearly aware of Canaanitish religion; and the apostle Paul said that he preached "Christ crucified, a stumbling block to Jews and folly to the Greeks" (I Cor. 1:23). Other early Christians, the Christian martyrs, say, must have suspected that not everyone believed as they did. The church fathers, in offering defenses of Christianity, were certainly apprised of this fact; Origen, indeed, wrote an eight-volume reply to Celsus, who urged an argument similar to those put forward by contemporary pluralists. Aquinas, again, was clearly aware of those to whom he addressed the *Summa contra gentiles,* and the fact that there are non-Christian religions would have come as no surprise to the Jesuit missionaries of the sixteenth and seventeenth centuries or to the Methodist missionaries of the nineteenth. In more recent times, when I was a child, *The Banner,* the official publication of the Christian Reformed Church, contained a small column for children; it was written by 'Uncle Dick', who exhorted us to save our nickels and send them to our Indian cousins at the Navaho

[2] Thus Joseph Runzo: "Today, the impressive piety and evident rationality of the belief systems of other religious traditions inescapably confronts Christians with a crisis—and a potential revolution." "God, Commitment, and Other Faiths: Pluralism vs. Relativism," *Faith and Philosophy* 5 (October 1988), 343.

[3] As explained in detail in Robert Wilken, "Religious Pluralism and Early Christian Thought," so far unpublished. Wilken focuses on the third century; he explores Origen's response to Celsus and concludes that there are striking parallels between Origen's historical situation and ours. What is different today, I suspect, is not that Christianity has to confront other religions but that we now call this situation 'religious pluralism'.

mission in New Mexico. Both we and our elders knew that the Navahos had or had had a religion different from Christianity, and part of the point of sending the nickels was to try to rectify that situation.

Still, in recent years probably more of us Western Christians have become aware of the world's religious diversity; we have probably learned more about people of other religious persuasions, and we have come to see more clearly that they display what looks like real piety, devoutness, and spirituality. What is new, perhaps, is a more widespread sympathy for other religions, a tendency to see them as more valuable, as containing more by way of truth, and a new feeling of solidarity with their practitioners.

There are several possible reactions to awareness of religious diversity. One is to continue to believe what you have all along believed; you learn about this diversity but continue to believe, that is, take to be true, such propositions as (1) and (2) above, consequently taking to be false any beliefs, religious or otherwise, that are incompatible with (1) and (2). Following current practice, I call this *exclusivism;* the exclusivist holds that the tenets or some of the tenets of *one* religion—Christianity, let's say—are in fact true; he adds, naturally enough, that any propositions, including other religious beliefs, that are incompatible with those tenets are false. Now there is a fairly widespread belief that there is something seriously wrong with exclusivism. It is irrational, or egotistical and unjustified,[4] or intellectually arrogant,[5] or elitist,[6] or a manifestation of harmful pride,[7] or even oppressive and imperialistic.[8] The

[4] Thus Gary Gutting: "Applying these considerations to religious belief, we seem led to the conclusion that, because believers have many epistemic peers who do not share their belief in God . . . , they have no right to maintain their belief without a justification. If they do so, they are guilty of epistemological egoism." *Religious Belief and Religious Skepticism* (Notre Dame: University of Notre Dame Press, 1982), p. 90 (but see the following pages for an important qualification).

[5] "Here my submission is that on this front the traditional doctrinal position of the Church has in fact militated against its traditional moral position, and has in fact encouraged Christians to approach other men immorally. Christ has taught us humility, but we have approached them with arrogance. . . . This charge of arrogance is a serious one." Wilfred Cantwell Smith, *Religious Diversity* (New York: Harper and Row, 1976), p. 13.

[6] Runzo, "Ethically, Religious Exclusivism has the morally repugnant result of making those who have privileged knowledge, or who are intellectually astute, a religious elite, while penalizing those who happen to have no access to the putatively correct religious view, or who are incapable of advanced understanding." "God, Commitment, and Other Faiths," p. 348.

[7] "But natural pride, despite its positive contribution to human life, becomes harmful when it is elevated to the level of dogma and is built into the belief system of a religious community. This happens when its sense of its own validity and worth is expressed in doctrines implying an exclusive or a decisively superior access to the truth or the power to save." John Hick, "Religious Pluralism and Absolute Claims," in Leroy Rouner, ed. *Religious Pluralism* (Notre Dame: University of Notre Dame Press, 1984), p. 197.

[8] Thus John Cobb: "I agree with the liberal theists that even in Pannenberg's case, the quest for an absolute as a basis for understanding reflects the long tradition of Christian

claim is that exclusivism as such is or involves a vice of some sort: it is wrong or deplorable; and it is this claim I want to examine. I propose to argue that exclusivism need not involve either epistemic or moral failure and that furthermore something like it is wholly unavoidable, given our human condition.

These objections are not to the *truth* of (1) or (2) or any other proposition someone might accept in this exclusivist way (although, of course, objections of that sort are also put forward); they are instead directed to the *propriety* or *rightness* of exclusivism. And there are initially two different kinds of indictments of exclusivism: broadly moral or ethical indictments and broadly intellectual or epistemic indictments. These overlap in interesting ways, as we shall see below. But initially, anyway, we can take some of the complaints about exclusivism as *intellectual* criticisms: it is *irrational* or *unjustified* to think in an exclusivistic way. And the other large body of complaint is moral: there is something *morally* suspect about exclusivism: it is arbitrary, or intellectually arrogant, or imperialistic. As Joseph Runzo suggests, exclusivism is "neither tolerable nor any longer intellectually honest in the context of our contemporary knowledge of other faiths."[9] I want to consider both kinds of claims or criticisms; I propose to argue that the exclusivist is not as such necessarily guilty of any of these charges.

Moral Objections to Exclusivism

I first turn to the moral complaints: that the exclusivist is intellectually arrogant, or egotistical, or self-servingly arbitrary, or dishonest, or imperialistic, or oppressive. But first three qualifications. An exclusivist, like anyone else, will probably be guilty of some or all of these things to at least some degree, perhaps particularly the first two; the question is, however, whether she is guilty of these things just by virtue of being an exclusivist. Second, I shall use the term 'exclusivism' in such a way that you don't count as an exclusivist unless you are rather fully aware of other faiths, have had their existence and their claims called to your attention with some force and perhaps fairly frequently, and have to some degree reflected on the problem of pluralism, asking yourself such questions as whether it is or could be really true that the Lord has revealed himself and his programs to us Christians, say, in a way in which he hasn't revealed himself to those of other faiths. Thus my

---

imperialism and triumphalism rather than the pluralistic spirit." "The Meaning of Pluralism for Christian Self-Understanding," in Rouner, *Religious Pluralism*, p. 171.

[9] "God, Commitment, and Other Faiths," p. 357.

grandmother, for example, would not have counted as an exclusivist. She had, of course, *heard* of the heathen, as she called them, but the idea that perhaps Christians could learn from them, and learn from them with respect to religious matters, had not so much as entered her head; and the fact that it *hadn't* entered her head, I take it, was not a matter of moral dereliction on her part. The same would go for a Buddhist or Hindu peasant. These people are not, I think, plausibly charged with arrogance or other moral flaws in believing as they do.

Third, suppose I am an exclusivist with respect to (1), for example, but nonculpably believe, like Thomas Aquinas, say, that I have a knock-down, drag-out argument, a demonstration or conclusive proof of the proposition that there is such a person as God; and suppose I think further (and nonculpably) that if those who don't believe (1) were to be apprised of this argument (and had the ability and training necessary to grasp it, and were to think about the argument fairly and reflectively), they too would come to believe (1). Then I could hardly be charged with these moral faults. My condition would be like that of Gödel, let's say, upon having recognized that he had a proof for the incompleteness of arithmetic. True, many of his colleagues and peers didn't believe that arithmetic was incomplete, and some believed that it *was* complete; but presumably Gödel wasn't arbitrary or egotistical in believing that arithmetic is in fact incomplete. Furthermore, he would not have been at fault had he nonculpably but *mistakenly* believed that he had found such a proof. Accordingly, I shall use the term 'exclusivist' in such a way that you don't count as an exclusivist if you nonculpably think you know of a demonstration or conclusive argument for the beliefs with respect to which you are an exclusivist, or even if you nonculpably think you know of an argument that would convince all or most intelligent and honest people of the truth of that proposition. So an exclusivist, as I use the term, not only believes something like (1) or (2) and thinks false any proposition incompatible with it; she also meets a further condition C that is hard to state precisely and in detail (and in fact any attempt to do so would involve a long and at present irrelevant discussion of ceteris paribus clauses). Suffice it to say that C includes (1) being rather fully aware of other religions, (2) knowing that there is much that at the least looks like genuine piety and devoutness in them, and (3) believing that you know of no arguments that would necessarily convince all or most honest and intelligent dissenters of your own religious allegiances.

Given these qualifications, then, why should we think that an exclusivist is properly charged with these moral faults? I shall deal first and most briefly with charges of oppression and imperialism: I think we must say that they are on the face of it wholly implausible. I daresay there are some among you who reject some of the things I believe; I do not believe that you are thereby oppressing me, even if you do not believe you have an argument that would convince me. It is conceivable that exclusivism might in some way *contribute to* oppression, but it isn't in itself oppressive.

The important moral charge is that there is a sort of self-serving arbitrariness, an arrogance or egotism, in accepting such propositions as (1) or (2) under condition C; exclusivism is guilty of some serious moral fault or flaw. According to Wilfred Cantwell Smith, "except at the cost of insensitivity or delinquency, it is morally not possible actually to go out into the world and say to devout, intelligent, fellow human beings: '. . . we believe that we know God and we are right; you believe that you know God, and you are totally wrong'."[10]

So what can the exclusivist have to say for herself? Well, it must be conceded immediately that if she believes (1) or (2), then she must also believe that those who believe something incompatible with them are mistaken and believe what is false. That's no more than simple logic. Furthermore, she must also believe that those who do not believe as she does—those who believe neither (1) nor (2), whether or not they believe their negations—*fail* to believe something that is true, deep, and important, and that she *does* believe. She must therefore see herself as *privileged* with respect to those others—those others of both kinds. There is something of great value, she must think, that *she* has and *they* lack. They are ignorant of something—something of great importance—of which she has knowledge. But does this make her properly subject to the above censure?

I think the answer must be no. Or if the answer is yes, then I think we have here a genuine moral dilemma; for in our earthly life here below, as my Sunday School teacher used to say, there is no real alternative; there is no reflective attitude that is not open to the same strictures. These charges of arrogance are a philosophical tar baby: get close enough to them to use them against the exclusivist, and you are

---

[10] Smith, *Religious Diversity*, p. 14. A similar statement: "Nor can we reasonably claim that our own form of religious experience, together with that of the tradition of which we are a part, is veridical whilst others are not. We can of course claim this; and indeed virtually every religious tradition has done so, regarding alternative forms of religion either as false or as confused and inferior versions of itself. . . . Persons living within other traditions, then, are equally justified in trusting their own distinctive religious experience and in forming their beliefs on the basis of it. . . . let us avoid the implausibly arbitrary dogma that religious experience is all delusory with the single exception of the particular form enjoyed by the one who is speaking." John Hick, *An Interpretation of Religion* (New Haven, Yale University Press, 1989), p. 235.

likely to find them stuck fast to yourself. How so? Well, as an exclusivist, I realize I can't convince others that they should believe as I do, but I nonetheless continue to believe as I do: and the charge is that I am as a result arrogant or egotistical, arbitrarily preferring my way of doing things to other ways.[11] But what are my alternatives with respect to a proposition like (1)? There seem to be three choices.[12] I can continue to hold it; I can withhold it, in Roderick Chisholm's sense, believing neither it nor its denial; and I can accept its denial. Consider the third way, a way taken by those pluralists who, like John Hick, hold that such propositions as (1) and (2) and their colleagues from other faiths are literally false although in some way still valid responses to the Real. This seems to me to be no advance at all with respect to the arrogance or egotism problem; this is not a way out. For if I do this, I will then be in the very same condition as I am now: I will believe many propositions others don't believe and will be in condition C with respect to those propositions. For I will then believe the denials of (1) and (2) (as well as the denials of many other propositions explicitly accepted by those of other faiths). Many others, of course, do not believe the denials of (1) and (2), and in fact believe (1) and (2). Further, I will not know of any arguments that can be counted on to persuade those who do believe (1) or (2) (or propositions accepted by the adherents of other religions). I am therefore in the condition of believing propositions that many others do not believe and furthermore am in condition C. If, in the case of those who believe (1) and (2), that is sufficient for intellectual arrogance or egotism, the same goes for those who believe their denials.

So consider the second option: I can instead *withhold* the proposition in question. I can say to myself; "the right course here, given that I can't or couldn't convince these others of what *I* believe, is to believe neither these propositions nor their denials." The pluralist objector to exclusivism can say that the right course under condition C, is to *abstain* from believing the offending proposition and also abstain from be-

---

[11] "The only reason for treating one's tradition differently from others is the very human but not very cogent reason that it is one's own!" Hick, *Interpretation of Religion,* p. 235.

[12] To speak of choice here suggests that I can simply choose which of these three attitudes to adopt; but is that at all realistic? Are my beliefs to that degree within my control? Here I shall set aside the question whether and to what degree my beliefs are subject to my control and within my power. Perhaps we have very little control over them; then the moral critic of exclusivism can't properly accuse the exclusivist of dereliction of moral duty, but he could still argue that the exclusivist's stance is unhappy, bad, a miserable state of affairs. Even if I can't help it that I am overbearing and conceited, my being that way is a bad state of affairs.

A Defense of Religious Exclusivism

lieving its denial; call him, therefore, 'the abstemious pluralist'. But does he thus really avoid the condition that, on the part of the exclusivist, leads to the charges of egotism and arrogance? Think, for a moment, about disagreement. Disagreement, fundamentally, is a matter of adopting conflicting propositional attitudes with respect to a given proposition. In the simplest and most familiar case, I disagree with you if there is some proposition p such that I believe p and you believe -p. But that's just the simplest case: there are also others. The one that is at present of interest is this: I believe p and you withhold it, fail to believe it. Call the first kind of disagreement 'contradicting'; call the second 'dissenting'.

My claim is that if contradicting others (under the condition C spelled out above) is arrogant and egotistical, so is dissenting (under that same condition). For suppose you believe some proposition p but I don't: perhaps you believe it is wrong to discriminate against people simply on the grounds of race, but I, recognizing that there are many people who disagree with you, do not believe this proposition. I don't disbelieve it either, of course, but in the circumstances I think the right thing to do is to abstain from belief. Then am I not implicitly condemning your attitude, your *believing* the proposition, as somehow improper—naive, perhaps, or unjustified, or in some other way less than optimal? I am implicitly saying that my attitude is the superior one; I think my course of action here is the right one and yours somehow wrong, inadequate, improper, in the circumstances at best second-rate. Also, I realize that there is no questions, here, of *showing* you that your attitude is wrong or improper or naive; so am I not guilty of intellectual arrogance? Of a sort of egotism, thinking I know better than you, arrogating to myself a privileged status with respect to you? The problem for the exclusivist was that she was obliged to think she possessed a truth missed by many others; the problem for the abstemious pluralist is that he is obliged to think he possesses a virtue others don't, or acts rightly where others don't. If, in conditions C, one is arrogant by way of believing a proposition others don't, isn't one equally, under those reflective conditions, arrogant by way of withholding a proposition others don't?

Perhaps you will respond by saying that the abstemious pluralist gets into trouble, falls into arrogance, by way of implicitly saying or believing that his way of proceeding is *better* or *wiser* than other ways pursued by other people, and perhaps he can escape by abstaining from *that* view as well. Can't he escape the problem by refraining from believing that racial bigotry is wrong, and also refraining from holding the view that it is *better,* under the conditions that obtain, to withhold that proposition than to assert and believe it? Well, yes, he can; then he has no *reason* for his abstention; he doesn't believe that abstention is better or more appropriate; he simply does abstain. Does this get him off the egotistical hook? Perhaps. But then, of course, he can't, in consistency, also hold that there is something wrong with *not* abstaining, with coming right out and *believing* that bigotry is wrong; he loses his objection to the exclusivist. Accordingly, this way out is not available for the abstemious pluralist who accuses the exclusivist of arrogance and egotism.

Indeed, I think we can show that the abstemious pluralist who brings charges of intellectual arrogance against exclusivism is hoist with his own petard, holds a position that in a certain way is self-referentially inconsistent in the circumstances. For he believes

(3)   If S knows that others don't believe p and that he is in condition C with respect to p, then S should not believe p;

this or something like it is the ground of the charges he brings against the exclusivist. But, the abstemious pluralist realizes that many do not accept (3); and I suppose he also realizes that it is unlikely that he can find arguments for (3) that will convince them; hence he knows that he is in condition C. Given his acceptance of (3), therefore, the right course for him is to abstain from believing (3). Under the conditions that do in fact obtain—namely, his knowledge that others don't accept it and that condition C obtains—he can't properly accept it.

I am therefore inclined to think that one can't, in the circumstances, properly hold (3) or any other proposition that will do the job. One can't find here some principle on the basis of which to hold that the exclusivist is doing the wrong thing, suffers from some moral fault— that is, one can't find such a principle that doesn't, as we might put it, fall victim to itself.

So the abstemious pluralist is hoist with his own petard; but even apart from this dialectical argument (which in any event some will think unduly cute), aren't the charges unconvincing and implausible? I must concede that there are a variety of ways in which I can be and have been intellectually arrogant and egotistic; I have certainly fallen into this vice in the past and no doubt am not free of it now. But am I really arrogant and egotistic just by virtue of believing what I know others don't believe, where I can't show them that I am right? Suppose I think the matter over, consider the objections as carefully as I can, realize that I am finite and furthermore a sinner, certainly no better than those with whom I disagree, and indeed inferior both morally and intellectually to many who do not believe what I do; but suppose

A Defense of Religious Exclusivism

it *still* seems clear to me that the proposition in question is true: can I really be behaving immorally in continuing to believe it? I am dead sure that it is wrong to try to advance my career by telling lies about my colleagues; I realize there are those who disagree; I also realize that in all likelihood there is no way I can find to show them that they are wrong; nonetheless, I think they *are* wrong. If I think this after careful reflection—if I consider the claims of those who disagree as sympathetically as I can, if I try level best to ascertain the truth here—and it *still* seems to me sleazy, wrong, and despicable to lie about my colleagues to advance my career, could I really be doing something immoral in continuing to believe as before? I can't see how. If, after careful reflection and thought, you find yourself convinced that the right propositional attitude to take to (1) and (2) in the face of the facts of religious pluralism is abstention from belief, how could you properly be taxed with egotism, either for so believing or for so abstaining? Even if you knew others did not agree with you? So I can't see how the moral charge against exclusivism can be sustained.

Epistemic Objections to Exclusivism

I turn now to *epistemic* objections to exclusivism. There are many different specifically epistemic virtues, and a corresponding plethora of epistemic vices; the ones with which the exclusivist is most frequently charged, however, are *irrationality* and *lack of justification* in holding his exclusivist beliefs. The claim is that as an exclusivist, he holds unjustified beliefs and/or irrational beliefs. Better, *he* is unjustified or irrational in holding these beliefs. I shall therefore consider those two claims, and I shall argue that the exclusivistic views need not be either unjustified or irrational. I shall then turn to the question whether his beliefs could have *warrant*: that property, whatever precisely it is, that distinguishes knowledge from mere true belief, and whether they could have enough warrant for knowledge.

Justification

The pluralist objector sometimes claims that to hold exclusivist views, in condition C, is *unjustified—epistemically* unjustified. Is this true? And what does he mean when he makes this claim? As even a brief glance at the contemporary epistemological literature shows, justification is a protean and multifarious notion.[13] There are, I think, substantially two possibilities as to what he means. The central core of the notion, its beating heart, the paradigmatic center to which most of the myriad contemporary variations are related by way of analogical extension and family resemblance, is the notion of *being within one's intellectual rights*, having violated no intellectual or cognitive duties or obligations in the formation and sustenance of the belief in question. This is the palimpsest, going back to Descartes and especially Locke, that underlies the multitudinous battery of contemporary inscriptions. There is no space to argue that point here; but chances are when the pluralist objector to exclusivism claims that the latter is unjustified, it is some notion lying in this neighborhood that he has in mind. (And, here we should note the very close connection between the moral objections to exclusivism and the objection that exclusivism is epistemically unjustified.)

The duties involved, naturally enough, would be specifically *epistemic* duties: perhaps a duty to proportion degree of belief to (propositional) evidence from what is *certain*, that is, self-evident or incorrigible, as with Locke, or perhaps to try one's best to get into and stay in the right relation to the truth, as with Roderick Chisholm,[14] the leading contemporary champion of the justificationist tradition with respect to knowledge. But at present there is widespread (and, as I see it, correct) agreement that there is no duty of the Lockean kind. Perhaps there is one of the Chisholmian kind;[15] but isn't the exclusivist conforming to that duty if, after the sort of careful, indeed prayerful, consideration I mentioned in the response to the moral objection, it still seems to him strongly that (1), say, is true and he accordingly still believes it? It is therefore hard to see that the exclusivist is necessarily unjustified in this way.

The second possibility for understanding the charge—the charge that exclusivism is epistemically unjustified—has to do with the oft-repeated claim that exclusivism is intellectually *arbitrary*. Perhaps the

[13] See my "Justification in the Twentieth Century," *Philosophy and Phenomenological Research* 50, supplement (Fall 1990), 45 ff., and see chap. 1 of my *Warrant: The Current Debate* (New York: Oxford University Press, 1993).

[14] See the three editions of *Theory of Knowledge* referred to in note 23.

[15] Some people think there is, and also think that withholding belief, abstaining from belief, is always and automatically the safe course to take with respect to this duty, whenever any question arises as to what to believe and withhold. But that isn't so. One can go wrong by withholding as well as by believing: there is no safe haven here, not even abstention. If there is a duty of the Chisholmian kind, and if I, out of epistemic pride and excessive scrupulosity, succeed in training myself not to accept ordinary perceptual judgments in ordinary perceptual circumstances, I am not performing works of epistemic supererogation; I am epistemically culpable.

idea is that there is an intellectual duty to treat similar cases similarly; the exclusivist violates this duty by arbitrarily choosing to believe (for the moment going along with the fiction that we *choose* beliefs of this sort) (1) and (2) in the face of the plurality of conflicting religious beliefs the world presents. But suppose there is such a duty. Clearly, you do not violate it if you nonculpably think the beliefs in question are *not* on a par. And, as an exclusivist, I *do* think (nonculpably, I hope) that they are not on a par: I think (1) and (2) *true* and those incompatible with either of them *false.*

The rejoinder, of course, will be that it is not *alethic* parity (their having the same truth value) that is at issue: it is *epistemic* parity that counts. What kind of epistemic parity? What would be relevant here, I should think, would be *internal* or internalist epistemic parity: parity with respect to what is internally available to the believer. What is internally available to the believer includes, for example, detectable relationships between the belief in question and other beliefs you hold; so internal parity would include parity of propositional evidence. What is internally available to the believer also includes the *phenomenology* that goes with the beliefs in question: the *sensuous* phenomenology, but also the nonsensuous phenomenology involved, for example, in the belief's just having the feel of being *right*. But once more, then, (1) and (2) are not on an internal par, for the exclusivist, with beliefs that are incompatible with them. (1) and (2), after all, seem to me to be true; they have for me the phenomenology that accompanies that seeming. The same cannot be said for propositions incompatible with them. If, furthermore, John Calvin is right in thinking that there is such a thing as the Sensus Divinitatis and the Internal Testimony of the Holy Spirit, then perhaps (1) and (2) are produced in me by those belief-producing processes, and have for me the phenomenology that goes with them; the same is not true for propositions incompatible with them.

But then the next rejoinder: isn't it probably true that those who reject (1) and (2) in favor of other beliefs have propositional evidence for their beliefs that is on a par with mine for my beliefs; and isn't it also probably true that the same or similar phenomenology accompanies their beliefs as accompanies mine? So that those beliefs really are epistemically and internally on a par with (1) and (2), and the exclusivist is still treating like cases differently? I don't think so: I think there really are arguments available for (1), at least, that are not available for its competitors. And as for similar phenomenology, this is not easy to say; it is not easy to look into the breast of another; the secrets of the human heart are hard to fathom; it is hard indeed to discover this sort of thing even with respect to someone you know really well.

But I am prepared to stipulate both sorts of parity. Let's agree for purposes of argument that these beliefs are on an epistemic par in the sense that those of a different religious tradition have the same sort of internally available markers—evidence, phenomenology, and the like— for their beliefs as I have for (1) and (2). What follows?

Return to the case of moral belief. King David took Bathsheba, made her pregnant, and then, after the failure of various stratagems to get her husband Uriah to think the baby was his, arranged for Uriah to be killed. The prophet Nathan came to David and told him a story about a rich man and a poor man. The rich man had many flocks and herds; the poor man had only a single ewe lamb, which grew up with his children, "ate at his table, drank from his cup, lay in his bosom, and was like a daughter to him." The rich man had unexpected guests. Instead of slaughtering one of his own sheep, he took the poor man's single ewe lamb, slaughtered it, and served it to his guests. David exploded in anger: "The man who did this deserves to die!" Then, in one of the most riveting passages in all the Bible, Nathan turns to David, stretches out his arm and points to him, and declares, *"You are that man!"* And David sees what he has done.

My interest here is in David's reaction to the story. I agree with David: such injustice is utterly and despicably wrong; there are really no words for it. I believe that such an action is wrong, and I believe that the proposition that it *isn't* wrong—either because really *nothing* is wrong, or because even if *some* things are wrong, *this* isn't—is false. As a matter of fact, there isn't a lot I believe more strongly. I recognize, however, that there are those who disagree with me; and once more, I doubt that I could find an argument to show them that I am right and they wrong. Further, for all I know, their conflicting beliefs have for them the same internally available epistemic markers, the same phenomenology, as mine have for me. Am I then being arbitrary, treating similar cases differently in continuing to hold, as I do, that in fact that kind of behavior *is* dreadfully wrong? I don't think so. Am I wrong in thinking racial bigotry despicable, even though I know there are others who disagree, and even if I think they have the same internal markers for their beliefs as I have for mine? I don't think so. I believe in Serious Actualism, the view that no objects have properties in worlds in which they do not exist, not even nonexistence. Others do not believe this, and perhaps the internal markers of their dissenting views have for them the same quality as my views have for me. Am I being arbitrary in continuing to think as I do? I can't see how.

And the reason here is this: in each of these cases, the believer in question doesn't really think the beliefs in question *are* on a relevant epistemic par. She may agree that she and those who dissent are equally convinced of the truth of their belief, and even that they are internally on a par, that the internally available markers are similar, or relevantly similar. But she must still think that there is an important epistemic difference: she thinks that somehow the other person has *made a mistake*, or *has a blind spot*, or hasn't been wholly attentive, or hasn't received some grace she has, or is in some way epistemically less fortunate. And, of course, the pluralist critic is in no better case. He thinks the thing to do when there is internal epistemic parity is to withhold judgment; he knows there are others who don't think so, and for all he knows, that belief has internal parity with his; if he continues in that belief, therefore, he will be in the same condition as the exclusivist; and if he doesn't continue in this belief, he no longer has an objection to the exclusivist.

But couldn't I be wrong? Of course I could! But I don't avoid that risk by withholding all religious (or philosophical or moral) beliefs; I can go wrong that way as well as any other, treating all religions, or all philosophical thoughts, or all moral views, as on a par. Again, there is no safe haven here, no way to avoid risk. In particular, you won't reach safe haven by trying to take the same attitude toward all the historically available patterns of belief and withholding: for in so doing, you adopt a particular pattern of belief and withholding, one incompatible with some adopted by others. You pays your money and you takes your choice, realizing that you, like anyone else, can be desperately wrong. But what else can you do? You don't really have an alternative. And how can you do better than believe and withhold according to what, after serious and responsible consideration, seems to you to be the right pattern of belief and withholding?

Irrationality

I therefore can't see how it can be sensibly maintained that the exclusivist is unjustified in his exclusivistic views; but perhaps, as is sometimes claimed, he or his view is *irrational*. Irrationality, however, is many things to many people; so there is a prior question: what is it to be irrational? More exactly: precisely what quality is it that the objector is attributing to the exclusivist (in condition C) when the former says the latter's exclusivist beliefs are irrational? Since the charge is never developed at all fully, it isn't easy to say. So suppose we simply consider the main varieties of irrationality (or, if you prefer, the main senses of 'irrational') and ask whether any of them attach to the exclusivist just by virtue of being an exclusivist. I believe there are substantially five varieties of rationality, five distinct but analogically[16] connected senses of the term 'rational'; fortunately, not all of them require detailed consideration.

(1) *Aristotelian Rationality.* This is the sense in which man is a rational animal, one that has *ratio,* one that can look before and after, can hold beliefs, make inferences, and is capable of knowledge. This is perhaps the basic sense, the one of which the others are analogical extensions. It is also, presumably, irrelevant in the present context; at any rate, I hope the objector does not mean to hold that an exclusivist will by that token no longer be a rational animal.

(2) *The Deliverances of Reason.* To be rational in the Aristotelian sense is to possess reason: the power of thinking, believing, inferring, reasoning, knowing. Aristotelian rationality is thus *generic.* But there is an important more specific sense lurking in the neighborhood; this is the sense that goes with reason taken more narrowly, as the source of a priori knowledge and belief.[17] An important use of 'rational' analogically connected with the first has to do with reason taken in this more narrow way. It is by reason thus construed that we know *self-evident* beliefs—beliefs so obvious that you can't so much as grasp them without seeing that they couldn't be false. These are among the *deliverances of reason.* Of course, there are other beliefs—$38 \times 39 = 1482$, for example—that are not self-evident but are a consequence of self-evident beliefs by way of arguments that are self-evidently valid; these too are among the deliverances of reason. So say that the deliverances of reason is the set of those propositions that are self-evident for us human beings, closed under self-evident consequence. This yields another sense of rationality: a belief is *rational* if it is among the deliverances of reason and *irrational* if it is contrary to the deliverances of reason. (A belief can therefore be neither rational nor irrational, in this sense.) This sense of 'rational' is an analogical extension of the fundamental sense, but it is itself extended by analogy to still other senses. Thus we can broaden the category of reason to include memory, experience, induction, probability, and whatever else goes into science; this is the sense of the term when reason is sometimes contrasted with faith. And we can also soften the requirement for self-evidence, recognizing both that self-evidence or a priori warrant is a matter of degree, and that there are many propositions that have a priori warrant but are not such that no one who understands them can fail to believe them.[18]

---

[16] In Aquinas's sense, so that analogy may include causality, proportionality, resemblance, and the like.

[17] But then (because of the Russell paradoxes) we can no longer take it that the deliverances of reason are closed under self-evident consequence. See my *Warrant and Proper Function* (New York: Oxford University Press, 1993), chap. 6.

[18] See my *Warrant and Proper Function,* chap. 6. Still another analogical extension: a *person* can be said to be irrational if he won't listen to or pay attention to the deliverances

Is the exclusivist irrational in *these* senses? I think not; or at any rate the question whether he is isn't the question at issue. For his exclusivist beliefs are irrational in these senses only if there is a good argument from the deliverances of reason (taken broadly) to the denials of what he believes. I myself do not believe there are any such arguments. Presumably, the same goes for the pluralist objector; at any rate his objection is not that (1) and (2) are demonstrably false or even that there are good arguments against them from the deliverances of reason; his objection is instead that there is something wrong or subpar with believing them in condition C. This sense too, then, is irrelevant to our present concerns.

(3) *The Deontological Sense.* This sense of the term has to do with intellectual *requirement*, or *duty*, or *obligation*: a person's belief is irrational in this sense if in forming or holding it she violates such a duty. This is the sense of 'irrational' in which, according to many contemporary evidentialist objectors to theistic belief, those who believe in God without propositional evidence are irrational.[19] Irrationality in this sense is a matter of failing to conform to intellectual or epistemic duties; and the analogical connection with the first, Aristotelian sense is that these duties are thought to be among the deliverances of reason (and hence among the deliverances of the power by virtue of which human beings are rational in the Aristotelian sense). But we have already considered whether the exclusivist is flouting duties; we need say no more about the matter here. As we saw, the exclusivist is not necessarily irrational in this sense either.

(4) *Zweckrationalität.* A common and very important notion of rationality is *means-end* rationality—what our Continental cousins, following Max Weber, sometimes call *Zweckrationalität*, the sort of rationality dis-

---

of reason. He may be blinded by lust, or inflamed by passion, or deceived by pride: he might then act contrary to reason—*act* irrationally but also *believe* irrationally. Thus Locke: "Let never so much probability land on one side of a covetous man's reasoning, and money on the other, it is easy to foresee which will outweigh. Tell a man, passionately in love, that he is jilted; bring a score of witnesses of the falsehood of his mistress, 'tis ten to one but three kind words of hers, shall invalidate all their testimonies. . . . and though men cannot always openly gain-say, or resist the force of manifest probabilities, that make against them; yet yield they not to the argument." *An Essay Concerning Human Understanding,* ed. A. D. Woozley (New York: World Publishing Co., 1963), bk. IV, sec. xx, p. 439.

[19] Among those who offer this objection to theistic belief are Brand Blanshard, *Reason and Belief* (London: Allen and Unwin, 1974), pp. 400 ff.; Antony Flew, *The Presumption of Atheism* (London: Pemberton, 1976), pp. 22 ff.; and Michael Scriven, *Primary Philosophy* (New York: McGraw-Hill, 1966), pp. 102 ff. See my "Reason and Belief in God," in Alvin Plantinga and Nicholas Wolterstorff, eds., *Faith and Rationality*: (Notre Dame: University of Notre Dame Press, 1983), pp. 17 ff.

played by your actions if they are well calculated to achieve your goals. (Again, the analogical connection with the first sense is clear: the calculation in question requires the power by virtue of which we are rational in Aristotle's sense.) Clearly, there is a whole constellation of notions lurking in the nearby bushes: what would *in fact* contribute to your goals, what you *take* it would contribute to your goals, what you *would* take it would contribute to your goals if you were sufficiently acute, or knew enough, or weren't distracted by lust, greed, pride, ambition, and the like, what you would take it would contribute to your goals if you weren't thus distracted and were also to reflect sufficiently, and so on. This notion of rationality has assumed enormous importance in the last one hundred fifty years or so. (Among its laurels, for example, is the complete domination of the development of the discipline of economics.) Rationality thus construed is a matter of knowing how to get what you want; it is the cunning of reason. Is the exclusivist properly charged with irrationality in this sense? Does his believing in the way he does interfere with his attaining some of his goals, or is it a markedly inferior way of attaining those goals?

An initial caveat: it isn't clear that this notion of rationality applies to belief at all. It isn't clear that in *believing* something, I am acting to achieve some goal. If believing is an action at all, it is very far from being the paradigmatic kind of action taken to achieve some end; we don't have a choice as to whether to have beliefs, and we don't have a lot of choice with respect to which beliefs we have. But suppose we set this caveat aside and stipulate for purposes of argument that we have sufficient control over our beliefs for them to qualify as actions: would the exclusivist's beliefs then be irrational in this sense? Well, that depends upon what his goals *are*; if among his goals for religious belief is, for example, not believing anything not believed by someone else, then indeed it would be. But, of course, he needn't have *that* goal. If I do have an end or goal in holding such beliefs as (1) and (2), it would presumably be that of believing the truth on this exceedingly important matter, or perhaps that of trying to get in touch as adequately as possible with God, or more broadly with the deepest reality. And if (1) and (2) are *true*, believing them will be a way of doing exactly that. It is only if they are *not* true, then, that believing them could sensibly be thought to be irrational in this means-ends sense. Since the objector does not propose to take as a premise the proposition that (1) and (2) are false—he holds only that there is some flaw involved in *believing* them—this also is presumably not what he means.

(5) *Rationality as Sanity and Proper Function.* One in the grip of pathological confusion, or flight of ideas, or certain kinds of agnosia,

or the manic phase of manic-depressive psychosis will often be said to be irrational; the episode may pass, after which he regains rationality. Here 'rationality' means absence of dysfunction, disorder, impairment, pathology with respect to rational faculties. So this variety of rationality is again analogically related to Aristotelian rationality; a person is rational in this sense when no malfunction obstructs her use of the faculties by virtue of the possession of which she is rational in the Aristotelian sense. Rationality as sanity does not require possession of particularly exalted rational faculties; it requires only normality (in the nonstatistical sense), or health, or proper function. This use of the term, naturally enough, is prominent in psychiatric discussions—Oliver Sacks's man who mistook his wife for a hat,[20] for example, was thus irrational.[21] This fifth and final sense of rationality is itself a family of analogically related senses. The fundamental sense here is that of sanity and proper function, but there are other closely related senses. Thus we may say that a belief (in certain circumstances) is irrational not because no sane person would hold it, but because no person who was sane and had also undergone a certain course of education would hold it, or because no person who was sane and furthermore was as intelligent as we and our friends would hold it; alternatively and more briefly, the idea is not merely that no one who was functioning properly in those circumstances would hold it but rather no one who was functioning *optimally*, as well or nearly as well as human beings ordinarily do (leaving aside the occasional great genius) would hold it. And this sense of rationality leads directly to the notion of *warrant*; I turn now to that notion; in treating it we also treat *ambulando* this fifth kind of irrationality.

Warrant

So the third version of the epistemic objection: that at any rate the exclusivist doesn't have warrant, or anyway *much* warrant (enough warrant for knowledge), for his exclusivistic views. Many pluralists—for

---

[20] Oliver Sacks, *The Man Who Mistook His Wife for a Hat* (New York: Harper and Row, 1987).

[21] In this sense of the term, what is properly called an 'irrational impulse' may be perfectly rational: an irrational impulse is really one that goes contrary to the deliverances of reason; but undergoing such impulses need not be in any way dysfunctional or a result of the impairment of cognitive faculties. To go back to some of William James's examples, that I will survive my serious illness might be unlikely, given the statistics I know and my evidence generally; perhaps we are so constructed, however, that when our faculties function properly in extreme situations, we are more optimistic than the evidence warrants. This belief, then, is irrational in the sense that it goes contrary to the deliverances of reason; it is rational in the sense that it doesn't involve dysfunction.

example, Hick, Runzo, and Wilfred Cantwell Smith—unite in declaring that at any rate the exclusivist certainly can't *know* that his exclusivistic views are true.[22] But is this really true? I shall argue briefly that it is not. At any rate from the perspective of each of the major contemporary accounts of knowledge, it may very well be that the exclusivist knows (1) or (2) or both. First, consider the two main internalistic accounts of knowledge: the justified true belief account(s) and the coherentist account(s). As I have already argued, it seems clear that a theist, a believer in (1), could certainly be *justified* (in the primary sense) in believing as she does: she could be flouting no intellectual or cognitive duties or obligations. But then on the most straightforward justified true belief account of knowledge, she can also *know* that it is true—if, that is, it *can* be true. More exactly, what must be possible is that both the exclusivist is justified in believing (1) and/or (2) and they be true. Presumably, the pluralist does not mean to dispute this possibility.

For concreteness, consider the account of justification given by the classical Chisholm.[23] On this view, a belief has warrant for me to the extent that accepting it is apt for the fulfillment of my epistemic duty, which (roughly speaking) is that of trying to get and remain in the right relation to the truth. But if after the most careful, thorough, thoughtful, open, and prayerful consideration, it still seems to me— perhaps more strongly than ever—that (1) and (2) are true, then clearly accepting them has great aptness for the fulfillment of that duty.[24]

---

[22] Hick, *An Interpretation of Religion,* p. 234; Runzo, "God, Commitment, and Other Faiths," p. 348; Smith, *Religious Diversity,* p. 16.

[23] See his *Perceiving: A Philosophical Study* (Ithaca: Cornell University Press, 1957), the three editions of *Theory of Knowledge* (New York: Prentice-Hall, 1st ed., 1966; 2d ed., 1977; 3d ed., 1989), and *The Foundations of Knowing* (Minneapolis: University of Minnesota Press, 1982); and see my "Chisholmian Internalism," in David Austin, ed., *Philosophical Analysis: A Defense by Example* (Dordrecht: D. Reidel, 1988), and chap. 2 of *Warrant: The Current Debate.*

[24] Of course, there are many variations on this internalist theme. Consider briefly the postclassical Chisholm (see his "The Place of Epistemic Justification," in Roberta Klein, ed., *Philosophical Topics* 14, no. 1 (1986), 85, and the intellectual autobiography in *Roderick M. Chisholm,* ed. Radu Bogdan [Dordrecht: D. Reidel, 1986], pp. 52 ff.), who bears a startling resemblance to Brentano. According to this view, justification is not *deontological* but *axiological.* To put it another way, warrant is not really a matter of justification, of fulfilling duty and obligation; it is instead a question whether a certain relation of fittingness holds between one's evidential base (very roughly, the totality of one's present experiences and other beliefs) and the belief in question. (This relationship's holding, of course, is a valuable state of affairs; hence the axiology.) Can the exclusivist have warrant from this perspective? Well, without more knowledge about what this relation is, it isn't easy to tell. But here at the least the postclassical Chisholmian pluralist would owe us an explanation why he thinks the exclusivist's beliefs could not stand in this relation to his evidence base.

A similarly brief argument can be given with respect to coherentism, the view that what constitutes warrant is coherence with some body of belief. We must distinguish two varieties of coherentism. On the one hand, it might be held that what is required is coherence with some or all of the other beliefs I actually hold; on the other, that what is required is coherence with my *verific* noetic structure (Keith Lehrer's term): the set of beliefs that remains when all the false ones are deleted or replaced by their contradictories. But surely a coherent set of beliefs could include both (1) and (2) together with the beliefs involved in being in condition C; what would be required, perhaps, would be that the set of beliefs contain some explanation of why it is that others do not believe as I do. And if (1) and (2) *are* true, then surely (and a fortiori) there can be coherent verific noetic structures that include them. Hence neither of these versions of coherentism rules out the possibility that the exclusivist in condition C could know (1) and/or (2).

And now consider the main externalist accounts. The most popular externalist account at present would be one or another version of *reliabilism*. And there is an oft-repeated pluralistic argument (an argument that goes back at least to John Stuart Mill's *On Liberty* and possibly all the way back to the third century) that seems to be designed to appeal to reliabilist intuitions. The conclusion of this argument is not always clear, but here is its premise, in John Hick's words:

> For it is evident that in some ninety-nine percent of cases the religion which an individual professes and to which he or she adheres depends upon the accidents of birth. Someone born to Buddhist parents in Thailand is very likely to be a Buddhist, someone born to Muslim parents in Saudi Arabia to be a Muslim, someone born to Christian parents in Mexico to be a Christian, and so on.[25]

As a matter of sociological fact, this may be right. Furthermore, it can certainly produce a sense of intellectual vertigo. But what is one to do with this fact, if fact it is, and what follows from it? Does it follow, for example, that I ought not to accept the religious views that I have been brought up to accept, or the ones that I find myself inclined to accept, or the ones that seem to me to be true? Or that the belief-producing processes that have produced those beliefs in me are unreliable? Surely not. Furthermore, self-referential problems once more loom; this argument is another philosophical tar baby.

For suppose we concede that if I had been born in Madagascar

[25] *Interpretation of Religion*, p. 2.

rather than Michigan, my beliefs would have been quite different.[26] (For one thing, I probably wouldn't believe that I was born in Michigan.) But, of course, the same goes for the pluralist. Pluralism isn't and hasn't been widely popular in the world at large; if the pluralist had been born in Madagascar, or medieval France, he probably wouldn't have been a pluralist. Does it follow that he shouldn't be a pluralist or that his pluralistic beliefs are produced in him by an unreliable belief-producing process? I doubt it. Suppose I hold

(4) If S's religious or philosophical beliefs are such that if S had been born elsewhere and elsewhen, she wouldn't have held them, then those beliefs are produced by unreliable belief-producing mechanisms and hence have no warrant;

or something similar: then once more I will be hoist with my own petard. For in all probability, someone born in Mexico to Christian parents wouldn't believe (4) itself. No matter what philosophical and religious beliefs we hold and withhold (so it seems), there are places and times such that if we had been born there and then, then we would not have displayed the pattern of holding and withholding of religious and philosophical beliefs we *do* display. As I said, this can indeed be vertiginous; but what can we make of it? What can we infer from it about what has warrant and how we should conduct our intellectual lives? That's not easy to say. Can we infer *anything at all* about what has warrant or how we should conduct our intellectual lives? Not obviously.

To return to reliabilism, then: for simplicity, let's take the version of reliabilism according to which S knows p iff the belief that p is produced in S by a reliable belief-producing mechanism or process. I don't have the space, here, to go into this matter in sufficient detail: but it seems pretty clear that if (1) and (2) are true, then it *could be* that the beliefs that (1) and (2) be produced in me by a reliable belief-producing process. For either we are thinking of *concrete* belief-producing processes, like your memory or John's powers of a priori reasoning (*tokens* as opposed to types), or else we are thinking of *types* of belief-producing processes (type reliabilism). The problem with the latter is that there are an enormous number of *different* types of belief-producing processes for any given belief, some of which are reliable and some of which

[26] Actually, this conditional as it stands is probably not true; the point must be stated with more care. Given my parents and their proclivities, if I had been born in Madagascar, it would probably have been because my parents were (Christian) missionaries there.

A Defense of Religious Exclusivism

are not; the problem (and a horrifying problem it is[27]) is to say which of these is the type the reliability of which determines whether the belief in question has warrant. So the first (token reliabilism) is the better way of stating reliabilism. But then, clearly enough, if (1) or (2) *is* true, it could be produced in me by a reliable belief-producing process. Calvin's Sensus Divinitatis, for example, could be working in the exclusivist in such a way as reliably to produce the belief that (1); Calvin's Internal Testimony of the Holy Spirit could do the same for (2). If (1) and (2) are true, therefore, then from a reliabilist perspective there is no reason whatever to think that the exclusivist might not know that they are true.

There is another brand of externalism that seems to me to be closer to the truth than reliabilism: call it (faute de mieux) 'proper functionalism'. This view can be stated to a first approximation as follows: S knows p iff (1) the belief that p is produced in S by cognitive faculties that are functioning properly (working as they ought to work, suffering from no dysfunction), (2) the cognitive environment in which p is produced is appropriate for those faculties, (3) the purpose of the module of the epistemic faculties producing the belief in question is to produce true beliefs (alternatively: the module of the design plan governing the production of p is aimed at the production of true beliefs), and (4) the objective probability of a belief's being true, given that it is produced under those conditions, is high.[28] All this needs explanation, of course; for present purposes, perhaps, we can collapse the account into the first condition. But then clearly it *could* be, if (1) and (2) are true, that they are produced in me by cognitive faculties functioning properly under condition C. For suppose (1) is true. Then it is surely possible that God has created us human beings with something like Calvin's Sensus Divinitatis, a belief-producing process that in a wide variety of circumstances functions properly to produce (1) or some very similar belief. Furthermore, it is also possible that in response to the human condition of sin and misery, God has provided for us human beings a means of salvation, which he has revealed in the Bible. Still further, perhaps he has arranged for us to come to believe what he means to teach there by way of the operation of something like the Internal Testimony of the Holy Spirit of which Calvin speaks. So on this view, too, if (1) and (2) are true, it is certainly possible that the exclusivist

---

[27] See Richard Feldman, "Reliability and Justification," *The Monist* 68 (1986), 159–74, and chap. 9 of my *Warrant and Proper Function*.

[28] See chap. 10 of my *Warrant: The Current Debate* and the first two chapters of my *Warrant and Proper Function* for exposition and defense of this way of thinking about warrant.

know that they are. We can be sure that the exclusivist's views lack warrant and are irrational in this sense, then, only if they are false; but the pluralist objector does not mean to claim that they *are* false; this version of the objection, therefore, also fails. The exclusivist isn't necessarily irrational, and indeed might *know* that (1) and (2) are true, if indeed they *are* true.

All this seems right. But don't the realities of religious pluralism count for anything at all? Is there nothing at all to the claims of the pluralists?[29] Could that really be right? Of course not. For many or most exclusivists, I think, an awareness of the enormous variety of human religious response serves as a *defeater* for such beliefs as (1) and (2)—an *undercutting* defeater, as opposed to a *rebutting* defeater. It calls into question, to some degree or other, the sources of one's belief in (1) or (2). It doesn't or needn't do so by way of an *argument*; and indeed, there isn't a very powerful argument from the proposition that many apparently devout people around the world dissent from (1) and (2) to the conclusion that (1) and (2) are false. Instead, it works more directly; it directly reduces the level of confidence or degree of belief in the proposition in question. From a Christian perspective, this situation of religious pluralism and our awareness of it is itself a manifestation of our miserable human condition; and it may deprive us of some of the comfort and peace the Lord has promised his followers. It can also deprive the exclusivist of the *knowledge* that (1) and (2) are true, even if they *are* true and he *believes* that they are. Since degree of warrant depends in part on degree of belief, it is possible, though not necessary, that knowledge of the facts of religious pluralism should reduce an exclusivist's degree of belief and hence of warrant for (1) and (2) in such a way as to deprive him of knowledge of (1) and (2). He might be such that if he *hadn't* known the facts of pluralism, then he would have known (1) and (2), but now that he *does* know those facts, he doesn't know (1) and (2). In this way he may come to know less by knowing more.

Things *could* go this way with the exclusivist. On the other hand, they *needn't* go this way. Consider once more the moral parallel. Perhaps you have always believed it deeply wrong for a counselor to use his position of trust to seduce a client. Perhaps you discover that others disagree; they think it more like a minor peccadillo, like running a red light when there's no traffic; and you realize that possibly these people have the same internal markers for their beliefs that you have for yours. You

<hr>

[29] See William P. Alston, "Religious Diversity and Perceptual Knowledge of God," *Faith and Philosophy* 5 (October 1988), 433 ff.

think the matter over more fully, imaginatively recreate and rehearse such situations, become more aware of just what is involved in such a situation (the breach of trust, the breaking of implied promises, the injustice and unfairness, the nasty irony of a situation in which someone comes to a counselor seeking help but receives only hurt) and come to believe even more firmly the belief that such an action is wrong—which belief, indeed, can in this way acquire more warrant for you. But something similar can happen in the case of religious beliefs. A fresh or heightened awareness of the facts of religious pluralism could bring about a reappraisal of one's religious life, a reawakening, a new or renewed and deepened grasp and apprehension of (1) and (2). From Calvin's perspective, it could serve as an occasion for a renewed and more powerful working of the belief-producing processes by which we come to apprehend (1) and (2). In that way knowledge of the facts of pluralism could initially serve as a defeater, but in the long run have precisely the opposite effect.

[9]

Non Est Hick

PETER VAN INWAGEN

Most of us probably remember from our childhoods a kind of puzzle called "What is wrong with this picture?" The child confronting one of these puzzles would be presented with a picture that contained details like a dog smoking a pipe or a woman writing a letter with a carrot instead of a pen. It would be announced that there were, say, ten such "mistakes" in the picture and the object was to find all ten.

There is a currently very popular picture of what are called "the World Religions" that looks to me a lot like those puzzle pictures from my childhood. The picture is done in prose, rather than in pen-and-ink outline. I shall have to provide you with a copy of it if am to proceed with this essay, but it will not be easy for me to do this, for I am constitutionally unable to write the kind of prose suited to the task. Nonetheless, here goes.

There are a number of entities called "religions"; the most important among them are called the "World Religions," with or without capitals. The world religions are the religions that appear in the history books, and appear not merely as footnotes or as clues to "what the Assyrians were like" or evidences of "the beginnings of cosmological speculation." The world religions are important topics of historical inquiry in their own right. Each of them, in fact, has a history of its own; the majority of them have founders and can be said to have begun at fairly definite dates. The list of world religions must include at least the following: Buddhism, Christianity, Confucianism, Hinduism, Islam, Judaism, and Taoism. But other religions are plausible candidates for inclusion in the list, and some might want to split some of the items in the list into two or more religions. It is the division of humanity into the adherents of the various world religions (of course, many people practice a tribal religion or belong to some syncretistic cult or have no religion at all) that is the primary datum of all responsible thinking about religion. Comparative studies of the world religions have shown that each of these religions is a species of a genus and that they have important common characteristics that belong to no other human social institutions. There are, of course, differences as well as similarities among the world religions, and some might think that there were *grave* differences, or even outright inconsistencies. It might be thought, for example, that the Middle Eastern or "Abrahamic" religions required their adherents to believe in a God who was a person and that other religions denied the existence of a divine person or subjected this thesis to "the death of a thousand qualifications" or even deprecated as a sign of spiritual immaturity any interest in a transcendent reality, whether personal or impersonal. It might be thought that Christianity taught that if your country was occupied by foreigners who despised you and your countrymen, and if a soldier of the occupying forces ordered you to carry his pack for a mile (which he was allowed by his own law to do), you should carry his pack for an extra mile; and it might be thought that Islam most definitely did not teach this. It might be thought that most forms of Buddhism taught that desire was intrinsically a bad thing, whereas Christianity taught that desire was made by God and that the Buddhist doctrine was therefore a blasphemous inveighing against the creation. It might be thought, moreover, that these apparent inconsistencies among the world religions were not matters of the surface. It might be thought that each of them pertained to the very root and essence of the religions involved.

It cannot be denied that the apparent inconsistencies exist. What can be denied is that they have anything to do with "the root and essence" of the world religions. Each of the world religions is a response to a single divine reality. The responses are *different*, of course; no one could dispute that. The world religions are different because they arose and developed under different climatic, geographical, cultural, economic, historical, and social circumstances. The God of the Abrahamic religions, for example, is male—that is, He is described almost exclusively in terms of male imagery. This is because He represents the response to the divine of a people who in their beginnings were nomads and herdsmen, and who therefore were little concerned with the craft of growing things in the soil. Growth in the soil is particularly associated in the human imagination with the female, and religions that have their roots in a community whose economy is based on sowing and reaping tend to incorporate a strong female element. It is because the ancestors of the Jews were herdsmen and not farmers that the God of the Jews and their spiritual children is, whatever refinements may have crept into His nature over the course of the millennia, at root an exclusively male sky-god—in fact, the Lord of Battles.

The divine reality that each of the world religions responds to is in an important sense beyond the reach of human thought and language. Therefore, any attempt to conceptualize this reality, to describe it in words, to reduce it to formulas, must be woefully inadequate. And when we reflect on the fact that all our religious conceptualizations, descriptions, and formulations are reflections of local and temporary conditions of human social and economic organization, we are led irresistibly to the conclusion that the letter of the creed of any particular religion cannot possibly be an expression of the essence of the divine reality toward which that religion is directed. What we can hope to see over the next couple of hundred years—as each of the great world religions becomes more and more separated from the conditions and the geographical area in which it arose, and as the earth becomes more and more a single "global village"—is a sloughing off of the inessential elements of the world religions. And we may hope that among these discarded inessentials will be those particular elements that at present divide the world religions. It may be that each will retain much of its own characteristic language and sacred narrative and imagery. Indeed, one hopes that this will happen, for diversity that does not produce division is a good thing. But it is to be hoped that the great religions will "converge" to the point at which the differences between them are not incompatibilities—not even apparent incompatibilities. We may look forward to the day when a sincere seeker after the divine may (depending on the momentary circumstances of his or her life) move back and forth among the world religions as easily and consistently as the late-twentieth-century American Protestant who attends a Presbyterian church in California and a Methodist church after moving to North Carolina.

This is as much of the picture as I can bear to paint. There is a lot more that I might have included. I might, for example, have said something more about the sense in which each of the great world religions is supposed to be a response to the divine. (I might have included the idea that the aim of each of the world religions is to lead humanity to salvation, and that the real essence of salvation is a move from self-centeredness to "reality-centeredness.") I might have said something about the "credentials" that each of the world religions can produce to support its claim to be a response to the divine reality. (I might have included the idea that the hallmark of a religion that is truly a response to a divine reality is its capacity for "saint production," its capacity to produce people who have left self-centeredness behind and become reality-centered.) But one must make an end somewhere.

Now what am I to do with this picture? I might treat it as the child is supposed treat the puzzle picture, and point out the dog smoking the pipe and the woman writing with the carrot. I will not do this. For one thing, there is (in my view) so much wrong with the picture that I hardly know where to begin. For another, the whole topic of "religious pluralism"—which is the standard name for what might be called the doctrinal basis of the picture—is surrounded with a nimbus of rhetoric (the defense of religious pluralism has always been entirely rhetorical), and this rhetoric is designed to make any criticism of religious pluralism look like mean-spirited hair-splitting. To attempt actually to analyze the rhetoric of the religious pluralists is to be drawn into a game the main rule of which is that the other side gets to make the rules. Rather than be drawn into this game, I will strike out on my own. I will present a sort of model or theory of "religion" that is intended to provide a perspective from which the traditional, orthodox Christian can view such topics as "the world religions," "the scandal of particularity," and "religious pluralism." I do not expect this theory to recommend itself to anyone who is not a traditional, orthodox Christian.

There is, to begin with, a God. That is, there is an infinite, perfect, self-existent person, a unique and necessarily unique bearer of these attributes. It may be, as many great Christians have said, that the language of personality can be applied to this being only analogically. It may be when we say things that imply that this being is conscious and has thoughts and is aware of other things than Himself and makes choices and has plans and acts to bring these plans to fruition, we are using language that is literally correct when we apply it to ourselves, and can be applied to God only in some way that is to be understood in terms of the concept of analogy—as we are using language that is literally correct when we say that Watson is following the suspect, and only "analogically correct" when we say that he is following Holmes's reasoning. And it may not be. It may be, as William Alston has suggested, that there is available a plausible functional account of personal language that has the consequence that the meanings of terms like 'conscious' and 'thought' and 'plan' are so abstract that it is possible for them to apply univocally to God and to human beings.[1] But even if the language of personality can be applied to God only analogically, it is the only language we Christians have been given and the only language

---

[1] William P. Alston, "Can We Speak Literally of God?" in his *Divine Nature and Human Language: Essays in Philosophical Theology* (Ithaca: Cornell University Press, 1989).

we have. It is not open to us to talk of God only in the impersonal terms appropriate to a discussion of Brahman or the Dialectic of History or the Absolute Idea or Being-as-Such or the *Elan vital* or the Force. (If it is the implication of "apophatic" or "negative" theology that it is improper to use personal language in speaking of God—I do not say that it is—then apophatic theology must be looked at as an assault by Athens on Jerusalem.) This is the meaning of Genesis 1:26–27. It is because we are made in the image of God and after His likeness that we can properly apply to Him terms that apply to human beings.

This God, although He is the only thing that is self-existent, is not the only thing that exists. But all other things that exist exist only because He has made them. If He had not, by an act of free will, brought other things into existence, there would be nothing besides Himself. When we say that He "made" other things than Himself, we do not mean that He formed them from some preexistent stuff that existed independently of His will. There could be no such stuff, for He is the Creator of all things, visible and invisible. Moreover, He did not produce the world of created things and then allow it to go its own way. Even He could not do that, for it is intrinsically impossible for anything to exist apart from Him—the *fons et origo* of being—even for the briefest moment. He sustains all other things in existence, and if He were to withdraw His sustaining power from any being—a soap bubble or a cosmos or an archangel—it would, of absolute, metaphysical necessity, immediately cease to exist. And He does not confine His interactions with the created beings to sustaining them in existence. He is, as we learn from St. John, love; He loves His creatures and, because of this love, governs the world they inhabit providentially.

Among His creatures are human beings, who were, as we have said, made in His image. They were made for a purpose. They have, as the Shorter Catechism of the Church of Scotland says, a "chief end": to glorify God and to enjoy Him forever. This end or purpose implies both free will and the ability to know God. Human beings have not been made merely to mouth words of praise or to be passively awash in a pleasant sensation of the presence of God. They have been made to be intimately aware of God and capable of freely acting on this awareness; having seen God, they may either glorify and enjoy what they have seen—the glorification and the enjoyment are separate only by the intellect in an act of severe abstraction—or they may reject what they have seen and attempt to order their own lives and to create their own objects of enjoyment. The choice is theirs and it is a free choice: to choose either way is genuinely open to each human being.[2]

---

[2] It may sound as if I am preaching Pelagianism here, but it will become evident in a moment that this can hardly be my meaning. In my view, in the present age of the world, this freedom comes to us only by Grace.

God wishes to be the object of human glorification and enjoyment not out of vanity but out of love: He is glorious and enjoyable to a degree infinitely greater than that of any other object. He has given us free will in this matter because it is only when a person, having contemplated the properties of something, freely assents to the proposition that that thing is worthy of glory, and then proceeds freely to offer glory to it, that a thing is truly glorified. And it is only when a person, having enjoyed a thing, freely chooses to continue in the enjoyment of that thing that true enjoyment occurs.

Unfortunately, the first human beings, having tasted and enjoyed God, did not persist in their original felicity. (Perhaps they chose to ignore some stricture on the course of their development that, in their pride, they thought they could bypass. We cannot say, for the form in which temptation could be present in the mind of an as yet unfallen creature is necessarily a mystery to us. The suggestion that it would be psychologically impossible for an Edenic human being to feel, or, at any rate, to succumb to, temptation to do wrong is, however, an assertion and not an argument. The idea that we are in a position to say what is psychologically possible for beings in circumstances that are literally unimaginable to us is nothing more than an illustration of the apriorism that is an endemic intellectual disease of philosophers and theologians.) They turned away from God—perhaps they did not describe what they were doing in that way, just as an alcoholic husband may not describe what he is doing as "turning away from his wife and children"—and ruined themselves. In fact, they ruined not only themselves but their posterity, for the separation from God that they achieved was somehow hereditary. This turning away from God and its consequences are known as the Fall.[3]

I find the following analogy helpful in thinking about the condition of fallen humanity. Imagine a great modern city—New York, say—that has been lifted several yards into the air by the hand of some vast giant and then simply let fall. The city is now a ruin. The mass of the buildings stand at crazy angles. Others have been totally destroyed or lie on their sides. Some few still stand more or less straight. The suitability of the buildings for human habitation varies. Most of the rooms in most of the buildings are now, in some measure, open to the wind and the rain, but a small proportion of them are still snug and dry. Water mains and gas mains and electrical cables have mostly been severed by the catastrophe, but here and there a building still has water or gas or

---

[3] For a discussion of the Fall that takes up some points that cannot be gone into here, see my "The Magnitude, Duration, and Distribution of Evil: A Theodicy," *Philosophical Topics* 16, 2, (1988) 161–87.

electricity. How these remnants of function are distributed among the various buildings of the city is simply a matter of chance: the fact that a particular building is snug and dry and more or less upright and still has running water is a consequence of the way a vast network of forces redistributed themselves when the city was dropped. Certainly it does not reflect any particular credit on the design of the building; no building could be designed to withstand such a catastrophe, and that this one emerged relatively intact (but in normal circumstances it would be condemned) is due to the fact that a complex array of forces happened to come close to "canceling out" at this location.

I have said that this story provides a model for the fallen human race. We are all ruins, in a sense very closely analogous to the sense in which the Parthenon is a ruin. That is, we cannot be said without qualification to be the products either of chance or of design. Each of us is at birth the product of two factors: the original plan of a wise and providential Creator, and the changes that chance—different in the case of every individual—has introduced into the original perfection that came from the Creator's hand. The effects of these changes are not grossly physical, of course, as they are in the buildings that are the other term of the analogy. They are moral and intellectual and aesthetic and spiritual. A particular human being may labor under a genetic predisposition to a vicious temper, or to an almost total lack of sensitivity to the needs of others, or even to a positive enjoyment of the sufferings of others. Another human being may be blessed with a genetic disposition to a sweet temper and great human sympathy and a horror of any human suffering. A particular human being may be born with almost no capacity for sustained rational thought, or with a tendency recklessly to disregard evidence, or with an inherent disposition to deprecate any use of the mind that is not directed toward what is immediately useful. Another human being may be genetically endowed with dispositions to intellectual virtue. Similar points may be made about our various genetic endowments as regards aesthetic matters. There is little more that needs to be said about our genetic endowments in these areas, except perhaps to stress the point that I have been talking about our *genetic* endowments, and that the bad dispositions we have been born with can no doubt be to some degree mitigated, and the good dispositions corrupted or rendered impotent, by social and other environmental factors.

What is most relevant to our present concerns is our "spiritual endowments"—that is, the degree to which the spiritual endowment that was a part of the Creator's plan for each individual has managed to survive the Fall. We have said that human beings were made to be intimately aware of God. It would not be profitable for me—whose spiritual life is devoid of the least tincture of mystical or religious experience—to speculate at any length on the nature of this awareness. I expect that this awareness was somehow connected with the subject's ordinary sensory awareness of physical objects (which endure and move and have their being in God). I expect that the way in which I am aware of the "invisible" thoughts and emotions of others through their faces and voices provides some sort of analogy.[4] I expect that the way the natural world looked to unfallen humanity and the way it looks to me are as similar and as different as the way a page of Chinese calligraphy looks to a literate Chinese and to me. But whatever the nature of our primordial awareness of God, we have largely lost it. Perhaps, however, none of us has lost it entirely, or only a very few of us have. And it may be that this awareness is present in various people in varying degrees. (The city is now a ruin. The mass of the buildings stand at crazy angles. Others have been totally destroyed or lie on their sides. Some few still stand more or less straight.) It is because some vestige of the capacity to be aware of God is present in all or most people that there is such a thing as religion. (We should note that an awareness of God does not necessarily seem to be an awareness of God to the person who has it: an awareness of a distant mountain range may seem to the person who has it to be an awareness of a bank of clouds.)[5]

It is because a capacity to be aware of God is present in people in varying degrees that people are more religious or less religious—or, at any rate, this is one reason among others for the varying degrees of engagement with religion exhibited by various people. It is because there are people in whom the capacity to be aware of God is relatively intact (the buildings that stand almost straight and provide shelter from the elements and perhaps even a trickle of water from the taps) that

---

[4] Cf. Rom. 1:20; Wisd. of Sol. 13:1–9.

[5] This useful analogy has a defect: it suggest that "misperceptions" of God are invariably as innocent as ordinary perceptual mistakes. But this is not so. I will make my point by means of an extreme example, without meaning to imply that this point is confined to cases of the extreme sort that I shall consider. There have been and still are those who believe in dark gods, gods whose favor can be gained only by ritual sodomy or by the immolation of babies or by tearing the heart out of a living victim. I see no reason to suppose that the remnant of our original awareness of God is any less a causal factor in the life of the religions of ancient Mesopotamia or pre-Columbian Central America (or current Satanism) than in the life of what the nineteenth century called "the higher religions." I do not believe, however, that God would allow any of His creatures *innocently* to perceive Him as a dark god. The belief that there were divine powers that demanded the immolation of babies can no more have been an "honest mistake" than the belief of the Nazis that a cabal of Jewish plutocrats arranged the defeat of Germany in 1918 can have been an innocent misreading of history.

there are great religious leaders and doctors and saints—or, again, this is one reason among others. And these people are not confined to any particular geographical area or to any historical period. This statement is of course consistent with the statement that it is only in certain social and cultural milieux that they will flourish spiritually or have any effect upon history.

In a way, what I have said in the preceding paragraph looks a great deal like the picture of the world religions that I have made it clear that I reject. Although I have talked about a personal Creator and a Fall, it might be argued that these are no more than details, and that the picture I have painted differs from the picture I have undertaken to attack in only a few background details. What difference does it make (someone might ask) what the exact nature of the relation between the great spiritual leaders and the divine reality is—as long as it is admitted that they are spread throughout the human race? In fact (the questioner might continue), don't your "details" undermine themselves? If you know about this "Fall," you know about it from certain great spiritual teachers: Augustine and Paul and the authors of the early books of Genesis. But their authority, if they have it, to pronounce on the relation of the human and the divine can be due only to their being in closer touch with the divine reality than most of us. And they are not in closer touch with the divine reality than, say, Lao Tzu or Gautama. (At least, you have not given us any reason to suppose so; and if it were so, how should *you*, who by your own admission are spiritually nothing out of the ordinary, know this?) If you are right, spiritual gifts are distributed more or less randomly in space and time, as randomly as intellectual and aesthetic gifts. Why, then, should a certain stream of stories told in the ancient Levant be normative for all of humanity? If things were as you say, if there has been a primordial catastrophe that has left us all, in varying degrees, spiritual ruins, then the details of our relation with the divine would have to be "blurry," too blurry to be read with confidence by such as you. Therefore, you can have no ground for your statement of the details, and when the details—which are of no great intrinsic importance in any case—have been erased, your picture is indistinguishable from the standard picture of the "world religions."

There is a great deal of merit in these pointed questions. Indeed, if I had no more to put into my "model" than this, they would be unanswerable. I do, however, have more to put into my model than this. The consequence of what I shall add is this: the standard picture of the world religions is not so much false as it is out of date. For God has not left us to deal as best we can with our state of spiritual ruin. If He had, then the picture of the world religions that I deprecate as false to the facts would have been true to the facts. But . . .

In many and various ways God spoke of old to our fathers by the prophets; but in these last days He has spoken to us by a Son, whom He appointed the heir of all things, through whom also He created the world. Let me expand on this theme, in rather a different vein from the author of Hebrews—or perhaps not so different.

The world religions, insofar as they have any reality at all (this qualification is an adumbration of a point I shall take up presently), are human creations. That is, they are the work of human beings, and their existence and properties are not a part of God's plan for the world. Other examples of human creations that are similar to religions in that they are in some sense composed of human beings would be the Roman Empire, Scotland, the Children's Crusade, Aunt Lillian's sewing circle, the Comintern, the Vienna Circle, the Gestapo, the American Academy of Religion, Tokyo, fauvism, the Palestine Liberation Organization, the *New York Times,* and the National Aeronautics and Space Administration.

The existence and properties of the institutions in this list are due to chance and to the interplay of a wide variety of "climatic, geographical, cultural, economic, historical, and social circumstances" that it is the business of the social sciences to identify and map. When I say that they are "not a part of God's plan for the world," I am assuming that there *are* things in the world that are not a part of God's plan for the world.[6] As to the individual items in the list, I am assuming that—given that there is *anything* that is not a part of God's plan for the world—it is fairly evident that none of these things is. Perhaps some will disagree with me about particular cases. And even if no one disagrees, it may be that we are all wrong. God's ways are mysterious, and I do not claim to be privy to them. I am proceeding only by such dim lights as I have. Nothing in the sequel really depends on whether the *New York Times* or the Vienna Circle is a part of God's plan for the world: the items listed are meant only to be suggestive examples. But I should make it clear that in saying that these institutions are not parts of God's plan for the world, I do not mean to deny that God may make use of them in carrying out His plan—as I may make pedagogical use of various physical objects that happen, independently of my plans and my will, to be among the fixtures of a lecture room in which I am giving a

---

[6] For a defense of the thesis that there are many things in the world that are not a part of God's plan for the world, see my essay "The Place of Chance in a World Sustained by God," in Thomas V. Morris, ed., *Divine and Human Action: Essays in the Metaphysics of Theism* (Ithaca: Cornell University Press, 1988), pp. 211–35.

lecture on perception. Indeed, I would suppose that God makes *constant* use of human institutions, human individuals, animals, inanimate objects, and transient psychological phenomena in His moment-to-moment shepherding of His creatures toward the fulfillment of His plan.

Like the *New York Times* and the Vienna Circle, the world religions have arisen amid the turmoil of the fallen world by chance and have developed and grown and acquired their peculiar characteristics partly by chance and partly by the interplay of the factors that a completed social science would understand. In the case of the world religions, however, a third factor is present, one that can hardly be supposed to have been involved in the development of the *Times* and the Vienna Circle: their growth and properties are affected by the innate awareness of God (both within their "ordinary" members and within their founders and great teachers) that is still present, in varying degrees, throughout fallen humanity. It is also possible—and we might make the same point about any things that exist in this present darkness—that the world religions have been partly shaped by God so that they may be instruments of His purpose. (If this is so, it does not follow that there is some *common* purpose that they serve. For all I know, God may have shaped Islam partly to be a reproach to a complacent Christendom, and it may be that no other religion has this purpose.)

"But if God has created the world, and if the world religions are parts of the world, how can they not be His creations?" It is important to realize that the following argument is invalid: God is the creator of all things visible and invisible; *hence,* God is the creator of Taoism (or of the *New York Times* or of the Vienna Circle). St. Augustine pointed out that the premise that God is the creator of all things does not entail the conclusion that God is the creator of evil, owing to the fact that evil is not a "thing" in the requisite sense: evil is not a substance. And just as evil is, ontologically speaking, not a substance, so religions are not substances; when a particular religion comes into being, this does not imply the coming to be of a substance but merely certain substances'— certain human beings—coming to stand in a new set of relations. And it may well be that God has not ordained that any human beings should stand in the particular set of relations that is the only being that a religion has. It is, of course, *possible* for God to create a religion; for Him to do this would be for Him to bring it about that certain human beings came to stand in a certain set of relations. I maintain, however, that He has not in fact done so: no religion is a divine creation. (But this conviction of mine is not essential to my point. If I am wrong about this, if God has created Taoism or Islam, I am wrong about a peripheral matter—as I should be wrong about a peripheral matter if the *New York Times* or the Vienna Circle were a divine creation.)

There are, I suggest, two and only two things that are in any sense composed of human beings and are both God's creations and a part of His plan for the world.[7] These are His people Israel and the Catholic Church.

By Israel I mean a *people*. I mean those descendants of Jacob who are the heirs of the promises made to Abraham. It was to this people, and not to a religion called Judaism, that the Law was given ("I have set before you life and death, blessing and curse; therefore, choose life that you and your descendants may live, loving the Lord your God, obeying his voice, and cleaving to him, . . . that you may live in the land which the Lord swore to your fathers, to Abraham, to Isaac, and to Jacob, to give them").[8] It was not "Judaism" whom David ruled and who heard the prophets, but a people.

By the Catholic Church I mean a certain *thing*. (The word is Chesterton's, and I have no better. God's people Israel are a unique people, but they are not the only people. The Church is the only thing of its kind, and we have, therefore, no useful general term under which it may be classified.) It was this thing which was created by the Holy Spirit on the day of Pentecost, of which Jesus Christ is the head and cornerstone, which has charge of the good news about Jesus Christ and the sacraments of Baptism and the Eucharist, which is specifically mentioned in the Creeds. There are, we believe, both a visible and an invisible Church. I might say a great deal about the invisible Church and its relation to the visible Church, but I will say nothing. As to the visible Catholic Church, the right to pronounce on its boundaries is a bone of contention among Christians. Roman Catholics, Anglicans, Orthodox Christians, and Protestants will have different ideas about the boundaries of the visible Church. It is not my intention to say anything controversial about this matter, so I will say nothing. (Nor will I say anything of consequence about the divisive question of the relation between Israel and the Church.)

It will be noted that my characterization of Israel and the Catholic Church has been in terms of God's action in history. If God has not acted in history, these things do not exist. If God has not spoken of

---

[7] From the premise that a certain thing has been created by God, the conclusion does not follow that it is a part of His plan for the world. It is possible—for all I know, it is true—that God has created the Red Cross, as a divine mitigation of the human invention of war. But if war is not a part of the divine plan for the world, then, even if the Red Cross has been created by God, it is not a part of His plan for the world.

[8] Deut. 30:19–20.

old by the prophets, then Israel does not exist. If He has not spoken in these last days by a Son, then the Catholic Church does not exist. (I do not mean to deny what is self-evidently true: that there are perfectly good senses of the words in which even an atheist can admit that there are such things as "Israel" and "the Catholic Church.")

The question naturally arises, Suppose that these two things, these two supernatural foundations, Israel and the Church, do exist; what is their relation to the two "world religions" Judaism and Christianity?

I do not know how to answer this question because I do not know what the words 'Judaism' and 'Christianity' mean. More exactly, although there are many contexts in which I understand these words (as, for example, if it is said that someone is a convert to Judaism, or has written a book that is critical of Christianity), there are many contexts in which I do *not* understand them and this question is an example of one. Let me concentrate on the word 'Christianity'. Most of what I say will be applicable, the appropriate changes being made, to my difficulties with the word 'Judaism'. Many statements that contain the word 'Christianity' can be easily rewritten as statements about Christians and their beliefs and their religious practices and their behavior in secular matters.[9] In most cases, I have no difficulty understanding statements of this kind. My difficulties are with statements that are not of this sort, with statements that imply, or appear to imply, that 'Christianity' is the name of a thing.

Is 'Christianity' really the name of a thing?—that is, is this word really a name, or is it simply a word that allows a speaker to take certain

[9] My difficulties with 'Christianity' do not extend to the noun 'Christian'. Like most English words, it has more than one meaning, but it has a "central" meaning that is something like this: a Christian is a person who has accepted Jesus Christ as his Lord and Savior, who has assented to certain creedal statements, and who has received the sacrament of Baptism. (There could, of course, be some dispute about what the creedal statements would have to contain and about when Baptism has been validly administered.) I am aware that, human beings being the contentious lot they are, there are those who would say that this definition was fundamentally inadequate—because, for example, real Christians must be *good* Christians, or real Christians must display gifts of the Holy Spirit. My purpose in this note is not to resolve vexed questions about who is and who isn't a Christian but simply to dissociate the question "What does 'Christianity' mean?" from the question "What does 'Christian' mean?"

The adjective 'Christian', unlike the noun, is very vague. Its vagueness, however, has nothing specifically to do with religion but is rather typical of adjectives of its type. Compare, say, 'Italian' or 'Asian'. An Italian, in the central meaning of the word, is a citizen of Italy; *an* Asian, in the central meaning of the word, is an inhabitant of Asia. But a definition of the adjectives 'Italian' and 'Asian' will have to make use of such extremely vague terms as 'pertaining to' and 'typical of'. This fact has the consequence that the meaning of the adjective 'Christian'—like the meanings of 'Italian' and 'Asian'—is highly sensitive to context.

statements about "Christians and their beliefs and their religious practices and their behavior in secular matters" and compress them into statements about a feigned thing called 'Christianity'? Is the word like, say, the *'New York Times'* or 'the Vienna Circle', which are names of real social entities? Or is it like the words 'morality' and 'violence', which (in many contexts, anyway) are no more than linguistic devices for compressing statements about moral or violent people and their behavior into statements about a feigned object ('The decline of morality in our time has reached serious proportions'; 'Violence never solves anything')?

I believe the latter. I think that a strong argument for this thesis is provided by the fact that one cannot "be a member of" or "belong to" Christianity. (Nor is there any more specific "membership word" like 'employee' or 'citizen' that can be used to describe the relation between an individual and Christianity.) One cannot say, "I am a member of Christianity," or "I belong to Christianity." A Christian is no more a member of Christianity than a violent person is a member of violence or a skeptic is a member of skepticism. (One can, of course, be a *convert* to Christianity, but conversion to Christianity does not imply membership in Christianity as conversion to Roman Catholicism implies membership in the Roman Catholic Church. To be a convert to Christianity is simply to become a Christian.) It should be evident from the way I have worded this discussion of 'Christianity' that its point has nothing to do with nominalism or the reality of social entities or any other abstract question of logic or metaphysics. I am perfectly willing to say that there is such a thing as, for example, the class of all Christians, and I have said that the Catholic Church and Israel—and the *New York Times* and the Vienna Circle—are real things. There is no logical or conceptual barrier to there being a real social entity that is, as one might say, coextensive with Christianity, a thing that people belong to if and only if they are Christians, as people belong to the Roman Catholic Church if and only if they are Roman Catholics. (Indeed, there is no logical or conceptual barrier to there being *more* than one social entity that is coextensive with Christianity.) But—unfortunately—no such thing exists in the world as it is.

I hope it is also evident that in saying that 'Christianity' is not a name for a thing, I am not denying the existence or reality of Christianity— just as I do not deny the existence or reality of violence when I say that 'violence' is not a name for a thing. Here is an analogy: In saying, with St. Augustine, that evil is not a thing—that it is among neither the *visibilia* nor the *invisibilia* mentioned in the Nicene Creed—one does not express agreement with Mary Baker Eddy.

What has been said of 'Christianity', and by implication of 'Judaism', applies equally to 'Islam' and 'Buddhism' and the other words that occur in any list of the world religions. None of these words is a real name; if it were a real name, it would name a social entity of some sort, and people could belong to it. But (although there are Muslims) no one is "a member of Islam," and (although there are Buddhists) no one is "a member of Buddhism."

Let us return to our question: What is the relation of the Catholic Church to "the world religion Christianity". I would say that insofar as this unclear question has an answer, it is contained in the following statement: All members of the Catholic Church are Christians, and some Christians are not members of the (visible) Catholic Church. In this answer, I have used the relatively clear word 'Christian' and have deliberately avoided the vague word (vague in this context, at any rate) 'Christianity'. If my suggestion that the word 'Christianity' is a "compression-word"—that it is a device for compressing statements about Christians into shorter statements about a feigned object—is correct, it should be possible to replace any meaningful statement in which the word 'Christianity' occurs with a statement in which this word does not occur. Therefore, if I am right, insofar as the question has an answer, it must have an answer in which the word 'Christianity' does not occur. There may be those who would wish to challenge my thesis. Perhaps not everyone will agree that my answer to this question is the correct answer; perhaps not everyone will agree that I have understood the question; perhaps not everyone will agree that all statements involving the word 'Christianity' can (insofar as they have any meaning at all) be replaced by statements containing no related word but 'Christian'.

I should have to see how a challenge to my thesis would be developed before I knew what to say in response to it. But I shall view any such challenge with suspicion. I think it is an important fact about compression-words that they are often used as devices of obfuscation. A notorious case is that of the statement 'Error has no rights', which in former days was used by some Roman Catholic apologists to defend the use of political coercion in religious matters. If we try to say what this statement says without using the compression-word 'error', we find that we must say either 'People who have erroneous beliefs have no rights' or 'If a thesis is erroneous, then those who sincerely believe it to be true have no right to defend it in public—or even publicly to express belief in it'. While 'Error has no rights' has an impressive and convincing ring to it, the same can hardly be said of these two statements.

The use of compression-words and the hypostatized abstractions they purport to denote may sometimes be harmless—I have no objection, for example, to the statement 'Violence never solves anything', although I believe I could think of more useful ways to express the thought behind these words. (It will be observed that in the sequel I allow myself to hypostatize "the Enlightenment.") But I am convinced that the practice often disguises a political or theological agenda, the advancement of an ideology.

Let me make a highly speculative suggestion (I put this forward as worthy of further reflection, rather than as a thesis whose truth I am convinced of): the list of world religions—indeed, the concept of a "religion"—is a piece of misdirection intended to advance what I shall call the "Enlightenment agenda."

The historical phenomenon that named itself "the Enlightenment" (it still exists, although it has abandoned the name) is, and always has been, an attack on the Catholic Church. Its social goal is the destruction of the Church. Its main intellectual goal is twofold: first, to show that there is no God, or at least no providential God who acts in history (and hence that all the Church teaches is false), and, secondly, that the Church is not only wrong about history and metaphysics and eschatology but is a socially retrograde force. An important part of this intellectual goal is to exhibit those things that the Church sees as unique as very much of a piece with lots of other things.

The Church, for example, has taught that the human species is radically different from all other species. The Enlightenment has sought to show that the human species is not all that different from many other species. Since it is blindingly, boringly obvious that humanity *is* radically different from all other species—although it is far from obvious whether the Church is right about the nature of or the reasons for this difference—any opponent of this thesis must proceed by misdirection. Thus it is pointed out by the proponents of the Enlightenment agenda that human DNA differs from chimpanzee DNA in fewer base-pairs than the number by which the DNA of grizzly bears differs from that of Kodiak bears. Or it is confidently stated that modern science has delivered a succession of "nasty shocks to human pride" (by its discovery of the vast reaches of geological time, or by its discovery that the earth is not at the center of the universe, or by its discovery that human beings and the other primates are descended from a common ancestor). Well, the point about the base-pair count is certainly true, and the statement about the nasty shocks to human pride is probably not true, but, whether their premises are true or false, these arguments are mere smoke and mirrors, for the fact is that human beings *are* radically different from all other animals, and a scientific discovery can no more challenge this fact than the transition from Ptolemaic to Copernican astronomy could challenge the fact of the alternation of day and night.[10]

It is a part of the Enlightenment agenda to undermine the confidence of Christians in the thesis—from the earliest times an undisputed axiom of Christian theology—that the Catholic Church is radically different from everything else in the world.[11] Is it "blindingly, boringly obvious" that this thesis is right?

Perhaps it is not so obvious that the Church is radically different from all other human institutions as it is that human beings are radically different from all other animals. But there is a closely connected fact that is just that obvious, and the connection is worth developing. Here is the fact: "Western Civilization" (that is, what used to be called Christendom) is radically different from all other civilizations and cultures. Modern Euro-American civilization has produced physical and biological science,[12] the rule of law, the independent judiciary, universal

[10] Another important example of this Enlightenment strategy is provided by the attempt of the Enlightenment to show that the creation-and-flood story in Genesis is really very much the same sort of thing as the Sumerian and Akkadian and Iranian and other creation-and-flood stories. All these stories are clearly historically related and share some structural features that are interesting to the student of comparative mythology. The strategy is to go on at great length about the historical relation and the structural similarities, while studiously ignoring the fact that in every respect that could matter to anyone who was not a scholar of comparative mythology, the Hebrew story is radically different from the Sumerian and Akkadian and Iranian stories (the average educated reader will find those three stories to be very similar)—and from all other creation-and-flood stories.

[11] With the possible exception of Israel. According to Christians, the Church is the New Israel, in which the promises that God made to Abraham are fulfilled (but not superseded). What the "differences" are between the New and the. Old Israel and whether they should be described as "radical" are delicate theological questions that do not fall within the scope of this essay.

[12] "But what about ancient Greek science?" What we today call Greek "science"—the Greeks, of course, did not call that, owing to the fact that they had no word meaning 'science'—is only a part of what we call science today. The achievements of Greek science, magnificent though they were, were entirely phenomenological, in the sense in which physicists use the term. That is, they pertained to such matters as size and motion and taxonomy. Modern astronomy is applied physics; Greek astronomy was applied geometry. There is no achievement of Greek science that can be in any way compared to Newton's derivation of Kepler's phenomenology of planetary motion from his laws of motion and universal gravitation. Greek science did not do that *kind* of thing, and it did not, therefore, *explain* things in the way in which modern science explains things. Greek science, having given what it regarded as an adequate description of all observed phenomena that it found of interest, had really nowhere to go, and, by the beginning of the Christian era, had ceased to make any significant advances. The scientific achievements of late antiquity were refinements, small increments of knowledge, and systematizations of what had already been discovered.

suffrage, the concept of human rights and its embodiment in working constitutions, and near-universal literacy. And it has a long list of "minor" innovations to its credit, such as drawing in perspective, scientific cartography and navigation, and anesthesia. (A good sense of the uniqueness of "Western Civilization" can be obtained by comparing the anatomical drawings of Leonardo with the best anatomical drawings from classical antiquity or the Islamic world or China or India.) It will no doubt be pointed out that "Western Civilization" also originated world wars, hydrogen bombs, and worldwide colonialism.[13] But I am not arguing that "Western Civilization" is morally superior to other civilizations and cultures; I am arguing only that it is radically different. Indeed, the horrible items in this second list simply go to prove my point, for no "non-Western" civilization has been in a position even to contemplate adding any of these things to the burden of humanity's ills. "Western Civilization" may or may not be morally superior to various other civilizations. That question could be argued interminably. What is certain beyond the shadow of a doubt is that it is vastly more dangerous than any of them, owing simply to its vastly greater knowledge of the workings of the physical world. (Anyone who suggests that our list shows that "Western Civilization" is somehow morally *inferior* to some or all other civilizations should meditate on Nietzsche's pointed remark about those animals that call themselves good because they have no claws.)

Why was the continent of Europe the scene of the development of a civilization that was radically different from all other civilizations and cultures? Why did this thing happen then and there and not in classical antiquity or in India or China? I think that a very plausible answer is that the Church has made the difference. The Church was the single greatest influence in the formation of modern European civilization, and it would be odd if it had nothing to do with the unique character of that civilization. (The Enlightenment was forced by its presuppositions into the odd position of holding that the unique appearance on the world stage of science happened at just that place on earth at which—owing to the presence of the powerful, antirational, and superstitious Catholic Church—conditions were most hostile to its birth.) Is it not plausible that science and the rule of law and the rest were products of the Church in much the same sense as that in which Gothic architecture was a product of the Church?

The analogy is instructive. I am not saying that science *et al.* were

---

[13] And industrial capitalism. I suppose it is controversial whether that invention should be listed with the rule of law or with the world wars.

inevitable products of the existence of the Catholic Church. If the whole Church had been as the Eastern Church was, then, quite possibly, none of these things would ever have come to be. And yet the Eastern Church is, and has always been, fully Catholic, in both its governance and its doctrine. To my mind, the Church did not *have to* produce the fruits (either the sweet or the bitter) that I have listed as the features that make "Western Civilization" unique; nevertheless, the Church *did* produce them, and nothing else that has ever existed could have. Whether or not this conviction of mine is true, it should be understood as strictly parallel with the following (presumably uncontroversial) thesis: the Church did not *have to* produce Gothic architecture; nevertheless, the Church *did* produce Gothic architecture, and nothing else could have.[14] If a tree bears unique fruit, then it is probably a unique tree, even if it might never have flowered.[15]

[14] But this analogy is in a way misleading. Gothic architecture is unique, but it is not, so to speak, *uniquely* unique. There are other architectural styles, each of them, I suppose, "unique," that can claim to rival Gothic architecture in beauty and sublimity. But the items in the list in the text have no rivals. They are not only unique in the way that any great architectural style must be unique, but simply *without parallel.*

[15] I will try to give some sense in this note of how it was in my view that the Church "produced" one of the things in our list, modern science. The Church taught that the material world was not an illusion. Hence it taught, in effect, that there was something for science to investigate. (All the "teachings" that I mention in this note are denials of beliefs that have had a significant number of adherents. The combination of teachings is unique to the Church.) The Church taught that the material world was not evil and hence that it could be investigated without moral contamination. The Church taught that no part of the material world was a divine being (as many of the ancients had thought the stars and planets to be) and thus that it could be investigated without impiety. The Church taught that the material world was the creation of a single perfectly rational mind and thus that it was not simply a jumble of things that had no significant relation to one another; its teaching therefore implied that the material world made sense, and that croquet balls were not going to turn into hedgehogs. The Church taught that the material world was a finite, contingent object; its teaching therefore implied that the nature of the world could not be discovered by a priori reasoning (a lesson Descartes was to forget). The Church taught that humanity was made in the image and likeness of God and thus encouraged the belief that the human mind, being a copy of the mind of the Creator, might be equal to the task of discovering the nature of the Creation. The Church taught that not only humanity but the whole physical universe was redeemed in Christ ("For God so loved the *kosmos* . . .") and thus that the investigation of that universe could be a Christian vocation, a way of glorifying its Creator and Redeemer. Assent to these teachings was second nature to the general run of educated Christians in the High Middle Ages, although some of them were disputed in the Schools. This assent produced a climate of thought and attitude that made the birth of modern experimental science possible. It is probably also worth mentioning that the Church's consistent condemnation of magic and astrology can hardly have hindered the development of science. (There is, of course, another relevant factor: the physical world cooperated. That is, it turned out to be the sort of thing whose nature *could* be investigated by the methods devised in Medieval and Renaissance Christendom.)

I do not mean to suggest that it was the purpose of the Church to produce these fruits, even the sweet fruits. To say that would make nonsense of the New Testament, where we are told that Christ's kingdom is not of this world. If we should "lose" science and representative government and the rule of law—as I am inclined to think we are in danger of doing—if these things should take their places among the "wrecks of time," the Cross will still be there. The purpose of the Church is that we should not lose the end for which we were made, a purpose beside which physical science and the rule of law are of literally infinitesimal significance. And yet it did produce these things. If, again, a tree bears unique fruit, then it is probably a unique tree, whether or not the fruit was a part of the central purpose of the planter of the tree.

If a thing is to be known by its fruits, then the Church is unique. But it does not follow that it is unique in every respect, and, in particular, it does not follow that the Church is spiritually unique. I have conceded that the fruits of the Church that have made "Western Civilization" radically different from all other civilizations and cultures are irrelevant to the purpose of the Church. (Logically and conceptually irrelevant: it is very plausible indeed to suppose that these fruits are in another way all too relevant to the purpose of the Church. The power and leisure and personal security that modern Euro-American science and social organization have given to great numbers of people in the West are no doubt the main causes of the long and continuing apostasy of the West.) May it not be that some or all of the world religions are the spiritual equals of the Church, even if they lack the Church's power to produce a wholly new kind of civilization? The Eastern Church apparently lacks the power of radically transforming the temporal aspects of civilization that the Western Church has displayed, and is nevertheless the spiritual equal of the Western Church.

May it not be that all the world's religions are instruments of God's salvation? May it not be that Islam and Buddhism are not merely accidental instruments of salvation, as literally anything under the sun may be, but intended instruments, spiritual equals of the Catholic Church?

I have no way to prove that this is false. If I had, I should be living not by faith but by sight. I can say only this: if that suggestion were true, then the Bible and the Creeds and all of Jewish and Christian history (as Jews and Christians tell the story) is an illusion. The teachings of the Church are quite plain on the point that the Church is a unique instrument by which Christ and the Holy Spirit are working (and the Father is working through them) to bring us to the Father. And the teachings of the Church are quite plain on a second point:

While the genesis and purpose of the Church belong to eternity, it has been given to us temporal creatures in time. (How else could it be given to us?) It was given to us through events that happened in Palestine in the first century of our era, and all possibility of our salvation depends on those events and on the Church's bringing us into the right relation with them. The Church is a thing that operates in history, and no hypostatized abstraction called Buddhism or Islam—or Christianity— is even in competition with the Church. These hypostatized abstractions, I speculate, are devices in the service of the Enlightenment agenda, and their purpose is to direct the attention of people away from the Church and to focus it on the abstraction "Christianity," which is the sort of thing that can be compared and contrasted with other abstractions like Buddhism and Islam. The comparisons, incidentally, are often extremely instructive. In reading or hearing them, the Christian is continually reminded of Chesterton's remark that, according to the students of comparative religion, Christianity and Buddhism are very much alike, especially Buddhism. (But nowadays Hinduism is the world religion that stands *prima inter pares*; it owes this preeminence to its proclivity for syncretism, to its ability to absorb what the proponents of the view of the world religions I have been discussing would regard as the essential features of all other religions.) But the nature of the comparisons is not central to my point. My point is that even if the comparisons were invariably honest and just, they would still be a piece of misdirection, a device to draw our attention away from the concrete reality of the Catholic Church and direct it toward the abstraction "Christianity."

I want to turn our attention away from this abstraction and back to the Church. I can hope to do no more than to attempt to convince a few people that this is where the attention of Christians who are interested in the question of their relation as Christians to the non-Christian religions of the world should be directed. I am certainly not particularly qualified to say anything in detail about the Church and Buddhism or the Church and Islam. It is not my business to tell Christians what they ought to think about Buddhism or Islam. If that is the business of any individuals (as opposed to, say, Ecumenical councils), it is the business of Christian historians and Christian students of Buddhism and Islam and Christian theologians. I have been concerned only to argue that Christians should think not in terms of, for example, "Christianity and Buddhism" but rather in terms of "the Church and Buddhism"—or, better still, "the Church and the Buddhists."

I will devote the remainder of this essay to an investigation of a difficulty that people sometimes feel in connection with the idea of the uniqueness of the Church. If I understand the phrase, this difficulty is what is sometimes referred to as "the scandal of particularity." Is there not something arrogant about the Church's claim to be unique? The odd thing is, the idea of there being such a scandal seems to make no sense at all.

Most of us have probably heard the old anti-Semitic quatrain, "How odd / Of God / To choose / The Jews." In addition to being morally rather nasty, this verse makes no sense at all. It presupposes that the Jews are "the chosen people" in the following sense: They were *about* somewhere, and God examined the various peoples of the world and, from among them, chose the Jews. But that is not how things went. The only thing that God chose in that sense was Abraham and his household—who were not yet "the Jews." God's people are a *product* of that choice. In a very straightforward sense, God did not choose, but made, or, one might even say, *forged*, Israel. The Hebrew scriptures are the story of that terrible forging ("for it is a terrible thing I will do with you").

If the Jews claim the distinction of being the one people among all the peoples in the world that God has made, do they call down a charge of scandal upon themselves? No, indeed. One can understand why it would be scandalous if the Jews claimed that God had chosen them from among all the peoples of the earth because of their excellent qualities, if they claimed to have bested all the other peoples of the earth in a contest for God's favor. (That is the claim that is ascribed to them in the nasty little verse I have quoted—together with the implication that they of all people are the most unlikely to be the winners of such a contest.) But that is not the story the Jews tell.

In a similar way, if the Catholic Church claims to be the unique instrument of salvation, there is no scandal. The United States and the Soviet Union and many other things have invented themselves, but the Church did not invent herself. The Church is God's creation, and what makes her the unique instrument of His salvation is no more the achievement of her members than the splendor and bounty of the earth are the achievements of her inhabitants. Those features of the Church that are the work of human beings (like those features of the earth that are the work of human beings) are mere details added to God's design. And those details, like all the other works of human hands, contain good, bad, and indifferent things, hopelessly intermingled.

"Well, isn't it fortunate for you that you just happen to be a member of this 'unique instrument of salvation'. I suppose you realize that if you had been raised among Muslims, you would make similar claims for Islam?" Yes, it is fortunate for me, very fortunate indeed. And I concede that if I and some child born in Cairo or Mecca had been exchanged in our cradles, very likely I should be a devout Muslim. (I'm not so sure about the other child, however. I was not raised a Christian.) But what is supposed to follow from this observation? If certain people claim to be the members of a body that is the unique instrument of God's salvation, who is supposed to defend their claim? Those who are *not* members of that body? It should be noted, moreover, that this style of argument (whatever its merits) can hardly be confined to religion. Consider politics. As is the case with religious options, a multitude of political options faces the citizens of any modern nation. And which of us can say that his political allegiances are coded into his DNA? Tell the Marxist or the liberal or the Burkean conservative that if only he had been raised in Nazi Germany he would probably have belonged to the Hitler Youth, and he will answer that he is well aware of this elementary fact, and ask what your point is. No one I know of supposes that the undoubted fact that one's adherence to a system of political thought and action is conditioned by one's upbringing is a reason for doubting that the political system one favors is—if not the uniquely "correct" one—clearly and markedly superior to its available rivals. And yet any argument to show that the Church's belief in her own uniqueness was arrogant would apply a fortiori to this almost universally held belief about politics. The members of the Church can, as I have remarked, take no pride in her unique relation to God, for that relation is His doing and not theirs. But the superiority of one's own political party to all others must be due to the superiority of the knowledge, intelligence, wisdom, courage, and goodness of one and one's colleagues to the knowledge, intelligence, wisdom, courage, and goodness collectively embodied in any other political party.

While we are on the topic of arrogance, I must say that if I am to be charged with arrogance, it had better not be by the authors of the picture of the world religions that I outlined at the beginning of this essay. Any of *them* that flings a charge of arrogance at me is going to find himself surrounded by a lot of broken domestic glass. I may believe that everything that the Muslim believes that is inconsistent with what I believe is false. But then so does everyone who accepts the law of the excluded middle or the principle of noncontradiction. What I do *not* do is to inform the Muslim that every tenet of Islam that is inconsistent with Buddhism is not really essential to Islam. (Nor do I believe in my heart of hearts that every tenet of Islam that is inconsistent with the beliefs of late-twentieth-century middle-class Anglo-American professors is not really essential to Islam.) Despite the fact that I reserve the right to believe things that are not believed by Muslims, I leave it to the Muslims to decide what is and what is not essential to Islam.

"But why should membership in the unique instrument of God's salvation depend upon accidents of birth? Isn't that rather unfair to those born at the wrong time and place to belong to it? Wouldn't God's unique instrument of salvation, if there were one, be universally available?"

This is a serious question. Before answering it let me remove a red herring. It is not necessary for Christians to believe that there is no salvation outside the *visible* Church. I do not know how widespread this belief has been in the past, but it is certainly not widespread today. (In my own lifetime, a notorious Roman Catholic priest—remember Father Feeney?—was excommunicated for obstinately teaching this doctrine.) Nor do very many Christians believe that those who died before the creation of the Church are denied salvation. (There would certainly be biblical difficulties with this idea, since the salvation of the Good Thief in St. Luke is explicitly stated, despite the fact that his death occurred not only before the creation of the Church on the day of Pentecost but before Christ was raised into the new life that is transmitted to us through the Church.)[16] The medieval legend of the Harrowing of Hell may be without any actual basis in the Apostles' Creed, but it testifies to the popularity of the belief that Christ's salvation is offered to those who died before His Incarnation.

So much for the red herring. Now for the serious question. This question would be unanswerable if Christians believed that salvation came through a religion called "Christianity" rather than through the Church. But I take the only sure condition of damnation in which Christian belief is involved to be the following: Anyone who has accepted Christian belief and rejects it and rejects it still at the moment of his death—and rejects it with a clear mind, and not when maddened by pain or grief or terror—is damned. ("Which Faith, except everyone do *keep* whole and undefiled, without doubt he shall perish everlastingly"; "which except a man believe *faithfully*, he cannot be saved.") What provision God makes for those who have never heard the Christian message, or who have heard it only in some distorted and falsifying form, I do not know. That is God's business and not ours. Our business is to see that as many as possible do hear the Christian message, and do not hear it in a distorted and falsifying form. (But I do know that

[16] The salvation of Enoch, Abraham, Moses, and Elijah seems to be clearly implied in various passages of the Old and New Testaments—and, indeed, the salvation of a great cloud of pre-Christian witnesses.

one of the things that may keep a person from hearing the Good News in its right form is the presuppositions of his native culture and religion. A Christian of our culture may know the words that a missionary has spoken to, say, a Buddhist who thereafter remains a Buddhist; he will not necessarily know what the Buddhist has heard. I do not know, but I suspect, that many people in our own culture who are, formally, apostate Christians may never have heard the Christian message in its right form. I certainly hope so, and the statements that many apostate Christians make about the content of the Christian message encourage me in this hope.)

The way for a Christian to look at the saving power of the Church is, I believe, like this: The Church is like an invading army that, having established a bridgehead in occupied territory, moves on into the interior, consolidating its gains as it goes. All those who do not consciously and deliberately cast in their lot with the retreating enemy and flee with him to his final refuge will be liberated—even those who, misled by enemy propaganda, fear and mistrust the advancing army of liberation.

If an army establishes a bridgehead, it must establish it at some particular place. "And why in Palestine?" Because that's where Israel was. "And why did God choose to locate His people there rather than in India or China?" Well, it would have to be *somewhere*. Why *not* there? The question borders on the absurd, although it has been pointed out that Palestine is approximately at the center of the great Euro-Afro-Asian supercontinent. Why did the Allied armies land in Normandy? No doubt Eisenhower and Montgomery had their reasons. But if a skeptical Norman farmer or Resistance fighter had heard rumors of the Allied landing and had asked "Why *here*?" you wouldn't have to know the reasons the Allied commanders had for choosing the Normandy beaches to answer him. It would suffice to point out that the same questions could be raised about any reported landing site by those who happened to be in its vicinity, and that the question therefore raised no doubts about the veracity of the rumor.

"But why should our salvation be accomplished by the institution of something that can be compared to an invading army?" I have no idea, although I am glad that God has chosen a method that allows some of His servants the inestimable (and entirely unearned) honor of being His co-workers in bringing salvation to others. Perhaps there was no other way. Perhaps there were lots of other ways, but this one recommended itself to the divine wisdom for reasons that surpass human understanding. Or perhaps the reasons are ones we could understand but that it would not, at present, be profitable for us to know ("What is that to thee? Follow thou me."). But I am sure of one thing. Anyone who believes in God, in a being of literally infinite knowledge and power and wisdom, and who believes that human beings require salvation, and who thinks he can see that God would not have used such a method to procure our salvation has a very high opinion of his own powers of a priori reason.

If we are Christians we must believe that salvation has not come to humanity through Confucius or Gautama or Mohammed. We must believe that the salvation of humanity began with events that were quite unrelated to the lives and teachings of these men. We must believe that it began when some women standing outside a tomb were told, "He is not here." Perhaps there is some authority who has discovered good reasons for thinking that these central Christian beliefs are false. If so, it is not John Hick.

[10]

Perceiving God, World-Views, and Faith: Meeting the Problem of Religious Pluralism

JOSEPH RUNZO

N ot so long ago, analytic philosophy of religion had largely relegated itself to a few relatively restricted topics, such as arguments for and against God's existence. Happily, the field is
now burgeoning with diverse issues—new *and* old. William Alston has
been a seminal force behind this sea change in the field. He is not only
the father of modern American analytic philosophy of religion; he has
brought an incisive and persistent approach to formerly dismissed or
unrecognized topics, illuminating their importance and bringing them
to the forefront of the contemporary discussion. In particular, he has
been a driving force behind the recent resurgence of epistemology
of religion.

Here I will address the main thesis of Alston's current cumulative
work in religious epistemology, *Perceiving God*. Alston argues that it is
rational to engage in the perceptual practice of Christian mysticism
and that this practice is "sufficiently reliable to be a source of prima
facie justification for the beliefs it engenders [about God]".[1] This is a
bold thesis. I agree with Alston's conclusion and with much of his defense of this view. But I think he has made a weaker case than he
thinks, and than he could. The most fundamental problem for his

Reprinted from Joseph Runzo, *World Views and Perceiving God* (London: Macmillan,
and New York: St. Martin's Press, 1993), © 1993 Joseph Runzo, by permission of the
author.

[1] William P. Alston, *Perceiving God: The Epistemology of Religious Experience* (Ithaca: Cornell University Press, 1991), p. 278. (Subsequent page references appear in parentheses
in the text.) Even if we focus on one doxastic practice, CMP, Alston points out that the
use of the overrider system means that other doxastic practices will also be brought
to bear.

position centers around religious pluralism. The solution centers around a greater recognition of the pivotal effect of diverse world-views, and a more prominent role for faith *vis-a-vis* religious belief, than Alston is willing to concede.

I

In general, Alston holds that one can be justified in holding (certain) beliefs about God in virtue of an experiential awareness of God, in virtue of "perceiving God". This is not presented as an argument from religious experience to God's existence. His more subtle line of reasoning proceeds in five stages. Alston argues (1) that the putative direct experiential awareness of God found in the Christian tradition—what he calls Christian "mystical perception"—is a *perceptual* mode of experience, and (2) that this mystical perception *could be* a perception of *God*. From this he concludes that (3) "the question of whether mystical perception does count as a genuine perception of God is just the question of whether it is what it seems to its subject to be" (p. 66). While Alston does not attempt to show that God *is* perceived (as doing so-and-so), he attempts to show that theistic perceptual beliefs of this sort are justified. Here he argues for the principle that (4) the percipient will be prima facie justified in his or her belief if the perceptual beliefs are formed within a well-established doxastic practice and if there are no sufficient considerations, or "overriders," to the contrary. And finally, given that the Christian mystical practice (CMP) is a well-established doxastic practice, (5) he defends this "mystical" practice of belief formation against potential overriders. Clearly, (4) and (5) are the crucial stages in Alston's reasoning.

Two points should be noted at the outset. First, Alston does not defend Christian beliefs about God and God-acts *taken in themselves.* Rather, he defends the justification of these beliefs as considered *within* an established doxastic practice—that is, CMP. Second, this means that on Alston's account, claims to justified beliefs about God on experiential grounds necessarily presuppose a background system of beliefs. The very doxastic practice itself involves a web of beliefs. But there is a background web of beliefs which serves as a check—an overrider system—against taking things always as they appear and so against the unacceptable conclusion that epistemically "anything goes" in religious experience. For when we acquire experiential religious beliefs, like acquiring sense-perceptual beliefs, as James says, "new ideas of ours must . . . take account of the whole body of other truths already in our possession."[2] This is particularly important for unusual experiences, such as religious experiences, and their resultant beliefs. As James puts it, when "this new idea is . . . adopted as the true one . . . it preserves the older stock of truths with a minimum of modification, stretching them just enough to make them admit the novelty, but conceiving that in ways as familiar as the case leaves possible. An *outree* explanation, violating all our preconceptions, would never pass for a true account of a novelty."[3]

Further, on Alston's view that "for any *established* doxastic practice, it is rational to suppose that it is reliable, and hence rational to suppose that its doxastic outputs are prima facie justified" (p. *183*; italics mine), it is the former rationality of the practice itself which is paramount. And a doxastic practice, P, is *itself* only prima facie justified if there are no overriders—either rebutters (reasons for following some other practice that entails not-P) or underminers (reasons for thinking that P is not adequately justified) (p. 72; cf. p. 194). These potential overriders are part of the background scheme of P and thus part of the, so to say, "extended" doxastic practice.

Now as Alston effectively argues, doxastic practices cannot be justified externally (that is, justified beyond the "extended" practice). There is no noncircular external justification for *any* doxastic practice. Theistic doxastic practices are obviously circular, since the check on the acceptability of a putative experience of God is the theological/praxis overrider system of the religious tradition in question. Yet the same sort of circularity "infects," for example, ordinary sense-perception. One cannot check a particular sensory belief for accuracy except against other sensory beliefs, thereby employing the general doxastic practice of perception and assuming that it *is* basically reliable. But this does not count against the general reliability of sense-perception. Likewise, since we have no idea what a noncircular proof of the reliability of the Christian mystical practice would be like, the lack of any such proof cannot count against CMP. Therefore, Alston can invoke the principle that apart from any reason for thinking that one of the "competing practices"—say, another world religion mystical practice—is more accurate than one's own religious doxastic practice, "the only rational course is for me to sit tight with the practice of which I am a master and which serves me so well in guiding my activity in the world" (p. 274).

[2] William James, "Pragmatism's Conception of Truth," in *Pragmatism*, ed. Bruce Kuklick (Indianapolis: Hackett, 1981), p. 96.
[3] William James, "What Pragmatism Means," in *Pragmatism*, p. 31.

In sum, Alston proposes a "modest foundationalism" (p. 300).[4] There are foundational beliefs that possess prima facie justification from experience, but they are subject to being overridden. Yet consequently, as Alston notes, since the outputs of CMP potentially can be overridden, the prima facie justification of CMP *itself* needs significant self-support if it is going to stand the test of competition in an age of religious pluralism.

II

Two additional elements in Alston's view of the justification for doxastic practices increase the difficulty of the task for CMP that it must "stand up to" the competition to be accounted reliable. For Alston is both a realist and an anticonceptualist about perception.

As a realist, Alston holds that "we mean what we . . . assert to be true of realities that are what they are regardless of what we or other human beings believe of them, and regardless of the 'conceptual scheme' we apply to them (except, of course, when what we are talking about is our thought, belief, or concepts)" (p. 4). Thus, Alston explicitly rejects the Wittgensteinian notion[5] that reality is relative to conceptual schemes (or language-games), as well as Carnap's idea that truth is an internal matter. Since he assumes that there is only one reality, the purpose of doxastic practices is to provide reliable methods for finding out what that one reality is like. But this means that different doxastic practices regarding the same subject matter are likely to—if not inevitably *must*, given a sufficiently strong notion of "different practice"— contradict each other about the nature of reality. In that case, as he insists, "only one practice can be right." This raises the problem of religious pluralism. Different religious traditions, with their correspondingly different doxastic mystical practices, make fundamental truth-claims which are mutually contradictory. What Alston believes they all have in common is a search for Ultimate Reality. What they do not share—indeed, cannot share—is any sort of roughly equal success in this endeavor.

Now one apparent way out of this conflict between religious tradi-

---

[4] On my agreement with Alston's modest foundationalism, see my "World-Views and the Epistemic Foundations of Theism," *Religious Studies* 25 (March 1989), 31–51, reprinted in my *World Views and Perceiving God* (London: Macmillan; New York: St. Martin's Press, 1993), chap. 6.

[5] And its more contemporary exponents in Quine, Putnam, Rorty, and others. See Alston, *Perceiving God*, pp. 154–55 and 165.

tions would be to turn to pure perceptual reports, setting aside the background scheme associated with each doxastic mystical practice, thereby enabling one to determine what is reliable solely on the basis of consensus among the reports. This move is not open to the conceptualist, who holds that the structuring of experience by the relevant concepts is an inextricable element of perceptual experience. But neither is it open to Alston, since, as he notes, this would eliminate the only checks—the overrider system—on taking whatever one seemed to perceive to be what one does perceive. Moreover, for Alston, support for the claim that one is in fact perceiving X is provided if the purported object (e.g., God) "presents itself as being or doing what it would be natural or reasonable to expect" (p. 98). And this again necessitates a heavy reliance on the background scheme of a doxastic practice, since it is that scheme which delineates what are the normal expectations for the perception of some object, X.

Another way to reconcile the (apparently) conflicting truth-claims of the world religions would be to allow that reality is in some sense relative to conceptual schemes, or world-views.[6] This would both explain why there can be such deeply established social practices as the vastly different world religions with their inexirpably different outputs about Ultimate Reality, and resolve the apparent conflict among the world religions without giving up one's own religious truth-claims.[7] But as a realist, Alston rejects this route. Part of his reasoning is that our world-views give us predictive success *because* they put us into cognitive contact with reality (p. 137). But this consideration, at least, in no wise tells against the possibility that different world-views correspond to different realities—each providing its own predictive success for the correspondent reality. And with the denial of this possibility, the problem of religious pluralism becomes all the more acute for Alston's account.

This brings us to the second additional element of Alston's view of the justification of doxastic pratices. In contrast to a conceptualist notion of perception, Alston offers a Theory of Appearing. According to this theory, "for S to perceive X is simply for X to appear to S as so-and-so" (p. 55). Thus for Alston, perception "is a mode of cognition that is essentially independent of any conceptualization, belief, judgment, or any other application of general concepts to the object" (p. 37; cf. pp. 186–87). The problem this raises for Alston's analysis of *mystical*

---

[6] I argue for this alternative in detail in "God, Commitment, and Other Faiths: Pluralism vs. Relativism," *Faith and Philosophy* 5 (October 1988), 343–64, reprinted in my *World Views and Perceiving God,* chap. 9.

[7] For a detailed defense that conceptual relativism can be reconciled with faith, see my *Reason, Relativism, and God* (London: Macmillan; New York: St. Martin's Press, 1986).

perception is that, once again, it leaves little room to account for the consistently different and socially well established perceptual experiences within the great world religions. Alston is forced to be an exclusivist and hold that the core truth-claims of only one religion can be correct, since, given the cognitive conflict among the world religions, only one can be correctly reporting the direct "appearing" of Ultimate Reality. However, there are at least three areas of confusion in Alston's analysis of perception that make the alternative, conceptualist account appear less attractive than it is. And a conceptualist account would offer a more inclusive resolution to the conflict among world religions than the exclusivism Alston ends up holding on his realist, anticonceptualist account.

First, Alston argues that conceptualists confuse the direct awareness of X (the "appearing" of X) and the awareness of X as possessing some particular property, mistakenly understanding the latter alone as genuine perception (p. 38). But how can I be aware of something—say, the tomato on the desk—except by being aware of properties it possesses? I can immediately and noninferentially see the object before me as a red sphere, or simply as red, or simply as a tomato—each a direct awareness but each conceptualized. So rather than the confusion lying with the conceptualist, I think Alston has confused perceptual activities like seeing with activities like merely *looking at* something, X, without seeing (i.e., without visually discriminating) X. To see something, X, is to see X *as* something.[8] True, to perceive a tomato is to perceive *the tomato* as well as to perceive that it is red or spherical or whatever. But *the tomato* is not one among several items we become aware of: to "perceive the tomato" just stands for the total set of facts of which we become aware—redness, spherical shape, tomatohood.[9] Each is a conceptualized seeing *as*. This is the basic conceptualist thesis. Assuredly, this issue between conceptualists and nonconceptualists will not be solved in this short space. But the point is that *if* perception inherently involves conceptualization, we would *expect* different percipients within different world religions to have different perceptions of Ultimate Reality. Further, percipients within different world religions could be perceiving the same object (say, God) though they have different, even contradictory, conceptualized perceptions.

Second, in emphasizing the *given* element in perception, Alston in-

---

[8] I argue for this in "The Radical Conceptualization of Perceptual Experience," *American Philosophical Quarterly* 19 (July 1982), 205–17, reprinted in my *World Views and Perceiving God*, chap. 2.

[9] See my "Propositional Structure of Perception," *American Philosophical Quarterly* 14 (July 1977), 211–20, reprinted in my *World Views and Perceiving God*, chap. 1.

correctly rules out the inextricable conceptualization of perceptual experience.[10] Granted, there is a given element. The question is whether this is sufficient for the content of perception. And granted that conceptualization is not sufficient for perception (for otherwise conception and perception would be indistinguishable), the question is whether conceptualization is a necessary element of the content of perception. I would argue that the given and conceptualization are jointly necessary and sufficient for perceptual content.[11] Again, we will not settle that issue here, but by attempting to eliminate the necessity for conceptualization, Alston has eliminated one clear way to explain persistent, diverse mystical perceptions: different mystical perceptions in different traditions are *necessarily* structured by the different respective conceptual schemes. In support of his opposing position, Alston cites examples from St. Teresa and Angela of Foligno (p. 42), where they in effect assert that their experiences (sometimes) are direct (that is to say, unconceptualized) perceptions of God. But this begs the question. It would do no more good to ask ordinary perceivers whether they seem to have pure perceptions or only conceptualized perceptions to try to settle this epistemological issue for the doxastic practice(s) of sense-perception (SP).

Third, Alston assumes that there is a single, worldwide overrider system for ordinary sense-perception, but if we consider the aspects of "a distinctive subject matter, a distinctive conceptual scheme, and an overrider system. . . . whereas SP presents virtually an identical picture in these respects across cultures, this is by no means the case with MP" (p. 188; cf. p. 192). This suggested contrast between SP and MP not only seems unlikely on Alston's own epistemology, it further weakens his means of responding to the problem of religious pluralism.

Transcultural (and transhistorical) differences in SP—while they may be different in degree—seem no different *in kind* than differences in MP. If we take the perceptual claims of ordinary percipients across cultures at face value,[12] it seems likely, given the phenomenological evidence, that the doxastic practices of, to use Alston's examples, a

---

[10] In his objection to John Hick's conceptualist analysis of religious experience (*Perceiving God*, p. 27), Alston equates conceptualization with interpretation. If interpretation is a conscious application of concepts, then there are three facts of perceptual experience to consider: the given, the conceptualized element, and then any additional interpretation. The conceptualization of experience need not be, and often is not, conscious.

[11] See "The Radical Conceptualization of Perceptual Experience," pp. 213–15 (*World Views and Perceiving God*, chap. 2).

[12] Earlier I argued against a different use of phenomenological reports: Alston's appeal to St. Teresa's reports of her experiences as supporting the meta-epistemological claim that no concepts are used.

bushman and a Manhattan stockbroker *are* different. Australian bushmen and Manhattan stockbrokers perceive a distinctively different subject matter[13] and employ distinctive conceptual schemes and overrider systems. Consider the Dow Jones Industrial Average. This is a highly complex object involving constitutive items like economic indicators, a market economy, a stock market, stocks themselves, and so on. Even if the aborigine can look at and read the number for today's DJIA, he or she does not *perceive* the DJIA. Unlike the stockbroker, the aborigine sees only a number; no information about stocks, the economy, or the DJIA is conveyed. So with respect to subject matter, perception terms like "see" do not govern transparent contexts.[14]

It is only with the imposition of a realist *metaphysics*—that there must be some one reality that both bushmen and stockbrokers are perceiving when they look in a certain direction—that we have reason to think that they are perceiving the same thing. But if we turn from that question of metaphysics, on Alston's *epistemology*, if there are different overrider systems, there are different perceptual practices (p. 189). So how do the overrider systems compare? The aborigine presumably checks his or her knowledge of numbers; the stockbroker checks against the ticker tape, calls to the floor of the NYSE, considers whether today's apparent DJIA *makes sense* given yesterday's DJIA, and so on— checks not available in the aborigine's overrider system. These certainly seem to be different overrider systems and hence would seem to imply different SP. That would explain the phenomenological differences in the percipients' perceptions. Similarly, for religion, as an overrider system the notion of a trinitarian God and of the Bible as the final Scripture and Thomas Aquinas as an authoritative theologian is as unacceptable and unusable to the committed, exclusivist Sunni as the notion of a market economy with stock indices is to an aborigine. If the differences in religious overrider systems imply differences in MP, do not the analogously different overrider systems of, for example, the aborigine and the stockbroker imply differences in SP?

Here again, the issue between the conceptualist and nonconceptual-

---

[13] Alston directly denies my claim that *what* is perceived, as well as how it is perceived, is, in part, determined by the percipient's conceptual scheme (*Perceiving God*, p. 39 n. 29). I offer supporting arguments for this claim in "The Radical Conceptualization of Perceptual Experience" and *Reason, Relativism, and God* (see pp. 96–99).

[14] As I argue in "The Radical Conceptualization of Perceptual Experience," unless a percipient S possesses the conceptual resources to discriminate some object O, S cannot see O except either when S sees that (what we call) O is F, or in the opaque sense that "S sees O as F." For examples within more narrow culture, such as Western science, see Thomas Kuhn's classic *The Structure of Scientific Revolutions* (Chicago: University of Chicago Press, 1970), 2d ed.

ist will not be settled in this brief space. But by assuming that the doxastic practice and overrider system of SP is unqualifiedly universal, Alston drives a wedge between SP and MP, making the differences among the various mystical doxastic practices appear much more radical and problematic than they are. If, as I believe, SP is more like MP, constituting a variety of (overlapping) doxastic practices, then reconciling differences in the outputs of diverse MPs will be more like reconciling the differences in diverse SPs, a far easier task than Alston has set himself.[15] Having cut off that alternative, Alston rightly acknowledges that religious diversity, the issue we will now directly focus on, is the most serious problem for his position.

III

Recall Alston's main thesis: "CMP is rationally engaged in since it is a socially established doxastic practice that is not demonstrably unreliable or otherwise disqualified for rational acceptance" (p. 194). Let us look more closely at the two principal elements of this formula for the rationality of the doxastic practice CMP.

Regarding the first condition for the rationality of engaging in CMP, positive support is supposed to be provided for CMP because it is so well established socially. But since this is true of the doxastic perceptual practices of all the great world religions, this will not particularly help the Christian practice over against its competitors. Indeed, Alston notes that it is rational to engage in a socially established doxastic practice "provided" it and its outputs have a sufficient coherence with *other* firmly established doxastic practices (p. 175). But given this principle, religious pluralism raises an even more serious problem. For the outputs of the world's diverse religious doxastic practices *do not* cohere. The situation is rather like competing and incompatible scientific doxastic practices. However, we have a (set of) methodology(ies) to resolve such conflicts within science. For religion, we have no such metamethodology, and hence a weaker case for accepting, among the competitors, the particular practice one in fact follows. True, in order to mitigate this problem for religious belief, Alston does appeal to faith at this

---

[15] For an analysis of how the background system for the mystical visions of the great mystics could *differently* link phenomenal properties with objective properties of the purported object for different MPs, see my "Visions, Pictures, and Rules," *Religious Studies* 13 (September 1977), 303–18, reprinted in my *World Views and Perceiving God*, chap. 3.

point. But as we shall see, faith plays a weaker role for Alston within CMP than it needs to play.

Moreover, there is a fundamental difficulty with the notion of justifying a mystical practice in part by appealing to its social establishment. On the one side, this criterion appears too strong: Does this mean that CMP was less justified—perhaps even unjustified—in the nascent period of Christianity? And does this mean that CMP would be less justified if Christianity largely died out as a practice—say, through the literal death of the vast majority of its followers? Would the few remaining Christians, like the first Christians, need to wonder about the epistemic justification of the practice they rely on? On the other side, the criterion appears too weak: For either the Christian tradition cannot evolve (and if so, this would rule out a conserving yet evolutionary theology like Sallie McFague's feminist theology,[16] or every sectarian "Christian" practice which diligently uses the "mainstream" canonical texts etc. as overriders—though now employed with their own idiosyncratic interpretation—must be accounted users of CMP. Consequently, being socially established at best lends weak support to a doxastic practice like CMP. There must be some other sort of support for CMP. I will address that support below: namely, the "fruits" of the practice (and eventually the role of faith).

Turn then to the second condition of rationality for a doxastic practice—that there are no sufficient reasons to regard it as *un*reliable (a form of "innocent until proven guilty"). Here Alston offers two basic defenses: A negative defense against the often supposed intractable conflict between science and religion, and a positive defense in terms of the fruits of the practice.

To take the former, it is the notion of a personal God, One who acts in history, which is supposedly incompatible with causal determinism and so incompatible with modern science. Yet surely in the practice of the theistic life—the life of prayer, of devotion, of asking for forgiveness, of a theocentric love of others for their own sake—it is essential to think of oneself as in genuine personal interaction with God.[17] Hence

[16] See Sallie McFague, *Models of God: Theology for an Ecological, Nuclear Age* (Philadelphia: Fortress Press, 1987).

[17] Historically, the God of the Judaic, Christian, and Islamic traditions is a God who *acts:* The Psalmist speaks of the Lord as one who "made known his ways to Moses, his acts to the people of Israel" (Ps. 103:7, RSV); in Matthew, Jesus says: "whatever you ask in prayer, you will receive, if you have faith" (Matt. 21:22, RSV); and in the Qu'ran we are told: "Wheresoever ye may be, Allah will bring you all together. / Lo! Allah is Able to do all things. . . . / And he who doesth good of his own accord . . . , lo! / Allah is Responsive" (from the surah Al-Baqarah [the Cow] 148 and 158, in *The Meaning of the Glorious Koran*, trans. Mohammed Marmaduke Pickthall [New York: New American Library, 1970]).

Alston's project of showing that God *can be* perceived (whatever my particular objections) is immensely important. For if one doubts that God can be perceived, then one cannot seriously believe that he or she knows what God is doing vis-à-vis one in the present.[18]

Now consider the supposed incompatibility of God's acts with causal determinism and modern science. As Alston argues, this objection ignores the fact that the "closed causal system" of science actually assumes no more than a *circumscribed* as well as *approximate* set of causal conditions, not a set of sufficient natural causal conditions *without* qualification. This allows for divine acts without in any way compromising the causal conditions set out by scientific theory and practice. The problem here is well illustrated by Stephen Hawking's recent attempt in *A Brief History of Time* to offer an analysis of "the origin and fate" of the universe, within the parameters of physics: of course, it turns out, as Carl Sagan puts it, that there is "nothing for a Creator to do."[19] The initial, circumscribed assumptions, restricted to physics, precluded any contrary conclusion.[20]

Moreover, the notion that modern science displaces religion rests on a misplaced veneration of the contemporary state of science. As Nicholas Rescher observes, we are led to "the humbling view that just as we think our predecessors of one hundred years ago had a fundamentally inadequate grasp on the furniture of the world, so our successors of one hundred years hence will take the same view of *our* knowledge (or purported knowledge) of things. No primacy—and certainly no finality—can automatically be claimed for our own conceptual posture."[21] However, this also points to a rather different challenge to

---

[18] In addition, one needs an account of how purposive actions could be *literally* attributed to God. Alston has developed such an account in "Divine and Human Action," in Thomas V. Morris, ed., *Divine and Human Action* (Ithaca: Cornell University Press, 1988); "God's Action in the World," in Ernan McMullin, ed., *Evolution and Creation* (Notre Dame: University of Notre Dame Press, 1986); and "Functionalism and Theological Language," *American Philosophical Quarterly* 22 (July 1985), 221–30. These three articles can also be found in William P. Alston, *Divine Nature and Human Language: Essays in Philosophical Theology* (Ithaca: Cornell University Press, 1989).

[19] Carl Sagan, Introduction to Stephen Hawking, *A Brief History of Time from the Big Bang to Black Holes* (New York: Bantam Books, 1990), p. x. See also Hawking, p. 174.

[20] For example, Hawking says that "if the universe is expanding, there may be physical reasons why there had to be a beginning. One could still imagine that God created the universe at the instant of the big bang, or even afterwards in just such a way as to make it look as though there had been a big bang, but it would be meaningless to suppose that it was created *before* the big bang" (*Brief History of Time*, p. 9). But Creation is "meaningless" here only on a verificationist view, where one is limited to knowledge about a state of affairs, X, which can be acquired only if the present laws of physics are in effect vis-à-vis X.

[21] Nicholas Rescher, "Conceptual Schemas," in *Midwest Studies in Philosophy*, vol. 5 (Minneapolis: University of Minnesota Press, 1980), p. 335.

Alston's position—one which he does not address—namely a principal motive *within modern theology itself* for the causal determinism/"modern scientific mind" objections to religion. Recent Christian theology often forgoes or flatly denies the notion that God literally, purposively carries out causally efficacious acts in history. This theological objection is rooted both in the influential historicist outlook of figures like Ernst Troeltsch, and in modern historical/critical biblical hermeneutics. The key idea is that theology must speak to the ever evolving, culturally conditioned mind of its contemporary audience, which precludes the idea of a God who acts in history.

Thus, what Troeltsch calls the "orthodox, supernatural apologetic" expects Christianity to be "traced to an immediate divine causality," something which Troeltsch feels cannot be found in the relativity of historical phenomena. In contrast, he argues for an "evolutionary apologetic" which recognizes the tension between the relativizing effect of human historicity and the "eternal content of Christian thought."[22] At the heart of modern biblical criticism we find Rudolph Bultmann's demythologizing hermeneutic: If the modern person "is prepared to take seriously the question of God, he ought not to be burdened with the mythological element in Christianity."[23] For "mythological thought regards the divine activity, . . . as an interference with the course of nature, history, or the life of the soul . . . —a miracle, in fact, . . . science does not believe that the course of nature can be interrupted . . . by supernatural powers."[24] And in the same vein we find John Macquarrie saying, "The way of understanding miracles that appeals to . . . supernatural interventions belongs to the mythological outlook and cannot commend itself in a post-mythological climate of thought."[25] Alston in effect circumvents this issue by rejecting the conceptualist account of the essential role of world-views (and changes in world-view) in perception, and thereby rejecting the very notion of historicity. As we have seen, though, this weakens his case for reconciling the problem of religious pluralism. But need a recognition of historicity lead to a rejection of the notion of God as acting in history? I think not.

[22] Ernst Troeltsch, *The Absoluteness of Christianity and the History of Religions*, trans. David Reid (Richmond, Va.: John Knox Press, 1971), pp. 52 and 54.

[23] Rudolph Bultmann, "A Reply to the Theses of J. Schniewind," in Hans Werner Bartsch, ed., *Kerygma and Myth: A Theological Debate* (New York: Harper and Row, 1961), p. 122.

[24] Rudolph Bultmann, "Bultmann Replies to His Critics," in Bartsch, *Kerygma and Myth*, p. 116; and Bultmann, *Jesus Christ and Mythology* (New York: Charles Scribner's Sons, 1958), p. 15 (cf. p. 38).

[25] John Macquarrie, *Principles of Christian Theology*, 2d ed. (New York: Scribner's, 1977), pp. 247–48.

In the first place, a recognition that our ideas are historically conditioned, that there is a plasticity over time to what we take to be the truth, actually obviates the conclusion of Bultmann, Macquarrie, and others[26] that modern "scientific" persons cannot accept the notion of miracles. For, (i) given the enormous variety of personal and historical factors affecting scientific paradigms, even within a scientific culture, there is no *one* scientific point of view, and (ii) today's science may be tomorrow's mythology. In the second place, it does not follow from the inextricable sociohistorical limitations and bias of our understanding that we cannot speak literally of, and correctly make literal reference to, God's actions. For how could we be certain that God *does not* carry out purposive actions in history? If we assume that this is not metaphysically impossible, this is just what a recognition of our own historicity should keep us from claiming *cannot* be so. This, however, is a consideration to which Alston cannot appeal. Hence, while Alston does successfully rebut the supposed "scientific" denial of the possibility of perceiving the acts of God, Alston does not take account of the historicist underpinnings of this denial within theology, historicist considerations which actually further undercut the validity of this challenge to religious experience.

IV

Let us turn, then, to Alston's positive defense of mystical perception in virtue of its fruits. He argues that if the only reason for following CMP was its social establishment, even if CMP were not shown to be unreliable, this would "severely reduce" its epistemic status (p. 275). Contrariwise, the epistemic status of CMP "will be strengthened if the practice generates significant self-support for its claims" (p. 278). The fruits of CMP which will lend this self-support are described as follows:

> Thus CMP proves itself, if at all, by the fact that it provides guidance in the all important enterprise of sanctification, guidance in the pilgrimage that leads, if things go right, to eternal loving communion with God. . . . It involves a radical turning (conversion) of oneself from preoccupation with the satisfaction of desires for sensory gratification,

[26] Others who have reached this conclusion include Langdon B. Gilkey, "Cosmology, Ontology, and the Travail of Biblical Language" (1961), reprinted in Owen C. Thomas, ed., *God's Activity in the World: The Contemporary Problem* (Chico, Calif.: Scholars Press, 1983), p. 31; and Gordon Kaufman, "On the Meaning of 'Act of God'," in Kaufman, *God the Problem* (Cambridge: Harvard University Press, 1972), pp. 134–35.

creature comforts, keeping up with the latest trendy consumer goods, one's own peace and serenity, one's status and reputation, and other self-centered aims; it involves turning away from this in the direction of an aim at loving communion with God and with one's fellows. It involves letting go of one's insistence on controlling one's destiny and opening up oneself to the Spirit, receiving the fruits of the Spirit— love, joy, peace, and so on—as free gifts, not as something one has earned by one's industry or one's own merits. (p. 251)

Alston says at the beginning of *Perceiving God* that he intends to address those who do not think that God is really perceived, as well as those who do. Let us set aside the atheist. Despite Alston's contention, the fruits of the spirit will not lend significant self-support to a theologically realist Christianity, either for those who are religious *non*realists or for those who deny Christianity but are theological realists—for example, Sunni Muslims.

Consider first, for example, the Christian theological nonrealism of Don Cupitt. Cupitt would readily agree with Alston's appeal to self-transcendence and invocation of the spiritual life: "What matters," says Cupitt, "is spirituality": "The highest and central principle of spirituality [is] . . . to attain the highest degree of . . . self-knowledge and self-transcendence. To achieve this we must escape from 'craving' or 'carnal lusts' and the false ego thereby created, and we must seek perfect purity of heart, disinterestedness, . . . and so on." But Cupitt holds that "a modern spirituality must be a spirituality for a fully-unified autonomous human consciousness, for that is the kind of consciousness that modern people have."[27] And he concludes that theological realism is inimical to the essential autonomy of ethical action: "it is a contradiction to suppose that my highest spiritual freedom could be determined for me from without, and by the act of another."[28] Consequently, Cupitt argues, "All reference to any supernatural world or beings or forces must be expunged or, at the very least, given a purely natural interpretation":[29] "What then is God? God is a unifying symbol that eloquently personifies and represents to us everything that spirituality requires of us. . . . God is the religious concern, reified."[30] Thus, Cupitt holds what he calls "Christian humanism," a view on which religion involves only naturalistic phenomena. While Alston rejects this view, the "fruits" which he feels offer self-support for a theologically *realist* CMP are

---

[27] Don Cupitt, *Taking Leave of God* (New York: Crossroad, 1981), p. 9.
[28] Ibid., p. 96.
[29] Don Cupitt, *The New Christian Ethics* (London: SCM Press, 1988), p. 51.
[30] Cupitt, *Taking Leave of God*, p. 9.

virtually identical to the "fruits" of Cupitt's Christian humanism. Again, we are left with the sense that something more is needed to offer full and final support for CMP over against its competitors, in this instance theological *non*realism.

Moreover, while Alston recognizes the value of offering an analysis of MP—and therefore of the fruits of spiritual development—which is applicable to all religions, the account he does develop is limited to the Christian tradition. In a 1991 essay, "The Fulfillment of Promises as Evidence for Religious Belief,"[31] he offers five "marks of the spiritual person": (1) being moral, (2) love and the transcendence of self-centeredness, (3) employment of a "different scale of values"—that is, eternal as opposed to worldly values, (4) a relation to God, devotion, and openness to the Holy Spirit, and (5) being imbued by the Holy Spirit and manifesting the "fruits of the spirit." Now (1), (2), and (5) (at least regarding the "fruits of the spirit" per se) are not specifically theistic,—though theological realists (like Alston and me) hold that (1), (2), and (5) *result* from God's actions, including God's promises. This is what a nonrealist like Cupitt denies. But (3) (employing an eternal scale of values) and, even more clearly, both (4) (a devout relation to God and openness to the Holy Spirit) and (5) (insofar as one is imbued by the Holy Spirit) are direct extensions of the Trinitarian Christian scheme. In important ways, this distinguishes Alston's view of spirituality from a view like Cupitt's. Yet (3), (4), and this part of (5) also exclude other world religion schemes, limiting this sense of "spirituality" to professed Christians.

In fact, this would disallow even an Inclusivist Christian account like Karl Rahner's, where, though salvation comes through Christ alone and there is no salvation outside the church, still, devout persons in other world religions can be "anonymous Christians," receiving salvation through Christ. This again illustrates the limitations of Alston's position for resolving the problem of religious pluralism, especially with respect to those in the nontheistic traditions who do not believe that God is perceived. (The question of nonreligious atheists is a somewhat different matter, which, following Alston, I will not address here.)

Now Alston argues that if many people have satisfied the conditions within CMP for receiving the "fruits of the spirit," and if they receive those fruits to a significant extent, this provides *evidence* for the truth of the Christian scheme. Significantly, Alston defends this thesis vis-à-vis Christian belief, he holds that, mutatis mutandis, this epistemic thesis is applicable to "any religious belief system that holds out promises

[31] *Logos* 12 (1991), 1–26.

of fulfillment to its devotees".[32] Still, the strongest support will be given to CMP if the Christian "fruits of the spirit" are unique to the Christian life, or a unique result of CMP. And indeed, Alston suggests in "The Fulfillment of Promises" that agape is a *distinctively* Christian form of love "not cultivated, and . . . perhaps rarely found, outside the context of Christian piety".[33] But this strongest-case scenario seems improbable.

In *An Interpretation of Religion*, John Hick argues that "all the great traditions teach the moral ideal of generous good will, love, compassion as epitomized in the Golden Rule."[34] Providing a detailed account from the various scriptural traditions of the world religions, Hick concludes that agape/Karuna (the latter is "limitless compassion" within the Buddhist tradition) constitutes the basic criterion by which moral judgments are made in all the world religions.[35] Of course, Hick's conclusion may be wrong. But prima facie the empirical data suggest that agape is not distinctively Christian. What, then, does Alston's notion of the "distinctively" Christian character of agape amount to?

Alston obviously means to say more than just that other-regarding love is *Christian* agape if it ensues from following the Christian life, from being a disciple of Christ, or if it results from the action of the Holy Spirit. What more can be said is that one can have *faith* that Christian discipleship and the indwelling of the Holy Spirit *leads to* agapistic love. It does not follow from this that this is the only operative causal sequence in all cases of agapistic love. The outcome provides evidence for the operation of Christ and/or the Holy Spirit, but it does not provide evidence that a *Christian* scheme is the sole explanatory scheme. Yet that in turn does not lessen the force of one's faith commitment that one *is* experiencing the fruits of the spirit.

As in his treatment of agape, Alston holds that "the degree of transcendence of self-centeredness that is characteristic of Christian spirituality" is also something that seems to be distinctive of that form of life.[36] I am less sure than Alston that this extraordinary mode of spirituality is ever very easy to identify. Perhaps the paradigmatic exemplar of this problem is St. Paul: "For I do not do what I want, but I do the very thing I hate" (Rom. 7:15, RSV). Yet even if we can successfully

---

[32] Ibid. Likewise, in *Perceiving God*, Alston suggests that his analysis of CMP, while applying to a *theistic* mystical practice, would apply to nontheistic ones as well (p. 30).

[33] Alston, "Fulfillment of Promises," p. 14.

[34] John Hick, *An Interpretation of Religion* (New Haven: Yale University Press, 1989), p. 316.

[35] Ibid., p. 326.

[36] Alston, "Fulfillment of Promises," p. 14.

apply this concept of the transcendence of self-centeredness in specific cases, it is not clear in what sense this notion of "agape" is distinctively *Christian*. A foundational element of Hick's comprehensive theory of Religious Pluralism is that the distinctive feature of *all* the world religions is the goal—and its present, even if partial, actualization—of the transformation from "self-centeredness to Reality-centeredness."[37] I have argued elsewhere that Hick's specific attempt to resolve the problem of religious pluralism by deemphasizing religious truth-claims or doctrines, and hence obviating their conflict, is misguided.[38] But the enormous empirical data Hick amasses from the world religions seems to support his central claim that in both theory and praxis the move from self-centeredness to a Reality-centeredness is elemental to all the great world religions. This, then, would not be a unique fruit of CMP. But as we just saw, it is at this point that an appeal to faith becomes crucial.

V

Thus, there is a rather tight circle in Alston's account of the evidential value of spirituality as self-support for CMP. Spiritual growth is evidence for the truth of the Christian scheme, but it seems that nothing can count as genuine spirituality for this purpose unless it comes out of—in the sense of (3), (4), and (5)—the Christian scheme. However, the tightness of this epistemic circle is not as serious as it appears. For I agree with Alston that we have no real alternative than to follow the doxastic practices we currently, successfully, use, unless we acquire good reasons to think them unreliable (p. 150; cf. 178). Of course, balanced against this, "a massive and persistent inconsistency between the outputs of two practices is a good reason for regarding at least one of them as unreliable" (p. 171). This is precisely the situation in our pluralistic age. And as Alston himself acknowledges (p. 270), the outputs of the other world religions which are not consistent with CMP, and the internal reliability of those other traditions, *in themselves* weaken the justification for continuing to follow CMP. Significantly, though, the awareness of religious diversity reduces, but does not obviate, the rationality of engaging in CMP (p. 275).

Alston's final conclusion is thus more subtle, and more inclusive, than it might initially have appeared. Consider, for example, Alvin Plan-

[37] John Hick, *Problems of Religious Pluralism* (New York: St. Martin's Press, 1985), p. 29.
[38] See my *Reason, Relativism, and God*, pp. 260–62; review of John Hick, *Problems of Religious Pluralism*, in *Faith and Philosophy* 5 (July 1988), 316–17; and "God, Commitment, and Other Faiths," pp. 353–54.

tinga's recent conclusion vis-à-vis this same problem in "Pluralism: A Defense of Religious Exclusivism."[39] Plantinga ends his analysis of religious pluralism by raising the possibility that a knowledge of the diversity of human religious responses might serve as an "undercutting" defeater (what Alston calls an "underminer") for core Christian beliefs. He observes that it is possible that knowledge of religious pluralism might reduce one's degree of belief, which would in turn reduce one's warrant and hence obviate one's knowledge of core Christian beliefs. But Plantinga concludes, in effect, that this is unlikely. Rather, for Plantinga, knowledge of religious pluralism might instead bring about a reappraisal of one's religious life and so a reawakening and deepened grasp of one's Christian beliefs. Here Plantinga's principal concern is to provide an internal apologetic. Alston's defense of the rationality of CMP is more external, and so he acknowledges the more serious undercutting effect of religious pluralism for Christian belief. Consequently, Alston is more open to the faith stance of others in our religiously pluralist world.

VI

What does this all finally come down to for those *inside* CMP? Ultimately, why should they continue their beliefs in the face of religious pluralism? Alston suggests that there is no other "final test" of the Christian scheme than "trying it out in one's life, testing the promises the scheme tells us God has made, following the way enjoined on us by the Church and seeing whether it leads to the new life of the Spirit" (p. 304). I have essentially argued that as a "test" this could not confirm but only disconfirm Christian belief. There must be more to the rationality of belief, more that keeps the believer engaged in the often arduous, often hard-to-fathom religious life. This has always been true; it is even more true in our age of religious pluralism. After all, the background schemes of the different world religions make different religious practices incompatible *even if* they produce the same experiential results. Something besides the fruits must most fundamentally keep the believer steadfast in holding to one practice over its competitors. And that foundational element is faith.

Alston is rightfully careful not to endorse a fideist view, given the potential excesses of a Kierkegaardian or Barthian or Wittgensteinian position. But it is an evidentialist trap to expect too much of the fruits

---

[39] Chap. 8 in this volume.

of the religious life as *demonstrating* internal support for CMP. It is too strong for Alston to hold that CMP "proves itself" by its fruits (p. 251). Even if one is epistemically justified in following CMP, faith provides its own, essential "overrider" against the "undercutter" of acknowledging religious pluralism. Indeed, with a greater emphasis on faith than Alston provides, his own analysis offers an opportunity for apologetics. True, his position involves a hermeneutical circle: if one has faith that there are divine promises, then the putative fulfillment of divine promises by a large number of persons provides a significant reason for continuing in and increasing one's commitment to the truth of the Christian scheme. But that is okay. What Christians can say to non-Christians is that they believe that the commitment of Christian faith becomes reinforced in the ensuing events of the Christian life and one's relation to God. This is an invitation to faith.

Humanism and theological nonrealism encourage us to be better persons by transcending our self-centeredness; theological realism—a belief in a personal God—enjoins us to be better persons by responding in the commitment of faith to a transcendent Thou. By exercising freedom and will, a person *can* sometimes transcend his or her present egotistical place in the natural order, but will remain in the natural order. But if there is a God who promises, a God with whom humans can *interact,* a transformation of our egotistic selves, not just within the social/psychological processes of the natural order but also *beyond* the natural order, becomes possible. And the fruits of the spirit are evidence *for the person of faith* of this divine-human interaction. This is the final conclusion to which Alston's analysis of perceiving God can lead us.

Of course, moving in this way beyond the relative security of the social establishment of CMP, and even beyond the internal support offered by the fruits of engaging in this doxastic practice, opens one to the *risk* of faith. We cannot deny our deepest faith commitments—"what other choice have we?"—but all faith commitments must be held with the humbling recognition that they can be misguided, for our knowledge is never sure. Our world-views are subject to our own historicity. Yet whatever the proper balance between faith and reason, humans are not saved by reason alone.[40] *That* is the ultimate idolatry of humanism; that is to deny the need for faith in a transcendent personal God.

[40] I argue against this view as classically articulated by Kant, in "Kant on Reason and Justified Belief in God," in Philip J. Rossi and Michael Wreen, eds., *Kant's Philosophy of Religion Reconsidered* (Bloomington: Indiana University Press, 1991), pp. 22–39, reprinted in my *World Views and Perceiving God*, chap. 5.

[11]

Polytheism

George I. Mavrodes

Ben-hadad had sent out scouts, and they reported to him, "Men have come out from Samaria." He said, "If they have come out for peace, take them alive; if they have come out for war, take them alive."

But these had already come out of the city: the young men who serve the district governors, and the army that followed them. Each killed his man; the Arameans fled and Israel pursued them, but King Ben-hadad of Aram escaped on a horse with the cavalry. The king of Israel went out, attacked the horses and chariots, and defeated the Arameans with a great slaughter. . . .

The servants of the king of Aram said to him, "Their gods are gods of the hills, and so they were stronger than we; but let us fight against them in the plain, and surely we shall be stronger than they.[1]

Almost all philosophy of religion in the West has assumed that any religion worth thinking about seriously is either monotheistic or else the nontheistic analogue of monotheism, a religion oriented toward a single impersonal ultimate. Polytheism has not gotten a fair shake in the philosophical casino; indeed, it has hardly gotten any shake at all, at least in the West. But perhaps that neglect is being remedied, to some small extent, now at the end of the twentieth century. I am thinking primarily of John Hick's published Gifford Lectures.[2] Hick is (in

[1] 1 Kings 20:17–21, 23. All the biblical quotations in this essay are taken from the New Revised Standard Version.

[2] John Hick, *An Interpretation of Religion* (New Haven: Yale University Press, 1989). This book is based on the Gifford Lectures for 1986–87. Page references appear in parentheses in the text.

my opinion, at least) probably the most important philosophical defender of polytheism in the history of Western philosophy. But I think he does not much care for that description himself. In any case, my own interest in polytheism has been largely stimulated by Hick's work, and his book provides a lot of material for philosophical rumination on that topic. In this essay I intend to explore some of the possibilities, and also some of the problems, associated with polytheism, with considerable reference to some of Hick's claims. But I have begun with an ancient reference to actual polytheistic religious thought (and practice?), an account from the Hebrew scriptures in the Bible.

The Aramean polytheists who figure in this passage were not, I suppose, philosophers in any profound sense. They were practitioners of their own religion but probably not deep reflectors on it. And the person who here described them—a Hebrew scribe—probably was not a philosopher either. I suppose the philosophical reflection and analysis must largely be ours, but some of the religions, and the religious thought, on which we are reflecting are theirs (and their neighbors'). I begin by trying to identify and clarify several prominent characteristics of the religious views of these ancient Arameans, as they are suggested in this text.

(1) *Realism.* The Arameans of this story are evidently realists with regard to the gods. That is, they think of the gods as belonging to the order of reality, as being real entities (rather than, say, hallucinations, imaginary beings, or fictions). I suppose they think that the gods are at least as real as they themselves are, and at least as real as ordinary physical objects, animals, and so on. A good clue to their realism is the fact that they evidently expect the gods to have effects in the ordinary world, in such a way that some happenings in the world can be explained by reference to the actions of the gods. They account for their own military defeat by citing the fact that they were foolish enough to fight in the hills, the home turf of the Hebrew gods. Naturally, they lost. And so they resolve not to make that mistake again. Next time they will fight on the plains, where presumably their own gods are at home and the Hebrew gods are strangers, and they expect to win there.

In this essay I adopt what I take to be the expectation of the Arameans as a minimal working account of a sufficient condition for something's being *real.* If some putative entity, x, can *itself* have a causal effect in the ordinary world, then x is real (or at least real enough for what I want to say here). But I stress the "itself" above. The fact that a belief in x, for example, or some other intentional attitude toward x, can generate effects in the world is not sufficient to make x real. Atheists deny the existence and reality of God (or the gods). So they do not suppose that God created the world; they do not expect the miraculous cure of a disease or the reversal of a tide of battle by an infusion of divine power. But they do not characteristically deny that *belief* in God, the *worship* of God, and so on have real effects in the world. On the contrary, they often bemoan those effects and sometimes praise them. I think such atheists have a grip on the notion of reality, and I am adopting it here.

(2) *Pure Descriptivism.* These Arameans appear to be pure descriptivists in their use of the term "god." That is, when they use this term, they presumably intend to identify and refer to a being of a certain kind, but they do not, merely by using this term, express any particular attitude of their own toward that being. In particular, they do not imply that they themselves worship the god to whom they refer, or that they are committed to serve or obey that god, or that they have any loyalty to him or her, and so on. This seems clear from the fact that they refer to the Hebrew deities ("their gods") even while plotting a way of defeating these gods and their Hebrew protegés.

No doubt the Arameans had gods to whom they did have some commitments of loyalty and obedience, whom they worshiped, and so on. Following the suggestion in this text, I use possessive pronouns ("my," "their," etc.) and similar locutions when I wish to indicate the gods who are linked to certain persons by relations such as worship and commitment, and use "god" without such indicators as a descriptive term without any implication of such relations.

Many, at least, of the attitudes and actions that link people with their gods are *intentional*. It isn't easy to define intentionality precisely. But perhaps we are familiar enough with it in statements such as "Debbie is looking for a perfect man." If I were to assert that, I would *not* be committing *myself* to the belief that there is such a thing as a perfect man, or even that there could be. (Nor, for that matter, would I commit myself to the view that there is no perfect man.) But I might well be describing Debbie's project in a way that she could recognize and accept. And what I would be saying about her could well be true even if there is no such thing as a perfect man. If I were to say, however, that Debbie had *found* a perfect man, then (in its ordinary interpretation) what I said could not be true unless there were in fact a perfect man. *Looking for* is an intentional notion, and it does not require that its object exist. *Finding,* on the other hand, is nonintentional, and it requires an existing object. And so I say that the Arameans worshiped gods of the plains, while remaining neutral myself about whether there really are any gods of the plains. The intentional objects of their worship are the gods of the plains, even if in fact there are no gods of the plains.

I say that the Arameans use "god" as a descriptive term, but nothing in the text indicates just what description they may have had in mind. They might be willing to accept a description suggested by Richard Swinburne, "a very powerful non-embodied rational agent."[3] At any rate, I begin with this as a sort of working description, and I will say something more later on about the possible attributes of a polytheistic god.

(3) *Pluralism.* I think these Arameans are pluralist about the gods in the sense that they think there really are *distinct* gods. It doesn't seem that they would have any enthusiasm at all for the suggestion that these various gods might really all be the very same god, going by different names. For they evidently think that these gods might be in conflict with one another, some of them backing the Hebrews and others supporting the Arameans. These people would take seriously the "poly" in "polytheist."

(4) *Descriptive Polytheism vs. Cultic Polytheism.* The Arameans evidently recognize some gods whom they do not worship or serve. But probably they were religious people themselves, worshiping and serving one or more gods. That fact suggests a distinction that is especially important in thinking about polytheism. A person who is both a realist and a pluralist about the gods is a *descriptive* polytheist. She thinks there are several distinct entities that fit some appropriate description, perhaps the description I suggested above. (And if she is also a pure descriptivist, she may use the term "god" for all these entities.)[4] If she herself worships and serves more than one distinct god, then she is a *cultic* polytheist. The Arameans were probably cultic polytheists (though nothing is said specifically about that in this text). But their cultic polytheism was not as broad as their descriptive polytheism, since they recognized the Hebrew gods[5] but did not worship or serve them.

Once we recognize this distinction, we can see that there are several other possible combinations of these two elements. One of the more

---

[3] Richard Swinburne, *The Concept of Miracle* (London: Macmillan, 1970), p. 53. Possibly, Swinburne meant merely to attribute this definition to David Hume. Someone may wish to add that a god must be the god of some actual religion, must actually be worshiped by some people, or something of the sort. The addition of such a clause will, I think, not make much difference to what is said here.

[4] But there may now be strong cultural reasons for even a pure descriptivist to avoid using "god" (or "God") in this way. I am myself a descriptive polytheist, but I characteristically use the term "God" in my own first-order utterances—i.e., when I am expressing my own religious convictions and not merely reporting other people's religion, etc.—to refer only to a single entity. This point becomes clearer, I hope, in the subsequent discussion.

[5] I use the plural here, since that is how the Aramean view of Hebrew religion is put in the text, but without prejudice to the question of whether the Hebrews themselves were monotheists or polytheists at the time.

interesting is that of combining descriptive polytheism with cultic monotheism.[6] Such a person would recognize the reality of several gods but would give his heart to only one of them. As we shall see below, John Hick might be just such a person. And I suppose there might be someone who was a descriptive polytheist (or a descriptive monotheist, for that matter) and a cultic atheist, recognizing several gods (or one) but worshiping and serving none at all.[7]

Might there be a person who is a descriptive atheist and a cultic monotheist (or polytheist)? I return to this question later, in connection with one of Hick's suggestions.

The distinction we have just been considering is closely related to a distinction that can be put in somewhat different terms, that between polytheism in *religion* and polytheism in *religious thought*. A person who worships and serves a single god might plausibly be said to be practicing a monotheistic religion, regardless of how many other gods she recognizes. But I suppose that a person who recognizes several gods would be a polytheist in her religious thought—or, perhaps better, in her thought about religion—regardless of how many gods (if any) she serves. In this essay I shall have occasion to comment on both polytheistic religion and polytheistic religious thought, but most of the discussion focuses on the latter.

(5) *Finitism.* The Arameans evidently considered the gods, both their own and those of the Hebrews, to be finite entities, limited in important ways. The most prominent version of this feature in the story at hand involves the way in which the Arameans believed the gods to be associated with various geographical regions. Other versions of polytheism limit the gods in other ways; for example, the polytheists of classical Greece and Rome assigned the various gods a particular influence and hegemony over various and distinct areas of human life and interest.

(6) *A Common World.* Though the gods, as the Arameans construed them, were finite and distinct, they were not isolated from one another. They shared a common world as at least one focus of their actions. They could collide with one another. Perhaps there could be direct, unmediated collisions and conflicts, though nothing is clearly said about that possibility here. It does seem pretty clear, however, that they could collide in a mediated way, through their effects on elements of the ordinary world, particularly through their sponsorship of, or actions against, various human beings and human groups. The Arameans and the Hebrews shared a common world (even if it was mostly a

---

[6] This combination is sometimes called "henotheism."
[7] Perhaps this is the position ascribed to the devils in James 2:19.

common border between the hill country and the lowlands), and so their gods, if they were to have effects in the world of their protegés, must also share that same common world.

So much, for the time being, about these characteristics of Aramean polytheism. How might they bear on polytheism now, especially philosophical polytheism?

I don't have much of an idea, in any detail anyway, about why the Arameans of this story believed in their own gods. But they probably did not make up the Hebrew gods out of whole cloth. They probably knew that the Hebrews had a religion, that they had ceremonies of worship, sacrifice, prayer, and so on. Perhaps they were even familiar with some Hebrew claims about their god or gods. Since they thought of their own gods in a rather limited and parochial way, it may have seemed natural to them to suppose that there must be other gods who had a similar parochial relation to other nations. And maybe they were generous enough to accept, more or less at face value, those other people's accounts of their own deities.

However that may be, we find ourselves in a somewhat similar situation, whether or not we have a religion of our own. For we too know that other people are religious, that (in the intentional sense, at least) they worship gods or contemplate impersonal absolutes, and so on. And so the question may arise for us too, as to how we are to think of the gods and absolutes that are not our own. One might say that in addition to the celebrated problem of other minds, there is, in a vaguely analogous way, a problem of other gods.

The hard-nosed (descriptive) atheist, I suppose, will not have much trouble with this question. Such a person has a single, all-purpose attitude toward the whole menagerie of divinities. They are all unreal. They do not exist, neither the Holy Trinity, or Allah, nor Shiva, nor . . . They do not belong to the order of the world.

The situation may be somewhat more complex for people who are themselves religious believers. Christians, for example, generally profess to be cultic monotheists. So they do not reject gods out of hand or universally. What are they descriptively? Many of them would also, I think, profess to being descriptive monotheists. And where does that leave the gods of the other religions? Here there seem to be two alternatives.

The first is that of saying that the gods of the other religions are real too, just as real as the god of Christianity. And how can that answer cohere with descriptive monotheism? It's easy. On this view the gods of the other religions are simply *identical* with the god of Christianity. And this is sometimes put by the slogan that God has many names. Of course, to be consistent, this view has to accept the consequence that some theologies—some bodies of belief that are integral to one religion or another—must be pretty badly mistaken. It doesn't seem possible, for example, that Muslims and Christians can both be right about the doctrine of the Trinity. But perhaps this consequence can be accepted, especially if we remember that saying that a certain theology is badly mistaken need not be the same thing as saying that the corresponding religion is evil, or useless, or anything of the sort.

I suspect, however, that rather few Christians have accepted the whole-hog view just described. More of them have been attracted to a somewhat weakened version of it, to the effect that the gods of *some* other religions are identical with the god of Christianity. The other religions usually turn out to be monotheisms themselves, and indeed monotheisms that seem to be rather like Christianity in some important ways.[8] In any case, this watered-down version leaves us with the question of what to do with the remaining gods.

The second option for those who want to be both cultic and descriptive monotheists is that of denying the reality of the other gods (or of some of them). Those Christians will be, one might say, theists with respect to the Holy Trinity and atheists with respect to the other gods.[9] So far as I can see, there is nothing radically incoherent in such a position, though it may strike some observers as ungenerous, chauvinistic, or the like. This position, however, might give rise to some penetrating and disturbing questions, questions about how so many people in the other religious traditions could be deluded into worshiping non-existent entities, and into building whole lives, sometimes lives of remarkable devotion and sacrifice, around gross unrealities. Such questions may be disturbing to the cultic monotheist because they (or their answers) tend to generate doubts about *her own* religious commitments. She, after all, does not write off the *whole* religious program as the atheist does. She will want to maintain the reality of her own god, even as she denies the reality of the others. But her denial of the reality of what *seems* real to so many other people of high intelligence and evident goodness may generate, in her own mind, doubts about the correctness of her judgment of her own religion and her own god. I say that such doubts may be generated, and that there is the potential for "distur-

---

[8] Some who profess to worship the same god as do modern Jews, and even the god of the Hebrew prophets, may find the Jahweh of earlier Hebrew religion too bloodthirsty for their tastes.

[9] This gives rise to the jibe that Christians are not much different from atheists after all—it is just a matter of one god. I suppose Christians might reply that there is a lot of difference between one and none, as, for example, with respect to having a wife.

bance" in such questions. But, of course, one or another monotheist of this general sort may find a way to resolve such doubts and to lay such disturbances to rest, at least to his or her own satisfaction.

Some Christians, however (and some other cultic monotheists, I suppose), are descriptive polytheists. That is, they are descriptive polytheists in fact, if not in name. A comparatively straightforward position of this sort is that of Christians who have held that the gods of other religions are devils. Of course, saying that the god of another religion is a devil seems to imply a strongly negative judgment, and no doubt that is what was usually intended. But that need not prevent this view from being a genuine descriptive polytheism. Possibly, the attitude of worship requires a judgment on the part of the worshiper that the object of his worship is good and/or holy. But *descriptive* polytheism does not imply an attitude of worship on the part of the descriptivist. And it is worth noting that the description of a god that I culled earlier from Richard Swinburne makes no mention of goodness or any similar value or virtue. A devil would seem to fit Swinburne's description perfectly well. And so it seems quite possible that some one entity should be both a god and a devil—a god in Swinburne's sense and a devil in some expanded sense that includes (negative) valuational elements. Furthermore, those Christians who think that the gods of other religions are devils are likely to think also that devils are real beings, at least as real as cantaloupes and giraffes. That is, they think that devils are actual creatures (on some views, angelic creatures who "fell"), created by the same divine power that created the rest of the existing universe.[10]

There are still other ways of being simultaneously a cultic monotheist and a descriptive polytheist. I mentioned John Hick as a distinguished modern defender of polytheism. Hick's position will be of special interest to philosophers, I think, because it is attached to a prominent, though highly controversial, philosophical tradition, that of Kantian epistemology and metaphysics. I turn now to a consideration of Hick's proposal as it was developed in his series of Gifford Lectures, exploring some of its promise and also some of its problems.

I begin with a quotation:

Within each tradition we regard as real the object of our worship or contemplation. If, as I have already argued, it is also proper to regard

---

[10] Whether devils (and angels) are *supernatural* creatures, as distinguished from natural creatures, is an obscure and difficult question. I set it aside, largely because I don't know much to say about it.

as real the objects of worship or contemplation within the other traditions, we are led to postulate the Real *an sich* as the presupposition of
the veridical character of this range of forms of religious experience.
Without this postulate we should be left with a plurality of *personae*
and *impersonae* each of which claimed to be the Ultimate, but no one of
which alone can be. We should have either to regard all the reported
experiences as illusory or else return to the confessional position in
which we affirm the authenticity of our own stream of religious experience whilst dismissing as illusory those occurring within other traditions. But for those to whom neither of these options seems realistic
the pluralistic affirmation becomes inevitable, and with it the postula-
tion of the Real *an sich*, which is variously experienced and thought
as the range of divine phenomena described by the history of religion. (p. 249)

In this paragraph, as indeed throughout the book, a monistic element is interwoven with the pluralistic strand of Hick's thinking. If for
the moment we leave out that monistic element—that is, the references
to "the Real *an sich*—then we get a view that seems, to me at least,
strongly suggestive of the Aramean picture with which this essay began.
We regard as real the gods and absolutes of our own religion, *and we
are to regard the gods and absolutes of the other religions also as real*. We may
or may not be cultic monotheists, depending on the architecture of our
own religion, but Hick argues that the only religiously proper and
justified *descriptive* stance is that of polytheism.

I say that on Hick's view this is the "religiously" proper stance because
Hick professes to give us here a *religious* interpretation of religion. His
interpretation, that is, is not one that is intended to reduce religion to
something else, accounting for it in terms of purely natural factors.
Rather, he intends to understand religion as a "human response to a
transcendent reality or realities" (p. 1). The reductionistic, naturalistic
mode of interpretation would yield the conclusion that *all* the gods
were unreal or illusory.[11] From the religious standpoint, however, we
come to regard them all as real.

I have already mentioned a view sometimes casually affirmed by
religious ecumenists which readily yields the conclusion that all the
gods are real, or at least that they are as real as our own god. This is
the view that all the gods of the various religions are really just one
and the same god, the view sometimes put by saying that God has many

---

[11] "The naturalistic response is to see all these systems of belief as factually false"
(p. 234).

names. But Hick seems to reject this view, on the grounds that the various gods are described, within the various corresponding religions, in mutually incompatible ways. "Surely these reported ultimates, personal and impersonal, are mutually exclusive" (p. 234). And if they are mutually exclusive, then, I suppose, they could not be identical.

It would be possible to reject this argument by holding that the enthusiasts of most religions—or all of them, for that matter—are substantially mistaken about their gods. They attribute to their gods properties they do not actually have, and it is these properties that generate the apparent incompatibility among the divine beings. So we might hold that the Muslim God and the Christian God are one and the same being after all, but that either the Muslims are mistaken in thinking that Allah is not a trinity or else the Christians are mistaken in thinking that there are three divine persons in the Godhead. And we might hold, perhaps even more radically, that the Holy Trinity is identical with Nirvana, but that Buddhists generally are mistaken in believing that Nirvana is nonpersonal, and so on. But maybe Hick thinks that the supposition that religious people could be so wildly mistaken about their own deities is too implausible to be taken seriously.

Comparing Hick's views with those I identified earlier in connection with the Arameans, we get (so far) the following results:

1. Hick, like the Arameans, seems to be both a realist and a pluralist about the various gods.

2. Again like the Arameans, Hick seems to be a pure descriptivist in his use of the term "god." He recognizes a wide variety of gods, and he calls them "gods," but he also makes clear (at least in conversation) that he intends his own religious commitments, worship, and so on, to find their place within the Christian tradition. In recognizing the reality of the Hindu gods, he does not become a Hindu.

3. Hick therefore, like the Arameans, seems to be a descriptive polytheist, but (probably unlike the Arameans) he is a cultic monotheist.

4. Is Hick, like the Arameans, a finitist with respect to the gods? Perhaps that question can be better answered after we consider the monistic strand in Hick's thinking.

Hick is pluralistic about the gods of the world's religions, but he declares himself to be monist about something else, something that is more ultimate in some final way, and hence metaphysically more basic, than any of these religious *personae* and *impersonae*. This item is what Hick calls "the Real." But though the Real appears to be on a different metaphysical level from that of the gods, it is not unrelated to them. I suppose it would not be far amiss to say that, on Hick's view, the Real is the ground and source of the gods.

Hick's own way of putting the point makes use of Kantian terminology and appeals to Kantian epistemology and metaphysics. Hick says, for example:

> In developing this thesis our chief philosophical resource will be one of Kant's most basic epistemological insights, namely that the mind actively interprets sensory information in terms of concepts. . . . For Kant God is postulated, not experienced. In partial agreement but also partial disagreement with him, I want to say that the Real *an sich* is postulated by us as a pre-supposition, not of the moral life, but of religious experience and the religious life, whilst the gods, as also the mystically known Brahman, Sunyata and so on, are phenomenal manifestations of the Real occurring within the realm of religious experience. Conflating these two theses one can say that the Real is experienced by human beings, but experienced in a manner analogous to that in which, according to Kant, we experience the world: namely by informational input from external reality being interpreted by the mind in terms of its own categorical scheme and thus coming to consciousness as a meaningful phenomenal experience. All that we are entitled to say about the noumenal source of this information is that it is the reality whose influence produces, in collaboration with the human mind, the phenomenal world of our experience. (pp. 240, 243)

This is not, of course, Kant's own account of religious experience or of divine beings. Hick has here taken Kant's way of treating our sensory experience of the ordinary world and has adapted it to serve as a way of understanding religious experience and its special objects, especially the gods and the impersonal absolutes. And he has broadened Kant's idea of the categorical machinery the mind brings to experience by allowing it to include elements that are not innate and universal but that are instead culturally conditioned and variable. And, according to Hick, the fact that different religious traditions provide their adherents with differing categories for conceptualizing the divine is what accounts for the diversity of divine beings that appear in these different religions.

This account, it seems to me, adds some further substance to my earlier claim that Hick can be thought of as a *realist* with respect to the gods and so on of the various religions.[12] For we can say that, on Hick's view, all the gods are real *in the same sense that cantaloupes are real on the Kantian view.* And, of course, on the Kantian view of things, ordinary cantaloupes such as one may buy in the supermarket are real in an important sense. They are not imaginary cantaloupes, they are not fictional melons, not hallucinations, and so on. They coexist with us and other things in the physical world, where they are causally significant. But, of course, Kantian cantaloupes are not metaphysically ultimate—they are not *Dingen an sich.* And neither are Hickian gods.

Is that a *religiously* satisfactory view? Probably that question has no single answer. Some people will certainly not find Hick's view satisfactory. They want their gods to be *more real* than cantaloupes—and not merely bigger or more powerful than cantaloupes. A watermelon, or even an elephant, would come no closer to filling the bill. And if those people cannot find gods who do seem to fill that bill, then they will give up on religion altogether. On the other hand, there have apparently been people who have built a religious and spiritual life around gods whose warrant (they believed) ended with the first line of hills, not twenty miles away, or with gods who took care of agriculture but had nothing to do with seafaring. Perhaps those people would not have found Hick's phenomenal gods all that unsatisfactory. (After all, those gods are thought to be at least a real as cantaloupes. And a cantaloupe is a real entity, a force to be reckoned with, something to be sought for the enrichment of human life.) For all I know, there may be people like that still.

There is, however, a deep ambiguity in Hick's way of thinking about the relation of the Real to the gods, an ambiguity that has an important bearing on the logical viability of any polytheism. And this ambiguity may be the reflection of a similar ambiguity in Kant's own discussions of the phenomenal world and the noumenal reality that is supposed to underlie it. It involves the difference between, on the one hand, thinking (or saying) that the phenomenon *is the noumenon* as experienced, as it appears, and so on, and, on the other hand, thinking (or saying) that the phenomenon *is a human creation* in reaction to some influence, input, or the like from the noumenon. I call these two ways of thinking about the phenomenon/noumenon relation the "disguise model" and the "construct model," respectively.

---

[12] But, at least in some moods, Hick seems ambivalent about this. On pp. 272–75 he suggests that two models, one strongly realist about the gods and one strongly nonrealist, are both compatible with his position. I discuss his nonrealist model below.

The difference between these models may perhaps be made plainer by thinking of two analogies. One of these is suggested by Hick himself. He says that we need not work through Kant's "complex philosophical architectonic" to arrive at the distinction between noumena and phenomena. "For it arises out of elementary reflection upon our experience. We quickly realise that the same thing appears in either slightly or considerably different ways to different people owing both to their varying spatial locations in relation to it and to differences in their sensory and mental equipment and interpretive habits" (p. 242). And, of course, Hick must be right about that. Things are not always what they appear to be, and they appear differently to one person and another. Thus we distinguish, early on, between appearance and reality.

The prince, let us suppose, wants to get an undistorted idea of what the lives of his people are like, what they are thinking, and so on. So he decides to visit the various provinces, but not openly as prince. He appears, therefore, in the marketplace of one town as an itinerant monk—that is, he comes barefooted, wearing a dark and shapeless gown made of rough cloth, cinched around the waist by a frayed robe, a cowl over his head, a wooden cross as a pendant upon his breast, perhaps a rosary in his hand. He does not appear to be a prince; he appears to be a monk. Of course, he might not appear to everyone to be a monk. There might be an ignorant person in the market that day, a person who has no knowledge at all of the monastic orders, who has never heard of monks, a person who has no idea at all, either accurate or stereotypical, of what a monk would wear. To that person the prince probably does not appear as a monk. To him, lacking in the appropriate interpretive categories, the prince may look simply like someone wearing funny clothes. But to the others who have the appropriate categories, the prince appears as a monk.

The prince need not always appear as a monk, even when not appearing as prince. In another province he may come to the Spring Fair as, say, a journeyman stonemason. He is wearing the heavy leather apron and openly carrying the tools of his purported trade. Perhaps he has even sprinkled stone dust into his beard. And thus (again to those who have the appropriate interpretive categories) he appears as neither prince nor monk but stonemason.

So much, for the moment, for the first analogy. I will come back to it. But here let us turn to a second analogy. Imagine several artists who sit, side by side, looking at a landscape. There is a country church there, a few tombstones beside it, trees nearby and a small stream, sheep on the hill beyond. The artists paint, looking back and forth from their easels to the landscape. And when the paintings are finished, we look at them.

We may imagine that these artists, or most of them at any rate, paint in the abstract and nonrepresentational manner. So the paintings do not strike us as looking much like the landscape itself. (If a stranger in the area told us he was looking for that church, we would not immediately think of giving him one of these paintings, and saying, "Take this. It will help you recognize the church when you come to it.") Furthermore, the paintings do not look much like one another. If we saw them hanging together on a gallery wall, we would not immediately suspect that they had been painted from the same location. Nevertheless, each artist assures us that his or her painting was indeed inspired by the actual landscape. And each is confident that if there had been a McDonald's restaurant there instead of the church, or perhaps even camels grazing instead of the sheep, then the painting would also have been noticeably different. So the landscape has contributed something to each painting. There is a real input there, and some sort of dependence. In some way, each painting is the way it is because the landscape is the way it is.

But, of course, the landscape does not provide the only input; it is not the only factor that goes into making the painting what it is. There is also the aesthetic creativity of the artist, his or her artistic interpretation, and so on. The painting itself is a construct, a humanly constructed entity, the product of an artistic reaction to, and interaction with, a (largely) natural landscape.

So we have two stories, the prince and the painters, and the corresponding two models for the phenomenon/noumenon distinction. But these models are not compatible. Which shall we use, if we are attracted by the Kantian project at all?

A crucial difference between these models, in the present connection, is this. In the disguise model there is an identity relation that holds among the various appearances. The (apparent) monk is identical with the prince, and the (apparent) stonemason is identical with the prince, and therefore the monk is identical with the stonemason. Hick recognizes this identity relation when he says, in the last passage I quoted above, "We quickly realise that *the same thing* appears in either slightly or considerably different ways to different people" (p. 242, italics mine). In this model there may be many appearances, but there is a single entity that has these appearances, a single entity that is experienced in these various ways. This identity is the basis for many hypotheticals. If the monk walks barefoot in the marketplace then the prince must endure the hot cobblestones beneath his feet. And if the stonemason drinks too much at the fair and drowns in the nearby river, then the life of the prince also ends in that river.

But may not the stonemason appear to be a middle-aged man, while the prince is a vibrant youth? Certainly. The stonemason may appear to have properties the prince does not have. But if the stonemason *is* the prince (in disguise), then the stonemason must *be* the same age as the prince. He can *appear* to be older, but that must be merely an appearance, and those who take it at face value are misled by an appearance.

The construct model, on the other hand, does not postulate an identity between the construct and its source, input, and so on, and consequently it does not support similar hypotheticals. The landscape is an important factor in making the painting what it is, but the painting is not identical with the landscape. The painting is not *the same thing* as the landscape. Therefore, a vandal who burns the painting does not thereby burn the church, and if he slashes the painting, he does not thereby kill a sheep.[13]

It is fairly common, I think, for philosophers to interpret the Kantian metaphysics along the lines of the construct model. We think, that is, that the ordinary world of Kantian metaphysics—the world of sense-experience as Kant construes it—is a human construct, the product of human cognitive operations reacting to some "kick" provided by an unknown and unexperienced noumenal reality. And the entities of the ordinary world, the cantaloupes, are phenomenal entities. On this interpretation, a cantaloupe is not a noumenon wearing a disguise, and when we take it to be a cantaloupe, we are not being misled by its appearance. It really is just what it appears to be. We *construct* the objects of our experience, and the only objects we experience are the objects we construct. These constructs belong to a different metaphysical level from that of the noumena, which are not human constructs at all and therefore cannot be identical with them.

Thinking of the gods in accordance with this model yields a genuine polytheism. The various gods are real—at least as real as the more ordinary furniture of the world, and possibly more real—and they are distinct from one another, again as the more ordinary entities of the world are distinct. The disguise model, however, when applied to the gods, does not yield a polytheism at all. Or at most it yields a polytheism

---

[13] It is not the nonrepresentational style of painting that cuts off these hypotheticals. Even if some of the artists in the story are representational painters, and their paintings are easily recognizable depictions of that particular landscape, it would nevertheless remain true that one would not destroy the church or injure a sheep simply by vandalizing the painting.

only of names. For according to this model, there is just one god who appears in all the various religions.

As I said above, Hick himself seems deeply ambivalent at this point. Often he speaks as though he adopted the disguise model both in understanding Kant and in adapting the Kantian machinery to his own purposes. So he says, for example, that "Kant distinguished between noumenon and phenomenon, or between a *Ding an sich* and that thing as it appears to human consciousness" (p. 241). And, speaking for himself, he says that "the divine Reality is not directly known *an sich*. But when human beings relate themselves to it in the mode of I-Thou encounter they experience it as personal. Indeed in the context of that relationship it *is* personal, not It but He or She. When human beings relate themselves to the Real in the mode of non-personal awareness they experience it as non-personal, and in the context of this relationship it *is* non-personal" (p. 245; Hick's italics). In the first of these quotations the phrase "that thing" must refer to the *Ding an sich,* and so the *Ding an sich* is the thing that appears to human consciousness. In a similar way, the repeated "it" of the second quotation refers to the previously mentioned divine Reality, which Hick here treats as a single entity. And, in a quotation I cited earlier, Hick tries to make Kant's views plausible by observing that "*the same thing* appears in either slightly or considerably different ways to different people" (p. 242; my italics).

Understood in this way, Hick is not a polytheist at all. His view turns out to be very much like that of those who say that God has many names. God has many appearances, many disguises. The divine reality can adopt many different *personae.* And the divine reality can appear without a *persona* at all, appearing instead as an *impersona,* a nonpersonal object of contemplation.

Sometimes, however, Hick speaks in a way that fits much better with the construct model, both in explaining Kant's views and in applying them for his own purposes. He says, for example, that "all that we are entitled to say about the noumenal source of this information is that it is the reality whose influence produces, in collaboration with the human mind, the phenomenal world of our experience" (p. 243). In this passage the phenomenal world is not "the same thing" as the noumenal world. It is rather something *produced* by the joint influence, the collaboration, of a noumenal reality and a human mind. And this is exactly the construct interpretation of Kantian metaphysics.

In addition, some of Hick's arguments make sense on the construct interpretation but not on the disguise interpretation. He argues, for example, that not all the intentional gods and impersonal absolutes could possibly exist, since they are described in ways that exclude one another. He says "The gods of the monotheistic faiths are thought of in each case as the one and only God, so that it is impossible for there to be more than one instantiation of this concept" (p. 234). But there is nothing impossible about there *appearing* to be more than one instantiation of a concept, even if it is impossible that it be instantiated more than once. There would be nothing impossible about a noumenon appearing to be the one and only god, Jahweh, and also appearing to be the one and only god, Allah. For something can appear to have a property without having it, and consequently to appear to instantiate a concept, even if it does not instantiate it. If we are to construe the reality and existence of the gods along Kantian or quasi-Kantian lines, and if we are to interpret Kant in terms of the disguise model, then Hick's line of argument here would fail entirely. But if phenomenal entities are construed not as noumena in disguise but as constructs generated by the joint action of noumena and human minds, then indeed no two such contructs could instantiate a concept that is intrinsically limited to a single instantiation. And so Hick's argument for the mutual exclusivity of some of the Gods would succeed.

Well, so much for this rather extended account of Hick's position, at least as I understand it. I turn again to a more general discussion of descriptive polytheism, with only occasional references to Hick. And I propose to discuss what reasons we may have for either accepting or denying descriptive polytheism. But I'm looking here for reasons particularly relevant to *polytheism*. For better or worse, I ignore reasons for theism in general, along with reasons for general atheism.

What reasons might we have for asserting the existence of *more than one* god? The reason Hick gives (p. 235) seems to me fallacious. He argues that "persons living within other traditions, then, are equally justified [as justified as we are] in trusting their own distinctive religious experience and in forming their beliefs on the basis of it." And he apparently wants to draw from this the conclusion that we cannot reasonably "claim that our own form of religious experience, together with that of the tradition of which we are a part, is veridical whilst the others are not." And so, since we assert the reality of our God, we must also accept the analogous assertions of others. This is fallacious because it confuses the notions of justification and truth or veridicality. Other people may be as justified as I am in relying on what seems to us to be our divergent experience. But that justification is largely independent of the veridicality of those experiences, and of the truth of the beliefs that they generate. As Hick himself says, "A proposition believed can be true or false: it is the believing of it that is rational or irrational"

(p. 212). And the rationality of a belief, unlike the truth of what is believed, is sensitive to the epistemic situation of the believer. So, contrary to what Hick seems to argue, there is nothing unreasonable in a person's asserting that someone else is justified in relying on a certain experience, but that nevertheless the experience is nonveridical.[14]

I don't know of any other attempt to provide a sort of general or philosophical reason in support of *poly*theism. I know of one religious or confessional reason, from within Christianity. And it is the reason for my saying earlier in this essay that I am now a sort of descriptive polytheist. The Christian tradition, both in the New Testament documents and in later theological developments, seems to me to take seriously the idea that human beings are not the only rational creatures in the realm of existence. And in particular it seems to countenance the existence of powerful and nonembodied intelligences. At least, that is how I understand the references to angels and devils within the Christian tradition. I don't take this to be a really central doctrine in Christianity, but for what it is worth it inclines me to think that there are many beings who satisfy Swinburne's definition of a god. And so in Swinburne's sense I am (even if a little tentatively) a descriptive polytheist.

Are any of these beings—could any of them be—the gods of some actual religion? Now that I come to think of it (and my thinking of it is very recent), I don't think of any strong reason for returning a negative answer. Playing such a role might, of course, be a usurpation of divine prerogatives. But I think that the possibility of such a usurpation is not entirely foreign to Christian thought. On the other hand, could such a role be divinely *assigned*, a service provided by the condescension of divine grace for the redemption of the world? The idea strikes me as strange, perhaps vaguely unsettling. But I do not now rule it out.

We can also divide objections to polytheism into two rough and nonexclusive categories: primarily religious objections and more general philosophical objections.

The primarily religious objections usually arise within a particular religion and are embedded in the theological or confessional apparatus of the religion. They can be prohibitions against polytheistic practice, as in "I am the Lord your God, who brought you forth out of the land of Egypt, out of the house of bondage. You shall have no other gods before me" (Exod. 20:2, 3). Or they can be ringing declarations of the

---

[14] I have discussed this point somewhat more at length, and developed some other criticisms of Hick's views, in "The God above the Gods," in Eleonore Stump, ed., *Reasoned Faith* (Ithaca: Cornell University Press, 1993), pp. 179–203.

monotheistic nature of the religion in which they appear, the insistence that "our" god is singular, not plural. One of the best-known examples of this is the *Shema*, "Hear, O Israel: The Lord our God is one Lord" (Deu. 6:4).

Such injunctions and declarations, however, are for the most part directed toward cultic polytheism, and do not seem to deny the thesis of descriptive polytheism—that is, they do not deny that there are other real gods who are, perhaps, the gods of other religions. Of course, there might be a religion that included such a denial in its theology. But (at least if we think of a god along Swinburne's lines) Christianity does not seem to be a strong candidate for such a religion.

Another sort of religious objection to polytheism, perhaps not dependent on the theology of a particular religion, would be the claim that polytheism is religiously unsatisfactory, religiously defective. This too, I suppose, would be a thesis about cultic polytheism, and even if true would not show that descriptive polytheism was mistaken. But perhaps some versions of this objection are closely related to some of the more general and philosophical objections, to which I now turn.

It has sometimes been supposed that descriptive polytheism must be mistaken because there could not possibly be more than one god. And why not? Because a god must have properties that cannot possibly (logically?) have more than one instantiation. Now, in the case of the unabashedly finite gods who are apparently the intentional objects of worship in some actual and historical religions, this objection seems to have very little force. The properties that are, or were, ascribed to them probably were no more incapable of multiple instantiation than the properties many Christians ascribe to angels and devils.

The objection might be pressed, however, by insisting that there is something profoundly unsatisfactory about religions of that sort. And here the objection connects with the second type of religious objection noted above. The finite gods, confined to the hill country or interested only in wine making, are not big enough to satisfy the fully developed and reflective religious impulse. We are not satisfied with Swinburne's minimalist definition. A god must have more than that, he must *be* more than that! And it might be suspected that gods described in such a way as to make them suitable religious principals will be so strongly endowed that they cannot possibly coexist.

It is certainly true that the theologies of the "high" religions tend to ascribe to their divinities extreme and unlimited versions of various attributes. (Cf. the "omni-" attributes that are stock items in Christian theologies.) And probably that does represent a genuine religious impulse. But is it clear that the divinities thus endowed must be incapable of coexistence?

No doubt that will depend on just what the unlimited attributes are. What seems initially most obvious is that not every unlimited attribute is intrinsically incapable of multiple instantiation. Think, for example, of perfect goodness, or of perfect love. I, at any rate, cannot think of any way at all of starting on an argument to show that there could not be more than one being who had these properties. In these cases, one instantiation does not seem to generate any special difficulty for a second. The same seems to be the case for omniscience and omnipresence. If it is coherent to suppose that some one being knows every truth, then why should it be impossible that there be a second being who also knows every truth? And if there is some being who, in some sense, is present everywhere (even in places that are also occupied by other objects), then why should not a second being also be omnipresent in that same sense? To me, at any rate, these properties, though they figure in the theology of my own religion, do not seem to be such as to belong *necessarily* to no more than one being.[15]

There is an "omni-" attribute, however, that seems to have more promise along this line. It is, of course, omnipotence. Here there seems to be more room, initially at least, for the suspicion that we have hit upon an "instantiation-exclusive" property. And, of course, it is the "omni-", the unlimitedness, that generates the exclusivity. Limited powers can be instantiated in distinct agents, and perhaps an unlimited power in one agent is compatible with limited powers elsewhere. But could there be two (or more) centers of *unlimited* power?

Well, why not? Intuitively, the attractive line of argument is captured in the hoary conundrum, What happens when an irresistible force meets an immovable object? If the force is thwarted, then it was not irresistible after all, and if the object is moved, then it was not immovable. In a similar way, one is to imagine the two putative omnipotent powers colliding, and then it will be seen that one of them was not omnipotent after all.[16] (If their contest ends in a draw, then I suppose we should think that neither was omnipotent.)

Though this argument is superficially attractive, I think that we cannot make it work. Ever since the time of Thomas, at least, Christian theologians have, for the most part, held that the power of God extends over what is logically possible, and *only* over what is logically possible.

---

[15] I am, of course, ignoring arguments to the effect that these alleged attributes are internally incoherent. That, if it were true, would show that *nothing* had such attributes. It would have no *special* relevance to polytheism.

[16] Hick seems to appeal to this line of argument (p. 79).

It has been surprisingly difficult to specify this version of omnipotence in a fully clear and satisfactory way. But suppose for the moment that the general idea of this version is correct and that this is how we should think of omnipotence. Then we could hold that God is omnipotent, even if we were to admit that He cannot create a mountain whose slopes run uphill only (the anathema of skiers). On this view of omnipotence, such "failures" as these do not damage an agent's claim to omnipotence.

Now let us assume, as the hypothesis that is to be explored, that there are two omnipotent agents, A and B. And let them be *essentially* omnipotent, so that they cannot survive the loss of power. And suppose they collide. Might A overpower B? Well, it certainly seems logically impossible that an essentially omnipotent agent should be overpowered. If that is so, then (given the Thomistic idea of omnipotence) A cannot overpower B. But it also follows that his inability to overpower B does not damage his omnipotence, any more than does his inability to create the mountain whose slopes run only uphill.

Might we have been mistaken in supposing that it is logically impossible for an essentially omnipotent agent to be overpowered? Maybe (though I cannot generate much doubt about it myself). But if we were mistaken in that, then being overpowered must be compatible with essential omnipotence. In that case, A might indeed overpower B, but this "defeat" would not damage B's omnipotence. In neither case, then, do we get the conclusion that one (or both) of these agents fails of omnipotence.

The situation between A and B is symmetrical, and we could have posed our questions in terms of B's thwarting A, rather than in terms of A's overpowering B. The results, however, are the same.[17]

This argument has been conducted on the assumption that the Thomistic idea of omnipotence is on the right track. A minority of philosophical theologians (Descartes perhaps) seem to reject the Thomistic restriction and to hold that omnipotence ought to be construed as encompassing even what is logically impossible. How does the collision fare under this assumption? It would seem that A could then overpower B, even though it is logically impossible for B (in virtue of his

---

[17] Someone may still feel unsatisfied with this result, because no definitive answer has been given to the question of what the outcome of such a collision would be. For what it is worth, my own view about that is that the outcome would not be determined by *force*. But an outcome might be generated in some other way—by love, perhaps, or justice, or chance (the flipping of a cosmic coin?), or . . . What is relevant to the present discussion, however, is the conclusion that omnipotence is not intrinsically an instantiation-exclusive attribute.

omnipotence) to be overpowered. In the same way, B could, in virtue of his omnipotence, also thwart A, and B could overpower A while A thwarted B. Indeed, so far as I can see, all these outcomes could be the result of a single collision. Of course, it seems logically impossible that it could be true *both* that A overpowers B and that B thwarts A. It certainly strikes me as logically impossible. But, *under the assumption with which we are now working,* that is just what omnipotent beings are supposed to be able to do. They can actualize impossible states of affairs. Under this assumption, therefore, the fact that a collision of omnipotent agents would result in an impossible outcome should not be taken to show that there cannot be a multiplicity of omnipotent beings.

Regardless, then, of whether we take omnipotence to be limited to the realm of the logically possible, it seems that there is no barrier to the multiple instantiation of this attribute.

I suppose that we could generate an instantiation-exclusive property out of just about any property by adding to it some restriction such as "the one and only." So even if more than one being could be perfectly loving, it seems plausible to suppose that no more than one could be *the one and only perfectly loving being.* And so if two or more distinct divinities were required to have this property, then I would suppose that no more than one of them could actually exist. But properties specified in this way have something of an ad hoc flavor about them. I don't know whether there are examples in actual religions of divinities that would exclude each other in this way.

There are, however, some closely related properties that do figure in actual theologies and that would seem to have that effect. I am thinking of exclusive relations, in which the divinity is said to bear a unique relation to some particular thing. Examples (taken primarily from Christian thought) are relational properties such as *being the creator of the world* and *being the judge of all the earth.* In such expressions it is rather natural to understand the definite article to mean "the one and only," and no doubt that is how it is usually taken by the theologians who attribute these relational properties to God. And so, if the Holy Trinity is the creator of the world, then no divinity who is distinct from the Holy Trinity could also be the creator of the world. And if it is required of a god that he (or she) be the creator of the world, then there could be at most only one god.

Christian theology certainly seems to involve relational properties with this feature, and I suppose that some other theologies do also. Probably there are cases in which one such property is ascribed (in different religions) to apparently distinct deities. At any rate, I would not be surprised if it were so. Would that show, or at least give one strong reason to suppose, that those two gods could not both exist?

I can think of only two ways of avoiding that conclusion. Both of them are of some interest, though neither in the end seems attractive to me. And both of them are suggested by Hick, in one way or another.

At one point Hick refers to "two alternative models for the status of the divine *personae*" (p. 272), both of which he says are compatible with his general hypothesis. One of these models is radically realist, and it is hard to imagine what more a person would have to assert to be taken to be a polytheist. According to the other one, however, the gods are

> projections of the religious imagination. . . . Applied to the divine *personae* this would mean that Jahweh, the heavenly Father, Allah, Shiva, Vishnu and so on are not objectively existent personal individuals with their own distinctive powers and characteristics. . . . They would be analogous to what have been called in the literature of parapsychology, 'veridical hallucinations'. . . . This experience is not caused by a particular invisible person—Jahweh or Vishnu, for example. It does however constitute a transformation of authentic information of which the Real is the ultimate source. (p. 273)

According to this model, the gods of the various religions are imaginary entities.[18] But they are *veridical* imaginary entities, in the sense that these imaginary entities are appropriate ways in which some genuine information derived from the Real can be represented and expressed by human beings. Perhaps the idea here is analogous to what we may have in mind when we say that a certain work of literature is "true to life," although every character and setting in it is purely fictional.

Now in fictional works, and perhaps in the realm of the imagination generally, it seems to be the case that distinct entities (fictional entities, of course) can bear exclusive relations to (what at least seems to be) a single object. There can be two novels in each of which there is a character identified as "the last king of France" and in which these two characters are otherwise described in wildly different ways. This need not involve an incoherence in either novel, nor is there any incoherence in the existence of the two novels (perhaps even written by the same author). And it is possible that we might find both these novels "true to life," expressive of deep truths about the human situation.

---

[18] On the other model, by way of contrast, the gods are "objectively existing, supramundane and subtle beings . . . real personal beings, independent centres of consciousness, will, thought, and emotion" (p. 274).

If the various gods—the Holy Trinity, say, and Allah—are really imaginary entities, then perhaps both of them can be, individually and distinctly, the sole creator of the world, in the same sense that two fictional characters can be, individually and distinctly, the last king of France. And so not even the occurrence of exclusive relations in the various theologies would rule out the plurality of gods.

I said that this option did not seem attractive to me. That is because, though it may salvage the element of plurality, it gives up what seems to me to be even deeper in any genuine theism—indeed, in any genuine religion—whether it be of the mono- or the poly- variety. That element is what I called "realism" in describing the Aramean view. Any theism at all, if it is to have a deep religious significance, will construe its god or gods as belonging to the order of reality, as being (at the very least) as real as the ordinary furniture of the world. Hick himself says that "within each tradition we regard as real the objects of our worship or contemplation" (p. 249). That sounds exactly right to me. And if we cease to think of those objects as real—if we come to regard them as hallucinations, fictions, projections of our imaginations, or something of the sort—then we have abandoned that tradition. Maybe we have moved to another religion, or perhaps to no religion at all. And maybe we were right to make that move. Maybe the old gods were fictions after all. But what we ourselves take to be a fiction, rightly or wrongly, will not sustain our religious life and cannot be the central object in it.

In comparing cultic and descriptive versions of polytheism and monotheism, I posed the question whether one could be a cultic mono-theist (or polytheist) and a descriptive atheist. The model we have just been discussing seems to me to be a descriptive atheism with respect to the gods (and absolutes) of the actual religions. And any view about religion that is compatible with this model must be compatible with atheism about these gods. Persons whose religious thought is compat-ible in that way could be worshipers of one of those gods, it seems to me, only by an extraordinary separation of their thinking from their religious life. But, of course, a person who counted all the old gods as fictions could be realist about something else, some new god or abso-lute. And if so, then that new divinity might be the ground of her religious life. That would be a new religion.

Well, I said that there might be two ways in which one could avoid the threat that exclusive relations pose for the plurality of gods. The second way turns on a problem (as I see it) in Kantian metaphysics, a problem Hick perhaps inherits. It would indeed seem that no two gods could be, individually and distinctly, the sole creator of the world, *pro-vided that the world is a single entity*. But if there is a plurality of worlds, and gods are matched to worlds, then various gods may be the creators of the various corresponding worlds. In thinking of a phrase such as "the creator of the world," then, we should have to think of the referential force of "the world" as being tied to the referential force of "the creator," so that the whole phrase refers successfully only if there is an appropriate match between these two included references.

I say that this is connected with a problem in Kantian metaphysics for the following reason. In that metaphysics (interpreted in terms of the construct model) the phenomenal objects of my experience are constructs related in some way to some noumenal reality and also to a categorical scheme that I supply. The "I think" that accompanies all my mental life unifies all the phenomenal objects of my experience into a single interrelated whole—one phenomenal world. But it is hard to see what, in the Kantian metaphysics, could account for, or even permit, a phenomenal world that was *common* to two or more perceivers. Rather, it looks as though each such perceiver must construct, and perceive, his or her own world. These worlds might be similar to one another (but how could any perceiver compare one world with another?), but they would be distinct worlds. Think, for example, of the situation in which I am initially alone in a melon patch, and I am the sole percipient of a cantaloupe there. It would seem, on the Kantian view, that this cantaloupe must be constituted by the categories I supply. When a second observer arrives, how could she observe *that very same* cantaloupe? Must she not rather observe a cantaloupe that is constituted by her own categorical contribution, and that is integrated into a world by *her* "I think" and not by mine? But then it would be her cantaloupe, in her world, and not mine.

For me, at any rate, the existence of a genuinely common world is one of the facts for which any satisfactory metaphysics must account, or which at least it must permit. The Kantian approach, therefore, does not seem likely to be satisfactory.

There is an analogue of this difficulty in the hypothesis we are considering here. We do sometimes talk loosely about the Hindu world view and the Hindu world, the Christian world-view and the Christian world, and so forth. And if we could take seriously the idea of there being distinct worlds associated with the various religions, then possibly we could also take seriously the idea that the various gods are the creators of the various worlds. But the fact seems to be that there is no distinctly Christian world or Hindu world. All of us—Hindus, Christians, atheists, Buddhists, and all the rest—live in one single and shared world. In that world we love one another and hate one another, help one another and kill one another, do business with one another and cheat one another, and so on down the line. If my god is real—if he can have an effect in my world—then he must also have an effect in the world of the Hindu, because (if for no other reason) I am a part of the Hindu's world. And mutatis mutandis for the Hindu god and my world. And (as for Kantian metaphysics in general) I can hardly imagine what an argument could have in it that would override the conviction that the world is in fact a single reality shared by many observers and participants.

What I have been calling the "exclusive relations," therefore, seems to set a limit to the plurality of gods. If the Holy Trinity is the creator of the world, then either Allah is identical with the Holy Trinity or else Allah is not the creator of the world. It is not possible that just any old set of intentional religious objects should be both real and distinct, and it is quite possible that some of the intentional objects, the gods or absolutes, of the world's actual religions are mutually exclusive in this way. But though these relations may rule out some putative polytheisms, they will not rule out all of them. For not all the candidate gods will be burdened with such relations.

Well, no doubt there is much more that could be said about this topic. In particular, I think, it would be worthwhile if we could find more incisive and conclusive arguments either for or against the reality of particular gods other than our own, and some usable criterion for determining the identity or nonidentity of the objects of worship. But I don't now know how to do that. Let me therefore close with just one suggestion. In the absence of strong reasons to the contrary, it might be wise to proceed on the assumption that we need not say the *same* thing about every case. We ought, for example, to allow the possibility that there may be distinct religions that have the very same god, and others that really do have distinct gods. There might be religions whose gods are purely fictional and imaginary entities, others whose gods are phenomenal beings in some Kantian or quasi-Kantian sense, still others whose gods are substantial creaturely beings, and still others whose god is the Real, the rock-bottom reality who gives the gift of being to everything else that exists. At least, assumptions such as these would provide a benchmark from which we might measure our progress in considering the possibility of polytheism.

Contributors

MARILYN MCCORD ADAMS is Professor of Historical Theology at Yale Divinity School.

ROBERT AUDI is Professor of Philosophy at the University of Nebraska.

WILLIAM HASKER is Professor of Philosophy at Huntington College.

NORMAN KRETZMANN is Susan Linn Sage Professor of Philosophy at Cornell University.

BRIAN LEFTOW is Associate Professor of Philosophy at Fordham University.

GEORGE MAVRODES is Professor of Philosophy at the University of Michigan.

ALVIN PLANTINGA is John A. O'Brien Professor of Philosophy at the University of Notre Dame.

WILLIAM ROWE is Professor of Philosophy at Purdue University.

JOSEPH RUNZO is Professor of Philosophy at Chapman University.

ELEONORE STUMP is the Henle Professor of Philosophy at St. Louis University.

PETER VAN INWAGEN is John Cardinal O'Hara Professor of Philosophy at the University of Notre Dame.

WILLIAM WAINWRIGHT is Professor of Philosophy at the University of Wisconsin at Milwaukee.

Index